DISTRUST

DISTRUST

Russell Hardin

EDITOR

VOLUME VIII IN THE RUSSELL SAGE FOUNDATION SERIES ON TRUST

Russell Sage Foundation • New York

The Russell Sage Foundation

The Russell Sage Foundation, one of the oldest of America's general purpose foundations, was established in 1907 by Mrs. Margaret Olivia Sage for "the improvement of social and living conditions in the United States." The Foundation seeks to fulfill this mandate by fostering the development and dissemination of knowledge about the country's political, social, and economic problems. While the Foundation endeavors to assure the accuracy and objectivity of each book it publishes, the conclusions and interpretations in Russell Sage Foundation publications are those of the authors and not of the Foundation, its Trustees, or its staff. Publication by Russell Sage, therefore, does not imply Foundation endorsement.

BOARD OF TRUSTEES
Robert E. Denham, Chair

Alan S. Blinder	Jennifer L. Hochschild	Cora B. Marrett
Christine K. Cassel	Timothy A. Hultquist	Eugene Smolensky
Thomas D. Cook	Kathleen Hall Jamieson	Eric Wanner
John A. Ferejohn	Melvin Konner	Mary C. Waters
Larry V. Hedges		

Library of Congress Cataloging-in-Publication Data

Distrust / [edited by] Russell Hardin.
    p. cm. – (Russell Sage Foundation series on trust ; v. 8)
    Includes bibliographical references and index.
    ISBN 0-87154-350-8
    1. Trust. I. Hardin, Russell, 1940– II. Series.
    BF575.T7D57 2004
    302'.1–dc22

2003068751

Copyright © 2004 by Russell Sage Foundation. All rights reserved. Printed in the United States of America. No part of this publication may be reproduced, stored in a retrieval system, or transmitted in any form or by any means, electronic, mechanical, photocopying, recording, or otherwise, without the prior written permission of the publisher.

Reproduction by the United States Government in whole or in part is permitted for any purpose.

The paper used in this publication meets the minimum requirements of American National Standard for Information Sciences—Permanence of Paper for Printed Library Materials. ANSI Z39.48-1992.

Text design by Suzanne Nichols.

RUSSELL SAGE FOUNDATION
112 East 64th Street, New York, New York 10021
10 9 8 7 6 5 4 3 2 1

The Russell Sage Foundation Series on Trust

The Russell Sage Foundation Series on Trust examines the conceptual structure and the empirical basis of claims concerning the role of trust and trustworthiness in establishing and maintaining cooperative behavior in a wide variety of social, economic, and political contexts. The focus is on concepts, methods, and findings that will enrich social science and inform public policy.

The books in the series raise questions about how trust can be distinguished from other means of promoting cooperation and explore those analytic and empirical issues that advance our comprehension of the roles and limits of trust in social, political, and economic life. Because trust is at the core of understandings of social order from varied disciplinary perspectives, the series offers the best work of scholars from diverse backgrounds and, through the edited volumes, encourages engagement across disciplines and orientations. The goal of the series is to improve the current state of trust research by providing a clear theoretical account of the causal role of trust within given institutional, organizational, and interpersonal situations, developing sound measures of trust to test theoretical claims within relevant settings, and establishing some common ground among concerned scholars and policymakers.

Karen S. Cook
Russell Hardin
Margaret Levi

SERIES EDITORS

Previous Volumes in the Series

Trust and Governance
Valerie Braithwaite and Margaret Levi, editors

Trust in Society
Karen S. Cook, editor

Evolution and the Capacity for Commitment
Randolph M. Nesse, editor

Trust and Trustworthiness
Russell Hardin

Trust in the Law: Encouraging Public Cooperation with the Police and Courts
Tom R. Tyler and Yuen J. Huo

Trust and Reciprocity: Interdisciplinary Lessons from Experimental Research
Elinor Ostrom and James Walker, editors

Trust and Distrust in Organizations: Dilemmas and Approaches
Roderick M. Kramer and Karen S. Cook, editors

Contents

		Contributors	ix
PART I		THEORIZING DISTRUST	1
	Chapter 1	Distrust: Manifestations and Management *Russell Hardin*	3
	Chapter 2	Distrust: Prudent, If Not Always Wise *Deborah Welch Larson*	34
	Chapter 3	Trust, Distrust, and In Between *Edna Ullmann-Margalit*	60
PART II		POWER AND DISTRUST	83
	Chapter 4	Trust, Distrust, and Power *Henry Farrell*	85
	Chapter 5	The Transaction Costs of Distrust: Labor and Management at the National Labor Relations Board *Margaret Levi, Matthew Moe, and Theresa Buckley*	106
	Chapter 6	Collective Paranoia: Distrust Between Social Groups *Roderick M. Kramer*	136
	Chapter 7	Compensating for Distrust Among Kin *Margaret L. Brown*	167

Chapter 8	Deadly Distrust: Honor Killings and Swedish Multiculturalism *Unni Wikan*	192
PART III	THE POLITICS OF DISTRUST	205
Chapter 9	Distrust and the Development of Urban Regulations *Patrick Troy*	207
Chapter 10	Coping with Distrust in Emerging Russian Markets *Vadim Radaev*	233
Chapter 11	Distrust as a Trade Impediment: European Trade Policy Toward Nonmarket Economies *Cynthia M. Horne*	249
Chapter 12	Terrorism and Group-Generalized Distrust *Russell Hardin*	278
Chapter 13	Corruption, Distrust, and the Deterioration of the Rule of Law *Gabriella R. Montinola*	298
Index		325

Contributors

Russell Hardin is professor of politics at New York University.

Margaret L. Brown is assistant professor of anthropology at Washington University in St. Louis.

Theresa Buckley is program and policy analyst at the U.S. Department of Education, Washington, D.C.

Henry Farrell is assistant professor in the Department of Political Science at the University of Toronto.

Cynthia M. Horne is assistant professor of international relations at the John C. Whitehead School of Diplomacy and International Relations at Seton Hall University.

Roderick M. Kramer is William R. Kimball Professor of Organizational Behavior at Stanford Business School.

Deborah Welch Larson is professor of political science at the University of California, Los Angeles.

Margaret Levi is Jere L. Bacharach Professor of International Studies in the Department of Political Science at the University of Washington.

Matthew Moe received his master's degree from the Department of Political Science at the University of Washington.

Gabriella R. Montinola is assistant professor of political science at the University of California, Davis.

Vadim Radaev is professor and chair of economic sociology and first vice-rector of State University—Higher School of Economics, Moscow, Russia.

Patrick Troy is visiting fellow at the Centre for Resource and Environmental Studies at Australian National University.

x   Contributors

Edna Ullmann-Margalit is professor of philosophy at the Hebrew University of Jerusalem.

Unni Wikan is professor of social anthropology at the University of Oslo, Norway.

PART I

THEORIZING DISTRUST

Chapter 1

Distrust: Manifestations and Management

Russell Hardin

Most of the contributions to this book assume, either explicitly or implicitly, that trust is cognitive, that it is de facto an assessment of the trustworthiness of the potentially trusted person or group or institution. If, on your own knowledge, I seem to be trustworthy to some degree with respect to some matter, then you trust me with respect to that matter. Similarly, if I seem to be untrustworthy, then you distrust me. If trust has grounds of particular kinds, we may expect distrust to have correlative grounds. Moreover, distrust is, like trust, a three-part relation: A distrusts B with respect to X. A might trust B on many matters but not on others. Like trust, distrust is also a matter of degree. I may distrust Ruth on some matter more than I distrust George. Finally, far more than could be true of trust, I might distrust a large number of people with respect to virtually everything. I typically would not trust many, if any, people with respect to virtually everything. It is sometimes important to recognize this asymmetry, not only for groups (as addressed in chapters 6, 8, and 12) but also for institutions and government (as in chapters 2, 3, 8, 10, 11, and 13).

One might think of distrust as the complement of trust, so that if I do not trust you with respect to something, I distrust you. Here distrust is commonly treated, most explicitly in chapter 3, by Edna Ullmann-Margalit, rather as the negative of trust with a somewhat neutral state in between. If I trust you, I have specific grounds for the trust. In parallel, if I distrust you, I have specific grounds for the distrust. I could be in a state of such ignorance about you, however, that I neither trust nor distrust you. I may therefore be wary of you until I have better information on you. Sometimes, I can create the grounds for trust by giving you incentive to be trustworthy, as Deborah Larson (chapter 2) and Rod Kramer (chapter 6) argue for international relations in the era of nuclear deterrence. If you then fail, I might sensibly thereafter distrust you and, therefore, avoid putting myself at risk from further attempts at cooperative endeavors with you. Unfortunately, I may have no choice in the matter and may be forced to deal with you even in matters on which I strongly distrust you. We may then have to secure some degree of cooperation through the use of such devices as Kramer, Larson, and Margaret Levi, Matthew Moe, and Theresa Buckley (chapter 5) discuss.

Apart from those by Gabriella Montinola (chapter 13), Patrick Troy (chapter 9), and Ullmann-Margalit, the following chapters do not specifically discuss distrust of government by its own citizens. There is a massive and growing literature on the claim that trust in government is declining in at least some democracies, especially the United States (see Pharr and Putnam 2000). Much of that literature supposes that such a decline is bad in that it is harmful to the working of government. That is a surprising supposition for the United States, whose Constitution frames a set of institutions explicitly designed to block government power as much as possible in order to deal with the fact that liberals of the era of James Madison and the other authors of the Constitution assumed that government cannot and should not be trusted. They thought that a good government is one that has extremely limited power to intervene in our lives.

Liberal political theory was largely founded on distrust of government, which David Hume, Madison, and to a lesser extent John Locke thought was the only intelligent stance for citizens to take toward government (Hardin 2002a; Bailyn 1967; Morgan 1999; but see Wills 1999). Theirs is a theory of liberal distrust. As Edmund S. Morgan (1999, 39) quips, "Between 1776 and 1789 Americans replaced a government over them with a government under them." The contest of views between contemporary advocates of trust in government and liberal theorist advocates of distrust in government is not of concern to many of the authors in this volume, who are more directly interested in the distrust that can color interactions between various parties who might, with less distrust, enter into cooperative relationships of many kinds. For many of these issues, the fact that government is there to help back up various interactions enhances the possibilities of developing trust relationships between the relevant parties.

Many of the contributions here are concerned with cases in which there is limited or no scope for government regulation of relevant interactions or in which government has failed to regulate them. They focus on intergroup, economic, political, and international relations. Higher-level government plays an active role in chapters 5 and 9, but it is not an active participant in many of the interactions here. Its failures in the studies of Unni Wikan (chapter 8), Vadim Radaev (chapter 10), Troy (chapter 9), Montinola (chapter 13), and myself (chapter 12), and its absence in the studies of Margaret Brown (chapter 7), Cynthia Horne (chapter 11), and Larson (chapter 2) are crucial and are the source of much of the distrust in these contexts. As Montinola argues, the executive, legislative, and judicial branches of government in emerging democracies must have the incentive and the capacity to hold one another accountable to block corruption and abuse of power. Only if liberal distrust is alive and well can citizens in new democracies be expected to have confidence in their governments.

It is a peculiar implication of the commonplace thesis that trust is inherently moral and of much of the current literature on the need for trust in society that distrust must evidently therefore be bad. But distrust is sometimes the only credible implication of the evidence. Indeed, distrust is sometimes not merely a rational assessment; it also is benign in that it protects against harms rather than causing them. For example, parents who do not entrust the safety of their children to unworthy caretakers, woefully including such institutionally selected caretakers as priests, or international institutions that do not act as though all nations are benign in their treatment of one another or even of their own populations, are acting morally according to almost any morality. Because distrust is benign whenever it is justified, it is implausible that trust is inherently a moral notion—as some authors suppose (see Hardin 2002b, 74–78). Brown argues, against a substantial tradition, that not even within familial relations is trust clearly grounded in moral commitments.

Relations between individuals are discussed in several of these chapters (2, 3, 6, 7, 8, and 10), but these relations are often embedded in larger contexts that drive the analyses or their analysis is used to extrapolate to collective and institutional behaviors. Of the contributions here, only those of Ullmann-Margalit and Brown focus primarily on interpersonal relations, but all generally extrapolate from such relations even when they address more complex relations involving collectivities and institutions. Most of the psychological work on trust has focused on individual-level interactions. Much of the sociological work has focused on trusting professionals. And most of the work in political science has focused on trusting government and political leaders. Montinola focuses on a major institution of the Philippine government, its Supreme Court, and gives a complex, nuanced account of how citizens and lawyers can know enough to distrust it as an agency often conspicuously hostile to their interests. Increasingly, scholars in all these disciplines have begun to study relations between groups, perhaps especially between racial and ethnic groups, and three of the chapters here (6, 8, and 12) focus on intergroup relations.

An important question about any conception of trust and distrust is whether it translates to diverse cultures. Contributions in this volume go some way to answering that worry. They deal with cases in Australia, China, France, Italy, Japan, Madagascar, the Philippines, Russia, the European Union, formerly communist nations, and the multicultural societies of Sweden and the United States, as well as interactions between some of these. The authors here do not all have identical notions of distrust, but they come close. Let us briefly lay out extant theories or conceptions of trust in the fast-growing literature on it.

Theories and Conceptions of Trust

Usually, to say that I trust you in some context simply means that I think you will be trustworthy toward me in that context. Hence to ask any question about trust is implicitly to ask about the reasons for thinking the relevant party to be trustworthy. Elsewhere (Hardin 2002b, chap. 1), I canvass the several most common reasons for thinking someone trustworthy. One of the most important and commonplace is trust as encapsulated interest, which I assume in the present discussion. On this account, I trust you because I think it is in your interest to take my interests in the relevant matter seriously in the following sense: You value the continuation of our relationship, and you therefore have your own interest in taking my interests into account. That is, *you encapsulate my interests in your own interests.* My interests might come into conflict with other interests you have, and those interests of yours might trump mine, and you might therefore not actually act in ways that serve my interests. Nevertheless, you at least have some interest in doing so. A minimal core part of a remarkable array of trust relationships is that there is a clear, fairly well defined interest at stake in the continuation of the relationship. For the issues of terrorism I address in chapter 12, this is surely the relevant account of trust to bring to bear.

Both the relatively limited relationship between yourself and a local merchant and the relatively rich relationship you might have with a friend involve trust as encapsulated interest. This is not merely to say that you and I have the same interests. Again, it is to say that you have an interest in attending to *my* interests because, typically, you want our relationship to continue. At a minimum, you may want our relationship to continue because it is economically beneficial to you, as in the case of your relationship to your merchant. In richer cases, you may want our relationship to continue, and not to be damaged by your failure to fulfill my trust, because you value the relationship for many reasons, including nonmaterial reasons. For example, you may enjoy doing various things with me, or you might value my friendship or my love, and your desire to keep my friendship or love will motivate you to be careful of my trust.

Note that *our merely having the same interests with respect to some matter does not meet the condition of trust as encapsulated interest,* although it can often give me reason to expect you to do what I would want you to do or what would serve my interests (because it simultaneously serves yours). The encapsulated-interest account does entail that the truster and the trusted have compatible interests over at least some matters, but such incentive compatibility, while necessary, is not sufficient for that account, which further requires that the trusted values the continuation of the relationship with the truster and has compatible interests at least in part for this reason.

Two other articulated theories of trust are common in the literature. One depends on an assessment of the trusted's moral commitments to be trustworthy. The other depends on an assessment of the trusted's psychological disposition to be the kind of person who is trustworthy. These might be important matters for individual-level trust relations. They are less likely to fit most trusters in the social contexts of most of the chapters of this volume. For example, relations between labor and management, emerging Russian markets, and relationships of citizens to governments cannot typically be motivated by beliefs that the potentially trusted party (management, other firms, or government) is morally motivated or primarily concerned with living up to some psychological disposition to have a trustworthy character. Virtually by definition, these two theories of trust fail in contexts in which distrust dominates trust. In the chapters here, neither of these theories is at issue.

Trust is, of course, a term of the vernacular, and in the vernacular it has manifold meanings. Perhaps the bulk of all academic work on trust in recent years is based on more or less vernacular uses of the term. For example, surveys ask people whether they trust a particular agent or virtually everyone. Surprisingly, much of this literature seems to have as its purpose merely to show that people do or do not trust in some vernacular sense. We might wish rather to explain a person's trust or to use the level of a person's trust to explain actions, such as cooperation, or at least taking a risk on cooperation. Often, the only explanations from levels of trust that are offered are correlations between changing levels of trust (such as supposedly declining levels of trust in government in the United States in recent decades) and some other change in the society. If such correlations are to be of any interest, they must be coupled with mechanisms that give a causal account of how levels of trust affect relevant other things. It is a great strength of the three theories of trust noted here that they can give explanations of important phenomena. It is similarly a strength of the chapters here that they give many such explanations. Atheoretical vernacular accounts have arguably yielded no compelling explanations of anything to date.

In this discussion, I have assumed that trust is a cognitive assessment of the other's trustworthiness. A large literature, mostly in psychology, treats it as a problem of the *psychology or traits of the person who trusts*. Some people are said to be high trusters and some low trusters. To measure such trustingness in the abstract—that is to say, independently of any particular relationship in which one might trust or not trust—Julian Rotter (1967) proposes an interpersonal trust scale. Thomas Wright and Richard Tedeschi (1975) break Rotter's scale into three orthogonal factors: political trust—beliefs that politicians and the media are trustworthy; paternal trust—beliefs that benign authorities (parents, experts, professionals) are trustworthy; and trust of strangers—beliefs that potentially exploitative, anonymous others are trustworthy. The implication of this finding is that the general trust scale is less predictive of risk taking in some domains than are the specific factors (see Cook, Hardin, and Levi 2004, chap. 2). One might speculate that there are different conceptions of trust in these realms.

In general, trust depends on two quite different dimensions: the motivation of the potentially trusted person to attend to the truster's interests and his or her competence to do so. One might therefore wish to have a broader range of questions for these scales in order to weigh the contribution of concerns with the motivations of the potentially trusted person versus judgments of the competence of the other. In most discussions of trust, as in many of the chapters in this volume, the relevant competence is taken for granted, although lack of such competence is often a major problem.

In the contributions to this book, there is substantial consistency in the conception of trust. In part that may be because the idea of distrust is inherently specific to a person or other agent or to some generalized collection of these. There is no aura of morality or of deep psychological commitments in distrust, which is almost necessarily grounded in a reading of the intentions of the object of distrust. I distrust *you* because of things you do or interests you have that conflict with mine. One might read backward from distrust to say that the conception of trust should mirror it. Accounts that make trust somehow part of the morality or the psychology of the potential truster do not mirror natural accounts of distrust. All of us sometimes distrust specific others for reasons we can articulate. Such instances of distrust in the midst of many trusting relationships cannot be part of our standard, almost fixed stance toward the world, whether moral, psychological, or rationally self-interested.

If we analyze distrust, therefore, we must either leave it untheorized (a common move when the discussion is at the vernacular level) or we must see it as something like the negative side of the encapsulated-interest theory of trust. The latter is what the contributions to this volume do, although the authors were not specifically asked to do any such thing.

It comes naturally to see distrust as a three-part relation (A distrusts B with respect to X) and as grounded in a reading of the other's motivations toward oneself, typically including the other's interests. This is one of the strongest lessons of these chapters taken together. If we think trust and distrust are conceptually tied together, we may be forced by the understanding of distrust to see trust as encapsulated interest. In a conversation many years ago, Robert Merton said I should analyze distrust if I wanted to get a clear understanding of trust. He then sent me several clippings on distrust. The authors of this book have implicitly shown the wisdom of Merton's advice.

Theorizing Distrust

In chapter 2, Deborah Larson analyzes the relations of the United States and the former Soviet Union, and subsequently Russia, by extrapolating from individual-level relationships and psychology. She notes that distrust varies across domains and that in any domain it may vary in degree. A central problem with trust and distrust is that they are essentially cognitive assessments of the trustworthiness of the other party and may therefore be mistaken. Hence they may be subject to type I (false positive) or type II (false negative) errors. The principal issue for nations is that misplaced trust can lead to grievous harms, so that a nation may be inclined to hedge its bets and, out of mere prudence, to act as though it distrusts another even more than it actually does. In some contexts, this makes for instability because it provokes the other nation to suppose it is distrusted and therefore to fear defensive actions. Prudential defensiveness can then produce instability and bring about the harms that are feared but not actually expected. In the development of the nuclear deterrent system, however, the United States and the Soviet Union actually secured a kind of institutionalized distrust that stabilized relations.

In the immediate postwar era, the United States distrusted the Soviet Union because the latter openly believed in the impossibility of peaceful coexistence with the capitalist world. (This stated view might have been provoked by Western hostility to the early communist regime immediately after World War I. Distrust can beget distrust.) This stance was renounced by Eduard Shevardnadze in 1988, thus setting the stage for the possibility of growing trust between the two adversaries. It took fairly dramatic events to change the atmosphere between the two nations. If they had been too trusting, they would quickly have had evidence that they were mistaken. As Larson says, misplaced trust is a self-disconfirming prophecy. If they were too distrusting, however, they would have been unlikely to enter into cooperative relations, and they therefore would have had less opportunity to notice that they were mistaken. The depth of the distrust between the Soviet Union and the United States made it difficult for them even to see that in many areas they actually shared interests and that they should have cooperated in those areas even while keeping a defensive posture in other areas. In Larson's term, the two nations were primed for hostility.

For nations, as for individuals, "favorable traits are hard to acquire but easy to lose, while unfavorable traits are easy to acquire and hard to lose." In military contexts, what seems defensive to one side might equally well seem offensive to the other side. Hence a state that distrusts another is apt to signal its distrust by stationing troops and weapons and refusing to negotiate on arms control or even to enter into trade agreements. These distrustful actions will quite likely be taken as hostile, and both sides may spiral their potential conflict into open and potentially disastrous confrontation. In the long run, distrust might block many potential small improvements in relations, improvements that would be advantageous to each side. We suffer such an accumulation of losses out of fear that, if we act as though we are trusting, we will incur enormous losses.

One of the great benefits of a well-enforced law of contracts is that parties to a contract can be secure in the expectation that especially large losses from the default of the other party will be blocked by courts. Hence the parties can deal with details in a far more trusting and amicable way. Where there is no such background of protection against large losses, nations might insist that the details of any treaty be carefully specified. Hence the treaty may be difficult to negotiate. If two nations in conflict can invoke the protection of a third party, such as the United Nations, they might more readily be able to reach a mutually advantageous settlement of their conflict. For the United States and the Soviet Union, there was neither a court with enforcement power nor a third party with the power to back any settlement.

The impasse between the United States and the Soviet Union was surmounted primarily by the extraordinary actions of Mikhail Gorbachev in renouncing control of central Europe and building down the Soviet army and nuclear forces. As in the much smaller world of the wayward husband in Brown's chapter 7, taking a step outside the range of ordinary expectations helped to secure the building of trust in the other party. Both that husband and Gorbachev reduced their own capacities for cheating on their other party. We might wish that many more people had the insight and strength of character to risk taking such steps.

In chapter 3, Edna Ullmann-Margalit supposes that to say I trust you means I believe you have the right intentions toward me and that you are competent to do what I trust you to do. The right intentions are to want to take my interests, as my interests, into account in your actions. Note here that the right intentions make you trustworthy for me. You and I could have coincidental interests, so that, while acting in your own interests, you happen also to serve mine. If I know this and no more about your intentions, I can be confident of your actions, but I cannot be said to trust you. Distrust must have a similar logic. If I distrust you, that is because I think that your interests oppose my own and that you will not take my interests into account in your actions. In this view, trust and distrust are cognitive notions or, in Ullmann-Margalit's term, they are epistemic terms. That is, they are in the family of terms that includes knowledge and belief.

Ullmann-Margalit is concerned with negations of trust and distrust. These help to define the full range from trust to distrust, with lack of trust and lack of distrust somewhere between them. The negation of trust includes both distrust and this in-between range. At either end of the full continuum, Ullmann-Margalit speaks of full trust and full distrust. These categories are meant to fit the three-part relation A trusts (or distrusts) B with respect to X because full trust (or distrust) is restricted to X. One of Ullmann-Margalit's examples of the possibility of full trust is in the relationship between a lawyer and her client. She supposes that the client could be confident in the lawyer because, among other things, the lawyer is ambitious and will become rich and famous from successfully defending her clients. Ullmann-Margalit does not count this as trust, however, because the lawyer's actions are not from the right reason to qualify as trustworthy—namely, from the reason that the lawyer's actions are directly motivated by the client's interests (Larson makes the same point in chapter 2). Ullmann-Margalit says, "When I fully trust my lawyer . . . I have good reason to believe that even in the case of a conflict of interests she will take my side." Here the trust is restricted to the specific matter of the defense of the client; it is not full trust in some more expansive sense that the lawyer could be trusted with respect to everything and anything.

Ullmann-Margalit then applies her conception of distrust and trust to the possibility of trust in institutions and other collectivities. Montinola (chapter 13) argues cogently that citizens cannot typically trust government because they cannot have the knowledge that it would take to define trust (see further Hardin 2002b, chap. 7). But they can have enough knowledge to distrust specific institutions that are, for example, demonstrably corrupt. Montinola astutely notes that when higher-level officials seem to take no action against openly corrupt officials, *they give citizens reason to distrust government generally.* Ullmann-Margalit takes a different tack. She questions whether it makes sense to say that institutions have intentions in anything like the way persons have intentions. Because we generally think such collective bodies do not and cannot have intentions in the ordinary sense, we cannot say that they can be trustworthy in the ordinary sense.

There are two ways that we might rescue the notion of trusting an institution. We could redefine intentions to accommodate institutional intentions, or we could eliminate the requirement of intentions for assessing trustworthiness. The latter change seems to wreck the meaning of trust and to reduce it to mere expectations. So how about redefining intentions? Ullmann-Margalit suggests that we might take certain leading figures in an organization to represent the trustworthiness of the institution. Hence if we trust the president or prime minister, we might be said to "trust" the government. A similar move would be to take a representative agent to stand in for the whole institution. I cannot attribute intentions to the institution, but I might have enough information from my own interactions with a particular agent of some government organization to trust that agent. Neither of these moves can work in any strong sense. They are shorthand devices that cannot meet the complaint that institutions do not have intentions. They also do not work for the knowledge that is required for trust. Therefore, Ullmann-Margalit concludes, that it is, strictly speaking, a misnomer to talk of trust of an institution.

There is one last move we could make to give some sense to the idea of an organizational intention. We might suppose that the incentive structure of an organization is adequate to get agents of the organization to act in ways that make the organization trustworthy. We could stipulate that the intention of the organization is whatever that incentive structure would bring about. But this move runs up against the grievous difficulty that few citizens, if any, could possibly know the incentive structures of various institutions, such as government and its agencies.

In these contexts, the knowledge constraints for distrust are much less severe than those for trust. Ullmann-Margalit cites the cases of the ultraorthodox and the Arab Israeli minorities in Israel. These communities, she says, want to be understood as imputing intentions to the Israeli government. She supposes that this is a natural response to apparent, pervasive unfairness. Here she is in general agreement with Montinola, who notes that I can know of the widespread corruption of an agency and can know that it seems to benefit relatively well defined groups of insiders and not ordinary citizens. That would be sufficient for me to conclude that the agency does not work in my interests, so that I can say it is untrustworthy toward ordinary citizens such as me.

Power and Trust

In a novel contribution to the theory of trust, Henry Farrell (in chapter 4) argues that trust and power have a close relationship. If neither party to a relationship had any power to withdraw from the relationship, their necessary mutual reliance would be sufficient to explain their cooperation, and neither would need to trust the other. This is not unlike the conditions of life in small, close communities, such as those of distant earlier times, where all are more or less stuck with one another and are subject to sanctions such as shunning from all others if they behave badly in their relationships with any other (Cook and Hardin 2001; Hardin 1999). On the other hand, if one party has a great panoply of alternative partners or has little need of the other party's continued cooperation, that party's power must disrupt the possibility of trust and trustworthiness and may even instill distrust. Hence modest power entails the possibility of trust, while great power asymmetry may commonly entail active distrust, and lack of power by either party blocks concern with trust altogether.

Moreover, if there is a moderate asymmetry of power, the more powerful party may be able to trust the less powerful party more (and over a wider array of issues) than the less powerful can trust the more powerful party. Indeed, this is an important way in which power is advantageous. It is useful not only in coercive relationships but also in fairly straightforward exchange relationships. In general, the relationship between power and the possibility of trust relations is curvilinear. If I have no power to withdraw from our relationship, you have no need of trust in me. If I have some power to withdraw, you may hope to develop a trust relationship. And if I can withdraw at will without cost to myself, you cannot trust me. Indeed, in this latter case, my interest does not encapsulate yours at all, so that the encapsulated-interest account of trust cannot apply. Farrell's measure of one's power in a relationship is essentially the level of cost one will incur if one unilaterally withdraws from the relationship. Low cost of withdrawal implies high power; high cost implies low power.

One party to a potential cooperative relationship may have such great power over the relationship that it can withdraw at will while the other party can withdraw only at great cost. Still, as Farrell argues, the more powerful party may be able to convince the other that it will be trustworthy if it can bind itself with credible commitments. Farrell defines these as "commitments that you know it is in my interest to fulfill once I have made them." This recalls Thomas Schelling's remark that the "right to be sued" may eventually turn out to be a liability, but it is a prerequisite to doing business in the first place (Schelling 1960, 43; Hardin 2002b, 46). The odd right to be sued is the power to make a commitment; it also helps us establish that we have a strong commitment. The Russian entrepreneurs whom Vadim Radaev surveys (in chapter 10) have only very weak power to make such a commitment because contract enforcement in their legal system is of limited effectiveness. The power of the English monarchy was enhanced in the long run by its capacity to bind itself to the repayment of loans that it sometimes needed, for example, in times of war or external threat.

Farrell applies these insights to three cases of industrial relations between suppliers and end-producers or "converters": in the weaving industry in Japan, machine production in France, and the packaging machinery industry in Italy. In Japan, there are long-term relationships that make for trust as encapsulated interest despite asymmetries of power. In his French case, end-producers strive to keep suppliers from depending too heavily on them, so that they are not threatened too severely by the clear power imbalance. This is a wise long-term policy because it helps to establish genuinely cooperative relations with the subcontractors (and it perhaps keeps the suppliers in business to compete with one another, to the collective advantage of the end-producers). This reduces the likelihood that subcontractors will hedge their own commitments and perform below standard.

In the Italian case, Farrell argues that increasing concentration in the packaging-tool industry has disrupted prior relations between suppliers and the end-producers. With great concentration, there cease to be many alternative partners for the suppliers, and they begin to be vulnerable to exploitation by the few end-producers. A given supplier may do almost all its business with a single end-producer and may therefore have almost no alternative partners if that company drops it, so that its financial security is almost entirely under the control of the single end-producer with which it primarily deals. Concentration in the end-producer industry has evidently led the end-producers to emphasize power over trust in their dealings with subcontractors. Farrell gives us an elegant array of relationships that show the broad range of interactions between power and trust.

In chapter 5, Levi, Moe, and Buckley study the workings of the National Labor Relations Board (NLRB) to determine how it affects relations between unions and employers. Their account is a study of the institutional creation of at least partially cooperative behavior by an institution that governs relations between the two potentially hostile parties. Because they need each other, arrangements that enable labor and management to reach agreements on wages and related matters can be mutually beneficial. There have surely been cases of employer-employee trust and trustworthiness, but these are probably common only in small firms in which the trust is de facto on an individual level. In early years in the United States, unions were denied the legal status of corporate persons (a status that was granted to joint stock companies), and they therefore could not sign legally enforceable contracts with employers, who could insist on individual contracts with each worker rather than a contract with a union. Hence collective bargaining was a weak device for labor. In that era, on Farrell's account of the relationship between power and trust, it would be wrong to say that the two parties could have trusted each other. Unions had little or no power of withdrawal from relations with relevant firms if firms could hire with impunity replacement workers from the reserve army of the proletariat and, in most years, from the ready pool of immigrants. Hence workers and nascent unions could have distrusted employers but could not have trusted them.

In firms with large workforces into the thousands of workers, as have arisen mainly in the past century, workers face a harsh logic of collective action that would make unions very weak if they were not given legal support (Olson 1965). In a study from relatively modern times, worker participation in union activities and, we may presume, worker solidarity were found to be greatest for shop sizes around two hundred, which was the size of the largest firms when Karl Marx wrote about the development of class consciousness on the factory floor. In both smaller and larger shops, solidarity falls off (Lipset, Trow, and Coleman 1956, 170–200). (That typesetters union has since been heavily affected by technological change that displaced labor.) Possibly, it is the individual-level interaction of workers with management in small shops that engenders trust relations that undercut commitment to a group bound by solidarity and hostile to management. Additionally, small shops might develop more diverse jobs and human capital that is specific to the firm, so that small-shop employers cannot replace all workers with trivial ease. For larger shops, the logic of collective action may be overwhelming, so that conflict between workers themselves over free riding undercuts solidarity. In the larger factories of the present time, solidarity may be difficult to build, so that legal protection of union prerogatives is a large part of the story of their success.

Relations between unions and firms in the United States changed when the National Labor Relations Board was created in 1935 to give unions greater power in their relationships with employers. If there is a curvilinear relationship between power and trust, we might therefore suppose that there is now some chance of trust between the two parties. The full story is complex, however, because we must keep in mind that trust is a three-part relation. Hence the two parties could trust each other with respect to some things while distrusting each other with respect to others. In particular, there could be trust in any context in which there is a mutual advantage in cooperating but not in any context in which there is only conflict.

Let us consider the range of possibilities. There is mutual advantage in cooperating at some level so that workers receive pay and firms receive labor. Both parties want to go to the bargaining table. (This was not so often true before the Wagner Act, which created the NLRB, and its regulation of employer-employee relations.) But there is a potentially wide margin of de facto pure conflict in the range of deals—all the points on the contract curve—any one of which would bring about a mutual advantage resolution. Suppose workers would quit if not paid at least $20 an hour and the firm would be unprofitable if it had to pay as much as $40 an hour, so that the contract curve for negotiations is the range of wage settlements between $20 and $40 an hour. Reaching agreement to be on the curve, and therefore coming to the table, is mutually advantageous.

But there is a $20 range over which there might be essentially pure conflict. There could be complexities in this argument. For example, if the quality of labor is affected by wage incentives, then this range is not entirely one of pure conflict because profits might increase as wages rise and give incentive for better performance over some part of that range, or worker quality might trade off with the number of workers. Still, both parties might reasonably suppose that part of their wage settlement is about how large are the shares that go to workers and employers from at least some of the difference between $20 and $40. For that part of their settlement, there can only be distrust because workers and employers can be confident that the interests of the other fully conflict with their own. All that they can trust each other to do, if the NLRB stands in the background to help equalize power, is to seek some settlement that will allow them both to continue in their worker-employer relationship.

On this account, the NLRB is not about overcoming distrust but about equalizing power relations, principally by giving unions recourse against certain actions by firms. Indeed, it does not overcome distrust except in the sense that it manages contract settlements over the pure conflict range. Any settlement at all allows the two parties to continue together. Primarily, however, the NLRB blocks strategic ploys by both employers and unions on side issues, such as unfair labor practices, and it is sometimes the venue and the timekeeper for contract negotiations. On these matters, its interventions might often be to the mutual advantage of both parties.

Levi, Moe, and Buckley say that the outcomes of NLRB activities serve the mutual advantage of both parties. This might be true at the margin of a particular interaction, but to show it is true overall would be difficult. There is apparently contrary evidence, which they cite, that effective unions lower profitability, so that NLRB activities and the legalization of union bargaining might seem not to serve the interests of firms (Freeman and Medoff 1984). Some scholars suppose that the overall effect of unions is a healthier economy. Perhaps one could argue that each individual firm would like to free ride on the system that produces a healthier economy and to negotiate much stricter settlements while other firms are more generous to workers. These are large and complicated issues that may not be settled convincingly. It seems likely, however, that if major employers had their way, the NLRB would have its powers curtailed substantially. If that is true, then on the views of employers, the NLRB generally serves not mutual advantage but primarily the advantage of labor. Depending on the party in power in Washington, however, unions commonly assert that the NLRB does not serve their interests.

Note that conflicts between union and management mirror intergroup conflicts in some ways. In particular, the parties to both kinds of conflict are collective entities. But unions and management have hierarchical structures that enable them successfully to negotiate almost as though they were individuals. Perhaps there would be something to learn from comparing the two forms of conflict and the roles of trust and distrust in them. Political and ethnic conflicts in many contexts combine hierarchical and relatively anarchic organizations. For example, Israel is hierarchically well organized and can respond systematically to actions by Palestinians, whereas Palestinian suicide bombers are more nearly anarchically organized. If they were hierarchically organized, they might long since have been defeated by Israeli forces. This is the reverse of the history of unionization: workers gained power from hierarchical organization.

In chapter 6, Rod Kramer seeks to understand the intensity of conflict between many groups as the result, in part, of problems of individuals' reasoning about other groups. He views group members in social contexts as "intendedly rational, vigilant, and discerning." They can be reasonably wary of other groups, although the psychology of heightened awareness might lead them to exaggerate difficulties and to undervalue positive possibilities. Wariness or suspicion is an important cognitive component of distrust, of the judgment that another is not trustworthy or is, in Ullmann-Margalit's phrase, in between. Kramer analyzes the dynamics of intergroup distrust from a social information–processing perspective. On this account, trust and distrust are cognitive. Hence he wishes to understand the factors that get in the way of an objectively correct understanding of the likely motives or trustworthiness of others, especially as these are exacerbated by in-group versus out-group relationships.

A major obstacle to trusting out-group members or an out-group as a whole is collective paranoia, which Kramer defines as "collectively held beliefs, either false or exaggerated, that cluster around ideas of being harassed, threatened, harmed, subjugated, persecuted, accused, mistreated, wronged, tormented, disparaged, [or] vilified . . . by malevolent others." Kramer explains how such beliefs arise and are maintained and then discusses devices that groups and their members can use to overcome the failure of beneficial cooperation with a seemingly hostile out-group. Among the reasons for paranoid perceptions are self-categorization in a separate group, perceptions of being evaluated by others, and uncertainty about social standing. Collective paranoia can have both cognitive and behavioral consequences. Among the former are hypervigilance in processing information, a tendency to dwell on negative readings of events (dysphoric rumination), a tendency to over-attribute hostile intentions to others (the sinister-attribution error), a tendency to organize one's personal history in a self-serving way (biased punctuation of interactional history), and exaggerated perceptions of conspiracy.

Devices that would overcome collective paranoia are implicitly devices for overcoming distrust and enabling cooperative relations. Among the most important of such devices are unilateral initiatives that show a willingness to take risks of cooperating with the other group, the use of third-party mediators, and structural devices for improving the accuracy of knowledge and thereby enabling trust relations. Sometimes, however, the more efficacious move is to reduce reliance on trust. In other chapters in this volume, both Larson and I discuss instances in which unilateral devices seem to have worked. Kramer's compelling example is the use by President John Kennedy and Premier Nikita Khrushchev of the so-called GRIT (graduated reciprocation in tension reduction) strategy, which Larson also discusses and which involved efforts to reduce tensions in the nuclear deterrent regime by taking unilateral, reciprocated steps toward reducing the risks of nuclear weapons and weapons tests (Osgood 1962; for discussion, see Hardin 1982, 209–11).

One can imagine going in the opposite direction, from some degree of trust to an increasing degree of distrust. For example, if their relationship is rocky, marital couples tend to avoid focusing on contentious current issues. This wariness about confronting ongoing issues in the relationship, perhaps out of fear that confronting them is to confront each other, "removes the opportunity to restore trust by showing concern and caring. As people pull back, diminished evidence of concern by one person is likely to be reciprocated by the other, creating a reality that mirrors their fears" (Holmes 1991, 95; also see Hardin 2002b, 90–93). Instead of taking chances on the relationship, distrustful parties put more effort into securing themselves against its breakdown by use of devices outside the relationship—and this reduces dependency on the partner. Hence distrust is circularly reinforced by the actions it provokes. Such reactions might eventually even lead to paranoid cognition, as in the awful superpower standoff that lasted four decades.

It is a commonplace that relations within families are grounded on moral commitments rather than rational or calculative commitments. They would therefore seem to be a poor context for the development of trust as encapsulated interest. Margaret Brown (chapter 7) argues, on the contrary, that distrust can pervade family relationships and that the devices to overcome distrust in families are not unlike those for overcoming distrust in other contexts. She focuses on three different kinds of intrafamilial relationships in a small community in Madagascar. All of these relationships are essentially economic: handling joint income in a marriage, buying property, and jockeying for inheritance. In that community, market institutions are weak or nonexistent, so that there are few alternatives to kin ties for economic opportunity, and formal institutions for handling relevant conflicts are weak. Brown's argument is that people will expend energy and resources to stabilize weak but important ties. In general, in her cases, the less trustworthy party typically must find informal devices to establish a commitment to being fair within the relationship. Indeed, Brown supposes that her villagers have to expend so much effort on securing familial ties that they have relatively little room to work on trust relations with nonkin. Hence, contrary to a standard view that the strength of family ties gets in the way of extending networks beyond the family (Banfield 1958), it is the weakness of even important family ties that forces all resources into maintaining them so that other networks cannot develop.

Although trust is strictly relational in Brown's account here and in the encapsulated-interest account (Hardin 2002b, chap. 1), what I can trust you to do cannot far exceed what others in like circumstances can be trusted to do. You can do something extraordinary to show your commitment to going beyond usual expectations. If the general communal context is one of distrust over the range of issues with respect to which I might wish I could trust you, you will have to make such a commitment, and it will have to be credible or I will not trust you. In Brown's community there is widespread distrust that comes from the fragility of marital relations. Extramarital affairs and divorce are common. Hence spouses distrust each other, and the children of mixed parentage distrust one another over property inheritance. The errant husband in one of Brown's cases establishes an unusually strong commitment by exceeding the demands of the community's norms governing food taboos, which differ by family. Although he is not expected to do so under prevailing norms, he takes on his wife's taboos to show that he is really committed to her despite his bad behavior. As Brown notes, that they share a value system does not lead to strong trust. "In fact, it signals to both parties the limits of their trustworthiness." That is, they cannot reliably be expected to go beyond prevailing norms.

In dealing with his siblings, a wealthier brother is careful to base his transactions with younger siblings on cash so that there can be no distrusting of the value of their exchange, as there might have been had they bartered his steer for part of their land. In this case, the wealthier brother has greater power in his relationship with his siblings than they have. As in Farrell's analysis of the effects of unequal power, this power is a clear source of heightened distrust. A common anthropological assumption is that family members engage in generalized reciprocity, without careful accounting of how much each gains from every exchange.

Brown's siblings, however, specifically want to avoid the potential for exploitation that such exchange permits. The fairly general distrust among siblings suggests that all exchanges even among themselves should be carefully calibrated and that, ideally, they should be in monetary terms.

Brown's third case involves intergenerational transfers of property. The promise of property in the future tends to secure good relations in the present. But children might prefer the gift of property now to block its partial inheritance by half siblings.

In Brown's study, the sometime view that trust is inherently moral is shown to be wrong. In her community, even family members base their relations on rational considerations. It is often supposed that strong moral ties make some societies kin based. Yet Brown's distrusting, calculative society has a kin-based organization. In her account, there is an absence of reliable alternatives to kin, and her villagers depend on only weak family ties. Such organization of society might suggest that the society would have an easy time making a transition to other forms, such as market organization. Alternatively, it may be that the difficulty of managing relationships, even among kin, impedes development of other bases of social and economic organization. If wives in Brown's village require an organization of the economy that enables them to monitor all cash flows to keep their husbands from cheating, economic change may be difficult. And if family members are more or less constrained to sell inherited land only to their own family members, they may make less investment in the land, and thus the land will be less productive than it could be. More generally, the pervasive distrust of her villagers even of their own kin may make the establishment of trust relationships with nonkin especially difficult. Strong norms over some activities seem actually to get in the way of better outcomes, as in Unni Wikan's study, in which divergent norms lead to extremely hostile conflict.

In chapter 8, Wikan presents the extraordinary and painful story of an intense clash of cultures that entails distrust on many levels. Fadime Sahindal is one of several young women who have been murdered in so-called honor killings in Scandinavia for violating their parents' cultural norms of arranged marriage with, usually, cousins from the homeland of the parents. In these cases, there is distrust between youths such as Fadime and their parents; between such parents and the state (in Fadime's case, Sweden); between imams and youngsters; between Muslims and non-Muslims; and even between different groups—more liberal or more conservative—of Muslims. The central problem is that illiberal immigrants to a liberal society may attempt to impose their own cultural order on the next generation of their own families, a generation that has grown up in a radically different society from that in which the parents reached adulthood. Some of the women who have suffered from familial impositions of cultural norms have even been born in the liberal society in which the family attacks them, and they know virtually nothing of the homeland of their parents. In the movie, *East and West*, a Pakistani man who has married an English woman and lives in England wants his half-Pakistani children to marry Pakistanis, and he even attempts to arrange a marriage for one of his sons. The children are English, independent, and liberal, and they want no part of these customs.

The cultural practices of the Islamic Kurdish community from which Fadime came are inimical, as Wikan says, to human rights—most especially to the rights of the child. These are rights that virtually define the Swedish social welfare state. Yet relevant government ministers have been reluctant to act against the violence of some of its immigrant societies because they feared that such action would fan racist sentiments. As Wikan notes, one minister balanced her concern for the welfare of immigrant girls with concerns about the racism and discrimination that immigrants might suffer if the state enunciated positions hostile to the immigrant cultures. One can see the likelihood of the collective paranoia that Kramer describes in the lives of the older generation of immigrants, who must feel isolated in their adopted communities and who presumably came to Scandinavia seeking their own freedom and prosperity. Yet once there, new immigrants often choose to live in isolated communities in which their women can be kept secluded. As Wikan observes, the problem of honor killing is a collective, not merely an individual, problem, because honor is joint. If Fadime is, by her father's lights, a whore, then by the community's lights so are her sisters, and even her brothers are shamed. Fadime's father may have pulled the trigger to kill Fadime, but many stood behind him when he did so, and many may have enabled him to find her.

One might note that the young women in these cases have torn allegiances. Are they members of the group of immigrants or of the group of Scandinavians? Having grown up in Scandinavia, they cannot escape the enticements of Scandinavian freedom and autonomy of choice, especially in such an important aspect of their lives as marriage. Their parents seem unable to see this conflict. Fadime, in a public speech, declared that she had to choose between freedom and her family. As Wikan notes, there is a problem of cultural translation when a father says in open court that, "If you had a daughter like this Fadime, you would have wished to shoot her too!" All of the Swedes in that courtroom must have recoiled in horror, and many of them must have thought Fadime an exemplary woman. In the end, Fadime could trust neither her family nor the Swedish state to care for her. Ironically, her family, as is true of perhaps most immigrants from the third world, left behind governments that could not be trusted at all, and their response to liberal governments is possibly as hostile and distrusting as their response to the governments of their homelands had been. Fadime and her sisters in Scandinavia face relatively generalized distrust of particular groups and institutions and not merely of specific individuals in those groups and institutions.

The Politics of Distrust

Patrick Troy notes, in chapter 9, that citizen distrust of government is more likely to arise with respect to those functions in which citizens frequently encounter government than those in which they seldom do so. One might suppose, therefore, that the successes of the introduction of safe drinking water and good sewerage systems have largely passed from public consciousness, while public awareness of continuing urban development can be a continuing source of public irritation and therefore distrust. Citizens might say they are confident in the water supply, but this is not likely to be a conscious thought unless they are surveyed or otherwise specifically asked about it. Governmental successes such as this one are often bygones and largely forgotten by the citizenry. Some of those successes were, after all, achieved by distant past governments and require little effort on the part of current governments.

A common, quasi-libertarian argument against government regulation is that citizens should make their own decisions about such things as how safely to build their homes. Troy's obvious response to this is that in urban contexts there are external harms that individuals typically would not care about in undertaking their own activities. Urban regulations and even urban services, such as the provision of clean water and good sewerage, are essentially collective problems that can be handled best if they are done for everyone at once. If individuals controlled their own building standards, Troy argues cogently, the result would be increased distrust between citizens, who would have to monitor one another's activities. Moreover, the introduction of regulatory standards in these contexts helped to secure the common law and led to fairer treatment of individuals who would have been at risk from the poor standards followed by others.

There is frequently a painful consequence of collective provision of early amenities such as clean water and good sewerage. Typically, all are treated more or less equally in what they will get, and all might even be forced to pay more or less equally. But the poor must generally place a lower value on such amenities than do the wealthy. Hence unless taxation for such provisions is carefully contrived to distribute the costs unequally, the poor de facto pay to help the wealthy achieve their interests less expensively than they could have done without collective provision. There is evidence from many contexts that this de facto redistribution from the poor to the well off is a common result of public provision. This result is called Director's law, from the early observation of Aaron Director that such public amenities as parks and many other facilities, supported by general revenues, benefit the well off far more than the poor (Stigler 1970; for further evidence, see Hardin 1982, 87–89). The wealthy of Sydney, Australia, tended to live in higher areas built on rock, where the costs of providing sewerage were much higher than in areas where lower-income citizens lived, and they may therefore have benefited from redistribution of costs to the poor.

A commonplace claim of recent work on trust in government is that trust in one area of a person's life might spill over to other areas. Hence if I find people in my daily life generally trustworthy, I might also think government, the church, and business trustworthy. There is little or no evidence to back this view, which arguably has roots in the writings of Alexis de Tocqueville. Troy suggests a more limited claim: that distrust of government in some areas may corrosively affect the level of distrust in other areas, which is also the argument of Montinola for the especially corrosive effects of untrustworthy, corrupt courts.

There seems to be a trend in the developments toward increasing distrust of local authorities on at least one of Troy's four main issues: urban planning (the other issues are regulations for structural safety, fire safety, and public health through, for example, public sewer systems). Troy argues that government's activities in regulating urban development result from three sources: regulations get out of date, developers and others sometimes evade regulations, and people are frustrated in their work by regulations that then seem invasive. He also discusses the general problems of the inherent discretion in applying regulations, especially in decisions on urban development, which can provoke a sense of unfairness, and the tendency for regulations to be excessive for normal circumstances, so that people think they are a matter of bureaucracy out of control. Still, Troy concludes that dissatisfaction with the results and procedures of urban planning has not had a significant effect on citizen's confidence in government in general.

On the positive side, Troy supposes that distrust of government is a healthy stance for keeping government regulations under review. Distrust keeps the system more beneficial than it would be if citizens were very trusting. Hence Troy shares with Hume, Madison, and many others the liberal theory that citizens are apt to benefit from distrusting their governments. Their arguments have mostly been principled rather than detailed, but Troy gives us a special context in which to see the force of liberal distrust. Urban regulation generally must, in a democratic society, be done in transparent and fair ways—it must be seen to be fair. Because virtually all of its detail is handled in agencies, it is apt to be less transparent than if those details were handled in open legislative sessions. Hence we have reason to distrust regulatory agencies, which are a massive part of government that did not even exist in the era of the early theory of liberal distrust. (The value of transparency might be compromised by the increased costs of decision making when there is far more participation in the decisions.)

In chapter 10, Vadim Radaev discusses the hard problems of establishing a stable contract regime in Russia after its transition to a market economy with substantially reduced state control of economic relations. Radaev works from recent surveys of nonstate enterprise managers and entrepreneurs. When asked what attributes they want their potential partners in trade to have, they rank honesty and trustworthiness as far and away the most important. They develop relationships that build from smaller initial deals to larger deals, and they choose to maintain relationships that are successful rather than to develop new relationships. One might suppose that there would be standard bidding by firms for various goods and services and that the firm that asks for the bids would choose the best combination of price and quality. Quality, of course, might involve creativity, and price might involve motivation to produce efficiently. In a well-developed, stable contract system, these last two attributes might be expected to govern choices of business partners. Where contract enforcement is essentially not available through credible courts, however, the first concern seems to be the development of alternative bases for securing desired outcomes by developing ongoing relationships that will be reliable.

The view of Radaev's managers seems clearly to be that using the courts is a poor guarantee of successful business dealings. Only about a quarter of them would go to court even to deal with malfeasance; a majority would use informal means. Fully privatized firms, however, more frequently resort to the courts. Part of the problem with the courts is that they are part of the very government that is distrusted by businessmen. As Radaev notes, businessmen join in solidarity against the government. Hence the use of the state's courts can undermine interpersonal trust rather than giving it a secure minimal basis on which to build.

Having to focus so strongly on mere reliability might have deleterious effects on the developing Russian economy. For example, the concern for trustworthiness may drive out concern for innovativeness, so that firms take a conservative, fail-safe stance. Avoiding or protecting against contract infringement is evidently the major concern of entrepreneurs and managers. Interestingly, Radaev's subjects think that contract infringement in general is more common than it is in their own experience. This echoes evidence from American studies of citizens and their relations with government bureaucrats, as noted in the claim that agents of the Internal Revenue Service (IRS) treat taxpayers viciously. Citizens commonly think bureaucrats are generally poor or even awful, although their own personal experience has generally been satisfactory

(Klein 1994). Perhaps there has been more progress in establishing good interfirm relations in Russia than firm managers believe.

Radaev also finds that business dealings with relatives and other close associates are not immune to contract infringement and nonpayment for goods or services rendered. This finding suggests affinities with the experience of the Frafras in the trading places of the migrant slums of Accra, Ghana. As Keith Hart (1988, 190) says, "Kinsmen make poor borrowers since they equate their interests with those of the lender." This is not a good foundation for exchange.

So what devices do Russian managers use when seeking to find reliable partners? They use third-party references, they check up on the behavior of their partners, and, if they are lucky, they are good psychological assessors of their potential partners. The transition has been under way long enough that reputations are commonly well established. Managers start with a new partner with small deals and work up to larger deals as the partner proves reliable. Each manager also is part of a network, in which performance in one relationship is apt to affect the possibility of other relationships (see Cook and Hardin 2001). Instant communication of default can get a potential partner cut off from the entire network. As Radaev notes, affect-based trust is being replaced by reputation-based trust. One might conclude from his account, however, that the final stage is an ongoing relationship with the same partner, so that reputation ceases to play a role (Hardin 2002b, 93). In that case, trust depends on a belief that the truster's interest is encapsulated in the interest of the trusted because each partner needs a stable relationship with the other.

Cynthia Horne, in chapter 11, asks why, in its trade policy, the European Union (EU) treats nations of the former communist world very differently from other nations at similar levels of development. In particular, the EU invokes antidumping policies as a form of trade protection against many goods from formerly communist states, as it had done earlier before those states began their transitions to market economies. Dumping means that goods are being sold to the importing nation at less than fair value, which roughly means at lower prices than they would be sold at in the exporting nation. Hostility to dumping partially grows out of concern that a firm might attempt to drive competitors out of business in order to establish a monopoly, as domestic firms have historically been thought to do. This is a fear that might seem credible for a major producer in an advanced society but not so credible for firms in the developing world.

An antidumping policy does not mean that imported goods cannot be sold more cheaply than goods produced in the importing nation. Indeed, it is the policy of the EU that developing nations should be able to benefit from their lower prices if these are the result of lower costs of various factors of production—especially labor—in the exporting nation. The EU implicitly supports development in poorer nations through the international division of labor. Comparing the price of a good, its "normal value," in the exporting nation to the price offered in the importing nation permits competitive advantages to poorer nations. If that were the whole story, dumping policy might be simple. Unfortunately, it is far more complex than this because some firms produce only for the export market. The EU policy on dumping accommodates pricing of such export-only goods by requiring evidence that the costs of production genuinely are lower. This move opens many possibilities for obstruction.

Horne argues that the EU uses antidumping claims to block trade from formerly communist states. Its apparent objective is to affect labor, environmental, and other social policies in those states, although such purposes are explicitly denied to the European trade agencies. She presents data to support her descriptive claims that the EU is much harder on formerly communist states than on others and that it uses shadier tactics in dealing with them. When comparative prices for a good in the exporting and importing nations cannot be used as a measure of dumping, the EU relies on comparisons to supposedly comparable nations to establish the costs of production. This device is used deceitfully and very effectively when production costs in, say, Russia are compared with those in Canada or Norway, where labor costs are much higher and environmental protections are much more extensive. If the nation for which such comparisons are being made is, say, Thailand, the EU would more likely compare its costs with those in Indonesia, where costs are apt to be fairly similar, rather than to costs in Canada or Norway.

Horne supposes that the EU bureaucrats act unfairly toward the formerly communist states because they distrust those nations, and she cites derogatory comments from her interviews with EU officials in support of her contention. She concludes that this distrust leads to discriminatory trade policies and, in the long term, undermines the ability of the EU to establish institutions that would foster credible trade commitments. This is a relatively informal assessment of the degree of distrust, and the claim of distrust is therefore somewhat speculative. What, one might ask, is the source or object of the distrust? Is it a residue of the justified distrust of the days before 1989? Or is it sparked by doubt that the formerly communist nations have genuinely made a transition, perhaps still only partial, to market economics?

There are two alternative theses. First, the formerly communist nations (still officially called nonmarket societies by the EU) have no natural supporters in EU circles, while many former European colonies have strong natural supporters. For example, for the EU to go against

India is to go against the United Kingdom and development policies it wants for India; and to go against Indonesia is similarly to go against the Netherlands. Second, EU nations have long had much richer trade relations with the noncommunist world than with the communist world, toward which they were long extremely hostile. If this is part of the problem with current practices, one might expect that the formerly communist states will slowly begin to be treated more equitably as a new generation of bureaucrats comes to control EU decision making and as trade relations between the two blocks become better established. One might expect the same longer-term development if the issue is primarily distrust, because increased interactions over time might eventually induce trust.

Finally, irrespective of whether the European Commission distrusts formerly communist nations, those nations must now distrust the EU, as Montinola and Ullmann-Margalit might be expected to argue. Such distrust, if not warranted by the current Eastern regimes and companies, might provoke responses that make the distrust a self-fulfilling prophecy.

Wikan's issues of intergroup distrust may be exacerbated during the present era of exported terrorism, as discussed in chapter 12 on such terrorism. Unfortunately, these two issues are not unrelated in the accounts here: they both arise from strong commitments to rigid variants of Islam. The heightening of distrust between ethnic groups might be a distressing side effect of the terrorist attack on the United States in September 2001. Though terrorism in many contexts, such as anarchist terrorism in the early twentieth century, has been more or less purely politically driven, without heavy overtones of ethnic or religious conflict, the most violent terrorist movements today are generally religiously or ethnically motivated. Concern with terrorism in the United States today has immediately raised issues of the civil liberties of various groups and individuals, and the imported terrorism has probably provoked intergroup conflict and distrust. This conflict between civil liberties and security against terrorism is an especially difficult problem in the United States. The regime of civil liberties in the United States arose first in the context of distrust of government, as in the discussion of Madison and his fellow constitutionalists. After the Civil War and the abolition of slavery, that regime was slowly expanded to cover specific problems of racial discrimination. The culmination of the long-developing regime of civil liberties brings these two strains together.

The usual concern with police power that animates libertarians is exacerbated when the police act from racial prejudice. To counter racism by police forces and even the justice system, American law and civil libertarians have developed a strong view of the wrongness of racial stereotyping. This is a complex issue because you and I commonly stereotype in many contexts to economize on the need for information and even investigation. More or less everyone must use stereotyping in varied contexts. If I am hiring workers, I will quite likely assume that some easy indicators are fairly good approximations to a more intensive assessment or testing of candidates. That might mean I make mistakes and treat some people unfairly. It is now legally prohibited under U.S. law to use mere race as a supposed indicator of performance. You might use such stereotyping in your private dealings with people, but you cannot do so when you are acting on behalf of a public agency or a large corporation.

To those who think such stereotyping wrong, Mayor Rudolph Giuliani's finest moment in office was when he told his fellow New Yorkers that we should not assume that our Arab neighbors had any responsibility for the attacks of September 2001. Yet if border control officials randomly checked those entering the nation to try to exclude potential terrorists, they would de facto harass people. Besides tourists, the largest single group of border crossers are Mexicans, who are coming to work and are extremely unlikely to be terrorists. Not to stereotype out of a concern for fairness to the different types would have perverse consequences of hassling vast numbers of people unnecessarily and of generally making air travel by tourists and others and border crossings by workers more cumbersome for everyone without greatly improving safety.

Americans may now face relatively generalized distrust of Arabs, who may be provoked into relatively generalized distrust of non-Arab Americans. That is a depressing effect of group identification in many contexts. Montinola and Troy, similarly, find relatively generalized distrust of whole institutions and not merely specific distrust of individual role holders in those institutions. As Montinola argues, generalized trust of these institutions can hardly make sense because individuals cannot know enough about them to trust them in any strong sense. At most they can be confident that an institution (or group) will continue to behave well, as it has done so far. They can distrust in a very general way because they can extrapolate to the contrary interests of many institutional role holders and of some ethnic or other group.

Such generalized distrust can be misplaced, as it arguably has been in the United States in the case of the IRS, which was loudly attacked in congressional hearings in 1997 and 1998 under the control of Republicans who evidently wanted to tarnish the image of government and who set themselves up as a kangaroo court to establish that the IRS had abused certain taxpayers. Unfortunately, as in typical kangaroo courts, they did not seek evidence from anyone other than complaining taxpayers. Afterward, independent agencies established that the taxpayers who gave testimony to the Senate investigating committee owed the taxes that the IRS had concluded they owed. The lasting result of those cynical hearings has been a radical decrease in audits of wealthier taxpayers and, quite possibly, undue damage to the reputation of an agency that is probably remarkably fair rather than abusive (David Cay Johnson, "Investigations Uncover Little Harassment by IRS," *New York Times*, August 15, 2000, p. A1; "Phantom Rogues at IRS," editorial, *New York Times*, August 19, 2000, p. A14). Agents of the IRS were portrayed as mean and vicious, but this is implausible on its face. More generally, there is a fairly strong tradition of libeling government in the United States, possibly increasing citizen distrust of government.

Montinola sets up her account of the Philippine judiciary in chapter 13 by noting the dramatic differences in the public reaction to arguably unjustified and politicized decisions about the nation's political leadership in the Philippines and the United States. When the Philippine Supreme Court legitimated the ouster of democratically elected Joseph Estrada as president, it sparked violent protests. Montinola argues that in part the reason for such a reaction was the weak credibility and apparent corruption of that court, whose decisions carry limited legitimate force. She takes an institutional approach to corruption—the misuse of public office for personal benefit—arguing that we must look to the structure of incentives to determine the likelihood and explain levels of corruption. Many nations have seen less benefit from transitions to democracy and the market than had been expected by theorists. Commonly, the reason for the failures is corruption in government.

Because government controls the supply of many costly benefits, officials are often in a position to exact a "fee" for letting contracts or giving out licenses. The institutional approach suggests several devices for limiting corruption. These include increasing the transparency of all governmental activities through open bidding, clear standards, and surveillance by a free press; raising the cost of corruption, especially by giving key actors the capacity to expose and ensure the punishment of offenders; and, for politicians, open elections to increase accountability. For the Philippine Supreme Court, requiring decisions by the entire membership of the Court once increased the number of people who must be corrupted and therefore reduced the likelihood of success.

Montinola is especially concerned to understand the relation of corruption on the Court to citizen's confidence in government. She supposes that the asymmetrical nature of trust and distrust allows for ready distrust of institutions and the government in general, even though it would not allow for trust of such institutions. Knowledge of its corruption is sufficient for a citizen to distrust a government agency because the corruption clearly is against the citizen's interest, so that the agency cannot be said to encapsulate the interest of the citizen. In the recent literature on trust in government, it is commonly supposed that trust can spill over from one arena to another, so that my trusting local organizations might contribute to my trusting the government. As noted above, there is little to no evidence of such spillover. With distrust, however, there might be a kind of spillover or generalization of distrust. If I know that government is broadly corrupt on many issues, I am likely to conclude that it is generally corrupt. Indeed, if I have knowledge of corruption, then those in high positions in government have access to much the same knowledge; and if they are not corrupt, they should take action against those who are. If corruption goes unpunished, I have reason to doubt the motivations of essentially all government officials. Trust does not similarly generalize by this logic. This is an important and apparently novel argument. Its conclusion seems likely to be reinforced by the apparent fact, noted by several writers here in addition to Montinola, that it is harder to repair distrust and create trust than it is to wreck trust and create distrust.

Finally, Montinola concludes that widespread government corruption tends to lead not only to distrust of government but also to lack of trust between officials within government and lack of trust—even distrust—among citizens. She spells out these relationships in her account of the Philippine Supreme Court. That particular institution most likely has more impact on these other relationships than do other governmental institutions because it is the foremost institution in establishing the rule of law that undergirds stable democracy. From a former status as apparently highly respected, the Court is now viewed by Filipinos as just another corrupt part of government. Its decline was driven by the politics of dictatorship under Ferdinand Marcos and the long transition to democracy. New rules for the organization of the Court in the 1987 constitution altered incentives for justices. The Court was given power to oversee political controversies, thus inviting corrupt entreaties; it was allowed to sit en banc in smaller groups, thus reducing the number of people who must be tempted into corruption on any given decision; it was given much greater autonomy, thus undercutting efforts at external control; it was given oversight over agencies that previously were under the Justice Department, including agencies that might have countered the Court in many arenas; finally, the process for appointments to the Court has been made less transparent and has largely been put in the hands of the president and the chief justice.

Newly emerging democracies, Montinola argues, must successfully design institutions that secure the liberal distrust of government. Otherwise, their governments will have such power as to be able easily to violate civil liberties. The new institutions must have the incentive and the genuine capacity to hold one another accountable. The consequences of failure and of corruption are pervasive distrust of government and, therefore, pervasive distrust among citizens and among those, such as entrepreneurs, who might build a dynamic economy.

Concluding Remarks

What general conclusions can we draw from the contributions presented here? A very general positive claim we can make is that these chapters show the value of understanding the nature of distrust (and trust) and of rigorously analyzing its role in various social contexts. There is great diversity of contexts and yet strong parallels in the analyses here.

When we try to understand collectivities and institutions, often we can start from analogies to individuals. For example, to some extent, one can see distrust between two nations as a relative of distrust between two groups or two individuals. A significant difference generally is that individual citizens of one nation are not so likely to develop paranoid cognitions about individual citizens of another nation as are individual members of two hostile groups. It is genuinely at the national level that problems of distrust arise, rather than at the level of individual citizens. What my nation might do to yours is not analogous to anything I might do to you. Hence we can suppose that whatever distrust there is between nations is institutional in some meaningful sense. Two chapters here discuss distrust between nations that can be analyzed as distrust by officials of the nations.

Patrick Troy tells a complex story of the rise of public regulation of urban space and activities in Australia and of the interactions between government and citizens, who have strong interests in how their space is used and regulated. One way to read his story is to note that, when there are failures of outcome or of procedure in urban regulations, citizens can know enough to begin to judge the government as untrustworthy.

In general, it appears to be difficult for citizens to judge their governments as trustworthy; at best, they can judge that a government seems to be competent and that it produces apparently good outcomes (Hardin 2002b, chap. 7; chapters 3 and 13 in this volume). Hence citizens can be more or less confident in government. Although they cannot be said to trust in any strong sense of that word, as spelled out in the three extant theories of trust, they can develop generalized distrust in response to seeming failures. At that point, they could say that government is either incompetent or badly motivated, but they might not have evidence to decide which of these is the problem. (It would be seen as badly motivated if, for example, its policy were thought to be a response to payoffs or to special interests.) If either incompetence or bad motivation is true of some area of government regulatory effort, however, citizens can distrust the government with respect to that area. In such contexts distrust and trust are asymmetric. Mere confidence, however, may not be as sharply asymmetric because it can be based simply on evidence of how well government does its job generally without any real understanding of how it does the job within its agencies.

If government handles crises and disasters well, it can be given credit for its seeming competence even while it is held accountable for failing to prevent the crisis or disaster—as the U.S. government received widespread praise for its handling of the al Qaida terrorist organization after September 11 but has been heavily criticized for its prior failures to follow up on leads that might have prevented the disastrous attacks that day. Similarly, urban citizens can do little more than react to government's failures that might set up disasters and then react to its immediate handling of the crisis. Evidence that it has failed can often be glaring and inescapable and can lead to citizens' distrust. Lack of evidence of government failures, however, is not sufficient to conclude in favor of generalized trust in government in many regulatory areas.

References

Bailyn, Bernard. 1967. *The Ideological Origins of the American Revolution.* Cambridge, Mass.: Harvard University Press.

Banfield, Edward C. 1958. *The Moral Basis of a Backward Society.* New York: Free Press.

Cook, Karen S., and Russell Hardin. 2001. "Norms of Cooperativeness and Networks of Trust." In *Social Norms,* edited by Michael Hechter and Karl-Dieter Opp. New York: Russell Sage Foundation.

Cook, Karen S., Russell Hardin, and Margaret Levi. 2004. *Cooperation Without Trust?* Unpublished manuscript.

Freeman, Richard B., and James L. Medoff. 1984. *What Do Unions Do?* New York: Basic Books.

Hardin, Russell. 1982. *Collective Action.* Baltimore, Md.: Johns Hopkins University Press for Resources for the Future.

———. 1999. "From Bodo Ethics to Distributive Justice." *Ethical Theory and Moral Practice* 2(4): 337–63.

———. 2002a. "Liberal Distrust." *European Review* 10(1): 73–89.

———. 2002b. *Trust and Trustworthiness.* New York: Russell Sage Foundation.

Hart, Keith. 1988. "Kinship, Contract, and Trust: Economic Organization of Migrants in an African City Slum." In *Trust: Making and Breaking Cooperative Relations,* edited by Diego Gambetta. New York: Blackwell.

Holmes, John G. 1991. "Trust and the Appraisal Process in Close Relationships." In *Advances in Personal Relationships,* vol. 2, edited by Warren H. Jones and Daniel Perlman. London: Jessica Kingsley.

Klein, Daniel B. 1994. "If Government Is So Villainous, How Come Government Officials Don't Seem Like Villains?" *Economics and Philosophy* 10: 91–106.

Lipset, Seymour M., Martin Trow, and James S. Coleman. 1956. *Union Democracy*. New York: Free Press.
Morgan, Edmund S. 1999. "Just Say No." *New York Review of Books,* November 18, 39–41.
Olson, Mancur, Jr. 1965. *The Logic of Collective Action.* Cambridge, Mass.: Harvard University Press.
Osgood, Charles E. 1962. *An Alternative to War or Surrender.* Urbana: University of Illinois Press.
Pharr, Susan J., and Robert D. Putnam, eds. 2000. *Disaffected Democracies: What's Troubling the Trilateral Democracies?* Princeton, N.J.: Princeton University Press.
Rotter, Julian B. 1967. "A New Scale for the Measurement of Interpersonal Trust." *Journal of Personality* 35(December): 651–65.
Schelling, Thomas C. 1960. *The Strategy of Conflict.* Cambridge, Mass.: Harvard University Press.
Stigler, George J. 1970. "Director's Law of Public Income Redistribution." *Journal of Law and Economics* 13(1, April): 1–10.
Wills, Garry. 1999. *A Necessary Evil: A History of American Distrust of Government.* New York: Simon & Schuster.
Wright, Thomas L., and Richard G. Tedeschi. 1975. "Factor Analysis of the Interpersonal Trust Scale." *Journal of Consulting and Clinical Psychology* 43(4): 470–77.

Chapter 2

Distrust:
Prudent, If Not Always Wise

DEBORAH WELCH LARSON

DISTRUST PERVADES ethnic wars, arms races, and enduring conflicts such as that in the Middle East. In 1955 President Dwight David Eisenhower commented to his advisers that he greatly regretted the deterioration of U.S.-Soviet relations in the postwar period. He felt that it was important to recognize "that in Moscow the Soviet version of events was put forth to their people and that in the United States the course of events was set forth as we saw them." As a result, "many millions of people in both countries had developed a state of fear and distrust of each other." Eisenhower did not expect that "any improvement could occur overnight, but would take some time until the present psychological state of distrust and fear were overcome" (Dwight David Eisenhower, Memorandum of conversation, July 20, 1955, in "Geneva Conference July 18–23, 1955 [1] (3)," Dwight David Eisenhower Papers, International Meetings Series, Dwight David Eisenhower Library, Abilene, Kansas).

Indeed, it took thirty-four years for the fear and distrust between the Soviet Union and the United States to be overcome. That psychological factors helped to prolong the cold war, however, does not imply that the United States had no reason to distrust the Soviet Union.

What is distrust? What factors enter into judgments to distrust? Distrust is often prudent, even if not always wise (for the distinction, see Leffler 1992, 502–6). The costs of misplaced trust can be devastating, whereas distrust merely impedes valuable cooperation or exchange. Because distrust is a judgment, however, it can be mistaken. In such instances, distrust may be self-perpetuating. Added up over time, the costs of unnecessary conflict and forgone opportunities for trade and cooperation can be substantial. In short, there is not only a "healthy" distrust that is a rational response to risk but also a distrust that is based on flawed reasoning; and it would be worthwhile to distinguish between the two and avoid the latter. Where it is unwarranted, how can distrust be overcome?

Trust and Distrust

Trust usually refers to a judgment that one can rely on another party's word or promise at the risk of a bad outcome should the other cheat or renege (Deutsch 1958; Luhmann 1979, 25; Coleman 1990, 91; Hardin 1993, 516; Dasgupta 1988, 51–52; Luhmann 1988, 97; Gambetta 1988a, 217). For example, a mother may decide to leave her baby at a day-care center. She trusts that the baby will be fed, changed, and cuddled and that the infant will not be neglected or restrained. To trust is to give discretion to another who is free to betray the faith placed in him or her (Gambetta 1988a, 218–19; Hardin 1993, 507). Trust differs from expectation in that it requires a choice between alternatives. If the other fails to keep his promises, the trusting party will feel regret for her trusting choice. The consequences of misplaced trust should be worse than not having relied on the other in the first place, because otherwise it is simply a matter of rational choice, for which no trust is required (Luhmann 1979, 24–25).

Distrust is a judgment that one cannot depend on the other's actions or promise because the other has an interest in cheating or wishes to harm oneself. Contrary to the conventional view of distrust as an emotional or irrational reaction, distrust is often a sensible response to potential dangers. The mother who decides that a day-care facility is unsanitary or unsafe is exercising appropriate care. Trust is demonstrated by reliance on someone's words or actions. In contrast, distrust may be concealed or may not be manifested in open behavior. One might have to find indirect indicators of distrust, such as information gathering, monitoring, protective measures, use of deterrence, or refusal to enter into long-term exchanges. For example, the mother may talk to other parents, consult a government agency in charge of regulating child-care facilities, make unscheduled drop-in visits, hire a babysitter, or stay at home with the baby herself.

Being unable to trust someone need not imply active distrust. I may not be able to trust an individual because I know too little to form an opinion. Trust and distrust both require at least some familiarity with the target, a state of knowledge somewhere between total knowledge and ignorance (Lewis and Weigert 1985; Jones 1996; Hardin 1998, 11; see also chapter 3 in this volume). People generally have reasons for distrusting someone else. Secretary of State John Foster Dulles did not distrust the Soviets because he was uncertain about their motives; he knew that they were devious, deceitful, and hostile (Jervis n.d.). Trust and distrust are functionally equivalent in that they tell us how to act when we do not know for sure the other's motives and intentions and being wrong could have undesirable consequences (Luhmann 1979, 71). Otherwise, we would merely be undecided.

What gives people confidence that they cannot rely on the other's actions or promises? Distrust is based not solely on risk aversion but also on information about the situation and personal history. That is, distrust is a judgment grounded in particular types of evidence. Distrust and fear are not the same, although they are often conflated in international relations. We fear someone if he or she has both the will and the capability to harm us. Similarly, one state views another as a threat if the second combines hostile intentions with substantial offensive capabilities (Walt 1987). I distrust someone if I believe that he is not telling the truth or will not fulfill a promise. My lack of confidence in him may reflect the belief that he is thoughtless, feckless, incompetent, or volatile, even if I do not believe that he intends to harm me or could do so if he so desired.

Fear has an emotional component that is not necessarily part of distrust. Fears are often automatic reactions to conditioned stimuli (LeDoux 1996, 146–48). Distrust, on the other hand, is cognitive in origin and impact. The United States may distrust Russia's renunciation of its empire and therefore refuse to allow it to join the North Atlantic Treaty Organization (NATO); at the same time, the United States does not believe that Russia has the military capability to invade Eastern Europe, much less to endanger American territorial integrity (Pruitt 1965, 396). It is true, however, that distrust of another state creates a propensity to view its military capabilities as threatening, which reinforces distrust in a vicious circle.

Distrust applies to particular statements or actions that the actor might take. A generalized predisposition to distrust everyone would be paranoia. Russell Hardin argues that trust and distrust describe a three-part relationship, whereby A trusts or distrusts B to do X (Hardin 1993, 506; Luhmann 1979, 92; Barber 1983, 17–18). I might trust you on some issues, be uncertain or skeptical about your reliability in another area, and distrust you on some other matter. I might trust a friend to repay a loan but not to drive my new car. Judgments whether to trust or distrust a state or its leader can be context specific. During World War II, American president Franklin D. Roosevelt trusted British prime minister Winston Churchill to fight against Hitler, but he distrusted Churchill's postwar colonial ambitions, especially in the Middle East. The United States trusts Britain in some respects but distrusts the British in others. Israelis may distrust Syrian leader Bashar Assad because of his support for Hezbollah in Lebanon but believe that he will observe a peace agreement that would return the Golan Heights to Syria. Distrust varies by issue and time period, and relations between states are therefore a mixture of trust, uncertainty, and distrust.

Trust and distrust are threshold points on a continuum of probability assessment (Gambetta 1988a, 218; Luhmann 1979, 45, 73). We would say that we trust someone if the likelihood that he will fulfill his obligation lies above a particular threshold. We distrust someone if the likelihood that he will carry out a promise is sufficiently low. In visual perception, a threshold is an artificial discontinuity on a continuum. Absolute trust would have a probability of one, complete distrust a probability of zero. In the real world, we would find few examples of complete distrust or absolute trust that were not products of psychological pathologies. We do not trust anyone without reservation. The idea of a continuum, a number line, captures the idea that trust and distrust are a matter of degree.

Where the threshold points are located depends on the party's innate suspiciousness and his potential losses. Individuals show consistent differences in their beliefs about whether other people in general can be trusted (Rotter 1971). Apart from individual differences, the risks associated with being betrayed also matter. On inconsequential issues, where trust costs little, an individual might be willing to gamble. When the potential dangers are greater, the person will not rely on the other unless the perceived probability that trust will be fulfilled is quite high. States require a higher level of assurance for arms control than for lowering their tariffs. When the other side has a gun—or an atomic bomb—pointed at you, then the probability that he will fire need not be very high for you to distrust him (Luhmann 1979, 42, 73).

In situations where misplaced trust could have devastating consequences, it is prudent to devise protective measures. Indeed, distrust can create the conditions necessary for trusting. Nuclear deterrence made superpower relations more predictable; thus institutionalized distrust led to a form of trust. Because it was not feasible to defend against a nuclear attack, both the United States and the Soviet Union could be certain that the other side would not knowingly launch a first strike as long as each maintained a sufficient number of weapons to retaliate. Mutual deterrence gave both sides an incentive to cooperate in reducing the number of nuclear weapons, because once the balance was achieved, superiority conferred no usable advantage (Jervis 1989, chap. 1).

Distrust may either be well founded or unwarranted, just as trust may be justified or misplaced. We may think of trust and distrust as subject to type I (false positive) or type II (false negative) errors. A decision rule that reduces the risk of falsely distrusting someone also increases the dangers that trust will be unjustified. As Dulles told Eisenhower in

1955, "The difficult problem for American statesmanship at the present time was to find policies which, on the one hand, would not rebuff the Soviet change in policy in case it were genuine, but, on the other hand, [would] not expose us to grave danger in case it turned out to be a pure maneuver for conquest" (Memorandum of conversation with the president at Fitzsimons Hospital, Denver, Colo., October 11, 1955, in "Meeting with the President 1955 (4)," John Foster Dulles Papers, White House Memoranda Series, Dwight David Eisenhower Library, Abilene, Kansas).

When Distrust Is Prudent

Distrust is often prudent because we cannot know fully the motives or intentions of many people we encounter in a complex society (Gambetta 1988a, 218). Trust may create the opportunity for mutually profitable interaction, but violating trust can sometimes be more attractive for at least one party. As Fritz Scharpf states, "Being able to trust, and being trusted, is an advantage—but exploiting trust may be even more advantageous" (Scharpf 1997, 89). Accordingly, relying on others or giving them discretion over our fate could be disastrous (Dasgupta 1988, 50).

Trusting is risky not because others are evil but because they are self-centered. For example, the day-care center can save money and make higher profits by not hiring enough staff or by paying them only the minimum wage. The financial officers at Enron were probably not trying to harm their employees or stockholders by concealing information about the firm's profit situation; they merely wanted to sell their stock for a higher price.

Trust would not be at issue if there were little possibility of its being betrayed. If it is in the other's interests to fulfill his obligation to you, if it is something that he would do anyway out of self-interest, then we do not need to trust him. As Edna Ullmann-Margalit (chapter 3 in this volume) observes, trust means that I believe that you will take my interests into account *because* they are my interests. We trust someone if we believe that he will forgo opportunities for short-term gain at our expense (Luhmann 1979, 42–43; Dasgupta 1988, 54; Scharpf 1997, 138). If trust is needed, distrust may be rational. As John Dunn (1988, 81) puts it, "The twin of trust is betrayal." Distrust follows naturally from the risks of trusting. Information about the other's lack of trustworthiness can make conditional distrust rational even if the potential gains from trust are high (Ziegler 1998).

This raises the question of why the trusted party, acting in his own self-interest, would ever fulfill the expectations of another. Why would an individual forgo an opportunity for gain at another's expense? The most obvious explanations are a continuing relationship, concerns about reputation, and identification with others.

Russell Hardin's formulation is an encapsulated-interest account: A trusts B if B's interests include taking A's interests into consideration. This might be because B wants to continue a profitable relationship. A relationship that benefits both sides increases the incentives for trustworthiness. Both parties may faithfully observe their obligations because the other party might otherwise retaliate or exit, thereby cutting off possible future benefits (Luhmann 1979, 36–37; Hardin 1991; chapter 1 in this volume). If one party has less to lose from breaking off the relationship, then the weaker side cannot rely on the other's prudence. Henry Farrell (chapter 4 in this volume) argues that asymmetries in a relationship can lead the more dependent party to distrust the commitments of the other. For example, the United States, as the world's sole remaining superpower, no longer needs its NATO allies to intervene militarily in other countries. Indeed, using allied forces can be a military liability, because they do not have the most technologically advanced, computer-guided weaponry or swift reaction capabilities. Because they lack leverage over U.S. policy, NATO allies do not trust the United States to act unilaterally but would prefer that it take action through the United Nations (James Traub, "Who Needs the U.N. Security Council?" *New York Times Magazine*, November 17, 2002, p. 46ff.).

Concern for maintaining a good reputation also inhibits people from lying or cheating (Dasgupta 1988). We give some weight to the verbal assurances of others, especially when the other's words are delivered face to face, as she looks us in the eyes. One reason for believing the other is that we know that a liar will gain a reputation for dishonesty that will inhibit others from relying on her in the future (Goffman 1969, 126–28; Jervis 1970, 78–83, 88–89). Leaders often give credence to their counterpart's personal assurances, even though relations between states are supposedly governed only by power considerations and Realpolitik. For example, President John F. Kennedy believed Premier Nikita Khrushchev's assurances that the Soviets were not installing offensive missiles in Cuba and was outraged by the deception when it was uncovered. In a secret meeting with Soviet ambassador Anatoly Dobrynin during the tense days after the missiles were uncovered, Robert Kennedy reportedly complained that the president "felt himself deceived and deceived intentionally," which was a "heavy blow to everything in which he had believed and which he had strived to preserve in personal relations with the head of the Soviet government: mutual trust in each other's personal assurances" (telegram from Soviet ambassador Dobrynin to the USSR ministry of foreign affairs, October 24, 1962, translated and reprinted in Woodrow Wilson International Center for Scholars, *Cold War International History Project Bulletin* [5, Spring 1995]: 72–73.).

In these cases, trust is based on an assessment of the interests of the trusted. Trust may also be justified by the belief that the other has a cooperative orientation, such that mutual trust is a more attractive outcome than unilateral defection. We may trust someone such as a close friend or relative because we believe that she is generally benevolent or that she derives utility from our well-being (Becker 1996, 54; Baier 1986, 234; Hardin 1991, 193–94; Yamagishi 1994, 131–32). Identification with others is a motive for group-based trust (Lewicki and Bunker 1996, 122; Kramer, Brewer, and Hanna 1996). Individuals derive part of their identity from membership in social groups. They tend to view members of their own group as more trustworthy, honest, and loyal than those from out-groups. Members of an ethnic or other social group may use their shared identity as a shortcut for decisions whether to trust, obviating the need to acquire personal information about the other (Brewer 1981, 351–52). Indeed, in Margaret Brown's study of villages in Madagascar (chapter 7 in this volume), the lack of any ethnic or other collective identity forces the inhabitants to develop trusting relationships with kin.

The absence of these conditions may account for lack of trust but not for distrust. What gives people confidence that the other's promises are false or his intentions hostile? We do not distrust someone merely because it is in his or her interest to behave in an untrustworthy manner, because that would apply to all situations in which trust is necessary. When a relationship is about to end, we may trust the other less than we did before, but that does not mean that we actively distrust him or her. An employee who has accepted a job with another company might steal proprietary secrets. But unless we already had some suspicions, we would not distrust him merely because he was leaving the firm.

A judgment to distrust is mediated by the individual's beliefs, experience, and information. Some beliefs are formed through interaction with relevant others. Information relevant to someone's trustworthiness may be contextual or conveyed by a third party. Beliefs trump experience and information, though, because beliefs influence whether we engage in experience and affect interpretation of information. Eventually, though, we may modify our beliefs if the contradictory information is unambiguous or overwhelming.

Individuals show consistent differences in their beliefs about whether other people in general can be trusted. If they have been fortunate in their experience with putting trust in others, people will attach a higher a priori probability that the other will fulfill obligations and that their expectations will be met (Rotter 1971; Hardin 1993, 508).

Other beliefs are induced from experience with a particular individual or type of person. Characterization of someone as untrustworthy may be a generalization, an abstraction from previous instances of lying or cheating by that person (Luhmann 1979, 28). For example, after trying to get along with Joseph Stalin after World War II, President Harry Truman concluded that the Soviets had broken every agreement since his meeting with Stalin at Potsdam. In September 1947, Truman explained to the press, "I have every kindly feeling in the world for the people who are causing us all the trouble now, and we made certain specific agreements, none of which has been carried out by the other party. And that is the cause of the present situation" (quoted in Larson 1985, 317). Since we can never be certain that a person will continue to behave in the same way, trust and distrust always go beyond available information in making inferences (Luhmann 1979, 26).

Distrust is also informed by beliefs about the lack of trustworthiness of different types of people. Where time or information is lacking, we may use social categories such as ethnicity, race, class, or gender to size up an individual quickly. A taxi driver, for example, must make snap judgments about whether potential fares are likely to rob him. As Hardin notes (chapter 12 in this volume), distrust of a member of another group may be justifiable and prudent, depending on the environment. African Americans in the South had particular reason to be wary of the police from 1880 until 1964, when lynching was commonplace.

The cold war was exacerbated by belief systems that portrayed the other side as hostile. Classic communist doctrine maintained that class conflict was inevitable. Leninist ideology held that capitalist states competing for overseas markets and territory would resolve their conflicts by going to war against the socialist bloc. In a February 9, 1946, speech that became known as the Soviet declaration of cold war, Stalin exhorted the Soviet people to invest in heavy industry so that the Soviet state would be guaranteed against all eventualities. Future wars were inevitable, he maintained, because the capitalist system could not peacefully resolve conflicts over markets and raw materials (Tucker 1971, 246, 248–49). The United States distrusted the Soviet Union because the latter believed in the impossibility of peaceful coexistence with the capitalist world. Commenting on Stalin's speech in his famous long telegram from the Moscow embassy, minister counselor George F. Kennan warned, "We have here a political force committed fanatically to the belief that with [the] U.S. there can be no permanent *modus vivendi*, that it is desirable and necessary that the internal harmony of our society be disrupted, our traditional way of life be destroyed, the international authority of our state be broken, if Soviet power is to be secure" (quoted in Larson 1985, 252, 256). In July 1988 Soviet foreign minister Eduard Shevardnadze argued, against vigorous opposition, that the Soviet Union had to renounce the doctrine of the inevitability of class conflict in order to overcome Western distrust of Soviet motives (Shevardnadze 1988, 13, 15).

Parties in conflict can find ample justification for their beliefs that the other cannot be trusted—a legacy of broken promises, attempts at subversion or assassination, betrayal, the seizure of disputed territory, and so forth. In Yugoslavia, Serbs and Croats had fought each other, as well as the Germans, during World War II. Yugoslav president Slobodan Milosevic stirred up Serbians' distrust of Croats by evoking images from the previous war, when fascist Croats or Ustashas had slaughtered Serbs, in order to defeat his political rivals for power in Yugoslavia. When Croatia became independent in 1990, minority Serbs believed that Croatian nationalists planned to reestablish a fascist state. Croatian extremists contributed to these fears by killing, intimidating, and expelling Serbs who tried to stay. Once violence had broken out, neither Croats nor Serbs knew whom they could trust (Glenny 1993, 11, 31, 92, 122–23). Similarly, the behavior of Soviet occupation forces in Germany after World War II left a residue of distrust. The German people might have welcomed Soviet troops as liberators from Nazi oppression and war, but the Red Army's widespread looting for food and liquor, pillaging and burning of German villages, and raping of German women instilled deep hatred among the Germans. Soviet troops may have raped as many as 2 million German women (Naimark 1995, 69–140; Smyser 1999, 38–39).

Contextual cues may provide information suggesting that the other cannot be trusted. Inferences from these indirect indicators draw on intuitive theories about others. For example, the other person may seem nervous or unwilling to make eye contact, indicators of lying. A state may send additional troops to the border despite its leader's pledges to reduce tensions with a neighboring country.

We may rely on third parties to provide testimony about others' trustworthiness (Coleman 1990, 180–81). For example, the Sicilian Mafia was in the business of attesting to the quality of goods such as horses in return for the payment of buyers who wished to avoid being cheated or defrauded (Gambetta 1988b, 171–73). Letters of recommendation to law school or graduate school serve a similar function of testifying about the validity of the applicant's qualifications.

Distrust is often prudent, given the high costs of being betrayed, uncertainty about others' motives, and material incentives to lie or cheat. Indeed, in a complex society or in international relations, where we cannot know everyone personally, it is not distrust that is problematic but trust. For that reason, trust has received more attention from scholars than distrust.

Why Distrust Is Sometimes Unwise

Most accounts of trust and distrust presume that actors are sensible and objective in judging others' trustworthiness. Distrust may be unwarranted, however, because it is based on categorical judgments or biased processing of information. Errors are inescapable because the same cognitive processes that are responsible for bias are highly functional for perception and social judgment. Distrust is based on inferences about the other's intentions, a process that is inherently subjective.

Group distrust may be decoupled from assessment of the other's interests or past behavior. To simplify the overwhelming confusion of reality, people divide up what they see into categories. The same is true for perception of individuals—they are categorized as members of social groups. Social groups accent differences between themselves and the other group while minimizing differences within their own group, a process that leads to stereotyping. Thus normal cognitive functioning leads to stereotyping and prejudice, without individuals being motivated to distort reality (Tajfel 1959; Hogg and Abrams 1988, 19–20, 23; Haslam et al. 1996, 186–89). The "dark side" of group-based trust is a corresponding suspicion of outsiders. Group members discriminate against out-groups even when the criteria for belonging are arbitrary, membership is anonymous, and there is no history of antagonism (Tajfel 1978, 63–64; Brewer 1979; Kramer 1999, 588) As Hardin observes in chapter 12 of this volume, members of close-knit groups ranging from terrorist cells to the Amish maintain cohesion by drawing sharp lines between "us" and "them." Unni Wikan (chapter 8 in this volume) observes that the isolation of Iranian Kurdish immigrants from Swedish society contributes to their deep distrust of government, freedom, and the cultural mores of their adopted country.

Politicians may exploit latent suspicions of out-groups to achieve purposes including distraction from economic problems, justification for defense expenditures, and their own personal aggrandizement. After World War II, for example, Joseph Stalin needed an external enemy to justify the continuing hardships and privations imposed on the Soviet people even after the defeat of Nazi Germany. Stalin also wanted to assert tighter control over Soviet society, including many returned soldiers and prisoners of war who had presumably been contaminated by their exposure to the higher living standards of the West, and over the regimes of Eastern Europe. Stalin's secret police apparatus institutionalized xenophobia, the belief that all foreigners were potential spies, and excessive secrecy (Zubok and Pleshakov 1996, 77, 114, 131, 133).

Like trust, distrust is grounded partly in learning and experience. It is not just raw experience that gives rise to distrust, though, but the way people interpret it. Group-serving biases distort the way people construe the history of interaction. To maintain a positive identity, social groups attribute negative behaviors by the other to internal characteristics, whereas similar undesirable actions by their own group are explained away as owing to external circumstances or outside pressures (Pettigrew 1979; Brewer and Kramer 1985; Hewstone 1990; Kramer,

Brewer, and Hanna 1996, 368). Assuming that the other's behavior is caused by internal factors, groups infer that the out-group's hostility is gratuitous and unprovoked by anything that they have done. Roderick Kramer calls this inferential pattern in which each group sees itself as responding to the other "biased punctuation" (Kahn and Kramer 1990, 150; chapter 6 in this volume). Who started it determines who is to blame (Michotte 1963; Kelley and Stahelski 1970).

In this way, groups may develop the belief that the other is largely responsible for the conflict. International adversaries from the Middle East to Bosnia to northern Ireland develop narratives in which they have been victims of the other's aggressive actions. If the other side started the conflict, then the other side is fundamentally untrustworthy. Moreover, conflicting groups view each provocation as part of a long chain of aggression rather than as a single, isolated incident (Baumeister, Stillwell, and Wotman 1990). The Serbs' belief that they have been historic victims of oppression and persecution leads them to portray Croats and Muslims as treacherous or bloodthirsty and to overlook their own role in instigating violence in Croatia and Bosnia (Finnegan 1999, 60ff.). Kramer calls false or exaggerated beliefs that portray one's group as being harassed, threatened, or harmed by a malevolent out-group or out-groups "collective paranoia" (chapter 6 in this volume).

Even when members of the other group have committed violent acts, category-based distrust is likely to be unwarranted because it assumes that out-group members are homogeneous, that all individuals are equally deceptive, disingenuous, untruthful, or treacherous. It also fails to consider the possibility that the other group might observe limited agreements or fulfill trust in particular issue areas. Despite their mutual distrust, the United States and the Soviet Union concluded several important arms-control agreements during the cold war, such as the Limited Test Ban Treaty and the Anti-Ballistic Missile Treaty, because both sides recognized that they had shared interests in regulating the arms race and in preventing an inadvertent nuclear war.

Erroneous distrust, however, is difficult to falsify and can elicit confirming behavior from the target. Beliefs that the other is untrustworthy color interpretation of his or her behavior. Ambiguous actions will be interpreted in the worst possible light. Refusal to answer a question, for example, will be viewed as evidence that the person has something to hide, not that he or she is naturally reticent or shy. Once people have been primed to suspect someone, they will interpret his or her behavior to support their suspicions. In one experiment, subjects instructed to interview a job candidate read a letter of recommendation that raised the possibility that the applicant might not be well rounded. The candidate, they were told, believed that the interviewers would be looking for applicants who had broad intellectual and cultural interests. Although the candidate gave a detailed list of extracurricular activities and interests, subjects chose a less qualified candidate whom they had no reason to distrust (Fein and Hilton 1994).

Kramer (chapter 6 in this volume) argues that people who are self-conscious or believe that others are evaluating them are apt to make overly personalistic attributions about others' behavior. Insecure individuals, for example, may construe an overheard conversation or laughter as gossip about them or ridicule (Kramer and Wei 1999). Instead of causing them to consider alternative interpretations, continued rumination over these alleged incidents causes people to become even more convinced of the validity of their erroneous interpretations. Because negative events have a disproportionate impact on impressions, what are perceived to be slights or betrayals loom large as justifying distrust.

Normally, if we place undue trust in someone else, we shall soon discover our mistake to our own detriment. When dealing with a personal friend, we may be willing to overlook repeated transgressions until a "bright line" is crossed. Then, when that boundary is crossed, like any threshold effect, the impact on beliefs is entirely out of proportion to the provocation—"the last straw." We tend to explain away a friend's unreliability by arguing that lapses or broken promises were unintentional, accidental, or made under duress (Luhmann 1979, 73; Williamson 1993, 483). It is entirely rational to hold on to one's well-grounded beliefs unless the contradictory evidence is overwhelming. In this case, the value of a long-standing personal friendship may be great enough to tolerate a few disappointments.

Nevertheless, unwarranted distrust is usually more difficult to falsify than is trust. Distrust inhibits one from engaging in the very behavior that might disprove it. A distrustful person will not rely on the other and so will have no reason to change his or her mind (Gambetta 1988a, 234). A bigot will refuse to have any contact with an African American and will therefore have no reason to revise stereotypical beliefs (Warner and DeFleur 1969).

Nor can an individual overcome the other's distrust by generally behaving in an upright, honest manner. The reason honesty is not always enough is that we cannot be sure of the causes. Telling the truth or keeping promises is socially preferred. A person who behaves honestly may be suspected of trying to create a good impression, conforming to social pressures, or ingratiating others (Skowronski and Carlston 1987).

Sometimes monitoring is proposed as a means of ensuring that others are trustworthy (Kreps 1990a, 528; Kreps 1990b, 106–7). Surveillance, however, can actually reduce estimates of the other's trustworthiness because it increases the ambiguity of its causes. In one experiment, a supervisor regarded an employee who worked under his close surveillance as less trustworthy than another worker who had received less supervision, even though both workers performed the same amount of work. The supervisor, though, could not be sure whether the employee had worked hard because he was conscientious or to avoid punishment (Strickland 1958; Kruglanski 1970).

When cheating is likely to be detected and punished, most people will observe the rules. Even a con man will pay traffic tickets or keep up with car payments. The Soviet Union could not prove that it had no intention of invading Western Europe merely by refraining from doing so, because it might have been deterred by the threat of U.S. nuclear retaliation. When the chances of being caught are lower and the potential gains of deception are higher, honest behavior is more diagnostic of trustworthiness. A woman who is truly of high integrity will pass up opportunities to lie or cheat even when she could get away with it (Reeder and Brewer 1979). Of course, if her actions truly cannot be monitored or observed, the other will not *know* that she behaved honestly.

That an individual appears to be honest and reliable in most instances does not prove that she can be counted on in a new situation where the stakes are higher. I may trust someone in the everyday dealings in with which we are engaged, but hesitate to rely on her for more important matters. During World War II, Stalin complained that "Churchill is the kind who, if you don't watch him, will slip a kopeck out of your pocket. Yes, a kopeck out of your pocket! . . . And Roosevelt? Roosevelt is not like that. He dips in his hand only for bigger coins" (Djilas 1962, 73). In Stalin's opinion, Roosevelt may have been trustworthy when the potential gains from deceiving his Soviet ally were low, but he too was unscrupulous when the prize was more attractive.

People ordinarily do not take notice when someone behaves honestly, whereas they may infer from a single highly dishonest action that the individual has no integrity (Reeder and Brewer 1979; Skowronski and Carlston 1987, 137–38). To illustrate, when President George Bush violated his pledge to "read my lips, no new taxes," the American public concluded that he was untrustworthy. The public was angered not just because their taxes went up but also because the president had broken a sacred compact (Jeffrey Schmalz, "Words on Bush's Lips in '88 Now Stick in Voters' Craw," *New York Times*, June 14, 1992, p. 16). A reputation for trustworthiness can only be established through consistent good behavior over time, but it can be lost in an instant (Dasgupta 1988, 62; Luhmann 1979, 28–29). If people are Bayesian information processors who incrementally update their beliefs in response to each new piece of data, then it may take a great deal of time and many occasions to disconfirm beliefs about the other's lack of trustworthiness (Hardin 1993, 508). As the psychologists Myron Rothbart and Bernadette Park (1986, 137–38) comment, "Favorable traits are hard to acquire but easy to lose, while unfavorable traits are easy to acquire and hard to lose."

Misplaced trust is a self-disconfirming prophecy. Confusing an aggressor state for a status quo power is an error that will soon be revealed. Unwarranted or exaggerated distrust, on the other hand, can stimulate behavior that confirms it, the familiar self-fulfilling prophecy. In the words of Robert Merton (1948, 195), "A self-fulfilling prophecy is, in the beginning, a *false* definition of the situation evoking a new behavior which makes the originally false conception come *true*." Distrust is a positive feedback system in which experience is self-reinforcing rather than equilibrating (Luhmann 1979). Being perceived as hostile, unfriendly, stupid, or incompetent can cause one to behave accordingly, thereby confirming the perceiver's original preconceptions or stereotypes (Darley and Fazio 1980). For example, in one experiment, interviewers were instructed to act toward white applicants for a position the same way that blacks had been treated, for example, giving them shorter interviews, creating greater physical distance, stuttering more, and so forth. The white applicants performed more poorly than a control group, according to independent raters who watched the interview on videotape (Word, Zanna, and Cooper 1974).

Trust and distrust are reciprocal. If someone makes himself vulnerable to us, we are more inclined to trust him. Conversely, if he behaves as if he distrusts us, or declines to put any faith in us, we are more likely to distrust him (Lewis and Weigert 1985, 971). In interpersonal relations, a distrustful person will behave defensively, for example, by refusing to disclose any information or declining occasions for conversation. The target of distrust cannot conceive of any reason for the other's suspicion and will not perceive the cause of it in himself. He will attribute the other's reserve to some attribute of the person who distrusts him. The target may at first try to explain away the other's hostility but may then return the distrust himself, feeling entitled by the unjust treatment he has received. It then becomes individually rational for the person to behave in an unfriendly manner, even if he originally had an optimistic assessment of prospects for a relationship, because to trust the other could expose him to ridicule or rejection (Luhmann 1979, 73; Gambetta 1988a, 234).

In a state of international anarchy, according to the security dilemma model, distrust of another state can elicit a hostile reaction from the other side even if the two states have had no previous conflict of interest. A state that distrusts another's intentions will build up its military, station troops along its border, refuse to negotiate on arms control, or impose trade sanctions in an effort to protect itself from attack. Not understanding how the other could suspect it of aggressive intentions, the target state will wonder why the other state is increasing its military capabilities. The distrusted state will conclude that the fearful state must itself have aggressive designs. Thus distrust can create or exacerbate conflict between two states that merely want to preserve the status quo (Jervis 1976, 1978). In support of the security dilemma thesis, researchers have produced experimental evidence that possessing high levels of coercive capabilities can cause interdependent actors to use more punishment tactics and produce a conflict spiral (Bacharach and Lawler 1981; Deutsch 1973; Rubin and Brown 1975; Pruitt 1982; Youngs 1986; Lawler 1992; Luhmann 1979).

A real-world conflict spiral occurred at the beginning of the cold war. In December 1947, the Truman administration decided to build up the western zones of Germany as an economically and politically viable entity instead of trying to negotiate with the Soviets for a unified Germany. State Department officials suspected that the Soviets were deliberately stalling to prevent German economic recovery and create chaotic conditions that would be conducive to a communist takeover. Stalin, on the other hand, feared that the Western countries were rebuilding West Germany to be the spearhead of aggression against the Soviet Union. In 1948 the Soviets blocked ground and water access to West Berlin to pressure the West into giving up its plans to form a separate West German government, an act that only strengthened the Western allies' determination not to allow the Soviets any role in West Germany. Stalin's heavy-handed attempts at coercion created the enemy he feared and helped to institutionalize mutual distrust. Western Europeans sought a defense guarantee from the United States, and Washington agreed to join an alliance, NATO. Yet neither the United States nor the Soviet Union desired a rebirth of German aggression or wanted Germany to become too powerful (Zubok and Pleshakov 1996, 37, 39, 50, 52, 74, 77; Leffler 1992, 512; Trachtenberg 1999).

Whereas misplaced trust can lead to large losses, unwarranted distrust may have high opportunity costs, as it can lead to a series of missed opportunities (Hardin 1993, 507). Distrust can exact its own costs. The mother who stays home with her child because she cannot find reliable child care loses salary and professional advancement. During the cold war, the United States and the Soviet Union acquired far more weapons than they needed for deterrence. The United States deployed thirty thousand nuclear warheads, while the Soviets accumulated more than forty-five thousand—totals vastly in excess of their actual security requirements (Robert Lee Hotz, "Cold War Foes Forge Warm Ties," *Los Angeles Times*, June 23, 1995, p. 1; Matthew L. Wald, "Today's Drama: Twilight of the Nukes," *New York Times*, July 16, 1995, p. E5). The arms race helped to contribute to the collapse of the Soviet Union and diverted resources in the United States from more productive investments.

There were numerous occasions on which it was at least possible and sometimes highly plausible that the superpowers could have achieved agreements—for example, German unification, a test ban, a ban on multiple-warhead missiles—that would made both more secure if they could have trusted the other to fulfill the bargain. After Stalin's death in 1953, Soviet leaders were worried that East Germany was falling apart owing to the regime's forced-pace imposition of Stalinist institutions. The head of the Soviet KGB (State Security Committee), Lavrenti Beria, and the prime minister, Georgi Malenkov, favored allowing East Germany to join with the Western half of the country in return for German neutrality, trading off an unstable client for guarantees against German rearmament. The Eisenhower administration, however, was unwilling to take the risk that the Soviets were proposing negotiations only to sidetrack or delay West Germany's impending membership in NATO.

In 1959 Khrushchev and Eisenhower had nearly agreed upon a ban on all nuclear tests above a certain threshold, but when a U.S. U-2 surveillance plane was sighted and shot down over Soviet territory less than two weeks before the Paris summit, Khrushchev felt that his trust in Eisenhower had been betrayed, and the opportunity to agree on a comprehensive nuclear test ban, which would have prohibited development of more accurate and destabilizing weapons, was lost. Finally, in 1969 and 1970, neither the United States nor the Soviet Union had tested missiles with multiple, independently targetable warheads (MIRVs), and satellites could have monitored a ban on their testing. But President Richard Nixon and his national security adviser, Henry Kissinger, did not trust Soviet motives for entering into arms-control negotiations. Such missiles later endangered mutual deterrence because of their accuracy and destructive power (Larson 1997).

Since missed opportunities refer to what might have been, they are less tangible and more difficult to interpret than actual losses. It is difficult to prove a counterfactual. People are more bothered by tangible losses than by opportunity costs. Nevertheless, the cumulative loss from missed opportunities can be quite substantial. Whereas misplaced trust can result in a few large losses, unwarranted distrust can result in an aggregate of individual missed opportunities, amounting to substantial losses over time (Hardin 1993, 507).

Overcoming Distrust

Distrust, where misplaced, can be undermined through unilateral actions and third-party mediation. An exogenous shock created by the emergence of a common enemy can swiftly overcome mutual distrust, but such events are not entirely under the control of the parties themselves. If trust is difficult to establish, the parties might try to reduce the need for it by structuring the incentives to encourage cooperation as a matter of rational calculation.

To prove his trustworthiness, a person can do something out of the ordinary that would not otherwise be expected if he were untrustworthy (Luhmann 1979, 42). That is why we speak of someone having to "prove" his trustworthiness. The actor should make a promise and keep it. Even better, he should carry out a promise in an area that is costly to him but does not impose many risks on the other. He might make a costly concession that would benefit the other in order to prove his sincerity (Swinth 1967). In her study of two villages in Madagascar (chapter 7 in this volume), Brown tells of an unfaithful husband who restored his wife's trust by refusing to eat her taboo foods, an act that went beyond the requirements of social norms and conventions.

More than one costly concession may be required to overcome the other's distrust. In the late 1950s the psychologist Charles Osgood (1962) proposed a strategy called GRIT (graduated reciprocation in tension reduction) whereby the initiator makes several small public concessions and then waits for the adversary to reciprocate. If the adversary responds, GRIT makes a slightly more risky concession. For example, President Kennedy's June 1963 speech at American University called for a "strategy of peace" consisting of small concessions by the Soviet Union and the United States that each could recognize and reciprocate. Kramer (chapter 6 in this volume) discusses psychological research that supports various components of the GRIT strategy.

Mikhail Gorbachev's actions toward the United States also fit the GRIT strategy. In August 1985 he initiated an eighteen-month unilateral moratorium on nuclear testing, which was not reciprocated by the Reagan administration. He agreed to on-site inspection and asymmetric reductions in Soviet medium-range missiles, which led to the Intermediate Nuclear Forces Treaty in December 1987. In a December 1988 speech at the United Nations, Gorbachev announced that he would unilaterally reduce Soviet troops by five hundred thousand, withdraw ten thousand tanks and eight hundred combat aircraft from Eastern European countries and the European portion of the Soviet Union, and reconfigure remaining Soviet forces so that they would be useful for defense rather than offense. Gorbachev's initiative convinced many in the United States that the Soviet leader was serious about ending the cold war. President George Bush took steps to end the Soviet Union's economic isolation at the December 1989 Malta summit. Finally, Gorbachev accepted the loss of East Germany to the Western bloc without insisting on assurances against NATO expansion (Larson 1985, 202, 223–24, 230–31).

Although it is not as fast or efficient a process as making a costly concession, honest behavior over time should help overcome distrust, if people are Bayesian information processors who modify their beliefs about the other's trustworthiness on the basis of experience. As evidence accumulates that the other can be trusted even in difficult situations, distrust may shade into trust as the threshold of probability is crossed (Luhmann 1979, 40–41; Dasgupta 1988, 62). The idea of a threshold suggests that small amounts of information can have large effects, if they cause judgments to "tip" over or under the required level of probability for trust. Although individuals receive information piecemeal, when their beliefs change, the beliefs change all at once (Luhmann 1979, 72).

To substitute for direct experience, a third party may act as a go-between, certifying one party's trustworthiness to the other. In his interviews with Russian entrepreneurs, Vadim Radaev (chapter 10 in this volume) finds that they consult business networks of friends and long-time associates to check up on new business partners. On the level of relations between states, British prime minister Margaret Thatcher told President Ronald Reagan, "I like Mr. Gorbachev. We can do business together." Since Reagan placed a great deal of reliance on Thatcher's judgment, he invited the new Soviet leader to a summit meeting (Shultz 1993, 507, 509; Garthoff 1994, 207n). Since the 1993 Oslo agreement between Israel and the Palestine Liberation Organization, Norway has on several occasions served as an intermediary for negotiations between rival states and ethnic groups. Norway has mediated agreements between the Indonesian government and separatists, Sri Lanka and Tamil rebels, and Guatemala and leftist guerrillas. A small state that is geographically distant, Norway is not perceived as a threat by conflict parties (Frank Bruni, "A Nation That Exports Oil, Herring, and Peace," *New York Times,* December 21, 2002, p. 3).

Perhaps the quickest way to overcome distrust is for the two parties to acquire a shared interest or a superordinate goal. Kramer (chapter 6 in this volume) discusses experiments by Muzafer Sherif and colleagues in which two rival groups of boys at a summer camp overcame their mutual distrust after they were required to work together. The history of international relations contains many examples of former enemies who allied with one another against a common threat—Britain and France against Germany in World War I, Britain and the United States with the Soviet Union against Nazi Germany. Most recently, the September 11 attacks reoriented U.S. relations with China and Russia, as each state feels threatened by radical Islamic movements and proliferation of weapons of mass destruction. The United States values Russia as a source of oil to make up for disruptions in supplies from the Middle East, a site for military bases directed against al Qaida in Afghanistan, and a diplomatic intermediary with Iran, North Korea, and Iraq. Russia, on the other hand, has a stake in being admitted to the "club" of advanced industrial states and in becoming a member of the World Trade Organization ("Reaching Out to Vladimir," *Economist,* May 25, 2002, p. 34). China has chosen to put aside former disputes with the United States over Taiwan and China's national missile defense because of concern about radical Islamic movements within its borders, regional security, trade, and weapons proliferation (Joseph Kahn, "Hands Across Pacific: U.S.-China Ties Grow," *New York Times*, November 15, 2002, p. 12).

If trust is scarce, then perhaps it makes sense to "economize" on trust by using a combination of coercion and incentives (Gambetta 1988a, 223–24). Two parties who distrust each other can still cooperate on some issues if they can structure the incentives so that they recognize that each has an interest in fulfilling an agreement. Despite their mutual suspicions, the United States and the Soviet Union concluded several important arms-control agreements during the cold war, such as the Limited Test Ban Treaty and the Anti-Ballistic Missile Treaty. Indeed, the superpowers negotiated more arms-control agreements than the United States and post-Soviet Russia because a declining sense of threat has reduced each side's interest in limiting the other's arsenal. The United States would not sign any agreements with the Soviet Union unless monitoring and enforcement provisions provided confidence that cheating could be detected and punished. As Ronald Reagan used to say, "Trust but verify."

Because ambiguous provisions can encourage cheating at the margins, the greater the distrust, the more detailed negotiators will insist that a treaty be, in order to cover all potential loopholes (Jervis 1976, 45). Distrust can motivate diplomats to craft more workable agreements. Negotiators will spend more time on developing monitoring arrangements and provisions for retaliation (Levi 1998, 78–79). The absence of distrust, on the other hand, reduces the motivation to craft precise agreements with provisions to ensure compliance. In May 2002 President George W. Bush and President Vladimir Putin signed a treaty to reduce their arsenal of nuclear warheads by two-thirds by 2012. In that year, however, either side can withdraw from the treaty with only three months' notice. Moreover, neither is required to dismantle or destroy the warheads but may keep them in storage for later reinstallation on missiles. Some U.S. senators have raised concerns that terrorists might get hold of stored Russian nuclear warheads (David E. Sanger, "Bush and Putin to Sign Pact to Cut Nuclear Warheads; Weapons Can Be Stockpiled," *New York Times*, May 14, 2002, pp. 1, 8; David E. Sanger and Michael Wines, "Bush and Putin Sign Pact for Steep Nuclear Arms Cuts," *New York Times*, May 25, 2002, pp. 1, 6).

The parties might reduce incentives to cheat by dividing up an agreement into smaller components. Although we might not trust the other to be prudent when a great deal is at stake, we might be willing to gamble a small investment. Not only would the other have less to gain from violating the agreement, but he or she would also lose the opportunity for future profitable interactions (Schelling 1960/1963; Blau 1964, 94). In the 1970s the West German Social Democratic Party pursued Ostpolitik, a policy of diplomatic engagement with the Soviet Union and Eastern Europe. Through trade, technology sharing, and diplomatic reassurance, the Social Democratic Party strategist Egon Bahr intended to give the Soviet Union a stake in better relations with West Germany. Although insufficient by itself to persuade the Soviets to relinquish control of their East German ally—for that, Gorbachev's ambitious strategy for achieving East-West trust was required—the policy of small steps did reduce Soviet fears of West Germany, making it politically easier for Gorbachev to agree to reunification (Ash 1993, 64–65, 364–65). Radaev's interviews (chapter 10 in this volume) indicate that Russian entrepreneurs sometimes protect themselves against noncompliance by beginning with small contracts to test the other side's good faith or by dividing up large transactions into several stages to ensure delivery of goods and services.

Such informal arrangements are necessary because Russia does not have well-developed, impartial public institutions. In contrast to Western industrial states, in which courts are available to enforce contracts, the international system is formally anarchic in the sense that there is no overarching authority. Nevertheless, a great power or international organization may help bring about a cooperative agreement between warring states or ethnic groups by mediating between the parties, preventing violence, and enforcing observance of a final settlement through the threat of external intervention. In enduring civil war settlements, an external party such as the United Nations has taken responsibility for maintaining peace, thus enabling the parties to lay down their arms, demobilize, and join a government (Walter 1997, 335–64). Historically, the United States has played an important role in negotiations to resolve the Middle East conflict by acting as an intermediary between the parties and providing guarantees that an agreement would be observed.

As Farrell discusses (chapter 4 in this volume), in line with the literature on credible commitments, a powerful actor may accept institutional constraints to make it possible for weaker parties to trust him to fulfill his commitments. Margaret Levi, Matthew Moe, and Theresa Buckley (chapter 5 in this volume) argue that institutions can help overcome distrust between parties of unequal power, as in the case of the National Labor Relations Board, which is available to adjudicate charges of unfair labor practices. The board helps equalize the bargaining power of workers and management by giving labor the option of filing a complaint rather than carrying out a costly strike.

After World War II, the United States reassured its weaker allies and persuaded them to accept an open economic and political order through "self-binding," that is, by agreeing to operate within multilateral institutions such as the Bretton Woods agreements and NATO (Ikenberry 2001, chap. 6). The Western allies still had to trust the United States not to dominate them, because no international organization can force a great power to act against its wishes. Nevertheless, the United States was able to convince Western allies that its interests were best served in a stable institutional order that would reduce the costs of obtaining compliance with liberal rules and norms—a good example of trust as "encapsulated interest."

Conclusions

In many situations, such as relations between rival nations or social groups, distrust is the baseline of expectation. Sometimes interests are conflicting, and each side would materially benefit from cheating or reneging. Distrust protects us from losses incurred by foolishly relying on those who would harm us. The United States exercised poor judgment in relying on the promises of Saddam Hussein or Slobodan Milosevic. Distrust can motivate us to acquire more information about the situation and the other party, contributing to better-quality decisions. Distrust can also stimulate us to erect defenses against potential dangers and exercise appropriate caution.

That distrust is often sensible, however, does not mean that it is always justified. Distrust can readily find grounds because we can always come up with possible reasons for the other to cheat or renege. In any exchange, there are short-term incentives to take advantage of the other. Then too, having been primed to suspect the other, people can always find information suggesting that the other has ulterior motives.

It is therefore important to find ways to distinguish good from bad distrust. How do we strike the right balance between the risks of misplaced trust and those of unwarranted distrust? One possible means is to assess the epistemological basis for our distrust. Where there is a possibility that distrust is based on snap judgments or automatic stereotyping, we might try to calculate the other's interests and assess the other's past behavior. If there is a chance that the other might benefit from an exchange, we should test the other side on small issues in which there is less risk before going on to more substantial matters.

Knowing the inferential grounds for distrust provides clues as to how to reduce distrust—by altering evidence concerning interests or character. Viewing distrust as a prudent response to risk means that we should take the other's concerns seriously. Croats and Serbs had reason to distrust and fear each other after the Yugoslav institutions broke down, given their previous shared history of murder and torture as recently as World War II. Providing rational grounds for trust, given such a history, is the next problem for theory and practice. Rival ethnic groups need to have some reason to believe that making themselves vulnerable to the other will not have a bad outcome. A third party may have to intervene to get the two sides talking to each other and assure that aggression will be punished. The end of the cold war and the Easter accords in northern Ireland give some grounds for expectation that practices and beliefs can be changed.

Just as distrust can be deliberately fostered by government action, through propaganda and educational programs, so perhaps may trust be replaced with greater tolerance for rival groups through public education. Along those lines, it is noteworthy that President George W. Bush emphasized in his early speeches after the terrorist attacks of September 11 that the American people were not at war with Muslims and that he spoke at a mosque.

For helpful comments and suggestions for revision, I thank Russell Burgos, Jennifer Kibbe, Russell Hardin, and three anonymous reviewers.

References

Ash, Timothy Garton. 1993. *In Europe's Name: Germany and the Divided Continent.* New York: Random House.
Bacharach, Samuel B., and Edward J. Lawler. 1981. *Bargaining.* San Francisco: Jossey-Bass.
Baier, Annette. 1986. "Trust and Antitrust." *Ethics* 96(January): 231–60.
Barber, Bernard. 1983. *The Logic and Limits of Trust.* New Brunswick, N.J.: Rutgers University Press.
Baumeister, Roy F., Arlene Stillwell, and Sara R. Wotman. 1990. "Victim and Perpetrator Accounts of Interpersonal Conduct: Autobiographical Narratives About Anger." *Journal of Personality and Social Psychology* 59(October): 994–1005.
Becker, Lawrence C. 1996. "Trust as Noncognitive Security About Motives." *Ethics* 107(October): 43–61.
Blau, Peter. 1964. *Exchange and Power in Social Life.* New York: John Wiley.
Brewer, Marilynn B. 1979. "In-group Bias in the Minimal Intergroup Situation: A Cognitive-motivational Analysis." *Psychological Bulletin* 86(2, March): 307–24.
———. 1981. "Ethnocentrism and Its Role in Interpersonal Trust." In *Scientific Inquiry and the Social Sciences,* edited by Marilynn B. Brewer and Barry E. Collins. San Francisco: Jossey-Bass.
Brewer, Marilynn B., and Roderick M. Kramer. 1985. "The Psychology of Intergroup Attitudes and Behavior." *Annual Review of Psychology* 36: 219–43.
Coleman, James S. 1990. *Foundations of Social Theory.* Cambridge, Mass.: Harvard University Press.
Darley, John M., and Russell H. Fazio. 1980. "Expectancy Confirmation Processes Arising in the Social Interaction sequence." *American Psychologist* 35(10, October): 867–81.

Dasgupta, Partha. 1988. "Trust as a Commodity." In *Trust: Making and Breaking Cooperative Relations*, edited by Diego Gambetta. New York: Basil Blackwell.

Deutsch, Morton. 1958. "Trust and Suspicion." *Journal of Conflict Resolution* 2(4): 265–79.

———. 1973. *The Resolution of Conflict*. New Haven, Conn.: Yale University Press.

Djilas, Milovan. 1962. *Conversations with Stalin*. New York: Harcourt, Brace and World.

Dunn, John. 1988. "Trust and Political Agency." In *Trust: Making and Breaking Cooperative Relations*, edited by Diego Gambetta. New York: Basil Blackwell.

Fein, Steven, and James L. Hilton. 1994. "Judging Others in the Shadow of Suspicion." *Motivation and Emotion* 18(2): 167–98.

Finnegan, William. 1999. "Letter from the Balkans: The Next War—What Will the New Serb Nationalists Do with Their Rage?" *New Yorker*, September 20, 1999, 60ff.

Gambetta, Diego. 1988a. "Can We Trust Trust?" In *Trust: Making and Breaking Cooperative Relations*, edited by Diego Gambetta. New York: Basil Blackwell.

———. 1988b. "The Price of Distrust." In *Trust: Making and Breaking Cooperative Relations*, edited by Diego Gambetta. New York: Basil Blackwell.

Garthoff, Raymond L. 1994. *The Great Transition: American-Soviet Relations and the End of the Cold War*. Washington, D.C.: Brookings Institution.

Glenny, Misha. 1993. *The Fall of Yugoslavia: The Third Balkan War*. 3rd ed. New York: Penguin Books.

Goffman, Erving. 1969. *Strategic Interaction*. Philadelphia: University of Pennsylvania Press.

Hardin, Russell. 1991. "Trusting Persons, Trusting Institutions." In *Strategy and Choice*, edited by Richard J. Zeckhauser. Cambridge, Mass.: MIT Press.

———. 1993. "The Street-Level Epistemology of Trust." *Politics and Society* 21 (4, December): 505–29.

———. 1998. "Trust in Government." In *Trust and Governance*, edited by Valerie Braithwaite and Margaret Levi. New York: Russell Sage Foundation.

Haslam, S. Alexander, Penelope J. Oakes, John C. Turner, and Craig McGarty. 1996. "Social Identity, Self-Categorization, and the Perceived Homogeneity of Ingroups and Outgroups: The Interaction between Social Motivation and Cognition." In *Handbook of Motivation and Cognition*, vol. 3, *The Interpersonal Context*, edited by Richard M. Sorrentino and E. Tory Higgins. New York: Guilford.

Hewstone, Miles. 1990. "The 'Ultimate Attribution Error'? A Review of the Literature on Intergroup Causal Attribution." *European Journal of Social Psychology* 20(4, July–August): 311–35.

Hogg, Michael A., and Dominic Abrams. 1988. *Social Identifications: A Social Psychology of Intergroup Relations and Group Processes*. London: Routledge.

Ikenberry, G. John. 2001. *After Victory: Institutions, Strategic Restraint, and the Rebuilding of Order After Major Wars*. Princeton, N.J.: Princeton University Press.

Jervis, Robert. 1970. *The Logic of Images in International Relations*. Princeton, N.J.: Princeton University Press.

———. 1976. *Perception and Misperception in International Politics*. Princeton, N.J.: Princeton University Press.

———. 1978. "Cooperation Under the Security Dilemma." *World Politics* 30 (2, January): 167–214.

———. 1989. *The Meaning of the Nuclear Revolution: Statecraft and the Prospect of Armageddon*. Ithaca, N.Y.: Cornell University Press.

———. n.d. "Hasty Notes on the Concept of Trust." Unpublished manuscript. New York: Columbia University, Department of Political Science.

Jones, Karen. 1996. "Trust as an Affective Attitude." *Ethics* 107(October): 4–25.

Kahn, Robert L., and Roderick M. Kramer. 1990. "Untying the Knot: De-Escalatory Processes in International Conflict." In *Organizations and Nation-States: New Perspectives on Conflict and Cooperation*, edited by Robert L. Kahn and Mayer N. Zald. San Francisco: Jossey-Bass.

Kelley, Harold H., and Anthony J. Stahelski. 1970. "The Inference of Intentions from Moves in the Prisoner's Dilemma Game." *Journal of Experimental Social Psychology* 6(4, October): 401–19.

Kramer, Roderick M. 1999. "Trust and Distrust in Organizations: Emerging Perspectives, Enduring Questions." *Annual Review of Psychology* 50: 569–98.

Kramer, Roderick M., Marilynn B. Brewer, and Benjamin A. Hanna. 1996. "Collective Trust and Collective Action: The Decision to Trust as a Social Decision." In *Trust in Organizations: Frontiers of Theory and Research*, edited by Roderick M. Kramer and Tom R. Tyler. Thousand Oaks, Calif.: Sage Publications.

Kramer, Roderick M., and Jane Wei. 1999. "Social Uncertainty and the Problem of Trust in Social Groups: The Social Self in Doubt." In *The Psychology of the Social Self*, edited by Tom R. Tyler, Roderick M. Kramer, and Oliver P. John. Mahwah, N.J.: Lawrence Erlbaum.

Kreps, David M. 1990a. "Corporate Culture and Economic Theory." In *Perspectives on Positive Political Economy*, edited by James E. Alt and Kenneth A. Shepsle. Cambridge, U.K.: Cambridge University Press.

———. 1990b. *A Course in Microeconomic Theory*. Princeton, N.J.: Princeton University Press.

Kruglanski, Arie W. 1970. "Attributing Trustworthiness in Supervisor-Worker Relations." *Journal of Experimental Social Psychology* 6(2): 214–32.

Larson, Deborah Welch. 1985. *Origins of Containment: A Psychological Explanation*. Princeton, N.J.: Princeton University Press.

———. 1997. *Anatomy of Mistrust: U.S.-Soviet Relations During the Cold War*. Ithaca, N.Y.: Cornell University Press.

Lawler, Edward J. 1992. "Power Processes in Bargaining." *Sociological Quarterly* 33(1): 17–34.

LeDoux, Joseph. 1996. *The Emotional Brain: The Mysterious Underpinnings of Emotional Life*. New York: Simon & Schuster.

Leffler, Melvyn P. 1992. *A Preponderance of Power: National Security, the Truman Administration, and the Cold War*. Stanford, Calif. Stanford University Press.

Levi, Margaret. 1998. "A State of Trust." In *Trust and Governance*, edited by Valerie Braithwaite and Margaret Levi. New York: Russell Sage Foundation.

Lewicki, Roy W., and Barbara Benedict Bunker. 1996. "Developing and Maintaining Trust in Work Relationships." In *Trust in Organizations: Frontiers of Theory and Research*, edited by Roderick M. Kramer and Tom R. Tyler. Thousand Oaks, Calif.: Sage Publications.

Lewis, J. David, and Andrew Weigert. 1985. "Trust as a Social Reality." *Social Forces* 63(4, June): 967–85.

Luhmann, Niklas. 1979. *Trust and Power.* New York: John Wiley.

———. 1988. "Familiarity, Confidence, Trust: Problems and Alternatives." In *Trust: Making and Breaking Cooperative Relations,* edited by Diego Gambetta. New York: Basil Blackwell.

Merton, Robert K. 1948. "The Self-fulfilling Prophecy." *Antioch Review* 8(2, June): 193–210.

Michotte, Albert. 1963. *Perception of Causality.* New York: Basic Books.

Miller, Dale T., and William Turnbull. 1986. "Expectancies and Interpersonal Processes." *Annual Review of Psychology* 37: 233–56.

Naimark, Norman M. 1995. *The Russians in Germany: A History of the Soviet Zone of Occupation, 1945–1949.* Cambridge, Mass.: Belknap Press of Harvard University Press.

Osgood, Charles E. 1962. *An Alternative to War or Surrender.* Urbana: University of Illinois Press.

Pettigrew, T. F. 1979. "The Ultimate Attribution Error: Extending Gordon Allport's Cognitive Analysis of Prejudice." *Personality and Social Psychology Bulletin* 5(4, October): 461–76.

Pruitt, Dean G. 1965. "Definition of the Situation as a Determinant of International Action." In *International Behavior,* edited by Herbert C. Kelman. New York: Holt, Rinehart and Winston.

———. 1982. *Negotiation Behavior.* New York: Academic Press.

Reeder, Glenn D., and Marilynn B. Brewer. 1979. "A Schematic Model of Dispositional Attribution in Interpersonal Perception." *Psychological Review* 86 (1, January): 61–79.

Rothbart, Myron, and Bernadette Park. 1986. "On the Confirmability and Disconfirmability of Trait Concepts." *Journal of Personality and Social Psychology* 50(1, January): 131–42.

Rotter, Julian B. 1971. "Generalized Expectancies for Interpersonal Trust." *American Psychologist* 26(5, May): 443–52.

Rubin, Jeffrey A., and Bert R. Brown. 1975. *The Social Psychology of Bargaining and Negotiations.* New York: Academic Press.

Scharpf, Fritz W. 1997. *Games Real Actors Play: Actor-Centered Institutionalism in Policy Research.* Boulder, Colo.: Westview Press.

Schelling, Thomas C. 1960/1963. *The Strategy of Conflict.* Harvard University Press (repr., New York: Oxford University Press, 1963).

Shevardnadze, Eduard. 1988. "The 19th All-Union CPSU Conference: Foreign Policy and Diplomacy." *International Affairs* (10): 3–64.

Shultz, George P. 1993. *Turmoil and Triumph: My Years as Secretary of State.* New York: Charles Scribner's Sons.

Skowronski, John J., and Donal E. Carlston. 1987. "Social Judgment and Social Memory: The Role of Cue Diagnosticity in Negativity, Positivity, and Extremity Biases." *Journal of Personality and Social Psychology* 52(4): 688–99.

Smyser, W. R. 1999. *From Yalta to Berlin: The Cold War Struggle over Germany.* New York: St. Martin's Press.

Snyder, Mark. 1992. "Motivational Foundations of Behavioral Confirmation." In *Advances in Experimental Social Psychology,* edited by Mark P. Zanna, vol. 25. New York: Academic Press.

Strickland, Lloyd H. 1958. "Surveillance and Trust." *Journal of Personality* 26(June): 200–15.
Swinth, Robert L. 1967. "Establishment of the Trust Relationship." *Journal of Conflict Resolution* 11(3): 335–44.
Tajfel, Henri. 1959. "Quantitative Judgment in Social Perception." *British Journal of Psychology* 50: 16–29.
———, ed. 1978. *Differentiation between Social Groups. Studies in the Social Psychology of Intergroup Relations*. New York: Academic Press.
Trachtenberg, Marc. 1999. *A Constructed Peace: The Making of the European Settlement, 1945–1963*. Princeton, N.J.: Princeton University Press.
Tucker, Robert C. 1971. *The Soviet Political Mind: Stalinism and Post-Stalin Change*. New York: W. W. Norton.
Walt, Stephen M. 1987. *The Origins of Alliances*. Ithaca, N.Y.: Cornell University Press.
Walter, Barbara J. 1997. "The Critical Barrier to Civil War Settlement." *International Organization* 51(3, Summer): 335–64.
Warner, Lyle G., and Melvin L. DeFleur. 1969. "Attitude as an Interactional Concept: Social Constraint and Social Distance as Intervening Variables between Attitudes and Action." *American Sociological Review* 34(2, April): 153–69.
Williamson, Oliver E. 1993. "Calculativeness, Trust, and Economic Organization." *Journal of Law and Economics* 36(April): 453–502.
Word, Carl O., Mark P. Zanna, and Joel Cooper. 1974. "The Nonverbal Mediation of Self-fulfilling Prophecies in Interracial Interaction." *Journal of Experimental Social Psychology* 31(2, March): 109–20.
Yamagishi, Toshio. 1994. "Trust and Commitment in the United States and Japan." *Motivation and Emotion* 18(2): 129–66.
Youngs, George A., Jr. 1986. "Patterns of Threat and Punishment Reciprocity in a Conflict Setting." *Journal of Personality and Social Psychology* 51(3, September): 541–46.
Ziegler, Rolf. 1998. "Trust and the Reliability of Expectations." *Rationality and Society* 10(4, November): 427–50.
Zubok, Vladislav, and Constantine Pleshakov. 1996. *Inside the Kremlin's Cold War: From Stalin to Khrushchev*. Cambridge, Mass.: Harvard University Press.

Chapter 3

Trust, Distrust, and In Between

EDNA ULLMANN-MARGALIT

THE NOTION of trust has been the focus of intensive research in recent years. Given the negation relation between trust and distrust, a good understanding of distrust may be a useful way of shedding additional light, even if indirectly, on trust. In a similar vein, the attempts in psychoanalysis to understand the pathological mind have always been taken as contributing to a better understanding of normalcy, and a grasp of "politica negativa" as a necessary step on the way toward a more solid foundation of a positive political theory. If I want to know about the bright side of the moon, I may do well to look at its dark side, too (Margalit 2001, 127–28).

I approach distrust as a problem in practical reasoning, one that deals with the rules and strategies of action that we are to adopt in situations of social interaction in which the question of trust versus distrust comes up. This approach distinguishes itself from the subjective probability approach, which asks under what conditions we are to accept a hypothesis of distrust.

Normal linguistic use suggests the existence of an interim zone between clear cases of trust and clear cases of distrust. Trust and distrust, while mutually exclusive, are not mutually exhaustive. That is, I cannot both trust and distrust you, at least not with respect to one and the same matter (say, with respect to your writing a genuinely warm letter of recommendation for me), though it is entirely possible for me neither to trust nor to distrust you with respect to the same matter—or, indeed, in general. I may, in other words, be agnostic in the matter of trusting you; trust and distrust negate each other but do not complement each other (Hardin 2001, 496).

Still, if I distrust you, this surely means that I do not trust you. The converse, however, does not hold: if I do not trust you, I may actually distrust

Figure 3.1 A Trust-Distrust Continuum

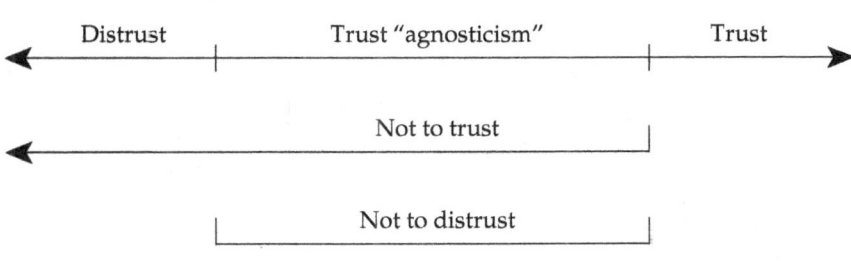

Source: Author's compilation.

you, but this is not necessarily so. And what if I do not distrust you? Does this mean I trust you? Ordinary use would not quite accept that. This set of relationships is represented pictorially in figure 3.1. Clear cases of trust are on the right; clear cases of distrust are on the left. In between lies the spectrum of cases characterized by neither trust nor distrust. Everything to the left of the area marked as "trust" is the complement of trust, namely, "not to trust." As can be read off the diagram, the area of "not to trust" covers the area of "distrust" along with the no-man's-land of neither trust nor distrust (in the figure, "trust agnosticism"). That is, if I do not trust you, this could mean either that I distrust you—that is, that I have reasons to positively distrust you—or, more minimally, that I just have no reasons to trust you (nor to distrust you either). All of this accords, I believe, with our normal and intuitive linguistic use.

Think of driving on the highway. A good driver will do well not to be too trustful of the other drivers and to resort to so-called defensive driving. At the same time, there is no reason for her to distrust all other drivers altogether. After all, she and they share an interest in not colliding and in completing their respective journeys safely. This is a common situation in which people find themselves interacting in an impersonal manner with others and in which the question of trust does come up in some "thin" sense, as relating both to the motivations and to the competence of the other(s). While there is no room for trust here, there are normally no specific reasons for distrust, either.

As can be seen from this example, the complement of "distrust" is not symmetrical to the complement of trust. Had there been symmetry, the complement of "distrust" would comprise everything to the right of the area marked as "distrust"—including, in particular, the area marked as "trust." This would mean that if I say "I do not distrust you," I could plausibly be interpreted as saying that I actually trust you. This, I believe, does not accord with accepted use.

When I say that I do not distrust my secretary, I take it that you will understand me as saying that I do not have reasons to distrust the secretary. I take it also that you will understand me, by implicature, as saying that neither do I have reasons to trust her. In other words, "not to distrust" is a narrower concept than a proper complement of "distrust" would be. "Not to distrust," then, is restricted to the middle section of the line in figure 3.1. It relates only to the no-man's-land area designated as "trust agnosticism," that is, to the area of neither trust nor distrust.

This asymmetry between the complementary notions of "not to trust" and "not to distrust" goes to the heart of the larger and much-discussed theme of asymmetries between trust and distrust. Against the backdrop of this larger theme, the bulk of the present study focuses on this middle ground, which comprises cases in which one has reasons neither to trust nor to distrust.

In the case of belief, too, there is a middle section, a no-man's-land, in which it is not the case that one believes that p nor is it the case that one believes that *not* p. However, this analogy indicates a connection between the notions of trust and belief that goes beyond the merely formal aspect. There exist, in fact, deep-level connections between the ideas of trust and belief. The Hebrew words for "trust," "belief," and "faith" all share the same three-letter root, "e-m-n." The faithful, that is, the believers, are the trustworthy, and to believe in God is tantamount to putting one's entire trust in him. When the Lord promised Abraham a son and heir, it is said of Abraham that "he believed in the Lord"—even though he knew that his wife Sarah was barren and beyond childbearing age. The traditional interpretation of this phrase is that Abraham trusted in the Lord. The Lord rewards him for this trust: "He counted it to him for righteousness" (Gen. 15:6; King James version).

Full Trust

The working analysis of trust presented here is an attempt to capture the conditions under which we would trust someone—or, rather, the conditions under which we would, with respect to a certain matter, trust someone in full. It relates primarily to the endpoint case, where I trust you fully about something. Note that the adjective "full" qualifies the degree of trust with respect to a given matter, not the range of matters with respect to which there is trust. When I say that he fully trusts his doctor I mean that he trusts her qua doctor to the fullest degree and without reservations. I do not mean by this that he trusts her about everything outside of their doctor-patient relationship.

I have good reason to fully trust you with respect to some matter when I believe that

1. you intend to behave or act in this matter so as to promote my interests and my general well-being;

2. you intend to promote my interests qua my interests (whether or not they coincide with your interests);
3. with respect to the matter at hand, you have the competence to behave or act so as to promote my interests.

In other words, my full trust in you requires that I attribute to you intention, right reason, and competence.

It is possible that the notion of full trust, the endpoint case, is not often applicable in practice. I start my account with it not because it is the most common case of trust but because it is a useful analytical strategy. Good grasp of the endpoint pure case gives one a handle on the range of deviations from it. The systematic possibilities of negating the notion of full trust provide us with the wide spectrum of cases that stretches from mere lack of trust to the opposing endpoint of full distrust.

Intention and Competence

Full trust, according to this analysis, is based in principle on reasons that include both intention and competence. These interact in subtle ways. They are not, in general, equal in weight: the competence component is secondary. If I have trust in your intentions—that is, if I have the required belief as regards your intentions or motives—but lack the required belief as regards your competence to act in a manner that will promote my interests, I would not say I distrust you. I may in fact still trust you. (Think of an incompetent mother: might not her children still trust her?) Not so in the converse case: if I have trust in your competence but not in your intentions, I would probably say that I distrust you. Note that when I say that I trust my surgeon, I may at times mean no more than that I think highly of his competence. That is, I assign a high probability to the surgeon's success in the operation. In such cases it will be more accurate to say that I *have confidence* in my surgeon, or that I *rely* on him, than that I trust him.[1]

In addition to the components of intention and competence, there is the additional "right-reason" component.[2] If I think someone intends to promote my interests but not for the reason that they are my interests, I do not necessarily distrust that person, though I cannot rightly say that I trust her, either. Suppose I hire a lawyer, whom I do not know personally, to represent my case strictly on the strength of what I have heard about her competence. In such a case, in which I assess that her chances of succeeding are good, I might say that I rely on her, or that I have confidence in her, or even that I have full confidence in her, but not that I fully trust her. Moreover, even if I believe that, being ambitious, she fully intends to win the case and thereby to promote my own interests, this still does not suffice to make it a case of full trust. Full trust, on the proposed analysis, requires that the lawyer's wish to promote my interests will be for the *right reason*—namely, for the reason that these are my interests, and not, say, because she wants to become rich and famous. When I fully trust my lawyer with respect to this (or any other) case, I have good reason to believe that even in the case of a conflict of interests she will take my side.

Less Than Full Trust

Still, in intermediary cases between full trust and full distrust, it may at times be in order to speak of trust. I may trust my travel agent or my teaching assistant or my representative in Congress about a given matter to some degree lower than full trust. This will be so if the conditions in the proposed analysis are relaxed in some appropriate ways. For trust that is less than full trust, we may, for example, consider dropping the condition of right reason, or the condition of competence, or both. Alternatively, we may consider weakening each or both of them rather than dropping them altogether. In the case of full trust, both of these conditions involve *good* reasons, based on full-fledged beliefs. An obvious way to weaken them, therefore, would be to turn them into conditions that involve less compelling reasons: "I have some reason to believe that—," or "I have prima facie reason to believe that—" might do.

The intention condition can be weakened in a similar manner, that is, from my having good reason for my belief in your intentions to having some reason or prima facie reason for my belief in your intentions to promote my interests.[3] This weakening notwithstanding, I am assuming that the intention component goes to the core of the notion of trust and therefore that it cannot be dropped. In one version or another, it is indispensable. This is, in principle, what distinguishes the notion of trust from the notions of reliance or confidence.

To the extent that I am in a position to assign a (sufficiently high) probability to your acting in a way that will promote my interests, I may rely on you or have confidence in you (to the appropriate degree). But it is my having reasons to believe that you *intend* to act so as to promote *my* interests that makes me trust you. This assumption becomes problematic, however, when attention is shifted from trusting an individual to trusting an institution, such as the Supreme Court or a university. The question then comes up, how are we to construe the intentions of institutions? This problem suggests that either it is possible to relax the intention condition in further ways or we must construe talk about trusting institutions in different terms.

Symmetry, Mutuality, and Familiarity

The trust relation as so far portrayed is a vector in the sense that it has direction. It is, therefore, asymmetrical: it flows from me to you. All three conditions in the proposed analysis involve my beliefs about you and not your beliefs about me. Not only does the notion of trust not emerge from the proposed analysis as a symmetrical relation, but experience shows that it is, in fact, often engendered within hierarchical relationships in which it is not—nor is it expected to be—reciprocated. Moreover, this is especially true in cases in which the hierarchical relations involve loyalty. When a secretary is known to the employer to be loyal to her, then the employer may develop trust in her secretary. Thus loyalty goes up in the hierarchy and trust goes down. This pattern characterizes such old-fashioned relations as those between kings and subjects, noblemen and vassals, and even husbands and wives in the old paradigm of marriage.

The account thus makes no assumption about mutuality. While my trustful relation toward you, as such, is asymmetrical, you may or may not trust me in return with respect to the same particular matter (or indeed with respect to additional matters). At the same time that it makes no assumption about mutuality, the trust relation emphatically does not *rule out* mutuality. Not only does it allow for mutuality, it may indeed expect it and call for it. Just consider the paradigmatic trustful relationship—a marriage of love, in which trust is assumed and expected to be symmetrical and mutual.

Note, as an aside, that the cluster of issues concerning symmetry, mutuality, and hierarchy extends in interesting ways to cases of relations of trust inside and outside of a group. Members of a family or clan may be loyal to one another and trust one another over a wide range of issues and distrust anyone from outside the family or the clan. (Consider the Mafia as an extreme case.) Moreover, a strong measure of distrust on a variety of issues on behalf of the members of some group—say, a minority—toward the members of another group—say, the majority—may create a strong bonding among the members of the first group. This bonding may even induce a relation of mutual trust among the membership of the minority group. In extreme cases, when the minority group resorts to violence against the majority, the phenomena of bonding and trust may eventually be engendered within the majority group itself (see Gambetta 1988; Banfield 1958).

The trust relation according to the proposed analysis does, however, make an assumption about mutual familiarity and acquaintance. It assumes some preexisting relation between the parties. My fully trusting you means that I believe that you intend to act so as to promote my own well-being and, moreover, that I believe that you intend to act in that way precisely in virtue of your wanting to promote my well-being. It is not reasonable that I should form these beliefs if I do not already know you, and you me, to some extent.

Trust relations can certainly flourish when the relationships between people qualify as thick: that is, when people are connected to one another by rich networks of family, clan, neighborhood, having grown up together or gone to school together, or otherwise sharing a past (Margalit 2002; see also Williams 1988). But when we move on to relations of trust that involve less than full trust, thick relations are neither required nor assumed. Indeed, the force of the account is supposed to derive, in part, from its applicability to cases of casual acquaintances, that is, to cases that qualify as rather thin relations. Nonetheless, the point here is that they cannot be entirely thin: trust is, after all, a personal, not an impersonal, relation. This point again poses a problem for the institutional case. If it can be said that you trust the police, what sort of "mutual familiarity and acquaintance" between you and the police is one talking about here?

Trust Differentiated

The problem of trust is here presented within the framework of practical deliberation. When I assess my options for action, given the situation I am in, my decision as to how to act may at times depend on whether or not I have reasons to trust the person I am about to interact with. Thus framed, this is different from the theoretical problem of assigning subjective probability to the hypothesis that that person is trustworthy.

Still, the approach here offered is epistemic. The analysis of trust cites three belief conditions as reasons for my fully trusting someone. The beliefs involved are propositional: they have to do with "belief that," not with "belief in." One's faith, as expressed in one's belief in God, is related in religiously important ways to one's trust in God. But this is not the notion of trust I wish to focus on here. "Belief in" is, then, a notion from which our notion of trust has to be distanced.

Another notion from which trust has to be differentiated is confidence or reliance. The latter notions do not essentially involve the imputing of intentions; they lend themselves more readily to the subjective probability approach. I may rely on, or have confidence in, some*thing* (a bridge, for example), not only in some*one*. Trust, in contrast, relates only to people.

Finally, trust as here approached must be distanced from emotions. To be sure, when I trust you, and more so when I fully trust you, and especially when I fully trust you with respect to a wide range of issues, it is likely that there is warmth between us and that various other feelings and emotions may be involved. Trust-related emotions are worthy of analysis, but they must be kept separate from the account of trust offered here (Barbalet 1996).

Negating Trust

Trust and distrust, though they do not complement each other, do negate each other. How is trust negated? The proposed analysis addresses three conditions—intention, right reason, and competence—each of which begins with a belief clause. A clause that begins with "I believe that p" can be negated weakly or strongly: compare "I do not believe that p" with "I believe that *not* p." The three conditions, all beginning with "I believe that," yield various combinations of these negations. As a result there are various negations of trust, at varying degrees of strength and located at different points in the space that opens up between full trust and full distrust.

Full Distrust

When I lack the belief that you intend to act in my best interests with respect to a given matter, I do not trust you. I begin to distrust you when I am in a position to form the actual belief that you do not intend to act in my best interests in that matter. My distrust in you increases when I become suspicious of your intentions, and it increases still further when I come to form the belief that you actually intend to act *against* my interests in the matter at hand. But this is not quite the extreme case yet. My belief that you intend to act against my interests may derive simply from my perception that our interests diverge and that you take your interests to trump mine. (When the difference between our interests is large, it might not even be seen as a violation of trust that you do what serves your interests but harms mine.) More generally, my belief that you intend to act against my interests may derive from the conjunction of my belief that you are concerned with promoting your own interests and not mine and my belief that your interests diverge from mine.

A more extreme case of distrust occurs when I believe that you intend to act against my interests with respect to the given matter, fully knowing that they are my interests. The most extreme case of distrust is encountered when I believe that you intend to act, with respect to that matter, against my interests qua my interests—that is, *because* they are *my* interests.[4] The extreme opposite of full trust is arrived at when, in each of the three conditions required of full trust, the expression "to promote my interests" is replaced with "to oppose (or harm or damage) my interests." Full distrust, then, also involves an intention component, a right-reason component, and a competence component.

I have good reason to fully distrust you when I believe that you intend to behave or act so as to harm my interests, with respect to a given matter, in virtue of their being my interests and that you have the competence to thus harm my interests. As in the case of full trust, the intention component and the competence component may interact in various ways, to different effects. Suppose that I believe that you want to harm my interests because they are my interests but that I also believe that you are generally powerless or incompetent. Here I would surely distrust you a lot, but at the same time this will be of little practical consequence, and I will have little to protect myself against. Henry Fielding (1743/1964, 94) gives the intricate advice, "Never trust the man who hath reason to suspect that you know he hath injured you." This advice serves as a reminder that human relationships that lead to trust and distrust are more complex and multidimensional than the account here offered may lead us to believe. This also helps underline that full distrust, like full trust, is a personal relationship that cannot be founded on entirely thin relations.

Self-Trust and Self-Distrust

The notion of symmetry was invoked earlier; let us here briefly consider reflexivity. Can one trust, or distrust, oneself? "If you can trust yourself when all men doubt you / But make allowance for their doubting too," says Kipling (1910/1999, 496), making self-trust an item on his famous list of what's required for one to be a man. Of course, the use of "trust" here is loose, such that your trusting yourself is not entirely distinguishable from your being self-confident or self-reliant. Still, the proposed analysis of trust does extend quite naturally to the idea of self-trust. It makes sense for me to believe of myself that I am motivated to promote my own interests precisely qua my own interests and also, at times, that I believe that I am competent to do so. It thus makes sense to comment on someone that she trusts herself—or, indeed, in special circumstances, that she does not.

At the same time, the proposed analysis of trust does not extend itself to the idea of self-distrust, and quite appropriately so. When John Armstrong (1744/1804, 141), a U.S. army officer and the secretary of war from 1813 to 1814, says "Distrust yourself, and sleep well before you fight / 'Tis not too late to-morrow to be brave," he does not quite mean literal distrust: "do not be over-confident" is roughly what he means. The idea that I may be suspicious of my own motivations, or that I may want to hurt my interests because they are my interests, does not quite make sense—or, if it does, it belongs in the pathological department.

Samson and Delilah

Contrary to the impression that the account here offered might have created, human relationships of trust and distrust are highly complex and not always easy to disentangle. The biblical Samson did not trust his wife Delilah with the secret of his great strength. He had his reasons to doubt whether his own well-being was closest to her heart, and he had his reasons to suspect that her loyalty was rather to her kinsfolk and his bitter enemies, the Philistines. Did he actually distrust her? Delilah thought so, and she made him pay a price for his distrust. Any personal relationship that one expects to be based on trust goes sour when distrust creeps in. The disclosure of secrets is commonly taken to be a hallmark of trust, and giving secrets away as a hallmark of betrayal. Delilah kept pestering Samson to disclose to her the secret of his strength. Samson's repeated refusal to do so marred their marital relationship. "And it came to pass, when she pressed him daily with her words, and urged him, so that his soul was vexed unto death" (Judg. 16:16, King James version). Finally, perhaps to save his marriage, Samson decided to confide to his wife the secret of his strength. "If I be shaven then my strength will go from me, and I shall become weak, and be like any other man" (Judg. 16:17, King James version). The price he eventually paid for confiding his secret to his untrustworthy wife was, of course, immense. He paid for his misplaced trust with his life.

Did Samson's distrust of Delilah change to trust when he told her his secret? Her behavior toward him up to that point certainly gave him no good reason to trust her. Could he have *decided to trust* her, even if he did not have the "right beliefs"? My account of trust precludes this possibility. But it does allow for the possibility that one who lacks the required beliefs will still proceed to act *as if* he had them. The facts (or fictional facts) remain that Samson entrusted Delilah with his secret and that she duly proceeded to betray him by making him sleep upon her knees, shaving off the seven locks of his hair, and turning him over to the Philistines. Whether by telling Delilah his secret Samson proved that his distrust in her had changed to trust or whether he was only acting as if he trusted her, thereby acting out a death wish, remains a moot interpretative question. But the possibility of lacking the requisite beliefs yet proceeding to act as if one had them occupies center stage in the discussion that follows.

The Presumption of Distrust

Both trust and distrust require reasons. You will trust me, to whatever degree, if you have sufficient reasons for that degree of trust; the same holds for distrust. But what if the reasons you have are not sufficient, or you have no reasons either way?

A seemingly straightforward answer in such a case would be that you should neither trust nor distrust but wait until you have reasons to do one or the other. Often, however, in situations of practical deliberation, the need to act, and therefore the need to trust or distrust, is pressing, and one cannot afford to wait it out. In our social interactions, many of our decisions and actions depend to some degree on the extent to which we trust or distrust other people. If we are in a position neither to trust nor to distrust, because we lack the requisite beliefs (about the others' intentions and competence), we may have to resort to acting as if we had them; we may have to decide to act as though we trust or distrust.[5]

The situation, then, is this: you must act, and you must act now. How you act turns in an essential way on whether you trust or distrust me. But, so we suppose, you have no (sufficient) reasons either way. How you solve this particular problem on this particular occasion may depend on what is at stake and on your personality. You may decide to play it safe and act as if you distrust me, or you may decide to take a risk on my trustworthiness and act as though you do trust me. But when you come to face this sort of situations repeatedly, and when we want to generalize from you to people in general, you may realize that what you need is a *default rule* that will tell you which way to turn in the absence of adequate reasons.

The kind of default rule we are looking for is a presumption (Ullmann-Margalit 1983). The very possibility of a trust-distrust gap—that is, of being suspended between trust and distrust—paradigmatically suggests a role for a default rule in the form of a presumption. The presumption thus provides a link between the separate categories of belief and action: it tells you how to behave when you do not have the beliefs that would normally tell you how to behave. In this respect the situation is analogous to the case of the guilt-innocence gap in the setup of a criminal trial. Between "proven guilty" and "proven innocent" there will be cases of "proven neither guilty nor innocent." What is a judge in a criminal case to do when the time comes for a decision between conviction and acquittal but the balance of evidence leaves him or her suspended between the two? Two alternative presumptions could, in principle, provide judges with the default rule that they need: to consider the defendant guilty unless proved innocent (beyond reasonable doubt, say) or to consider the defendant innocent unless proved guilty (beyond reasonable doubt). We know which of the two our society chooses.

Regarding trust and distrust, one possible presumption would be this: In case of doubt, act as if you trust—unless or until you have (sufficient) specific reasons for distrust. Once you have such specific reasons in the concrete situation in which you find yourself, the presumption is rebutted. The alternative presumption would be this: In case of doubt, act as if you distrust—unless you have (sufficient) specific reasons for trust. This, too, is rebuttable. Of course, it is hard to know whether to act as if you trust or distrust in the abstract, without a sense of the consequences and the alternatives. Suppose I am in a situation in which I will die unless I take a risk on some stranger's trustworthiness (with respect to a given matter): I would best act as though I trust the stranger. On the other hand, suppose that a friendly reporter, or my dinner date, asks me some personal questions whose public disclosure might be embarrassing to me. It might be best to presume distrust here, or at least to act as though I do not trust. Some rapid balancing of costs and benefits may be at work here, possibly with a bit of "maximin" thinking.

Still, in some of the literature on trust it sometimes seems to be taken for granted that "fairly generalized distrust might make sense in a way that generalized trust does not" and that, in abstraction from any specific context, suspicion and distrust are "inherently well grounded" (Hardin 2001, 500).[6] Cannot these statements be taken to constitute a sweeping recommendation for the presumption in favor of feigning distrust over the presumption of feigning trust? If so, how is this recommendation justified? After all, we all know that our world would be a much more pleasant place if it supported a general, contextless presumption in favor of trust. The issues involved need further exploration.

This exploration requires a shift of gear. The remainder of this chapter adopts a "game-theoretical," strategic approach that no longer resorts to the highly personalized notions of full trust or full distrust. General lack of beliefs that justify my trusting (or distrusting) you are assumed. Yet I take it that it is nevertheless possible for me to decide to act as if I had the requisite beliefs. This is the intended meaning of the phrase I use here, "adopting the trust (or distrust) strategy."

With these understandings, let us note that the presumption in favor of distrust is first and foremost justified on the ground that it is considered the safer of the two alternative presumptions. Consider the following rough calculation of best and worst scenarios. First, the case of trust: Acting as if you trust when trust is in fact reciprocated can lead to successful cooperation and hence to mutual benefit and potentially to significant gain. Acting as if you trust when your partner is untrustworthy and trust is not reciprocated inevitably involves disappointment. It often involves worse: being betrayed or exploited. It may lead to serious damage. Consider next the case of distrust: Acting as if you distrust when distrust is reciprocated leads to whatever gains you are able to achieve on your own. But what does acting as if you distrust, when your partner is trustworthy and does not reciprocate with distrust, lead to?

Here we may want to look at two different possibilities. One involves situations in which, when you adopt the distrust strategy, your gains are not affected by whether or not your distrust is reciprocated by your partner. Your gains remain the same regardless of whether your distrust is unilateral or reciprocated. This kind of case may in the long run breed lone distrusters who essentially expect nothing from their partners, individualists who "go it alone." They would be indifferent as to whether their partners trust them or not. The other possibility involves situations in which unilateral distrust does benefit the distrusters, at the expense of their trusting partners. In these situations the trusters are being exploited by their partners. Note that it is not two psychological types that are differentiated here but rather two different types of situations.

"Soft" Distrust

Let us refer to the two possibilities just presented as "soft" distrust and "hard" distrust, respectively. The adjective "soft" is justified by the fact that the lone distruster exhibits mere *lack of trust*. Distrust here is benign: it does not cause harm but merely protects against harm (see Hardin 2001, 495–96). "Hard" distrust, in contrast, is exploitative of and harmful to one's partner; it involves betrayal of the partner's trust.

When payoff matrices are drawn for these two types of cases, it is easily, and unsurprisingly, revealed that cases of "hard" distrust have the structure of a prisoner's dilemma (PD) game. (For the matrices, and for further elaboration on the ideas presented in this section, see Ullmann-Margalit 2002.) In PD-structured situations, the noncooperative choice, which in the case at hand means acting as though one distrusts, dominates the cooperative choice of acting as though one trusts. Since the PD structure and its implications are well known, I focus on cases of "soft" distrust. Here too, as in the case of "hard" distrust, adopting the trust strategy can lift you high or make you fall. It can be disappointing; it is risk dominated. Adopting the distrust strategy, in contrast, is in this sort of case basically even. It leaves one on some in-between plateau that is insensitive to changes in one's environment—as well as insensitive to the disappointments one may cause to others. One neither exploits possibilities nor exposes oneself to being exploited by others.

To the extent that "playing it safe" means hedging your bets, minimizing your potential losses, being risk averse, to act as though you distrust thus seems to be the safer choice not only in the cases of hard distrust but in the case of soft distrust, as well. But suppose rather than a one-round encounter the partners are in a situation that repeats itself. If the partners start by playing it safe and adopting the distrust strategy, they will remain stuck with a suboptimal equilibrium in future repetitions of the situation (see Hardin 2002, chap. 5). If, however, they succeed in coordinating on acting as if they trust, whether through communicating with each other or somehow independently, then both will reap the fruits of their cooperation. Neither of them will be tempted to "defect" to the distrust strategy in future repetitions of the situation.

If the situation is further generalized, not just from a one-round to a repeated situation but also from two participants to a community, is the presumption of distrust justified? This may be conceptualized as a Wild West community of rugged individualists. They are honest folks who are used to relying on no one and to exploiting no one. Still, in the long run, they need be neither blind nor averse to the possibility of trustful cooperation and to its mutual benefits. In such a community the argument of "playing it safe" does not justify the adoption of the presumption in favor of distrust.

Hobbes's State of Nature

When people think of paradigmatic cases of having to choose between acting as if they trust and acting as if they distrust, it is PD-structured situations that they commonly have in mind—namely, cases of hard distrust. Many people seem to take it for granted that the distrust strategy dominates the trust strategy paradigmatically. To act as though you trust when you lack the requisite beliefs seems much worse than simply to take a chance: it seems as though it actually *means* to be a sucker, to expose yourself to exploitation.

The general outlook of hard distrust may well derive from the powerful hold that Thomas Hobbes's grim picture has over us, the picture of the state of nature as a state of suspicion of all in all and of a war of all against all. Indeed, Hobbesians often tend to interpret social interactions, whether on the micro- or macro-level, as one-round games. To the extent that these are PD-structured situations, this outlook tends to justify a general presumption in favor of feigning distrust.

But even Hobbes himself, in presenting what he calls the "precept, or general rule of Reason," distinguishes between two situations. Hobbes (1651/1968, 190) says that "every man ought to endeavour Peace, as farre as he has hope of obtaining it and when he cannot obtain it, that he may seek, and use, all helps, and advantages of Warre." The first part of this precept contains what is for Hobbes the fundamental law of nature: to seek peace and follow it. The second part sums up what he refers to as the right of nature: to defend ourselves by any and by all means we can. There is nothing far-fetched or strained, as far as I can see, in interpreting the first part of the precept as applying to situations of soft or mild distrust and the second as applying to situations of hard or harsh distrust.

True, Hobbes did not believe that endeavoring peace in the hope of obtaining it would get one very far. A close reading of the relevant passages reveals how deeply convinced he was that we are doomed constantly to seek and use the advantages of war to defend ourselves. But the important point is that he did seem to recognize the possibility that the state of nature might be construed in terms of soft distrust as well as hard distrust.

The fact that not every situation of distrust is structured as a prisoner's dilemma is crucial here. As in those cases that fall under the category of soft distrust, mutual trust not only leads to a jointly beneficial outcome but it is a stable equilibrium, and it is accessible to the participants. This in itself suffices to cast serious doubt on the idea that the presumption in favor of distrust should be considered a universal "default" presumption.

Further Observations

To be sure, trust is fragile. As soon as breach of trust occurs, for whatever reason and by however small a number of people, a tipping-point phenomenon is likely to occur, and distrust will rapidly prevail. Like Humpty Dumpty, trust, once shattered, may be beyond repair. But to the extent that situations of soft distrust exist and are recognized as such, the precariousness—as well as the preciousness—of trust in such situations may at the same time be recognized, too. Furthermore, it is not impossible to imagine situations in which, because I decide to act as if I trust you, I eventually bring it about that you do become trustworthy and deserving of my future trust. This is what happened with Victor Hugo's priest, who chose to take the risk of acting as though he trusted Jean Valjean, thereby making him trustworthy (Hugo 1862/1992). Perhaps this is what Samson hoped against hope would happen with Delilah.

As small children we have to start out with something like an instinctive conclusive presumption in favor of sweeping trust in the adults who care for us. After all, it is hard to imagine how small children could generally get on, let alone learn a language, if they started out with an instinctive attitude of suspicion and distrust. If this is crudely true, then a case can be made that, at least developmentally, it is the trust strategy that is for many the default strategy and distrust is learned. So perhaps distrust is not a foregone social conclusion on this consideration, as well.

In thinking about the default presumption it must be noted, finally, that not only do people divide empirically into instinctive trust presumers and instinctive distrust presumers: contexts divide, too, in paradigmatic ways. We naturally catalogue situations involving economic transactions, for example, as ones in which a presumption in favor of feigning distrust is justified. Familial and communal situations, in contrast, we are often quite happy to approach with a presumption of trust. When we go abroad or are otherwise outside of our habitual contexts, we are typically in doubt. But even in such cases it is too crude to counsel in favor of acting as though we distrust. We are often able to use various social cues, sometimes quite subtle ones, to sort out different contexts and to identify those that justify taking the risk of trust. Who of us has not encountered the classical yet puzzling case on the beach, when the total strangers who happen to sit next to us ask us to "keep an eye" on their belongings until they return from their dip in the water?

It may thus be the *content* of the situation in which we find ourselves, in its wider social context, that will argue against a pessimistic and suspicious adoption of the distrust presumption. Alternatively, it may be the game-theoretical *structure* of the situation that will achieve the same purpose, once the distinction between soft and hard distrust is internalized and correctly applied. For one reason or another, it may, after all, be the case that distrust shall have no dominion.

Institutional Trust and Distrust

There is an impressive volume of social-psychological literature about trust and distrust within organizations. The bases of trust, the benefits of trust, and the barriers to trust have been studied extensively (a useful survey of this literature is given in Kramer 1999). Quite separate from this body of research that is concerned with the antecedents and consequences of trust and distrust within organizations, political theorists are also concerned with institutional trust or distrust. Their concern, however, is with the question to what extent the public displays trust or distrust toward this or that social institution, and with what implications to the polity.

It is taken to be a necessary condition of a well-functioning democracy that its citizens trust its institutions. In a sense—a somewhat ironic sense—social institutions are sometimes seen as trust mediators. On the one hand, there is the fact that in modern mass democracies, in contrast to the intimate city-states of ancient times, no level of general interpersonal familiarity and trust can be assumed. An important role of institutions, then, is to facilitate social transactions by essentially replacing the need for personal trust among citizens (see Hardin 2001, 518; also see Hardin 2002, chaps. 7, 8)—consider, for example, the role of legally binding contracts as a replacement for promises. On the other hand, there is the further consideration that once the institutions are in place, in order for them to fulfill their role as trust replacers, it is often supposed that citizens need to trust *them*. In terms of the example just cited, in order for contracts to work it is commonly said that people need to trust their country's legal system and its enforcement mechanisms.

A number of writers seem to diagnose a malaise in many contemporary democracies, which they believe to exhibit a general decline in institutional trust. This relates to both public and private institutions. There is substantial evidence, for example, that institutional trust in the United States has been declining for several decades—in federal government, universities, medical institutions, and journalism as well as in several major private companies (see Coleman 1990; Carnevale 1995; Ney, Zelikov, and King 1997).[7] These finding are alarming if the ability of institutions to function properly depends in no small measure upon public trust in them.

According to another view, representative democracy and distrust go together. "A certain amount of distrust," says Russell Hardin (2001,

517), "may be useful to a society or government. Certainly, large, modern democracies work better if we can be sure that there are professional distrusters or cynics or skeptics, people who act as watchdogs, raise alarms, or provide contrary information."[8]

Much can be said in an attempt to explore these two views and possibly reconcile them. How threatening—or healthy—to a democracy are various degrees of institutional distrust? Is the sort of distrust one is talking about when arguing that it is threatening quite the same as the sort of distrust one is talking about when arguing that it is healthy? Moreover, there may be interest in following the further body of research that tries to advance explanations, from a variety of perspectives, for the sources of the erosion in public trust in institutions in various countries. But the question I pursue is a different and, in a sense, a prior one. What does it mean to trust or distrust an institution?

Institutional Trust

As it stands, the proposed account of trust and distrust will not do for the institutional case. The analysis requires that for me to trust X, I need to entertain certain beliefs about X's intentions and about what motivates those intentions. Since it is to persons, not institutions, that we attribute such intentions and motivations, it would seem to be the case that X can only be a person and not an institution. If one accepts this line of thinking, it follows that our common, everyday talk of trust or distrust in institutions may have to be rethought and possibly revised.

Still, in an attempt to make sense of talk about trust or distrust in institutions, several ways may seem to be available to go around this obstacle. In principle, one may either see one's way to attributing intentions to institutions, if not directly then somehow indirectly, or one may see one's way to weakening the intention component or dropping it altogether from the analysis of distrust.

One may acknowledge, for example, that even though we attribute intentions primarily to individuals, we can nevertheless attribute intentions to institutions in some derivative or secondary sense. This line of thought puts the onus of the argument on clarifying the derivative sense in which it may be coherent to talk about the intentions of an institution. One way may be to argue that it is often the person who is the figurehead of an institution that embodies for us the institution as a whole. Roderick Kramer cites a speculation that "people may use the behavior of institutional leaders as reference points for gauging their basic beliefs . . . when appraising the trustworthiness of society's institutions in general. In other words, people may draw general inferences about institutional trust from the behavior of highly visible role models" (Kramer 1999, 589). Insofar as this is so, the question of trust in the police, say, or in the

Supreme Court is translated into people's beliefs about the intentions and motivations of the commissioner of police or of the chief justice.

A different route is to tinker with the intention component of the analysis of trust. Given that I trust (or distrust) you, is it really necessary that I entertain beliefs about how you intend to act and about what motivates your intentions? Is it not enough perhaps that I entertain beliefs and assess probabilities about how you are actually going to act?

I believe that this is not enough. The attribution of intentions is of the essence, so far as trust is concerned. Entertaining beliefs and probabilities about the future course of action of a person or of an institution has to do with the notions of reliance and confidence but not with trust. I believe, indeed, that as far as trust is concerned, talk of trusting an institution is misplaced. To say that we trust an institution is to be construed, rather, in terms of our reliance on an institution or of our degree of confidence in its competence and performance. This can be expressed, for example, in the probability we assign to its achieving its set goals—provided its goals accord with our interests. (I can also have confident expectations that an institution will achieve its goal and *therefore* distrust it because its goal is against my interest.)

More specifically and more crucially, talk of trusting an institution ought to be construed in terms of our degree of confidence that the institution will continue to pursue its set goals and to achieve them regardless of who staffs the institution. There is a *principle of substitutability* at work here: whenever the idea of substitutability comes up, the question to ask is what remains constant under the substitution. In the case at hand, when we express trust in an institution we express our belief that, even if the present officeholders in that institution were to be replaced with others, the performance of the institution would remain constant. In other words, so-called trust in an institution is tantamount to a belief in the *impersonality* of its performance, in addition to the belief that its goals are compatible with our interests. Given our account of trust, it is precisely this impersonality that prevents this attitude from counting as trust.

When we trust an individual, we expect his or her attitude toward us to be entirely personal. When we say we trust an institution, we expect its attitude to us to be impersonal. Can it be the same notion of trust that is invoked in both cases? I think not. Strictly speaking, in the institutional case it is a misnomer to talk of trust.

This may have to be somewhat qualified, though. Often, talk of trust is bound up with social role. I may trust my dean; you may trust the U.S. president; he may trust the federal court. What is meant here is something not entirely impersonal yet less personal than in the noninstitutional case.[9] In trusting the dean, I trust that she will not be corrupt, that she will not play favorites, that the interests of the institution will have priority at her heart, that she is competent, that she will try to do her best. These express confident expectations, not trust in the full personal sense. Nevertheless, it must be acknowledged that talk of trust here is consistent with ordinary usage and cannot easily be dispensed with.

Institutional Distrust

The case of distrust in institutions, however, is different. Here, I believe that we do attribute intentions and motivations, and not just to the figureheads of the institution.

Consider, for example, the case of the ultraorthodox in Israel, who in recent years have expressed growing distrust in the Israeli Supreme Court. Consider also the case of the Arab Israeli minority, whose members now talk of having lost whatever trust they had in the Israeli police.[10] In expressing their distrust in the respective institutions, these people are conveying something other than a mere factual prediction to the effect that the Court or the police will act in ways that will not further their interests but will rather collide with them. Their expression of distrust has a surplus element that goes beyond expressing nonreliance or low degrees of confidence. Rather, I believe, these communities want to be understood as imputing intentions, diffusely, to those who staff the respective institutions.

What intentions can these be, given that there is no personal acquaintance and there are no personal relations between the individuals involved? At bottom, I suggest, the question of distrust in an institution boils down to one's belief in the unfairness of the institution—and to the ancillary belief that the unfairness works against one's interests. When an institution faces a crisis of trust, which is at the same time a crisis of legitimacy, this means that segments of the populace in need of recourse to the institution in question suspect it of operating in an unfair manner, a manner that goes against their interests. More specifically, in many cases this means that these members of the public tend to impute discriminatory intentions quite generally to the officeholders at all levels of hierarchy in the institution—for example, to all the judges or to all the policemen and policewomen. The discriminatory intentions may be racist, sexist, homophobic, anti-Semitic, antireligious, or what have you.

The flip side of any discriminatory intentions that make some people distrust an institution is that the very same institution may become highly trustworthy to people with other, opposing, interests. In a city where the police favor the Mafia, it may be expected that the general citizenry will distrust the police. Can we say that the members of the Mafia trust the police? Well, they sure do, in some sense. But their trust in the police is in the personal sense of trust, not in the institutional sense that is premised on impersonality and substitutability.

The mafiosi's trust in the police cannot be the trust we are after when we reflect upon the role of institutional trust in a healthy democracy.

Their trust is a perversion of the trust in institutions that is claimed to be required for mass democracy to work. A necessary condition for institutional trust worthy of its name is confidence in the fairness and impartiality of the institution. (It is not a sufficient condition, though, as the element of competence is missing.) When this condition is fulfilled, there is no imputing of personal intentions to those who staff the institution; the principle of substitutability holds.

The point, then, is that in contrast to the case of institutional trust, institutional distrust does involve the imputing of intentions. It involves a shared belief among groups of citizens about the personal intentions of the officeholders of the institution. These intentions are taken to be operative while the officeholders are executing the duties of their office. The typical belief here is that these officeholders are infected with discriminatory intentions against the members of the relevant groups and that these intentions result quite generally in unfair practices. The unfair practices are believed to operate in principle against the interests of those groups of citizens.

Another possibility for institutional distrust occurs when there is widespread belief that the institution is corrupt. David Hume (1748/1987) suggests that institutions should be designed in such a way that they would work well even if, in his well-known phrase, they were staffed by knaves. Should the design fail, however, or should the level of corruption of the knaves pass a certain threshold, the institution qua institution may be perceived to be corrupt. Here, too, the attitude toward the institution turns in an essential way on people's beliefs about the personal motives of officeholders of the institution at its various hierarchical levels. Once their personal motives become suspect—as, for example, when there is a shared belief that they serve foreign interests or are open to bribes—then general distrust in the institution qua institution reigns.

There may be an interesting difference between cases in which institutional distrust is based on partiality and those in which it is based on corruption. The first tend to be cases of *group* distrust, based on membership in groups defined by race, gender, ethnic origin, sexual orientation, and so forth. The second tend to be cases of *class* distrust, in which the institution is taken to operate in such a way that the rich can get away with things that the poor cannot. The two kinds of institutional distrust may of course overlap, and there may be various intermediate cases, too.

Conclusion

The account of trust offered in this chapter is a belief-based account: roughly, I trust you when I believe that you have the right intentions toward me. Trust can be differentiated from the related but importantly different notions of reliance and confidence. The analysis also affords some insights into questions worthy of future attention, such as why trust is not, in general, a symmetrical relation and why trust can be reflexive but distrust not (that is, why it makes sense to say that I trust myself but not that I distrust myself).

The problem of trust as presented in this chapter is a problem of practical deliberation: how is one to act in a situation in which trust (or distrust) is required but the requisite beliefs are lacking? This is a problem because trust and distrust are exclusive but are not exhaustive: the absence of reasons to trust does not entail distrust, and the absence of reasons to distrust does not entail trust. Regarding those situations in which one has reasons neither for trust nor for distrust, can there be a reasoned policy in favor of acting as though one had reasons for either? The commonly held idea that the presumption in favor of acting as though you distrust is better and safer than the opposite presumption is probed. On the basis of the notion of soft distrust, this chapter argues that a pessimistic and suspicious adoption of the distrust presumption as a general rule of behavior is unfounded.

The account of trust in relation to institutions requires some modifications. Because institutions cannot have intentions in anything like the way persons have intentions, to say that we trust an institution cannot involve an ordinary ascription of intentions. What we ordinarily mean by trusting an institution should be construed not in terms of trust but rather in terms of our confident prediction that the institution will pursue its goals. Moreover, when we say that we trust an institution we expect the institution to be impersonal, whereas in trusting an individual we expect his or her attitude toward us to be entirely personal. In light of such considerations, in the institutional case it is a misnomer to talk of trust. Not so, however, in the case of distrust. Distrusting an institution is not a matter of confident predictions, and it does involve the assigning of intentions. Institutional distrust embodies one's belief that the intentions of the officeholders of the institution are discriminatory and that the institution is consequently unfair in ways that work against one's interests.

I owe gratitude to Russell Hardin, Cass Sunstein, and Avishai Margalit for discussing this chapter with me and for their valuable comments and ideas.

Notes

1. I learned about the role of competence in trust from Sidney Morgenbesser.
2. It is mostly this condition that distinguishes my account from Hardin's encapsulated-interest account of trust (elaborated in Hardin 2002). Strictly speaking, intention is subsumed under right reasons. The focus of the two conditions, however, is different.

3. The intention condition can also be strengthened. It may be the case that I believe that you intend to behave or act so as to promote my interests and my general well-being not only with respect to a particular matter but in all matters. This may be because I believe that you love me, as a parent or a spouse, or because I believe that you value me highly as a friend. We may say that in such cases my trust in you is not only *full* but also *complete*. That is, it relates both to the full degree to which I trust you with respect to any given matter and to the complete range of matters with respect to which I fully trust you: I trust you with everything and anything. Cases of full and complete trust may be rare, but they are not nonexistent. (See also note 4 for the analogous notion of *complete* distrust.)

4. Note that one may speak also of *complete* distrust, in analogy to complete trust (see note 3). My distrust is complete when it is not relativized to a particular matter, that is, when I distrust you with respect to everything and anything. This may be because you are my bitter enemy and I believe that you thoroughly hate me.

5. For a relevant discussion of an analogous distinction, between believing a proposition true and deciding to behave as if we believe it true, see Ullmann-Margalit and Margalit (1992).

6. While these are quotes from Hardin's article, they do not express his view.

7. See also Slovic (1993) for a discussion of distrust in nationwide institutions responsible for risk management in connection with technological hazards. It would surely come as no surprise if the Enron-Anderson debacles of late were shown to have produced serious new waves of distrust in financial institutions.

8. "Although often portrayed in the popular press and social science literature largely in negative terms, distrust and suspicion may constitute appropriate and even highly adaptive stances toward institutions. Vigilance and weariness about institutions, some have argued, constitute essential components of healthy and resilient organizations and societies. From this perspective, distrust and suspicion may, in a fundamental sense, constitute potent and important forms of social capital" (Kramer 1999, 590.) See also Ely (1980) and Warren (1999).

9. When I trust my lawyer qua my lawyer, this is less than full personal trust in a friend qua friend but more than just full confidence in *a* lawyer, as distinct from *my* lawyer. (Compare the lawyer example under the section "Full Trust.")

10. The acute crisis in Israel goes back to early October 2000, when the Israeli police shot to death thirteen Arab Israeli citizens during demonstrations that erupted in connection with the Palestinian uprising.

References

Armstrong, John. 1744/1804. *The Art of Preserving Health*. "Prefixed," a critical essay on the poem, by John Aikin. Philadelphia: Printed for Benjamin Johnson.

Banfield, Edward. 1958. *The Moral Basis of a Backward Society*. New York: Free Press.
Barbalet, Jack M. 1996. "Social Emotions: Confidence, Trust and Loyalty." *International Journal of Sociology and Social Policy* 16: 75–96.
Carnevale, David J. 1995. *Trustworthy Government: Leadership and Management Strategies for Building Trust and High Performance*. San Francisco: Jossey-Bass.
Coleman, James. 1990. *Foundations of Social Theory*. Cambridge, Mass.: Harvard University Press.
Ely, John Hart. 1980. *Democracy and Distrust*. Cambridge, Mass.: Harvard University Press.
Fielding, Henry. 1743/1964. *Jonathan Wild: The Journal of a Voyage to Lisbon*. Introduction by A. R. Humphreys. London: J. M. Dent & Sons Ltd.
Gambetta, Diego. 1988. "Mafia: The Price of Distrust." In *Trust: Making and Breaking Cooperative Relations*, edited by Diego Gambetta. New York: Basil Blackwell.
Hardin, Russell. 2001. "Distrust." *Boston University Law Review* 81(3, June): 495–522.
———. 2002. *Trust and Trustworthiness*. New York: Russell Sage Foundation.
Hobbes, Thomas. 1651/1968. *Leviathan*, edited by C. B. Macpherson. London: Penguin.
Hugo, Victor. 1862/1992. *Les Miserables*. Translated by Charles E. Wilbour. New York: The Modern Library.
Hume, David. 1748/1987. "Of the Independency of Parliament." In *David Hume: Essays Moral, Political, and Literary*, rev. ed., edited by Eugene F. Miller. Indianapolis, Ind.: Liberty Fund.
Kipling, Rudyard. 1910/1999. "If." In *Rudyard Kipling*, edited and with an introduction by Daniel Karlin. Oxford: Oxford University Press.
Kramer, Roderick M. 1999. "Trust and Distrust in Organizations: Emerging Perspectives, Enduring Questions." *Annual Review of Psychology* 50: 569–98.
Margalit, Avishai. 2001. "Recognition." *Aristotelian Society* Suppl. 75: 127–39.
———. 2002. *The Ethics of Memory*. Cambridge, Mass.: Harvard University Press.
Ney, Joseph S., Philip D. Zelikov, and David C. King. 1997. *Why People Don't Trust Government*. Cambridge, Mass.: Harvard University Press.
Slovic, Paul. 1993. "Perceived Risk, Trust and Democracy." *Risk Analysis* 13(6): 675–82.
Ullmann-Margalit, Edna. 1983, "On Presumption." *Journal of Philosophy* 80(3): 143–63.
———. 2002. "Trust out of Distrust." *Journal of Philosophy* 99(10): 532–48.
Ullmann-Margalit, Edna, and Avishai Margalit. 1992. "Holding True and Holding As True." *Synthese* 92(2): 167–87.
Warren, Mark E. 1999. "Democratic Theory and Trust." In *Democracy and Trust*, edited by Mark E. Warren. Cambridge, U.K.: Cambridge University Press.
Williams, Bernard. 1988. "Formal Structures and Social Reality." In *Trust: Making and Breaking Cooperative Relations*, edited by Diego Gambetta. New York: Basil Blackwell.

PART II

POWER AND DISTRUST

Chapter 4

Trust, Distrust, and Power

Henry Farrell

THE SO-CALLED encapsulated-interest account of trust, developed by Russell Hardin and other interested scholars, draws together an important body of thought about trust and its meaning in social and personal relations. Trust, under this account, involves considered expectations about the interests of others to behave in a trustworthy manner. Some scholars argue that trust of this sort is not trust at all. Laurence Becker (1996), for example, argues that "cognitive" trust, of the sort discussed in the encapsulated-interest account, is indistinguishable in the final analysis from knowledge and power. Becker oversimplifies considerably; it is clear that in many instances, neither power over another nor knowledge of another's interests create trust and that, even when power may engender trust, the concepts remain distinguishable. For example, as Russell Hardin (2002) argues, trust does not apply when I am holding a gun to your head; while I certainly have power over you and know that you have an overwhelming interest to do what I tell you to do, the degree of certainty that I have about your interests renders trust irrelevant. While power, and knowledge of the effects of power on interests, may clearly affect trust under certain circumstances, the concepts should not be conflated.

This said, the relationship between power, trust, and distrust in the encapsulated-interest account has yet to be properly teased out. Under some circumstances, power seems to drive out trust. When I have a gun to your head, not only is it difficult to describe my relationship to you in terms of trust, but also, quite obviously, it is nearly impossible for you to trust me. When I hold such power over you, there is no reason for me to take your interests into account.[1] At the same time, trust clearly must sometimes be possible between actors of unequal power. Otherwise, the concept's applicability is confined to a relatively small set of human relationships, those between genuine equals.

Thus an account of the relationship between trust (under the encapsulated-interest account) and power should fulfill two criteria. It should account for the difficulties of maintaining trust in a situation of extreme disparities of power between actors and it should also be able to accommodate trust in relationships in which disparities of power between actors exist but are less marked. Clearly, it must thus be able to distinguish between those social situations in which power drives out trust (and often leads to distrust) and those situations in which power and trust are not mutually exclusive.

In this chapter, I canvas one set of arguments that draws such a distinction. The literature on credible commitments, which shares much common ground with the encapsulated-interest account of trust, discusses the need to "tie the king's hands" in certain instances (North and Weingast 1995; Miller 1992). Certain actors may be too powerful to be trusted because they have no incentive not to renege on their commitments. However, their power may not actually serve their interests; because they cannot be trusted, other actors will seek, as much as they can, to avoid dealings with them that require trust. Thus as Douglass North and Barry Weingast argue, the ability of the early modern British state to raise monies was greatly increased when its power to break its commitments was curbed. Creditors could lend money to the government in the reasonable expectation that it would be returned, with interest. North and Weingast use this train of reasoning to draw general lessons for political economy; however, their arguments also provide a basis for arguments about the relationship between trust, distrust, and power.

One can plausibly maintain that under the encapsulated-interest account of trust, your relationship with me may involve trust, even if I am more powerful than you, *up to the point at which I am so powerful that I am no longer capable of making credible commitments to you*. Before this point is reached, power and trust are not mutually exclusive; while disparities in power may certainly affect the way in which the proceeds of trust-based cooperation are distributed, they will not necessarily prevent trust from arising. After this point, it is difficult, if not impossible, to use trust to describe your relationship with another who is so powerful that he or she cannot make credible commitments to you. If I am so much more powerful than you that I am no longer capable of giving credible commitments, then it follows that our relationship is insufficient to bind me to act in your interest. You will have no reason to trust me and in many circumstances will actively distrust me. This further means that insofar as you have no reason to trust me, I will have no reason to trust you.

Incorporating Power into the Encapsulated-Interest Account of Trust

The encapsulated-interest account of trust argues that trust involves expectations about interests.[2] I trust you to the extent that I believe that you have an interest in fulfilling my trust. Trust is not diffuse; it is likely to be limited to a particular matter (or matters). A trusts B to do X but may not trust B to do Y. Trust is an expectation, but it is a quite particular sort of expectation; it involves A's expectations on the basis of B's specific interests with regard to A. As Hardin argues, trust is a *relational* concept. That is to say it depends on the specific relationship between A and B; A's trust of B usually depends on their relationship, and the interest that relationship creates for B in behaving in a trustworthy fashion.[3]

This suggests how the encapsulated-interest account might incorporate power. Power, like trust, is a notoriously difficult concept to pin down; here, I follow Jack Knight (1992, 41), who argues that "to exercise power over someone or some group is to affect by some means the alternatives available to that person or group." Knight goes on to argue that a good index of power in bargaining situations is the set of alternatives faced by a party in the case of breakdown. Parties who have many possible attractive alternatives should a particular relationship not work out will be more powerful than parties who have few such alternatives because they can more credibly threaten to break off bargaining, thus affecting the other's feasible set. Power, under this definition, is clearly relevant to trust. If I am capable of affecting the set of feasible actions that you may undertake, I have influence over your ability to pursue your interests. This may affect your trustworthiness with regard to a particular matter; you have to take my interests into account.

Viewed in this way, power is clearly relevant to the encapsulated-interest account of trust (although, again, the terms "power" and "trust" should not be conflated, and extremes of power do not translate into extremes of trust). Merely redescribing trust relations in terms of power does not tell us much. However, examining the relationship between power and trust may lead us to two interesting conclusions. First, power may affect trust insofar as it touches on parties' evaluation of the relative worth of the relationship. Second, to the extent that power affects the possibility of trust and trustworthiness, it also may affect the kinds of cooperation that take place on the basis of trust and trustworthiness.

The first point follows more or less clearly from Hardin's emphasis on trust as a relational concept. As Hardin (2002, 4) puts it, "I trust you because I think it is your interest to attend to my interests in the relevant matter. This is not merely to say that you and I have the same interests. Rather, it is to say that you have an interest in attending to *my* interests because, typically, you want our relationship to continue." It may be in your interest to behave in a trustworthy fashion because of the economic benefits flowing from our relationship or, in thicker relationships, because of the nonmaterial benefits that you receive from it. In both cases one might say that your interest in being trustworthy is affected by my power to break off the relationship, or to redefine its terms to your disadvantage, should you behave in an untrustworthy fashion. If one party wishes to continue the relationship, and the other party values it more lightly and has scope to affect the relationship to the first party's advantage or disadvantage, that second party may be said to have power over the first. In many circumstances, the parties in a relationship will have roughly symmetrical power; neither will want to break off or alter the relationship much more than the other. In such circumstances, power will not be especially relevant to explanations of the existence and form of trust.

However, substantial asymmetries may exist, even in "thick" relationships, that carry a considerable emotional weight. In the presence of such asymmetries, power may have an important impact on trusting relationships. To the extent that one individual has many possible attractive alternatives to a given relationship, that relationship will be less valuable to the individual in question. The other individual in this relationship may not have so many alternatives and thus may be more dependent on the continuation of the relationship.[4]

This conclusion leads to the second point: that asymmetries in power are one source of asymmetry in trusting relationships and thus in the forms of cooperation that take place on the basis of trust in these relationships.[5] If asymmetries of power exist, they are likely to have an impact on trustworthiness and thus on trust. When I have many attractive alternatives to my relationship with you, and I know that you have few, I may be more inclined to take advantage of you in some circumstances. This may happen in thick relationships as well as in thin ones; everyday life provides evidence, for example, of friendships in which one party is considerably more socially "attractive" than the other and treats his or her less fortunate acquaintance badly. Power asymmetries may play an important role in family relationships, too, as Margaret Brown (chapter 7 in this volume) vividly demonstrates. This said, relationships that involve genuine emotional attachments are less likely to be highly asymmetrical in this sense; both parties may have sunk considerable resources into the relationship and will be unwilling to abandon it lightly.

Thus power may affect trust and trustworthiness insofar as it impinges on a relationship that both parties value. If one party values the relationship more lightly than the other (perhaps because of the existence of other potentially attractive relationships), she may be said to have power, in the sense that she can affect the set of feasible actions available to the other by credibly threatening to end the relationship, in order to redefine it to her advantage. Trust remains possible in such relationships; to the extent that both parties attach some value to the continuation of the relationship, they each have some reason to take the other's interest into account and thus to behave in a trustworthy manner. The point is that such trustworthiness (and trust) may be asymmetrical; insofar as one party values the relationship more lightly than the other, she has less need to be trustworthy for the relationship to continue. If A values the relationship less than B, A may still trust B over a wide range of issues (or over more important issues), but B may only be able to trust A over a narrower (or less important) range. While B may distrust A over many issues, he may prefer to continue the relationship, given his alternative options, provided that the relationship still offers him some overall benefit.

Encapsulated Interest and Credible Commitments

Under certain circumstances, then, trust may coexist with asymmetries of power. This, however, leads to a troubling question. If, as Hardin has argued, trust is not present in relationships involving extreme disparities of power, at what point do power asymmetries change their causal weight, so that they no longer merely affect trust relations but instead make them impossible? Here I wish to point to similarities between the debate about trust in relationships between individuals and the ongoing debate in political economy about the role of the state. While I do not want to gloss over the important differences between these two levels of analysis, political economy provides important lessons that may (with some care) be applied to trust between individuals.

The power of the state, and its implications for relations with society, has been an important question for political economists and economic sociologists since the foundations of the two disciplines. Some scholars, especially paternalist conservatives, have held that an absolute ruler may be trusted to rule for the common good because his particular interest is commensurate with the general interest. The historian Edward Gibbon (1776/1995, 95), for example, in his account of the reign of Septimius Severus, makes the claim that "the true interest of an absolute monarch generally coincides with that of his people. Their numbers, their wealth, their order, and their security, are the best and only foundations of his real greatness; and, were he totally devoid of virtue, prudence might supply its place, and would dictate the same course of conduct." However, most social science suggests the opposite, finding that the nonaccountability of the ruler to other social actors has negative consequences for general welfare. Max Weber (1922/1978), for example, distinguishes between Oriental and European varieties of feudalism. In the former, the ruler had absolute power over his nobles, granting and taking away authority from functionaries at whim. In the latter, the monarch granted land in return for military services, creating a complex web of reciprocal obligation (fealty) between monarch and liege-lord, which constrained the former and was crucial to the later development of the rule of law and the economic development of the West. Most recently, a body of scholarship associated especially with Douglass North (1981) and Margaret Levi (1988) has clarified the often fraught relationship between state and other actors in the sphere of economic development.

It is not difficult to show that this work is relevant to the relationship between trust and power. It asks whether, under what circumstances, and to what extent powerful actors (state actors) may take the interests of less powerful actors (typically, the general public or economic agents) into consideration or, in a broad sense, when more powerful actors may be expected to be trustworthy toward weaker ones. Nowhere is this clearer than in North and Weingast's (1995) work on "credible commitments" and the Glorious Revolution. These authors argue that the degree to which the sovereign is himself bound by the rules governing commercial exchange is crucial to the development of markets. In early modern Europe, sovereigns were not necessarily bound to repay the debts that they had incurred; they could repudiate them at will. Their power to do this was not necessarily to their advantage, however, as it made merchants unwilling to advance them loans. Because they were unconstrained by law, they had difficulty in making credible commitments.

North and Weingast note two possible solutions to this problem. Monarchs could establish a reputation for repaying debts, which could become a valuable asset (see Kreps 1990), providing them with an incentive to repay and thus reassuring merchants that they were trustworthy. This solution was impracticable in early modern Europe, where states were frequently at war with one another, so that the temptation for the sovereign to renege was often overwhelming. Alternatively, the crown could itself become subject to the law. The Glorious Revolution, and the departure of the Stuarts, saw the British crown becoming subject to legal and institutional constraints but simultaneously becoming vastly more credible to lenders, so that the level of public debt grew fiftyfold between 1688 and 1720.

The problem faced by the British crown—that it was too powerful to give credible commitments easily—can be generalized to many other social situations. Gary Miller (1992, 2001) has shown the relevance of this problem to the political economy of the firm. Many aspects of the internal hierarchy of the firm, from piecework to deferred compensation of workers, require that the owners of the firm credibly commit ex ante not to take ex post advantage of workers, even though opportunism would be to their immediate benefit. The hierarchical advantage enjoyed by owners and managers means that it is difficult for them to make these commitments; to do so, they have to constrain themselves, either by creating an appropriate "culture" or by creating a firewall between shareholders, whose interest is in short-term profit, and managers and directors, who ideally should have a longer-term perspective, and be prepared to make the necessary commitments over time. Only through these means can the stakeholders in a firm coordinate on an efficient equilibrium (or at least an equilibrium that is superior to the never-trust–never-honor-trust equilibrium that strictly dominates the one-shot trust game).

These arguments provide the basis for two important conclusions. First, one may identify conditions under which asymmetries of power will almost certainly prevent trust from arising and will lead to distrust. A certain degree of asymmetry in power may be tolerated in a relationship, although it is likely to have distributional effects. But if I am so powerful that I may renege without significant consequences, you may reasonably doubt my interest in continuing the relationship; my most attractive option may be to abuse your trust. In other words, I am incapable of making credible commitments to you—commitments that you know it is in my interest to fulfill once I have made them. To say that I am incapable of making credible commitments to you is to say (among other things) that you are incapable of retaliating effectively should I betray your trust. The hurt that you can inflict by breaking off your relationship with me is potentially outweighed by the benefit I would receive from abusing your trust. Furthermore, there is no reason external to our relationship for me to behave in a trustworthy manner within it. The point at which I am so powerful that I can no longer make a credible commitment to you is just that point at which I am so much more powerful than you that you can no longer trust me.[6]

Clearly, under circumstances in which you cannot trust me, you will avoid relationships with me that require trust. You will rationally distrust me and expect me to take advantage of you at every opportunity, so that you will be unlikely to benefit from any such relationship. Even in the unlikely event that you were to engage in such a relationship (you were somehow coerced), I would probably be unable to trust you, either. The relationship provides you with no good reason to behave in a trustworthy fashion because you know that it provides me with no good reason. To the extent that you cannot expect me to be trustworthy, your particular relationship with me has no value, so that (all other things being equal) you will not be trustworthy, either, and I will not trust you. You are likely only to "cooperate" to the extent that you are forced to do so.[7] Extreme disparities of power mean that both the stronger and the weaker actor will have good reason to distrust each other.

Second, however, this literature points to the existence of a gray zone in which asymmetries of power are not so great as to lead inevitably to mutual distrust but may nonetheless significantly hamper the development of trust. As the more general literature on trust and trustworthiness emphasizes, trust invariably involves some degree of uncertainty; one can never fully divine another's interests, and thus one can never be entirely sure that another will behave in a trustworthy manner, although one may have reasonable expectations. Where there are substantial (although not overwhelming) asymmetries of power, such uncertainties may have important consequences. The less powerful actor may be unsure whether his relationship with the more powerful actor gives the latter sufficient reason to behave in a trustworthy fashion.

As Roderick Kramer (chapter 6 in this volume) argues, social psychology provides us with good evidence that less powerful actors will often misconstrue more powerful actors' intentions, interpreting them in the worst possible light. In these situations, even when the more powerful actor genuinely wishes to behave in a trustworthy manner, she may have difficulty in persuading the less powerful actor of her good intentions. Even where the latter does not fall victim to the kinds of paranoid cognition that Kramer identifies, he may be unsure as to the interests of the former in borderline cases. Furthermore, he may reasonably worry that even if the more powerful actor has an interest in behaving in a trustworthy fashion now, circumstances may easily change so that it is no longer in her interest to be trustworthy in the future.

North and Weingast (1995) and Miller (2001) discuss the implications of such uncertainty.[8] First, actors may have variable time horizons. A monarch may wish to borrow money and may be willing, most of the time, to commit to repay her debts; the shadow of the future may loom long enough to give her reason to be trustworthy. However, her time horizons may shift rapidly if war threatens, so that she has a strong interest, perhaps even an overwhelming interest, in defecting in order to avoid extinction. A potential lender, knowing that there is a substantial chance of war (which may not be quantifiable so as to transform uncertainty into risk), may be unwilling to advance money, however sincere the monarch may appear to be. A similar logic may apply within firms, in which owners' commitments to reward their workers are rendered less credible by the possibility of economic downturn, which will give them a strong interest in reneging. Creditors and workers, knowing that wars and economic downturns are not extraordinary events, are often disinclined to believe the promises of kings and owners that they will give full return over time.

Second, and more profoundly, many problems of trust may be treated as problems of equilibrium selection in an infinitely repeated game, in which actors may be uncertain of each other's ultimate intentions (Miller 2001). Here, asymmetries of power may make it more difficult to coordinate on a mutually beneficial equilibrium. One or both actors may have a strong incentive to renege in the short term. If there is uncertainty that one actor will play an honorable strategy, then the other actor must always worry that the first actor will violate trust, thus making it more difficult for both to converge on a mutually beneficial equilibrium. The most obvious solution to this problem is for one or both of the actors to make a binding commitment that he or she will behave honorably. However, if one of the actors is much more powerful than the other, it will be difficult for her to make that commitment. She will have difficulty in using the relationship as surety for good behavior insofar as there are other attractive options available to her. Even when she genuinely desires to cooperate, she may have difficulty in convincing the weaker actor to extend the necessary trust for cooperation.

To remedy this problem, Miller's logic suggests that she is best advised either to establish an appropriate "culture," which may be linked to reputational sanctions (Kreps 1990), or to subject herself to external institutions or organizational forms that would make it difficult or impossible for her to abuse trust.[9] By pursuing either of these courses she is constraining herself, and limiting her future ability to exercise power, in order to convince others that she will not use that power to traduce their trust. Brown (chapter 7 in this volume) provides a detailed analysis of how a more powerful actor may pursue a strategy that both limits his power and serves as a token of future intentions. She notes that both a Madagascar villager and his younger siblings may prefer to undertake certain transactions on the basis of cash rather than more informal means of exchange; this both limits the elder brother's ability to abuse his greater bargaining power and reassures his siblings of his future good intentions. Levi, Matthew Moe, and Theresa Buckley (chapter 5 in this volume) explain how external institutions may at least alleviate distrust between actors with asymmetric power, even where they do not necessarily create trust. However, they also demonstrate that such institutions have their own costs and may be captured over time by more powerful actors. These quandaries are beyond the scope of my discussion.

Thus trust may be affected by power: power asymmetries impinge on the value of the relationship between the trusting and trusted parties. Relationships involving trust may be asymmetrical: I may trust you with matters over which you do not trust me, and you may trust me with matters about which I do not trust you. One important source of such asymmetries is likely to be differences in power between individuals. To the extent that I have many other options outside our relationship and you do not, I may have less reason to behave in a trustworthy fashion toward you; the breakdown of our relationship (when you accuse me of untrustworthy behavior) is likely to hurt you more than it hurts me, and we will both know this. Our relationship may still be characterized by trust, but I will probably be able to trust you over a wider range of matters than you will trust me.

At a certain point, however, power asymmetries can become so marked as to drive out trust. When one actor is much more powerful than the other, she does not have to take the other's interests into account. Thus she has no reason to be trustworthy and is incapable of giving credible commitments. Furthermore, one can extend the argument to say that the less powerful party has no interest in being trustworthy, either. Extreme disparities of power are likely to give rise to mutual distrust.

Thus one can distinguish between situations in which asymmetries of power exist but are not so marked as to prevent trust and situations in which such asymmetries are so pronounced that they make credible commitments (and therefore trust) impossible. One may also identify an intermediate area at the cusp between these two, where uncertainty means that the less powerful actors are unsure as to whether power disparities and interests are sufficient to make trust impossible. Here, if the more powerful party wishes to create the possibility of cooperation, it behooves her to constrain herself in such a way that her power to defect is lessened, so that others may reasonably trust her (or, at least, have less reason to distrust her).

Trust, Distrust, and Relations Between Firms

The relationship between power, trust, and distrust that I have described is likely to apply to many areas of social life, including economic relations. More particularly, it may help to explain subcontracting relations between firms. At first glance, such relations might appear to involve institution-induced expectations rather than trust; indeed, Oliver Williamson (1993) argues that the concept of trust has little purchase on economic relations. However, institutions, whether they be based on formal laws or informal social rules, will not fully determine outcomes in real-life situations, providing scope for quite rich varieties of trust (and distrust).[10] Subcontracting relations frequently involve quasi-personalized relationships between individual actors of the sort emphasized in the encapsulated-interest account. Furthermore, these relationships provide a good test case for the argument that power affects trust relationships. Such relationships usually involve imbalances of power; typically (although by no means universally), the final firm making the order has more options, and thus more power, than the subcontractors.

If the theory outlined in the previous section has empirical merit, and if the power imbalances between final firms and subcontractors are indeed substantial, final firms will face a difficult balancing act. On the one hand, their power may allow them to shape long-term relationships with subcontractors to their particular advantage. On the other hand, they may run the risk of finding themselves too powerful for their own good: to the extent that subcontractors have difficulty in trusting them, final firms may be incapable of reaching cooperative equilibriums in which both parties would benefit. To examine the potential relevance of power to choices made by actors and to their outcomes in terms of trust and cooperation, I turn to three examples drawn from the literature on "thick" subcontracting relationships: Japanese subcontracting practices in the weaving industry; relations between metalworking firms in France; and relations in the packaging machinery industry in Italy.[11]

Weavers in Japan

Much of the recent literature on subcontracting relations has focused on Japan,[12] even if the Japanese model of industrial organization seems less successful than it did a decade ago. Many of the key arguments about Japanese subcontracting practices were set out in a classic article by Ronald Dore (1992) on "goodwill" in the Japanese economy. Dore argues against the persistent skepticism in classical and neoclassical economics about economic behavior that is not motivated by self-interest. As a counterexample, he proposes the existence of relations between economic actors in Japan, which he sees as involving "moralized trading relationships of mutual goodwill" (Dore 1992, 163). In Dore's argument, such relationships have important economic benefits; they lower transaction costs and decrease the likelihood of opportunism. In addition to making certain kinds of coordination and "X-efficiencies" available, relationships of goodwill make it easier for economic actors to trust one another.

Dore turns to the fragmented Japanese weaving industry for evidence of goodwill in practice. Weaving in Japan relies extensively on subcontracting relations in which "weavers," who own the automatic looms, produce for "converters." Typically, smaller weavers are monogamous—they tend to produce for only one converter—whereas larger weavers may have relationships with three or four converters. Dore suggests that relationships between these firms do not involve the kinds of open confrontation found in many occidental trading relationships, in which bargaining is seen as a zero-sum game. Instead, both sides of the relationship recognize a moral obligation to try to maintain the relationship. When the relationship breaks down, it usually involves one or both of the parties making accusations of "insincerity." A similar logic of relations is found within the larger "grupu," or groupings, which involve stable, obligated bilateral trading relationships between large firms (Dore 1992), as well as in the Japanese economy more generally, where survey evidence suggests a widespread reliance on long-term relationships involving trust between economic actors (Sako 1991).

"Goodwill," as Dore defines it, is clearly closely connected with trust, a connection made explicit in Mari Sako's (1991) portmanteau term, "goodwill trust." What is noteworthy is that Dore's "goodwill" relations seem to involve substantial imbalances of power. Dore argues that weavers are more dependent on converters than are converters on weavers, so that the converter is in a position of hierarchical superiority. There are many weavers in competition with one another and relatively few converters. This has implications for the way the benefits of cooperation are distributed. Especially in hard times, the weavers may find their profits squeezed by the converters (Dore 1992). More generally, the converters have less need to behave in a trustworthy fashion toward weavers than weavers do toward converters. Weavers with verbal contracts are more likely to have their goods returned for quality deficiencies than weavers with written contracts. Furthermore, such returns curiously become more common when prices are falling, so that a rejected lot can be replaced with a newly contracted, cheaper one. Dore finds that the weaker partner has to show considerably more "sincerity" to the more powerful partner than the latter must show to the former.

However, as Dore is keen to emphasize, even if these mutual obligations are asymmetrical, they are not one-sided. Although converters may take advantage of weavers, they do so within certain limits. Both the losses of bad times and the profits of good times are shared, even if in an unequal fashion. Furthermore, the converter is expected to refrain from using his superior bargaining power to push weavers to the verge of bankruptcy. His obligation not to do so (as well as the obligations of the weavers to show sincerity) is reinforced by reputational mechanisms (Dore 1992).

As should be immediately apparent, the kinds of subcontracting relationship identified by Dore in Japan may easily be recomposed in the terms of the simple theory of trust, distrust, and power outlined in the first section of this chapter. Subcontracting relations between converters and weavers clearly involve trust. Economic actors find themselves bound into long-term relationships, and thus each partner may reasonably believe that the other partner has an interest in behaving in a trustworthy fashion in order to continue the relationship. However, converters have many more weavers with whom they can potentially do business than weavers have converters. Because converters have more options outside the relationship, they have more power inside it, as well. This translates not only into an asymmetrical division of the benefits of cooperation but also into differences in trustworthiness and trust. Converters can behave in an openly untrustworthy fashion in some aspects of the relationship without causing it to fail; weavers typically cannot. This said, while the asymmetry of power between converters and weavers is enough to shape their relationship and the forms of trust it involves, it is not enough to prevent trust from arising in the first place. Converters are restrained by reputational mechanisms, and quite possibly by social norms, from using their power to reshape the relationship so that weavers derive no benefit from it (and are potentially driven into bankruptcy).[13] Weavers can thus rationally trust converters, at least over some matters, even if converters may sometimes take advantage of them.

Machine Production in France

The quandaries of power may also help explain a puzzling finding reported in the literature on subcontracting: that final firms may tend to discourage subcontractors from becoming too dependent on them. What is perhaps the most developed account of this phenomenon may be found in the work of Edward Lorenz (1988, 1993, 1999) on trust between machinery producers in the Rhône-Alps region of France. Lorenz finds that technological changes led these firms to adopt new forms of production and, in particular, to decentralize productive activity. Certain standardized stages of the production process, which had previously been carried out in-house, were put out to smaller subcontractors. As in Japan, relationships between final firms and subcontractors involved trust between the relevant economic actors. Lorenz's interviewees describe their relationships in terms of partnership, loyalty, and trust. Because the production process might involve unexpected contingencies, neither institutional enforcement nor reputational incentives, on their own, could provide a sufficient basis for cooperative relations (Lorenz 1993, 1999). Instead, so called moral contracts ("contrats moraux") that involved basic procedural rules for how unexpected events might be handled provided the basis for cooperation. These moral contracts did not necessarily involve genuine emotional or normative commitments; while business actors spoke of their commercial relations in terms of friendship, this language was intended to coordinate expectations (in situations of difficulty, actors should behave "as if" they were friends) rather than to express deeper forms of commitment. In Lorenz's (1988) lapidary phrase, business actors were "neither friends nor strangers."

Lorenz's evidence indicates that these firms sought to diversify their relations in order to mitigate the risks of undue dependency. Final firms would solicit tenders from at least three subcontractors before engaging in a relationship, and they preferred to split orders between a minimum of two so that they could switch to one if a problem with the other arose.

More unusually, final firms not only sought to avoid becoming dependent on particular subcontractors, they also actively sought to discourage subcontractors from becoming too dependent on them. The final firm and the subcontractor sought to create a partnership in which the final firm would account for no less than 10 percent and no more than 15 percent of the total output of the subcontracting firm. Less than that would mean that the subcontractor did not have sufficient incentive to take account of the particular needs of the final firm, while more meant that the subcontractor would become unduly dependent on the final firm, so that it would be crippled if the final firm ran into serious difficulties.

The interesting question is why final firms would encourage a situation that protected subcontractors from becoming too dependent on them, given Lorenz's assertion that they did not possess genuinely other-regarding motivations. Why should decision makers within the final firm care enough about the possible effects of their own economic difficulties on others that they were prepared to discourage these others in advance from becoming too dependent on them?

One may plausibly argue that the reason for this behavior lies in the dilemmas of power discussed in this chapter.[14] Final firms that wish to encourage genuinely cooperative relations with subcontractors may have good reason to ensure that power disparities do not prevent their doing so. If a subcontractor becomes overly dependent on a particular final firm, the owners of the subcontracting firm have greater difficulty in trusting the decision makers in the final firm not to renege on informal commitments by pocketing the additional effort given by the subcontractor without rewarding it in return. Trust may be especially difficult in times of economic hardship, when the final firm may face an overwhelming temptation to defect by using its power to squeeze the subcontractor for short-term profits. If the owners of subcontracting firms know that difficult periods are likely at some point in the future but are unable to predict when, it may be difficult for them to enter into a genuinely trusting relationship with the final firm. Under these conditions, it may be wise for both the final firm and the subcontractor to create a relationship in which trust is possible (that is, both have a sufficient stake in the relationship for trust to arise) but in which the subcontractor does not become unduly dependent on the final firm (for fear that this dependency might tempt the final firm too much). The arrangements reached by firms in Lorenz's case study seem designed as compromises between these two exigencies.

Production of Packaging Machinery in Italy

Finally, the packaging machinery industry of Bologna, capital of the Italian region of Emilia-Romagna, is a case in which power relations are currently changing.[15] Packaging machinery manufacturers and subcontractors are both located in a relatively well defined geographic area, known as "Packaging Valley," where there has historically been a high degree of cooperation in the production process. Indeed, production is radically disintegrated, so that final firms are generally responsible only for sales, design, and assembly of the final product. The actual manufacture of individual parts and components is carried out by subcontractors, working from designs provided by the final firms.

This extraordinary level of vertical disintegration is typical of Italian "industrial districts," in which cooperation between a multitude of smaller firms has typically served as a substitute for hierarchical production within the firm (Brusco 1990). There must be extensive trust between final firm and subcontractors if the risks of exploitation (on the part of final firms) and hold-up (on the part of subcontractors) are not to prevent cooperation. This trust is possible because of informal institutional rules at the local level, which provide for a high level of honesty in personal dealings, and the sanctioning of firms that behave opportunistically (Farrell 2001; Farrell and Knight, forthcoming). These rules have permitted a set of understandings to come into being that have themselves become institutionalized, in which final firms commit to providing work over time in exchange for the subcontractor's flexibility and honesty. However, as in many other Italian industrial districts, power relations between firms are shifting in a manner that has important implications for trust and cooperation.

Two sets of relationships are important here: relationships among final firms themselves and relationships between final firms and subcontractors. Final firms in the packaging machinery industry have traditionally been highly specialized. Each firm might specialize in machines for a particular stage of the packaging process in a particular industry. For example, one firm might produce dosing machines that fill gelatin capsules with a drug for the pharmaceutical industry, whereas another quite different firm might produce the machines that pack these gelatin capsules in blister packs. Thus several different final firms might come together to provide the machines for the packaging line ordered by a customer firm.

Increasingly, however, larger firms in the industry have bought out smaller firms so that they can provide a complete line of machinery. This is driven by customer demand: large firms in the pharmaceutical and food industries no longer wish to deal with several smaller firms, preferring instead to create closer ties with a single packaging machinery supplier that can provide all their needs. As large final firms buy out their smaller counterparts, they assume ever-increasing control over the packaging machinery district. Because of their strong relationships with their customers, they have no reason to fear competition from smaller firms, which are increasingly hierarchically subordinated. As described in an interview with me by the managing director of one of the largest firms in the district,

> In this field we exist really, when we have the control of the final customer. In manufacturing of industrial or capital equipment like this, if you manufacture capital equipment you have got to have the grip on the customer yourself. What you could say is that there is a space for a small company, but they will supply mostly through the sales organisations of larger companies. That means they are nothing, they can be purchased easily, or destroyed or eliminated. Because the market here is not for this machine, it is for these customers, and if you don't have these customers, you don't exist. You have got to have these customers to exist.

Thus the district is increasingly becoming dominated by a small number of final firms, which are buying up most of their competitors. This has consequences in turn for the relationship between final firms and subcontractors. Previously, subcontractors in the district had considerable latitude in their relations with final firms. Although many subcontractors were in competition with one another, there were also many final firms for which they could work. The result was a situation of rough equality in bargaining between final firms and subcontractors; both had many alternative options if they failed to reach agreement in a particular set of negotiations. Now, in contrast, there are rather fewer final firms for which subcontractors can work.

The result is an increase in hierarchy. Final firms, which face the demand for ever-higher quality from their customers, seek to bring this about by hierarchically organizing their subcontractors in a "Christmas tree arrangement" in which the final firm is at the vertex, certain key subcontractors, which organize the production process, are beneath the final firm, and a large number of smaller subcontractors who report to the "key" subcontractors are at the base. Final firms now have more power over their subcontractors, and they can use that power to extract concessions (such as greater flexibility) without providing the quid pro quo (guaranteed levels of work in the long run) that had previously been given. A senior manager in another large firm in the district describes in an interview with me how they have built up dependent subcontractors, which rely on the firm for up to 80 percent of their turnover but have to agree to terms that are "very favorable" to the final firm, without any guarantees of future income: "We ask for a lot of flexibility from our suppliers! That is the main concern they have normally. They don't like to be treated in that way, because for us it is difficult to predict what is the workload that we would pass to our suppliers. So normally our projection is always pretty wrong. But on the other side, for them we are very important. So they just complain."

Here, final firms, unlike their counterparts in the Rhône-Alps region, are deliberately reorganizing their relationships in such a way as to emphasize power over trust. It remains to be seen whether this strategy will be successful in the long run; certainly, it is difficult to see how the traditional advantages of the industrial district can be maintained if it continues. Subcontractors no longer have good reason to trust final firms, which have the power to squeeze their profits at will. They are expected to provide flexibility without receiving any guarantees in return, becoming what Klaus Semlinger (1993) describes in his title as "flexibility reservoirs." This may, over the longer run, lead to distrust and persistently inefficient equilibriums of the sort that have characterized final firm–subcontractor relations in sectors such as the European car industry (McMillan 1995). It may be possible to solve this problem through reputational means and by creating an appropriate "culture" within these quasi-hierarchical structures (Miller 1992). It is far more difficult, however, to mitigate problems of distrust within hierarchy, where there are substantial asymmetries of power between actors, than in situations in which such asymmetries are less marked or nonexistent.

Conclusions

Asymmetries of power, up to a certain level, are by no means incompatible with trust. Even when trust and its outcomes are asymmetric, trust may still be possible. Nonetheless, there is a point at which asymmetries are such that it is impossible for the more powerful actor to give credible commitments to the weaker. At this point, disparities of power prevent trust from arising and make distrust the likely outcome. Where substantial asymmetries of power coexist with uncertainty, it may be difficult for actors to be sure which side of this dividing line they are on.

This relationship between trust, distrust, and power may be shown to have implications for cooperation in the real world. In particular, it helps explain behavior in subcontracting relations between firms. If final firms wish to create the conditions for cooperation with their subcontractors, they are well advised to constrain their power in some way, whether through credible commitments, subjection to outside agencies, or other appropriate technologies. Failing this, they may find themselves in an inefficient equilibrium in which subcontractors rationally refuse to be trustworthy because they perceive that the more powerful party may simply take advantage of their good faith without reciprocation. Indeed, this last may be the default condition; conscious effort on the part of final firms (as in the Rhône-Alps region) or the existence of external reputational mechanisms (as in Japan) may be required to avoid it. Indeed, in many cases, final firms may prefer to pursue the profits possible through exploiting their power over the difficult and complex task of nurturing cooperation.[16]

Thus while Becker (1996) and other critics of the encapsulated-interest account of trust are surely wrong when they argue that trust reduces under this account to power, the encapsulated-interest account may incorporate power and its consequences. Indeed, precisely because it can provide a plausible account of the relationship between trust and power that helps explain the behavior of actors in the real world, it has an important advantage over those other accounts that have difficulty doing so.

This chapter had its beginnings in a conference in the Russell Sage Foundation's Series on Trust, jointly hosted by the Max-Planck Project Group on the Law of Common Goods in Bonn and the Max-Planck Institute for the Study of Societies in Köln in December 2000. I am grateful to Russell Hardin for having seen the germ of a paper in my arguments and for having encouraged me to write it. I am grateful to the other participants in the conference, especially Margaret Levi, Fritz Scharpf, and Marco Verweij, for their comments in discussion and to Jack Knight, for later conversations on the topic. I am also grateful to Brad DeLong for a clarificatory observation.

Notes

1. "That we might not trust those who have power over us, especially when they have little reason to care for us individually, is no surprise. I depend very heavily on your favor while you depend not at all on mine. You can therefore do me substantial harm while I can do you little or none. The mutual trust that depends on reciprocal relations cannot easily develop in such unequal, non-reciprocal contexts" (Hardin 2002, 100).

2. I do not engage in an extended discussion of the encapsulated-interest account here, only mentioning those points that are necessary to my argument. Extended descriptions of the encapsulated-interest account can be found in Hardin (2002) and Levi (1998).

3. Many authors disagree with this claim; specifically, there is dispute as to whether one can describe more general social relationships, such as citizens' relationship with their government, in terms of trust. I wish to bracket this set of issues. In this chapter, I follow Hardin's definition, which emphasizes the relational aspects of trust. Some parts of my argument depend on such a definition; to the extent that one makes use of other concepts of trust, the force of my arguments will be vitiated.

4. This point is made in Hardin (2002).

5. This argument adapts Jack Knight's (1992) discussion of the distributional aspects of power.

6. This point is the crux of Ken MacLeod's (1998) science fiction novel, *The Cassini Division*. MacLeod, who has some acquaintance with game theory, asks whether it is possible for actors who are potentially immensely powerful and are unconstrained by the "shadow of the future" to make binding commitments. His protagonist reasons (correctly, as it turns out) that they cannot.

7. As in North and Weingast's (1995, 810) example, when the Stuarts demanded loans under threat.

8. These situations are not incompatible, and they may reinforce each other.

9. This suggests how one may account for the effects of institutions and organizational forms on trust in a way that does not reduce trust to mere institution-induced expectations. Insofar as institutions and organizational forms provide a technology that allows actors credibly to limit their future ability to use power in a manner that is inimical to trust, they may make trust between actors possible, without dictating the precise form that it takes. Even where they do not produce trust, they may at least alleviate distrust. See further, Levi, Moe, and Buckley (chapter 5 in this volume). For an insightful treatment of the circumstances under which hegemonic states may wish to restrain themselves through institutional frameworks, see Ikenberry (2000).

10. Future collaborative work with Jack Knight will explore the relationship between institutions and trust in greater detail. For a useful critique of overly deterministic accounts of economic cooperation, see Lorenz (1999).

11. Note the limits of my ambitions here. I do not offer an explanation of why different outcomes may be reached in different settings; instead, I wish simply to show that actors in each setting face a broadly similar dilemma.

12. See, for example, Holmström and Roberts (1998), Sako (1991), and Sako and Helper (1995). The literature on this subject is voluminous.

13. While Dore notes the presence of reputational mechanisms, his explanation clearly privileges social norms as an explanation and, in particular, what he describes as "benevolence." While he is very likely right, most of the evidence that he advances is also compatible with a "narrow" rational-choice explanation, albeit a more sophisticated one than the neoclassical market framework provides.

14. The following explanation builds on Lorenz's own explanation of business actors' reasoning, recomposing his arguments, as best as I understand them, within the theoretical framework used in this chapter.

15. I here summarize findings that are laid out in much greater detail in Farrell and Knight (forthcoming) and Farrell (2001).

16. Susan Helper (1993) discusses the respective merits and problems of "exit" and "voice" strategies on the part of final firms. These closely parallel the strategies of pursuing power, or creating the conditions of cooperation, that I discuss here.

References

Becker, Laurence C. 1996. "Trust as Noncognitive Security about Motives." *Ethics* 107: 43–61.
Brusco, Sebastiano. 1990. "The Idea of the Industrial District: Its Genesis." In *Industrial Districts and Small Firm Cooperation in Italy*, edited by Frank Pyke, Giacomo Becattini, Werner Sengenberger. Geneva: IISS.
Dore, Ronald. 1992. "Goodwill and the Spirit of Market Capitalism." In *The Sociology of Economic Life*, edited by Richard Swedberg and Mark Granovetter. Boulder, Colo.: Westview Press.
Farrell, Henry. 2001. *Trust and Political Economy: Institutions and the Sources of Inter-Firm Cooperation*. Unpublished paper. Max-Planck Project Group, Bonn.
Farrell, Henry, and Jack Knight. Forthcoming. "Trust, Institutions and Institutional Evolution: Industrial Districts and the Social Capital Hypothesis." *Politics and Society*.
Gibbon, Edward. 1776/1995. *The Decline and Fall of the Roman Empire*. Vol. 1. New York: Modern Library.
Hardin, Russell. 2002. *Trust and Trustworthiness*. New York: Russell Sage Foundation.
Helper, Susan. 1993. "An Exit-Voice Analysis of Supplier Relations: The Case of the U.S. Automobile Industry." In *The Embedded Firm: On the Socioeconomics of Industrial Networks*, edited by Gernot Grabher. London: Routledge.
Holmström, Bengt, and John Roberts. 1998. "The Boundaries of the Firm Revisited." *Journal of Economic Perspectives* 12(4, Autumn): 73–94.
Ikenberry, John. 2000. *After Victory: Institutions, Strategic Restraint, and the Rebuilding of Order after Major Wars*. Princeton, N.J.: Princeton University Press.
Knight, Jack. 1992. *Institutions and Social Conflict*. Cambridge, U.K.: Cambridge University Press.
Kreps, David M. 1990. "Corporate Culture and Economic Theory." In *Perspectives on Positive Political Economy*, edited by James E. Alt and Kenneth A. Shepsle. Cambridge, U.K.: Cambridge University Press.
Levi, Margaret. 1988. *Of Rule and Revenue*. Berkeley: University of California Press.
———. 1998. "A State of Trust." In *Trust and Governance*, edited by Valerie Braithwaite and Margaret Levi. New York: Russell Sage Foundation.
Lorenz, Edward H. 1988. "Neither Friends nor Strangers: Informal Networks of Subcontracting in French Industry." In *Trust: Making and Breaking Cooperative Relations*, edited by Diego Gambetta. Oxford, U.K.: Basil Blackwell.
———. 1993. "Flexible Production Systems and the Social Construction of Trust." *Politics and Society* 21(3): 307–24.
———. 1999. "Trust, Contract and Economic Cooperation." *Cambridge Journal of Economics* 23(3): 301–15.
MacLeod, Ken. 1998. *The Cassini Division*. London: Orbit.

McMillan, John. 1995. "Reorganizing Vertical Supply Relationships." In *Trends in Business Organization: Do Participation and Cooperation Increase Competitiveness?*, edited by Horst Siebert. Tübingen, Ger.: J. C. B. Mohr.

Miller, Gary J. 1992. *Managerial Dilemmas: The Political Economy of Hierarchy*. Cambridge, U.K.: Cambridge University Press.

———. 2001. "Why is Trust Necessary in Organizations? The Moral Hazard of Profit Maximization." In *Trust in Society*, edited by Karen Cook. New York: Russell Sage Foundation.

North, Douglass C. 1981. *Structure and Change in Economic History*. New York: Norton.

North, Douglass C., and Barry R. Weingast. 1995. "Constitutions and Commitment: The Evolution of Institutions Governing Public Choice in Seventeenth-Century England." In *Empirical Studies in Institutional Change*, edited by Lee J. Alston, Thráinn Eggertsson, and Douglass C. North. Cambridge, U.K.: Cambridge University Press.

Sako, Mari. 1991. "The Role of 'Trust' in Japanese Buyer-Supplier Relationships." *Ricnerche Economiche* 45: 449–74.

Sako, Mari, and Susan Helper. 1995. "Determinants of Trust in Supplier Relations: Evidence from the Automotive Industry in Japan and the United States." Unpublished paper. Said Business School, University of Oxford.

Semlinger, Klaus. 1993. "Small Firms and Outsourcing as Flexibility Reservoirs of Large Firms." In *The Embedded Firm: On the Socioeconomics of Industrial Networks*, edited by Gernot Grabher. London: Routledge.

Weber, Max. 1922/1978. *Economy and Society*. Berkeley: University of California Press.

Williamson, Oliver E. 1993. "Calculativeness, Trust, and Economic Organization." *Journal of Law and Economics* 36(1p2): 453–86.

Chapter 5

The Transaction Costs of Distrust: Labor and Management at the National Labor Relations Board

Margaret Levi, Matthew Moe, and Theresa Buckley

Distrust at the workplace between managers and workers and especially between employers and unions can reduce productivity and increase inefficiencies—as well as make the workplace an unappealing place to be. Distrust may be the problem, but trust is not always the solution (Levi 2000, 137, 152–53). In situations in which there are mutual advantages from cooperation but also the combination of conflicting interests and reasons to fear hostile behavior by the other, the rational baseline position is distrust, not trust. This is particularly the case where the parties or individuals each control resources on which the other depends, resources whose withdrawal could inflict serious damage or loss. In some instances and over many kinds of issues, distrust is not a problem at all; it is a sensible stance. But when distrust leads to suboptimal outcomes, then the parties have an incentive to find ways to overcome distrust. Often the mechanisms are the creation not of trust relations, which would be unlikely and quite fragile in such instances, but of laws and other institutional devices.

The distrustful relationship between employers and employees is illustrative. The distrust is grounded in divergent interests and asymmetric power. Employers seek the highest performance they can get at the lowest pay possible. They generally resist efforts by their employees to unionize and by the state to impose labor standards. Workers seek the highest possible pay for their effort, and they often conflict with employers over hours and working conditions. They attempt to organize at the workplace and in the political sphere to compel employers to improve compensation, hours, and working conditions. The partners in this conflict are not equal, however. The right to hire, fire, and pay gives employers far greater power over workers than workers have over employers. The development of strong unions, tight labor markets, and certain institutional arrangements may level the playing field somewhat, but the power of the employers still tends to be greater, especially in depressions and recessions and when state administrations are particularly beholden to business elites. Opposing and hostile interests is one source of distrust. Following the line of reasoning offered by Henry Farrell (chapter 4 in this volume), the power disparity further fuels distrust.

Unionization increases the power of employees in relation to their employers. Through collective bargaining, the threat of strikes, and increased control of the shop floor, organized labor provides workers with significant leverage. The development of unions reduced the asymmetries of power between employers and employees sufficiently to compel employers to encapsulate the interests of their workers to some extent. Before unions gained clout, the power asymmetries were such as to foreclose credible commitments by employers. With the development of unions as a major force, asymmetries of power still existed but in a form in which credible commitments became feasible.

The existence of unions does not necessarily reduce distrust but sometimes dramatically increases it by intensifying the antagonism of the conflicting parties and by giving workers more resources to resist employer demands. Instead of particular individuals in a hierarchy of bosses, supervisors, and workers, the decision makers are collective actors: labor and management. Monitoring and enforcement of rules are less likely to be the means of resolving disruptive tensions than are negotiation and the exercise of power, such as the firing of agitators by employers or the use of strikes by employees. The withdrawal of resources—jobs or work—on which the other depends is an important credible threat for bringing the recalcitrant to the bargaining table. The strategy of withdrawal of resources can have negative side effects, however. Both parties may lose income, and both may develop resentments and, possibly, paranoid cognitions (see chapter 6 in this volume), with long-term destructive impact on workplace relationships and productivity. Where distrust between labor and management is pervasive, conflicts of interest may be more likely to evoke behaviors that further offend the other party.

The consequences of distrust may motivate the creation of institutional arrangements meant to make the parties, particularly the more powerful party, trustworthy (Levi 2000; also see chapter 4 in this volume).[1] Given the power asymmetry and, therefore, the credible threat employers possess of firing workers who engage in organizing activity, workers and unions followed the strategy of tying employers to a set of formal rules. The 1935 National Labor Relations Act (NLRA, also known as the Wagner Act) and the National Labor Relations Board (NLRB) were the results. Employers may initially have agreed only reluctantly, but over time they realized that the NLRB created a forum for interaction with unions from which they could benefit strategically.

As a device for institutionalizing trustworthiness, the NLRB constrains both management and labor, affects the balance of power between them, and promotes trust or, more likely, alleviates some of the worst consequences of distrust. The price for this outcome includes additional transaction costs imposed on the parties and the public, which pays for the government institution. Does the NLRB produce sufficient benefit to justify the cost? It is not easy to determine the transaction costs entailed or to evaluate the social gains from reducing distrust, although this chapter offers an initial effort.

The Attempt to Level the Playing Field

At the root of distrust are conflicts of interest, power asymmetries, and lack of credible commitments. It should be made clear here, however, that it is the distrust that requires a palliative; conflicts of interest and power asymmetries will continue to exist and are probably impossible to eradicate, although it may be possible to create some capacity to constrain actors by institutionalizing credible commitments. This might enable actors to overcome distrust sufficiently to take their conflicts to the bargaining table or to appeal resolution to a third party. While the conflicts and power disparities will not disappear, compromises and negotiated settlements might become feasible. The parties are likely to become more trustworthy; each becomes more motivated to act in a way compatible with—or at least not destructive to—the other's interests, and each develops capacities for solving the problems that stand in the way of a better working relationship.

For labor to believe management is trustworthy, labor must have assurances of its rights to organize the workplace and engage in collective bargaining. For management to believe labor is trustworthy, it must have assurances that slowdowns and work stoppages will be a last, not a first, resort. Both must feel free from harassment. In the absence of such assurances between the parties, it is difficult to build trust; however, the establishment of institutions that protect both employers and employees provides a basis for the parties to cooperate by institutionalizing credible commitments.

It is also conceivable that the institutional arrangements will facilitate new forms of strategic action and amplify rather than reduce distrust in the long run. If one side knows how to rig the game to its advantage, then dysfunctional distrust again becomes the norm. If one or the other side in the bargaining relationship is able to capture the purportedly neutral third party who is managing the conflict, then the institution itself becomes unreliable, and new sources of distrust emerge. New forms of strategic action also arise from the perception of institutional bias in day-to-day decisions. Institutional capture requires evidence of intent on the part of the capturing party; no intent is necessary, however, for institutional bias, which can result from the structure of the formal rules or from the unintended consequences of standard practices within the agency. But be it institutional bias or capture, the result is likely to be an increase in distrust by the party who neither controls the institution nor benefits from its bias. In these cases, the commitment of the more powerful party is no longer credible. In Farrell's terms (chapter 4 in this volume), its power is now too great, and the institution designed to constrain abuse and enable cooperation is no longer effective.

If we start with distrust as the baseline position and institutions as a response, it is possible to begin to develop a model of how institutions stimulate cooperation by creating credible commitments. An individual, A, will distrust another individual, B, when A has a rational belief that it is in B's interest and within B's capacity to harm A in regard to some specific purpose, X. This belief depends on sufficient information about B's interests and capacities. This leads to the transaction costs of acquiring and assessing information about B, monitoring B's behavior, and establishing means to enforce B's behavior in ways that ensure that B acts consistently in the interests (or at least not against the interests) of A. To prevent probable injury or to ameliorate its effects implies a credible alteration of B's interest in doing harm.

There are two basic mechanisms, and both involve transaction costs:

1. Ongoing relationships that alter the conception of interest from the short-term to the long-term, even in the absence of third parties;
2. The establishment of rules with third-party enforcers that alter the incentives the actors face.

The first is a viable mechanism only when the relationships are ongoing, interdependent, and face-to-face and when the parties are relative equals. The parties can then rely on intracommunity means for punishing those who have been trusted and have violated common norms of reciprocity and fairness (Taylor 1987; Cook and Emerson 1978; Cook and Hardin 2001). Supervisors and workers often have long-term and interdependent relationships that build trust relations,[2] but in large-scale industries or in firms with distant owners there are unlikely to be such relationships with top management. Although there can exist intracommunity sanctions, there are likely to be at least two communities rather than one; managers and workers answer to separate groups. Moreover, managers and workers are rarely equals, especially in the early stages of union organizing, when the balance of power so strongly lies with the employer who can fire or speed up at will. Some of the worst working conditions and the angriest workforces have emerged in just those industries, such as mining and textiles, in which the workers, their parents, and their children were lifetime employees of a particular firm. Relations were ongoing, but the disparities of power remained so great that any existing trust relations rarely survived serious conflicts, layoffs, or industrial tragedies.

Labor's distrust of management is often the effect of a significant imbalance in bargaining power and in access to critical information. Without union representation, workers are unlikely to have the necessary parity with management to feel confident that they can bring management's interests more in line with their own. Managers, too, can suffer from what appears to be intractable distrust of unions, if not the workers. They fear that unions will gain too much power, disrupting the workplace arbitrarily, destroying rapport and goodwill among the managers and the workers, undermining profits severely, and ultimately destroying the business itself. Informal institutions or norms of reciprocity will seldom be stable, given such strong incentives to exploit power imbalances.

Reputational mechanisms for ameliorating distrust are effective in the labor-management domain only when there is already sufficient confidence that rules of the game are in place that can ensure orderly negotiation and protect each party against the excesses of the other. Formal institutions provide the background conditions for the partners in ongoing interactions to transform their relationships from feuding to cooperative. They alter the incentives for untrustworthy behavior by creating severe punishments for failing to act according to certain established guidelines of behavior. Although the negotiators may have good reason to distrust the unconstrained behavior of the other actors, they can trust each other in a regulated setting to the extent that they have confidence that the laws and rules are effectively enforced by third parties.

But these rules and enforcement procedures have potential drawbacks. First, they come with costs, the costs of establishing collective bargaining and of enforcing the laws that protect labor and management rights in the process. The second drawback is the susceptibility of the NLRB to manipulation and transformation. What works at one point in time may not work so well over time. The effect may be to reproduce or even increase distrust. With changes in the ability of actors to use the system for their own ends, there are also likely to be variations in the relative costs and benefits of using the system.

For example, as unions gain recognition and bargaining power, an institution set up to equalize power relationships between labor and management may undermine the trustworthiness of unions, who can end-run a reluctant employer. Alternatively, managers may find means to ensure that initially impartial institutions are either crippled or captured. The possibilities abound, given the difficulties of designing an institution that adequately constrains owners, managers, or other agents.[3]

The National Labor Relations Board provides an opportunity to assess the pressures on an institution. It was intended to make credible the commitments of a powerful player and thereby reduce some of the consequences of distrust. Established as the major enforcement machinery of the National Labor Relations Act, the NLRB regulates representation elections by unions and the unfair labor practices, as determined by law, of employers. The NLRB may have been designed to level the playing field between two unequal players and to improve labor's bargaining power vis-à-vis management, but legislative and rule changes have altered the nature of the NLRB over time in order to also alleviate management's distrust of unions and of the NLRB as a union-captured regulatory agency. The Taft-Hartley Act (1947) extended the regulatory apparatus to the unfair practices of unions, and the Landrum-Griffin Act (1959) further constrained organized labor.

The analysis that follows investigates the filing behavior of labor and management as indicators of their reliance on the NLRB to bring their opposition into line. Variation in filing over time and between the parties could reflect differences in relative bargaining power or differences in the parties' perception of the bias of the institutional decision makers.

Another focus of this chapter is comparison of the transaction costs expended and saved by the creation of the NLRB. There have been only a few notable attempts to measure transaction costs (Wallis and North 1986; North and Wallis 1994), and one of our goals is to extend this effort into additional domains. In particular, we are interested in figuring out how to measure the transaction costs created by governmental regulatory agencies. Determining the transaction costs of the NLRB work is relatively straightforward—although time consuming. What is more difficult to estimate is the trade-off between costs and benefits. Do the benefits of government intervention outweigh the additional costs to society? Hernando DeSoto (1989) gives a clear no to that question in his analysis of the effect of regulation on the Peruvian economy. We believe the issue deserves further investigation and consideration. We are not so certain DeSoto is right, and part of our task is to think through the problem of how to measure the effects on productivity and on labor relations as well as on time, price, and the other factors DeSoto discusses.

Evaluating the Playing Field

Some of the earliest research on the NLRB, by John Spielmans (1940), explores the agency's effectiveness by focusing on the use of labor's complaints to the NLRB as a substitute for strikes and on employers' compliance as measured by the number of disputes over unfair labor practices. Spielmans concludes that the NLRB is effective in enhancing the power of labor vis-à-vis management. However, this work covers only the first four years and is marred by a lack of sophisticated statistical technique. Subsequent changes in the law increased employer power and weakened the union position. The Taft-Hartley Act not only enabled employers to file charges of unfair labor practices against unions, it also prohibited labor organizations from using secondary boycotts and other devices that enhance the power of a strike. Unions now generally perceive the NLRB as undermining rather than facilitating their efforts (Levi 2003).

The extent to which this belief has a basis in reality is the subject of some analysis. An ongoing historical debate indicates the difficulties of making an objective assessment (Gross 1974, 1981; Tomlins 1985). There is a voluminous literature on the National Labor Relations Act, the Taft-Hartley amendments, and the cases and behavior of the National Labor Relations Board itself. However, a major survey of this literature more than a decade ago (Delaney, Lewin, and Sockell 1985) reveals that relatively little attention has been paid to the issues of power equity and cost raised in this chapter.

There is, however, considerable evidence that the rules of the NLRB frustrate labor's organizing efforts. The *Wilmar 8*, a documentary film about female bank employees who tried to unionize in the 1970s, illustrates the long administrative delays that made it difficult for these women to sustain their labor action. They continued their strike against all odds but were ultimately denied recognition based on the NLRB's interpretation of a technicality of the law. There are also narrative accounts by former members of the NLRB. A recent and compelling documentation of personal experience is *Labored Relations*, by William B. Gould (2000). Gould, a professor of law at Stanford University, was appointed president of the NLRB by President Bill Clinton. After a grueling Senate approval, Gould took on the mission of reducing delays, inefficiencies, and biases in the process. His success was, at best, limited.

Other scholars have noted that such delays are particularly damaging to unions trying to gain recognition or their first contract. William Cooke (1985) finds that employers facing a newly elected union can effectively use the slow administrative pace of the NLRB to their advantage and thus gradually pick away at the solidarity of the workers. They file charges with the agency to directly challenge the results of union elections and refuse to bargain while they await the findings. The unions often counterattack with charges of their own. However, NLRB decisions can take a year or more. It is this lengthy delay in conflict resolution—coupled with the dismissal of union activists—that erodes the strength of the newly organized union. Cooke finds that the greater the delay between the union election victory and the resolution of all related cases filed at the NLRB, the greater the chances that the union will fail to gain a first contract.

Other work explores the political bias among the members of the board. It finds that those appointed by Democrats tend to support unions and those appointed by Republicans tend to favor employers in their decisions (Delaney, Lewin, and Sockell 1985, 50–51). Terry Moe (1985) offers one of the most sophisticated quantitative and theoretical analysis to date of the role of politics. He finds that employers and unions consider the probability of success in their decisions to initiate cases involving allegations of unfair labor practices, and one of the most significant determinants of perceived probability of success is the composition of the board. The NLRB, he argues, is composed of an endogenous core of relationships among the constituents who file charges, the staff who filter the charges, and the board members who make the final determinations. Each can be affected by exogenous political pressures from the president, the Congress, and the courts or exogenous economic circumstances such as inflation and unemployment. He concludes that the formal outcomes result from "mutually adaptive behavior" among the core actors and that this produces "a distinctive logic and dynamic process" in the NLRB (Moe 1985, 1114).

Robert Flanagan (1989) also uses the data on unfair labor practices to consider the nature of the NLRB as a regulatory apparatus. For him, the puzzle is that the relative stability of labor relations activity, as measured by representation elections, work stoppages, and collective bargaining negotiations, is accompanied by a significant increase in the volume of charges of unfair labor practices (Flanagan 1989, 257–61). He argues that this growth reflects changes in the incentives to comply and in the incentives to evoke enforcement of the NLRA by employers and unions, who are engaged in strategic interaction with each other. He then models the compliance and enforcement game and, finally, subjects its implications to empirical test. He concludes that the most important influences on the "compliance and enforcement choices that determine the volume of unfair labor practice charges" are not NLRB policy but "incentives that are determined in the market and through collective bargaining. In particular, the growth of the union relative wage during the 1970s, by reducing the incentives of employers to comply with the

NLRA and by increasing the incentives of unions to challenge potentially illegal behavior, had a profound influence on the growth of regulatory litigation" (Flanagan 1989, 278).

Cooke et al. (1995; also see Cooke and Gautschi 1982) look at a sample of board-level decisions between 1957 and 1986 and discover that very different board behavior characterizes the minority of cases, about 20 percent, that actually shape policy. In the other 80 percent of cases, decision making is routine; the board members generally rubber-stamp recommendations by those below them in the NLRB hierarchy. In the more important and complex cases, board-level decisions reveal political bias, but board members exhibit concern with their accountability to Congress as well as to the president. Moreover, they are sensitive to market conditions and are more likely to find for labor when unemployment is high.

Flanagan and Moe offer two distinct models of the variation in charges of unfair practices. In Flanagan's (1989) account, the strategic interaction is effectively between labor and management, whose choices are affected mostly by economic circumstances that alter their incentives to comply with or evoke regulation. In Moe's (1985) account (see also Cooke et al. 1995) the strategic actors also include the staff and board of the NLRB; exogenous political and economic factors induce adjustments in their mutually adaptive system. We, too, use the volume of regulatory litigation as a dependent variable, and we follow all these authors in their choice of independent variables—at least in part of our analysis.

In our analysis, the key strategic actors are labor and management. Their incentives are affected by many of the variables Flanagan identifies, but the actors also must consider the probable behavior of the NLRB staff and the board itself, as both Moe and Cooke and colleagues argue. We explore the extent to which the NLRB affects relative bargaining power as defined by Neil Chamberlain (1951, 221):

> If the cost to B of disagreeing on A's terms is greater than the cost of agreeing on A's terms, while the cost to A of disagreeing on B's terms is less than the cost of agreeing on B's terms, then A's bargaining power is greater than that of B. The NLRB imposes constraints on the parties, and it also imposes transaction costs, including the costs of negotiation, litigation, and delay.... When party A believes the NLRB raises the costs to B of disagreeing to A's terms and reduces the costs to A of disagreeing with B's terms, the NLRB has enhanced A's bargaining power.

The decision tree for filing cases with the NLRB is captured in figure 5.1. The first mover can be either management or labor, but it is the second mover who files—or not. Even when the first mover has been cooperative, the second mover may decide to file if he either misreads the behavior of the other or believes that there is an advantage to be gained by

Figure 5.1 Decision Tree for Case Filing at the National Labor Relations Board

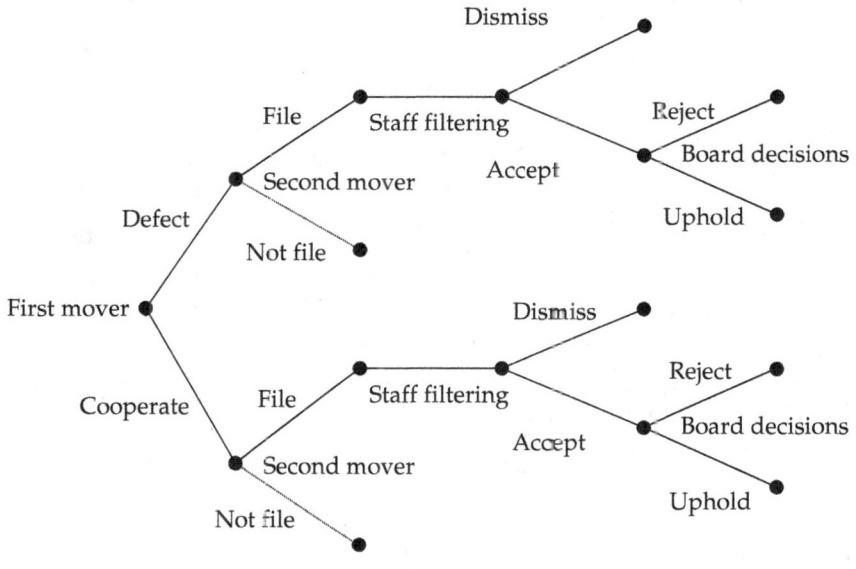

Source: Authors' compilation.
Note: First mover can be either management or labor.

filing. It is then the turn of the NLRB staff to decide whether to dismiss outright or accept the complaint. If the staff accepts the complaint, then it is the up to the board to reject or uphold the complaint.

Our model assumes that the key actors have conflicting interests and reasonable bases for distrust and that they vary across time in their relative power to cause harm. We define labor as "weak" when both overall union membership—the number of people belonging to unions—and union density—the percentage of workers who belong to unions—are low. These factors reduce the capacity to strike. The relative weakness of unions is an effect of laws and job market power as much as of internal union organization. When management is "weak," it cannot tolerate a strike or effectively prevent unionization among its workforce. This, too, is an effect of law and job markets but also of worker control over the shop floor. Of course, both unions and management will try to prevent each other from having complete information about their weaknesses and will attempt to present a picture of strength. This is a major source of imperfect and incomplete information.

From this perspective, filing behavior becomes another means for improving one's bargaining position, making oneself stronger vis-à-vis

Figure 5.2 Simple Strike Game, Perfect Information (Without Institutional Framework)

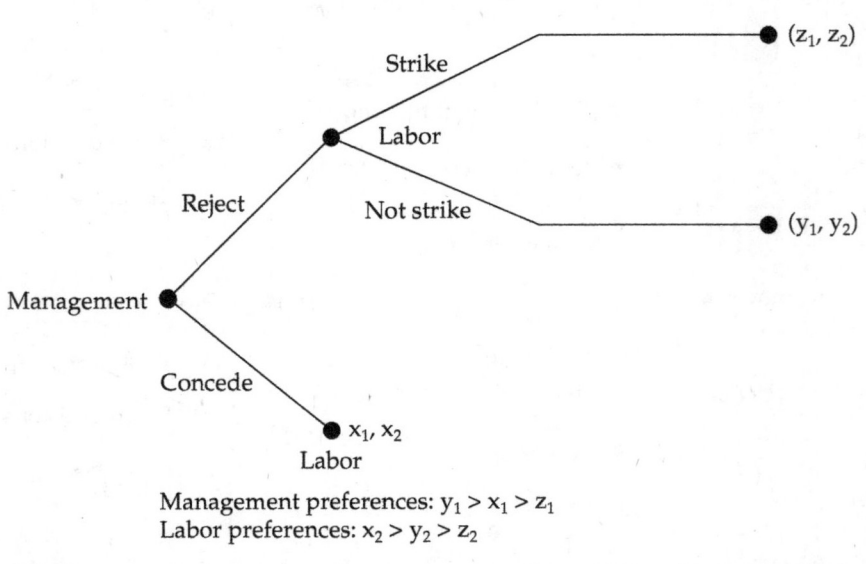

Management preferences: $y_1 > x_1 > z_1$
Labor preferences: $x_2 > y_2 > z_2$

Source: Authors' compilation.

one's opponent. Although both labor and management may benefit from cooperation created by regulation, each will also attempt to exploit the other if possible. Thus we can model their interaction as a game, and we can vary some key attributes of the players and the environment in ways that should enable us to infer some testable implications from our model. We derive our games from those developed by Miriam Golden (1997, 28–37) to investigate labor and management strategies when the firm threatens job reductions, but we revise them to reflect strategies relevant to union demands for recognition and bargaining rights.

To make the point that the existence of an institution such as the NLRB will change the nature of the relationship between labor and management, let us consider the case in which there is no regulatory apparatus (figure 5.2). This is analogous to the situation Golden (1997, 29) models in her "simple job loss game." Management would prefer to avoid both concessions (x_1) and a strike (z_1); its preference is for labor to acquiesce to its demands (y_1). Labor would prefer to obtain concessions from management (x_2). If management refuses to concede to its demands, labor will threaten to strike, but management knows that the union would prefer to acquiesce (y_2) than strike (z_2). The equilibrium is management resistance to the union and union quiescence (y_1, y_2). With the

Figure 5.3 Simple Filing Game, Perfect Information (with Institutional Framework)

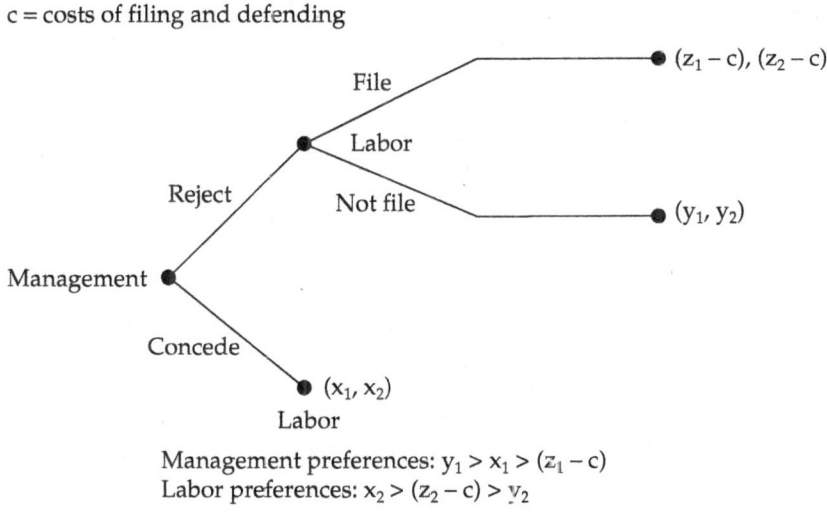

Management preferences: $y_1 > x_1 > (z_1 - c)$
Labor preferences: $x_2 > (z_2 - c) > y_2$

Source: Authors' compilation.

introduction of the NLRB, the calculation changes. The costs of filing are considerably lower than the costs of striking and provide labor with an alternative strategy, a strategy that, in principle, may be as effective as a strike in compelling management to acquiesce to its demands for recognition and bargaining. In this simple game (figure 5.3), both labor and management have perfect information about the intentions and ability of the other and about the likely behavior of the NLRB. This game models a situation in which labor is attempting to organize a union and hold a representation election. It is in management's interest to block the election or ensure that labor loses the election. It is in labor's interest to hold the election and win it. Thus when management concedes to labor's demands, there is no reason for labor to file.

Within this simple framework, x_1, x_2 represents mutual cooperation for management and labor, respectively. The situation in which management defects and labor strikes is represented by y_1, y_2. Finally, rejection by management followed by filing on the part of labor is represented by $(z_1 - c)$, $(z_2 - c)$, where c represents the costs to each party of filing and defending cases. Management's preferences are $y_1 > x_1 > (z_1 - c)$, and labor's preferences are $x_2 > (z_2 - c) > y_2$.

This game suggests that the very existence of an institution such as the NLRB should reduce distrust between the players, reduce overt conflict and hostility, and enhance cooperation, ceteris paribus, but only after an initial increase in the costs to the public of establishing the NLRB and to the players in using and learning to use its machinery. By solving this game through backward induction, we can see that cooperation emerges as an equilibrium outcome. Management will choose to cooperate from the start because labor will always choose to file whenever management defects, that is, refuses to recognize or bargain with labor. This will hold as long as the payoff y_2 never becomes greater than $(z_2 - c)$.

The outcome in the first simple game depends on management's capacity to predict that the union will not strike; in the second it depends on certainty that the NLRB is effective, that is, timely in its intervention and able to actually compel management to recognize a legally organized union. A more realistic version of the first game (in which there is no institutional framework) is a situation of imperfect information, in which management does not know whether labor is strongly or weakly organized, whether it is strike prone or not. The perception of the threat of unionization will encourage management to act to block the union unless a strike is extremely credible and the costs it is likely to impose extremely high. However, without an institutional framework to regulate the situation, and with no certainty in the assessment of labor's strength, management's best strategy is unclear. Moreover, without an institutional framework, poorly organized or timid labor unions lack any credible bargaining threat for inducing management to make concessions to them. On the other hand, an institution such as the NLRB may provide a basis for believing that the other party will act in a trustworthy manner, that is, that it can be trusted not to sucker a player who chooses to be cooperative. This, in turn, may reduce overt conflict and its associated costs.

But the game is not really so simple. Labor and management do not always have perfect information about each other or about the nature of the NLRB. The next game (figure 5.4) illustrates what happens when labor files but can be reversed to apply to management filing. In this game, c represents the cost of filing, s represents the costs to each party of a strike, and p represents the probability that labor is strong or weak. If labor is relatively strong, then we are in upper branch of figure 5.4; if labor is relatively weak, then we are in the lower branch. When management possesses imperfect information about whether labor is strong or weak, it lacks certainty about how to behave. If it rejects, labor could file or could file and strike, possibly pushing the two players toward their worst outcome. The converse is true for labor. Management's preferences are $y_1 > x_1 > (z_1 - c_1) > (z_1 - c_1 - s_1)$. Labor's preferences are $x_2 > (z_2 - c_2) > y_2 > (z_2 - c_2 - s_2)$. There are several equilibria. The key to understanding why one equilibrium is more likely to occur over another hinges largely on the perceived value of probability p, but it also depends on the values of c and s.

Figure 5.4 Labor Filing Game, One-Sided Imperfect Information (with Institutional Framework)

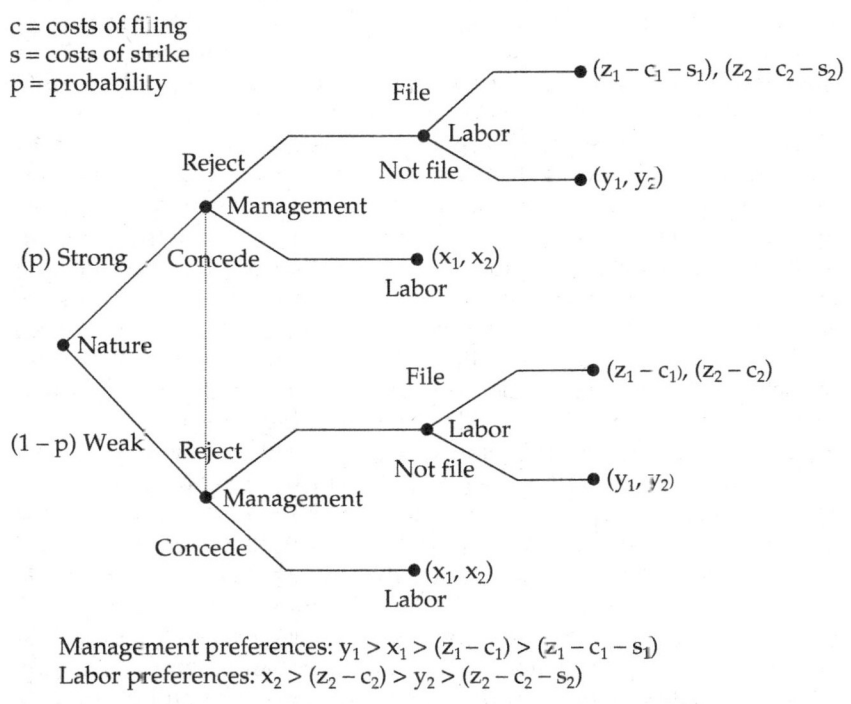

Management preferences: $y_1 > x_1 > (z_1 - c_1) > (z_1 - c_1 - s_1)$
Labor preferences: $x_2 > (z_2 - c_2) > y_2 > (z_2 - c_2 - s_2)$

Source: Authors' compilation.

We can infer from the logic of this game that a few major factors will affect decisions to reject or to concede and to file or not to file. These factors largely relate to relative bargaining strength: union density, overall union membership, the unemployment rate, inflation, and the political bias of the NLRB. However, as we know from the facts of the case, the establishment of the institution creates a dynamic among the players that leads to changes in the rules and interactions—perhaps in predictable and perhaps in indeterminate ways. The extent to which the institution can be manipulated and transformed reflects the extent to which the NLRB actually facilitates credible commitments. The narrative of the institution suggests that it can be manipulated; the filing behavior reveals that it has been.

The first implication of the game has to do with the initiation of filing activity. Filing is more likely to be initiated by the weaker party or the party that is most likely to have to respond to a possibly illegal action.

Unions tend to fit both of these criteria more than management. Unions tend to have the weaker bargaining position and are more likely to be put in the position of the second player in a filing game by the nature of the institutional and organizational obstacles they face in gaining recognition or calling a legal strike. Thus we expect that unions will initiate more charges of unfair labor practices than management unless—that is, they think they have no chance of winning.

This leads to the second implication. Filing activity is likely to be dampened if staff filtering decisions consistently work against one particular party over the other. Dismissal of cases by NLRB staff, we believe, provides information to potential filing parties on the probability of a successful and favorable resolution. For example, we expect that employers who face higher dismissal rates are less likely to file future cases than those who face lower dismissal rates. Similarly, if dismissal rates are in decline we expect filing activity to be enhanced. A further implication is that there will be temporal variations in filing activity that reflect the combination of the relative bargaining power of the parties and the nature of the institutional arrangements themselves.

We initially assumed that the NLRB is an institution designed to arbitrate differences between the key actors and to impartially enforce the law, which would mean an inverse relationship between unions and employers in terms of filing activity; that the weaker party would file more was our first intuition, and one we continue to explore. However, the NLRB is subject to a myriad of influences. Moreover, both the relative bargaining power of labor and management and their presentation of misinformation about that power should affect the equilibrium outcome. Flanagan (1989) and Moe (1985) expect (and find) a long-term equilibrating tendency toward statistical parity in the filing of charges of unfair labor practices by employers and employees. With Moe and Flanagan, we expect an equilibrating tendency over time with temporary shifts. However, we have different expectations that emerge from the comparative statics of our game models and from our understanding of transaction costs and institutional theory. Our predictions are as follows:

1. Unions will initiate more charges than management, ceteris paribus.
2. A decline in the bargaining power of either party will lead to a rise in its filing activity as a means of enhancing its bargaining power—unless it believes that it has no chance of winning, in which case it will be unable to justify the expenditure of resources.
3. Political bias against the weaker party will influence its filing behavior in a negative manner; it knows it cannot win.
4. Political bias for the stronger party will influence its filing behavior in a negative manner; it can impose bargains without having to resort to the NLRB.

5. The effect of structural variables on the initiation and level of filing activity should differ within different time periods that reflect major rule changes in the NLRB.

There are other potentially testable implications of the model that we do not address here, given the lack of any plausible measures. For example, it is evident that changes in the costs and reliability of information about each other's relative strength should affect the strategies of the parties. However, we have no means of assessing either the costs or the credibility of the information at this point in time.

Bases for Evaluating the Hypotheses

Our first hypothesis requires simple statistics on the trends in union and employer filing. The second rests on measures of labor strength and institutional bias. Measures of labor strength are union density, high employment (Hibbs 1976), and, following Moe (1985), a political and legal climate favorable to labor. The measures of employer strength are high unemployment, low inflation, and a political and legal climate favorable to business. There are a number of reasons why these measures are pertinent in measuring relative strength of labor.

First, economic conditions can affect the manner in which labor and management interact. Inflation can increase the pressure on management to keep costs low; at the same time, high inflation may encourage workers to fight for higher wages as the value of their salaries declines. High unemployment can also affect the quantity of cases submitted to the NLRB. In times of substantial unemployment, for example, management may submit additional cases to the NLRB to exacerbate labor's problems, thereby strengthening its power in relation to labor. Similarly, both labor and management may send cases to the NLRB during a work stoppage as a way to force the opponent to divert resources away from the strike toward defending its case to the board.

Second, the degree of union density also may alter the propensity of unions and management to submit complaints to the NLRB. We expect both parties to rely upon an independent institution such as the NLRB when they are at a disadvantage but only if they believe it will assist them. As total union membership in the workforce declines, so, too, should labor's power in relation to management. This is particularly true when union density also is low. Therefore, we expect to see labor send more cases to the NLRB in periods of relative weakness as a way of compensating for its diluted bargaining position. However, this is the expectation only if the NLRB is actually providing a level playing field. If, in fact, the NLRB tends to favor management, labor may not want to expend limited resources on working within an institution biased against it. Thus there will be fewer cases initiated by labor when it is weak.

In contrast, if management faces a high degree of union density, especially during times of tight employment, it is unlikely to use up resources appealing to the NLRB. To do so will only antagonize labor, when it is most able to impose job disruptions. Under such circumstances it may make more sense to bargain than to fight.

Our third hypothesis requires us to measure the effect on filing activity of any observable bias in the NLRB staff filtering decisions. We believe dismissal rates by the NLRB staff are one such measure of bias provided to potential filers. This information allows the potential filers to estimate rough probabilities that their case will be successfully resolved.

The fourth hypothesis requires periodicity of the institution of the NLRB. Drawing on the history of legislative and case law that seemed to alter the rules governing labor-management relations (Raza and Anderson 1996; Gold 1998), we established four major periods: from the establishment of the NLRA (1935) until the passage of Taft-Hartley (1947); from the passage of Taft-Hartley until the passage of Landrum-Griffin (1959); from the passage of Landrum-Griffin until the election of Ronald Reagan (1980); and (4) from Reagan's election until the present. Since until 1947 only workers could file charges of unfair labor practices, we focus primarily on the last three periods to understand the effect of bargaining power on filing activity. However, for understanding the last hypothesis, the first period is also important. Owing to changes in methods of data recording at the NLRB and to a lack of some measures up to the late 1990s, testing of this hypothesis will be postponed until further data are collected and made consistent across the given time periods.

Analysis and Findings

All data on the National Labor Relations Board were obtained from the *Annual Report of the National Labor Relations Board* (NLRB 1948–99). We first focused on total cases received by the NLRB from 1948 to 1997. Detailed tables describe the number of complaints filed by each party: national unions, local unions, the AFL-CIO (American Federation of Labor–Committee for Industrial Organization), employers, and individuals. In addition, we also aggregated and analyzed data, which describe, in detail, each category of cases involving charges of unfair labor practices since 1965. With the total number of cases received by the National Labor Relations Board established as an initial base for evaluating transaction costs, data regarding the personnel levels and budgetary allocations of the NLRB were then obtained from the Budget Office of the U.S. government.

Figure 5.5 Unfair Labor Practice Cases Filed at the National Labor Relations Board, 1944 to 1998

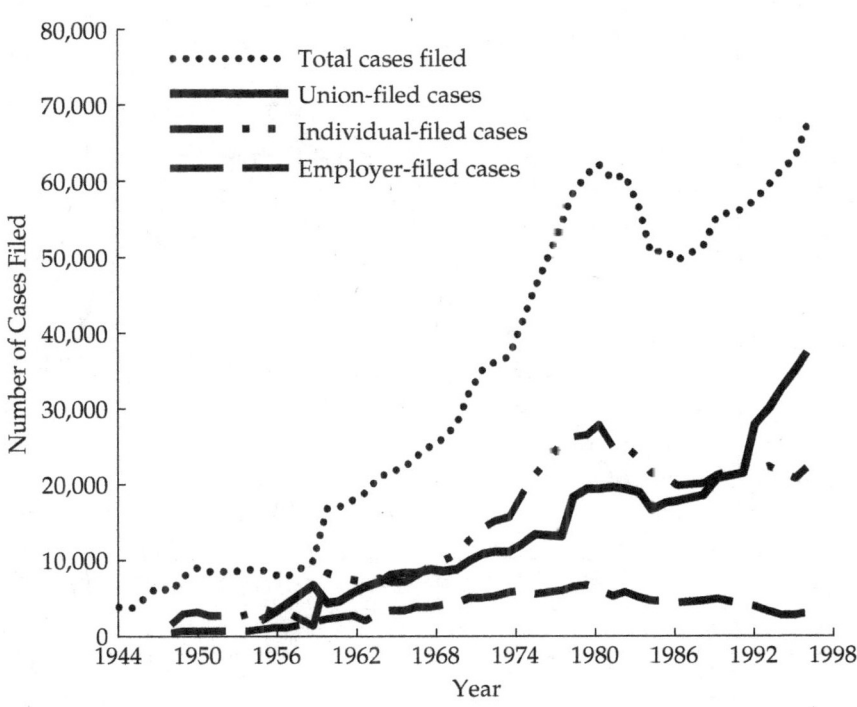

Source: NLRB (1948–99).

While the data generally indicate an increasing trend in the total number of cases filed at the NLRB, analyzing the source of the charges of unfair labor practices reveals some interesting results. Figure 5.5 indicates that union-filed cases have tended to increase steadily over time, except for a small decrease in the early 1980s and a rapid increase in the 1990s.[4] The number of cases filed by individuals followed a similar pattern through the early 1980s, but instead of increasing into the 1990s, they remained relatively constant from the mid-1980s until the late 1990s. In contrast, the number of cases filed by employers steadily increased from the late 1940s, peaked in the late 1970s, and experienced a steady decline thereafter (figure 5.6). Clearly, in relation to labor, employers initiate far fewer cases involving unfair labor practices at the NLRB. This supports our initial expectation that labor, the weaker party, will be more active and will more readily make use of the NLRB.

Figure 5.6 Employer-Filed Unfair Labor-Practice Cases, 1948 to 1998

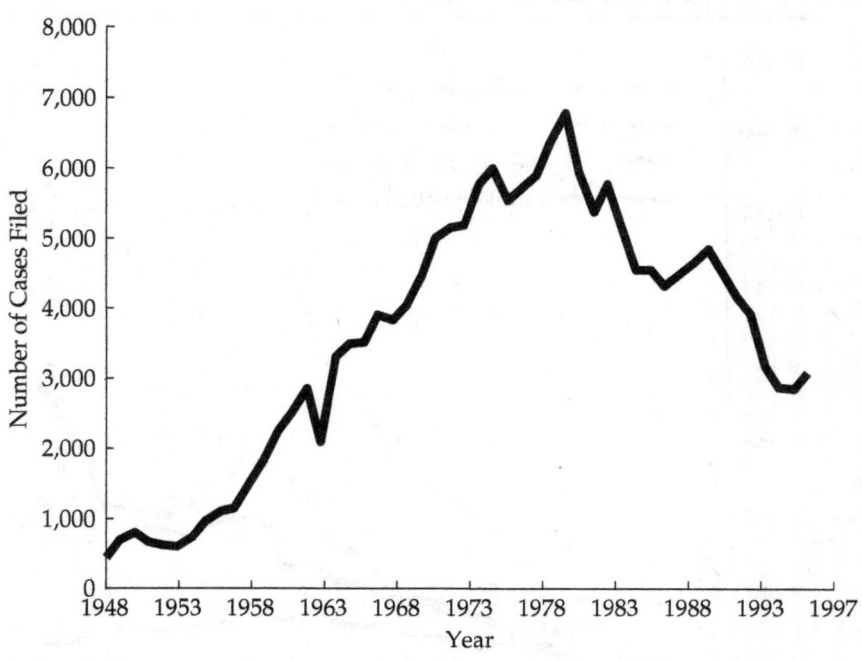

Source: NLRB (1945–99).

Examination of the raw data suggests that the decline in union membership in the 1980s is correlated with a sharp increase in the number of cases sent to the NLRB by labor (Farber and Western 2001). The increase in union-sponsored cases in the 1980s confirms our expectation that a weakened position of organized labor will precipitate an increase in total cases filed by unions. Conducting a linear regression analysis using the unfair labor cases submitted to the NLRB as the dependent variable adds some support to but also detracts from our earlier hypotheses.

Using employer-initiated cases as the dependent variable yields the following results (the first column in table 5.1). Inflation, unemployment, and union membership produce a positive and statistically significant relationship with the dependent variable, employer-initiated cases of unfair labor practices. This lends support to our earlier claim that during inflationary times, management and employers become more willing to file cases against labor. On the other hand, union density, Republican leadership, and NLRB staff dismissal rates produce a negative and significant relationship on employer filing activity. As expected, greater union density appears to dampen filing on the part of employers, but

Table 5.1 Political and Economic Effects on Case-Filing Behavior, 1945 to 1999

	Employer-Filed Cases			Labor-Filed Cases		
Variable	Beta Statistic	t Score	p Value	Beta Statistic	t Score	p Value
Constant		2.84	.012		7.620	.000
Inflation (GDP[a] deflator)	.411	4.82	.000	.251	2.540	.022
Unemployment rate	.268	3.57	.003	.241	2.930	.010
Total union membership	.571	5.87	.000	−.082	−.609	.551
Union density	−.732	−4.03	.001	−.788	−8.150	.000
NLRB staff dismissal rates	−.328	−2.27	.037	−.069	−.740	.470
Republican president (t − 1)	−.131	−2.36	.031	−.126	−1.880	.078
R	.982			.976		
R-squared	.965			.953		
Durbin Watson	2.13			1.30		
N[b]	23			23		

Source: Data from U.S. Department of Labor (1946–1999); NLRB (1945–1999); Golden, Wallerstein, and Lange (2002); World Bank (1998).
[a]Gross domestic product.
[b]The N of 23 represents the number of years for which there was full data.

greater union membership appears to enhance filing activity. Perhaps this is because there is more likely to be employer filing against first contracts (Cooke 1985), an issue we have not fully explored here.

Changing the dependent variable to labor-initiated cases produces results similar to those in the earlier regression (the second column in table 5.1).[5] Inflation and unemployment are positively related to the dependent variable, labor filing activity, as they are for employer-filed cases. Union density and Republican leadership have a negative influence on labor filing activity. This would lead us to believe that the number of labor-filed cases of unfair labor practices is influenced by the degree to which unions permeate the workforce. That is, in periods of low union density, labor becomes more active in filing charges, while in periods of high union density, labor becomes less active. The results from this regression also add support to our claim that a stronger relative position of labor should be accompanied by a decrease in filing activity by labor at the NLRB. Interestingly, a Republican president had a negative influence on filing behavior in both regressions. This presidential effect strengthens our claim that Republican leadership dampens filing activity by labor. We also find that a Republican president dampens filing activity by employers. This is not surprising given that the unions, knowing they are in an antiunion environment, are more likely to come to terms with management, who during these periods relies less on the NLRB. The Reagan presidency, in particular, supported antiunion behavior by management in so many other ways that management had cheaper and more effective alternatives. At the same time, it raised the costs to the union of disagreeing with management.

The NLRB may have initially leveled the playing field by ensuring credible commitments by management to recognize labor unions and engage in collective bargaining. However, the legal changes documented in the historical and administrative analyses of the NLRB suggest that the long-term effect of the NLRB may have been to impose constraints on unions that reduced their power while providing employers with means to evade their commitments (Levi 2003). The analysis of filing activity offers additional evidence for this perspective.

Transaction Costs

The NLRB as an institution intended to make the parties more trustworthy and to manage the effects of distrust is subject to exploitation when there is a significant power imbalance between the two key parties. This implies that there should be considerable variation in the timing and extent of reliance on the NLRB by the two parties. We have already demonstrated that the relative costs to each party of using the NLRB might affect their relative bargaining power, but further documentation of some of those costs is still required. Moreover, there are costs to the citizenry of an institution supported by the taxpayers. To the extent that the NLRB raises the transaction costs of labor-management relationships without producing Pareto-superior outcomes, it has failed to achieve its public purpose.

Filing complaints and defending against those complaints involve myriad costs ranging from the simple transaction costs of completing the necessary paperwork to more complex (and high-priced) costs of hiring lawyers to either defend or make charges against opponents. Compiling and collecting accurate data on the "private" costs of litigation is beyond the scope of this chapter. A more thorough analysis would attempt to generate estimates of this type. At this point it seems reasonable to assume that both labor and management bear considerable private litigation costs directly related to increased levels in the caseload at the NLRB and that these costs, too, have risen over time.

Our model and concerns lead us to look at data that Flanagan (1989) and Moe (1985) do not. Whereas they wish to explain the variation in the volume of litigation, that is only one of our measures of the transaction costs of the NLRB as an institution created to manage conflict and reduce distrust. We wish also to assess the absolute level of transaction costs over time and whether the transaction costs of the NLRB as an institution represent deadweight loss or productive uses of public resources. Thus we also measure changes in the personnel and budget of the NLRB. In our preliminary effort to determine the relative costs and benefits of the NLRB, we consider such factors as person-days lost in work stoppages, the forms for reaching agreement over unfair labor practices, and, to a limited extent, productivity. This is a highly speculative discussion but one that, we hope, points to the kinds of empirical research and theoretical development required to assess the transaction costs created by an institution such as the NLRB.

Our dependent variable is the change in the transaction costs of institutions of labor-management relations as measured by the trends in caseload, personnel, and budget of the NLRB. Our independent variables include political factors, particularly the party of the president and NLRB staff filtering decisions as a measure of political and institutional bias (Moe 1985); economic conditions, of which inflation and unemployment (Hibbs 1976, Flanagan 1989) are the most important, that affect the relative strength of unions and management; and other aspects of labor strength, including union density and union membership.

In evaluating the transaction costs of the NLRB over time, we briefly consider trends in caseload, personnel, and budget of the NLRB. The empirical expectation is a sharp increase in the early years as the weaker party, labor, begins to make use of the new machinery. After the initial increase, we expect a leveling off as both parties file cases that are more meritorious.

Our initial findings concerning the basic trends in transaction costs of conflict between labor and management are both consistent and incongruent with our expectations. First, it is apparent that the budget, adjusted for inflation, and the number of cases submitted to the NLRB generally have increased over time (see figure 5.7). Second, personnel levels consistently increased into the late 1970s and then steadily decreased into the late 1990s. The increase in budget and caseload suggests that the board has become more institutionalized since its inception, indicating higher transaction costs for labor-management interaction. The decrease in personnel levels in face of budgetary and caseload increases could suggest a turn toward greater efficiency in the NLRB organization as a whole. It is more likely, however, that this decrease is indicative of the political climate of the time (the Reagan-Bush years), when most government-funded organizations witnessed cutbacks in personnel and budgetary outlays.

Figure 5.7 Total Cases Filed, Personnel, and Budget at the National Labor Relations Board, 1944 to 1998

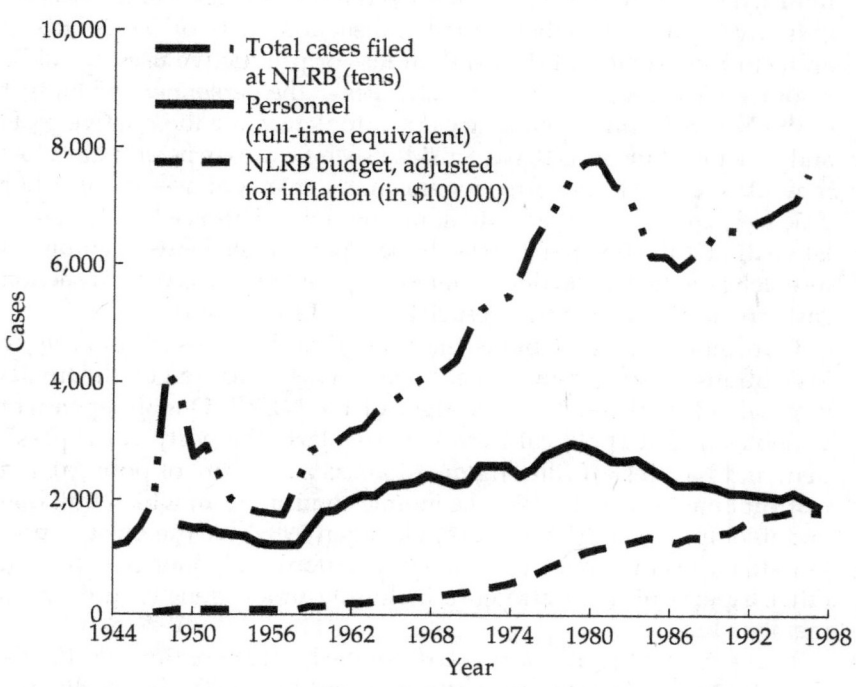

Source: NLRB (1945–99).

Benefits from the Investment in Transaction Costs

After examining the variables that influence labor and management transaction costs, we then consider the degree to which the NLRB facilitates labor-management cooperation in general. More specifically, we wish to find out whether the increasing transaction costs that we have documented diminish labor-management discord. To measure increasing discord or accord, we collected data on the method and stage of disposition of all cases involving charges of unfair labor practices. Four main methods of disposition of such cases are listed by the NLRB: agreement of the parties, withdrawal of the complaint, dismissal of the charge, and compliance with judicial or board decisions. Agreement of the parties involves a resolution of the problem before the case reaches the board level. In these situations, the cases are not withdrawn but rather are resolved by the parties in question. "Withdrawal" denotes a

Figure 5.8 Disposition of Unfair Labor Practice Cases, 1965 to 1997

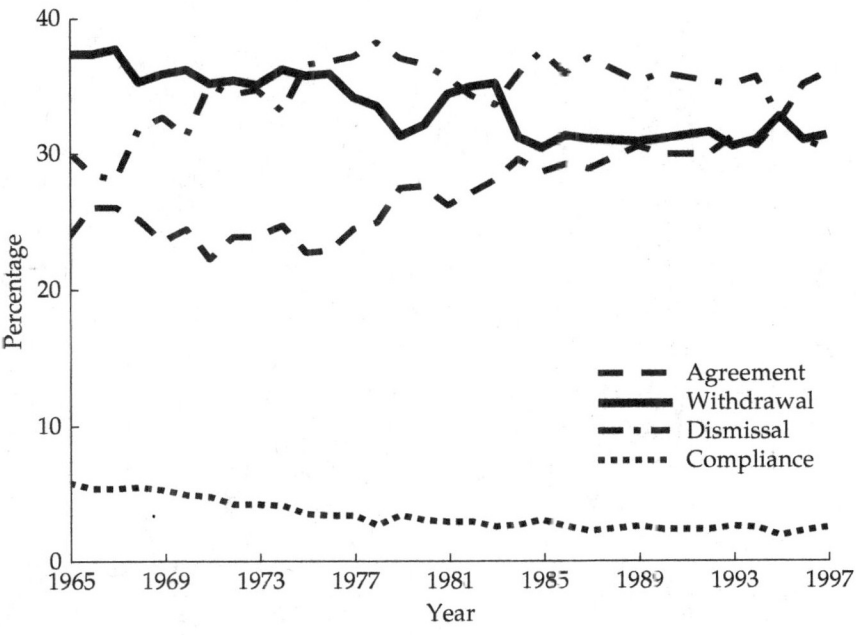

Source: NLRB (1966–99).

situation in which a party completely retracts a case that has already been filed and of which it is assumed no resolution has occurred. A dismissal of a case occurs at the staff level at the NLRB. When a case is dismissed it is deemed by the staff to be unworthy of a hearing at the board level. Of course, no resolution occurs in these situations. Finally, "compliance" refers to the few situations in which a case is decided upon at the board level and each party is compelled to abide by the board decisions. Figure 5.8 presents the trends in these four methods of disposition from 1965 to 1997.

Figure 5.8 indicates that agreement has become increasingly more common as a method of disposition; agreement has seen a more or less steady increase from the early 1970s. Moreover, the frequencies of both withdrawal and compliance have decreased steadily as a method of disposition. The rate of dismissal, on the other hand, increased through the late 1970s and remained consistent until the early 1990s, only to experience a considerable decline after 1994. These trends suggest that even in the face of increasing transaction costs, as reflected by total caseload, labor and management are more frequently settling disputes by agreement.

Figure 5.9 Days Idle and Work Stoppages, 1945 to 1997

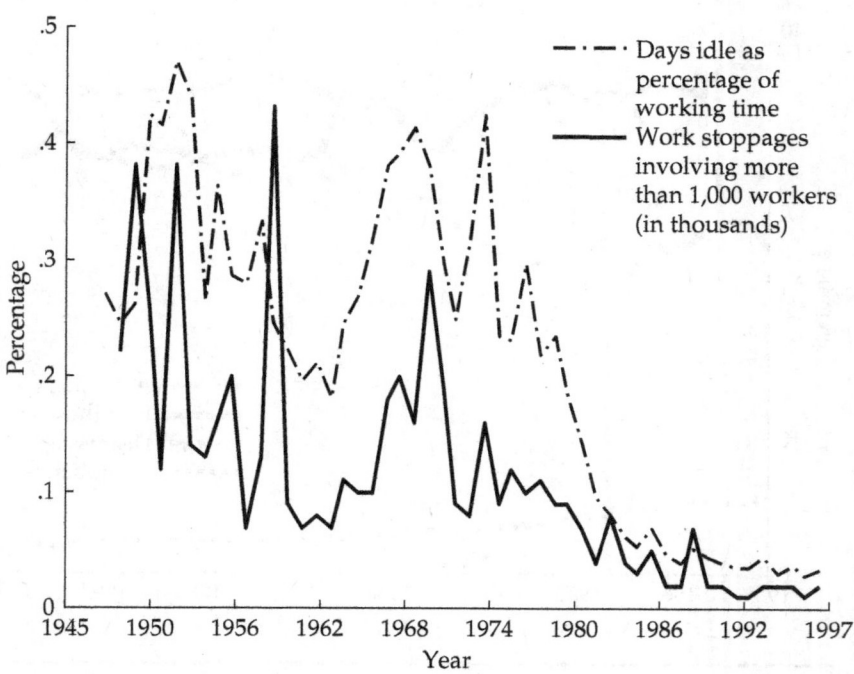

Source: U.S. Department of Labor (1946–99).

In fact, by 1995 agreement had become the most common method of disposition. More interestingly, fewer cases are being resolved by reference to board or higher judicial decision makers. This trend suggests that labor and management are resolving disputes at a lower level—preferring to reach agreement or withdrawing complaints altogether. Finally, the fact that withdrawal has seen a steady decrease as a method of disposition may indicate that the NLRB is being used more often as an organization to settle disputes than as a tool for labor to harass management—or for management to harass labor.

While further research is needed to fully evaluate our claims, the trends we document do suggest that the NLRB has the potential to become more effective as an arena for promoting sincere dispute resolution. However, distinguishing between significant and more routine cases, as Cooke and his colleagues (1995) advocate, may show that mutually beneficial dispute resolution is more likely in the easier than the harder cases.

Finally, the data on work stoppages and days idle as a percentage of working time (figure 5.9) suggest that there are benefits to the public of the observed increase in transaction costs in labor-management relations. Although there is considerable variation across time in both days idle and work stoppages, these measures in the long run trend downward. From the beginning to the middle of the 1970s, both measures dramatically decreased, a pattern that continued through to the late 1990s. The reduction in labor and management conflict probably has several sources, including the weakening of the labor movement and the increased power of management (Levi 2003; Farber and Western 2001). However, the evidence drawn from the NLRB data also suggests that labor and management are finding alternative venues and methods in order to settle their disputes.

Our final measure of benefits from this investment in transaction costs is by far the most speculative. There is reason to believe that unionization brings productivity gains to the firm (Freeman and Medoff 1984, chap. 11; also see Gordon 1996) and for precisely the reasons we suggest at the beginning of this chapter. Unionization appears to improve industrial relations by ameliorating the sorts of distrust that block cooperation. The history of U.S. labor relations makes apparent the importance of the NLRA, the NLRB, and other labor laws and institutions in enabling workers to unionize. If this were the whole story, it would be possible to infer that there is a clear Pareto-superior outcome to the transaction cost investments the NLRB requires.

However, as this chapter suggests, the NLRB, by frustrating union efforts through its legal constraints on their activities, administrative delays, and employer bias, may actually foster distrust. It may promote the kinds of collective paranoia that Roderick Kramer (chapter 6 in this volume) discusses, leading the parties, especially the weaker party, to suspect even the good intentions of employers and certainly to be wary of, possibly even resistant to, agreements management proffers.

Conclusion

The standard economist account of the role of trust is Oliver Williamson's (1993), in which trust operates only at the personal level; otherwise, all can be accounted for by costs and incentives. While alterations in these factors are critical to enhancing the conditions for cooperation, our findings suggest a role for establishing institutionalized trustworthiness. The NLRB is an institution that attempts to make labor and management more trustworthy by enforcing credible commitments. This can happen only when labor is sufficiently organized to reduce the power asymmetry sufficiently to allow labor—and government—to impose constraints on management. This analysis fuels the fires flamed by Kenneth Arrow (1974), Partha Dasgupta (1988), Douglass North (1990), James Coleman (1990), and other social scientists who recognize the important role trust and trustworthiness can play in a wide variety of economic relationships. More significantly, we hope to have clarified how distrust catalyzes institutional emergence and change while also suggesting how those institutions can, under certain conditions, diminish and, under other conditions, create distrust.

If institutional arrangements such as the National Labor Relations Act and the National Labor Relations Board can in fact reduce the negative effects of distrust by promoting cooperation through the establishment of credible commitments, and if enhanced perceptions of trustworthiness in fact produce Pareto-superior outcomes, then the public, labor, and management investment in them is well worth the cost. The problem is that the NLRB did not arise, as some institutions do, from the mutual requirements of the two parties, who are then locked into a self-sustaining equilibrium from which both benefit. The NLRB was imposed by a third party, government, in response initially to labor demands and then modified in response to the interests and concerns of management. Not surprisingly, it is an institution that changes with the political winds and with variations in the power of labor and management. It is also an institution whose board decisions are highly susceptible to political bias.

In its early years, employers objected to the NLRB, which they perceived as having been captured by organized labor. Today, the NLRB, indeed the whole NLRA apparatus, is particularly unpopular with organized labor. When the NLRB becomes ineffectual or develops a bias toward business interests, the door is open to the kind of considerable employer resistance to unionization we are witnessing today (Bronfenbrenner and Juravich 1998; Cohen and Hurd 1998). Labor no longer perceives management as trustworthy in its likely treatment of employees, and industrial relations deteriorate. Given the bias perceived in the institutional arrangements and the costs of filing, labor unions often cannot use the NLRB to enhance their ability to achieve recognition or sustained and effective bargaining.

The evidence and argument of this chapter suggest that the NLRB, while hardly ideal as a mechanism for resolving disputes or leveling the playing field, has nonetheless reduced some of the worst consequences of labor and management distrust. It has facilitated the recognition of unions (albeit not all unions) and collective bargaining once unions have been recognized. Despite delays, administrative hassles, and various transaction costs for labor, management, and the general public, the NLRB is an institution that ensures that the more powerful party will have to cooperate—to some extent. It does not build trust between labor and management, but it does make each more trustworthy in relation to important issues in the employer-employee relationship. The National Labor Relations Board manages distrust by institutionalizing trustworthiness, but it neither manages distrust nor institutionalizes trustworthiness as well as we might like. We join with those in the labor relations field who advocate a search for better institutional design. Yet we conclude that it is better to have the NLRB than no institution at all.

We have received useful feedback on this chapter from Karen S. Cook, Jean Ensminger, Avner Greif, Bryan Jones, Linda Kaboolian, Mark Smith, and Paul Zak. We also wish to thank the participants in the Harvard-MIT Seminar in Positive Political Economy, the American Public Policy colloquium at the University of Washington, the Political Economy Drinks and Discussion Society (PEDDS), and especially the three anonymous reviewers. This research could not have progressed without the assistance of the Russell Sage Foundation.

Notes

1. The conceptions of trust, trustworthiness, and distrust used here draw heavily on the collaborative work in progress by Karen S. Cook, Russell Hardin, and Margaret Levi. See also Hardin (2002).
2. There is a large literature on this subject. Within the volumes of the Russell Sage Foundation Series on Trust, see, especially, Brehm and Gates (2004).
3. This is the argument Gary Miller (1992, 2000) makes in his critique of principal-agent theory.
4. The category "union-filed" is the sum of cases filed by the AFL-CIO, other national unions, and other local unions, taken from table 1 of the appendix in the *Annual Report* (NLRB 1945–99).
5. Our strongest results are found when we use employer-filed cases as the dependent variable. The Durbin Watson test also indicates that the results from the second regression are more reliable than those of the first, which tests the independent variable, labor-filed cases. The low score on the Durbin Watson test for the first regression suggests we cannot rule out some collinearity among the independent variables. While transforming some of the independent variables could eliminate this concern, we preferred to maintain the variables in their raw unaltered form. Our only transformation was to lag the presidential variable by one year. This allows time for newly appointed board members to make their way into and begin to influence the NLRB apparatus.

References

Arrow, Kenneth. 1974. *The Limits of Organization*. New York: Norton.
Brehm, John, and Scott Gates. 2004. "Supervisors as Trust Brokers in Social-Work Bureaucracies." In *Trust and Distrust in Organizations: Dilemmas and Approaches*, edited by Roderick M. Kramer and Karen S. Cook. New York: Russell Sage Foundation.

Bronfenbrenner, Kate, and Tom Juravich. 1998. "Preparing for the Worst: Organizing and Staying Organized in the Public Sector." In *Organizing to Win*, edited by Kate Bronfenbrenner, Sheldon Friedman, Richard W. Hurd, Rudolph A. Oswald, and Ronald L. Seeber. Ithaca, N.Y.: Cornell University Press.
Chamberlain, Neil. 1951. *Collective Bargaining*. New York: McGraw-Hill.
Cohen, Larry, and Richard W. Hurd. 1998. "Fear, Conflict, and Union Organizing." In *Organizing to Win*, edited by Kate Bronfenbrenner, Sheldon Friedman, Richard W. Hurd, Rudolph A. Oswald, and Ronald L. Seeber. Ithaca, N.Y.: Cornell University Press.
Coleman, James S. 1990. *Foundations of Social Theory*. Cambridge, Mass.: Belknap Press of Harvard University Press.
Cook, Karen S., and Richard M. Emerson. 1978. "Power, Equity and Commitment in Exchange Networks." *American Sociological Review* 43(5, October): 721–39.
Cook, Karen S., and Russell Hardin. 2001. "Norms of Cooperativeness and Networks of Trust." In *Social Norms*, edited by Michael Hechter and Karl-Dieter Opp. New York: Russell Sage Foundation.
Cooke, William N. 1985. "The Failure to Negotiate First Contracts: Determinants and Policy Implications." *Industrial and Labor Relations Review* 38(2): 163–78.
Cooke, William N., and Frederick H. Gautschi III. 1982. "Political Bias in NLRB Unfair Labor Practice Decisions." *Industrial and Labor Relations Review* 35(4): 593–649.
Cooke, William N., Aneil K. Mishra, Gretchen M. Spreitzer, and Mary Tschirhart. 1995. "The Determinants of NLRB Decision-Making Revisited." *Industrial and Labor Relations Review* 48(2): 237–57.
Dasgupta, Partha. 1988. "Trust as a Commodity." In *Trust: Making and Breaking Cooperative Relations*, edited by Diego Gambetta. Cambridge, Mass.: Basil Blackwell.
Delaney, John Thomas, David Lewin, and Donna Sockell. 1985. "The NLRA at Fifty: A Research Appraisal and Agenda." *Industrial and Labor Relations Review* 39(1, October): 46–75.
DeSoto, Hernando. 1989. *The Other Path*. New York: Harper and Row.
Farber, Henry S., and Bruce Western. 2001. "Accounting for the Decline of Unions in the Private Sector, 1973–1998." *Journal of Labor Research* 22(3): 459–85.
Flanagan, Robert J. 1989. "Compliance and Enforcement Decisions under the National Labor Relations Act." *Journal of Labor Economics* 7(3): 257–80.
Freeman, Richard B., and James L. Medoff. 1984. *What Do Unions Do?* New York: Basic Books.
Gold, Michael Evan. 1998. *An Introduction to Labor Law*. Ithaca, N.Y.: Cornell University Press.
Golden, Miriam. 1997. *Heroic Defeats*. New York: Cambridge University Press.
Golden, Miriam, Michael Wallerstein, and Peter Lange. 2002. "Data Repository for the Golden-Wallerstein-Lange Project on Unions, Employers, Collective Bargaining and Industrial Relations for 16 OECD Countries, 1950–1995." Available at: http://www.shelley.polisci.ucla.edu/data (accessed on January 26, 2004).
Gordon, David M. 1996. *Fat and Mean*. New York: Free Press.
Gould, William B., IV. 2000. *Labored Relations*. Cambridge, Mass.: MIT Press.
Gross, James A. 1974. *The Making of the National Labor Relations Board: A Study in Economics, Politics, and the Law, 1933–1937*. Vol. 1. Albany: State University of New York Press.

———. 1981. *The Reshaping of the National Labor Relations Board: National Labor Policy in Transition, 1937–1947.* Vol. 2. Albany: State University of New York Press.

Hardin, Russell. 2002. *Trust and Trustworthiness.* New York: Russell Sage Foundation.

Hibbs, Douglas A. 1976. "Industrial Conflict in Advanced Industrial Societies." *American Political Science Review* 70(4, December): 1033–58.

Levi, Margaret. 2000. "When Good Defenses Make Good Neighbors." In *Institutions, Contracts, and Organizations: Perspectives from New Institutional Economics,* edited by Claude Menard. Colchester, Eng.: Edward Elgar.

———. 2003. "Organizing Power: Prospects for the American Labor Movement." *Perspectives on Politics* 1(1, March): 45–68.

Miller, Gary. 1992. *Managerial Dilemmas.* New York: Cambridge University Press.

———. 2000. "Why is Trust Necessary in Organizations: The Moral Hazard of Profit-Maximization." In *Trust in Society,* edited by Karen S. Cook. New York: Russell Sage Foundation.

Moe, Terry. 1985. "Control and Feedback in Economic Regulation: The Case of the NLRB." *American Political Science Review* 79(4): 1094–1116.

National Labor Relations Board (NLRB). 1936–. *Annual Report of the National Labor Relations Board.* Washington: U.S. Government Printing Office.

North, Douglass C. 1990. *Institutions, Institutional Change, and Economic Performance.* New York: Cambridge University Press.

North, Douglass C., and John J. Wallis. 1994. "Integrating Institutional Change and Technical Change in Economic History: A Transaction Cost Approach." *Journal of Institutional and Theoretical Economics* 150(4): 609–24.

Raza, M. Ali, and A. Janell Anderson. 1996. *Labor Relations and the Law.* Upper Saddle River, N.J.: Prentice-Hall.

Spielmans, John V. 1940. "Measurements of the Effectiveness of the National Labor Relations Act." *American Economic Review* 30(4): 803–13.

Taylor, Michael. 1987. *The Possibility of Cooperation.* Cambridge: Cambridge University Press.

Tomlins, Christopher. 1985. *The State and the Unions: Labor Relations, Law and the Organized Labor Movement in America, 1880–1960.* New York: Cambridge University Press.

U.S. Department of Labor, Bureau of Labor Statistics. 1947–99. *Current Population Survey.* Available at: http://www.bls.census.gov/cps/cpsmain.htm (accessed on January 12, 2004).

———. 1946–99. *Monthly Labor Review Online.* Available at: http://data.bls.gov/cgi-bin/surveymost?ws (accessed on January 12, 2004).

Wallis, John J., and Douglass C. North. 1986. "Measuring the Transaction Sector in the American Economy, 1870–1970." In *Long-Term Factors in American Economic Growth,* edited by Stanley L. Engerman and Robert E. Gallman. Chicago: University of Chicago Press.

Williamson, Oliver E. 1993. "Calculativeness, Trust, and Economic Organization." *Journal of Law and Economics* 33(April): 453–500.

World Bank. 1998. *World Development Indicators.* Washington, D.C: International Economics Department Development Data Group. CD-ROM.

Chapter 6

Collective Paranoia: Distrust Between Social Groups

RODERICK M. KRAMER

THE STUDY of intergroup relations, and intergroup conflict in particular, has occupied a prominent place in the social sciences for decades (see, for example, Brewer and Campbell 1976; Sherif et al. 1961; Worchel and Austin 1986). Although few social scientists would probably dispute the importance of trust and distrust as a factor in intergroup relations, surprisingly little systematic theory and research has been conducted on this topic (Brewer [1981] constitutes a notable exception in this regard). Accordingly, this chapter develops an original perspective on the origins and consequences of a deleterious form of distrust and suspicion I term "collective paranoia." To set the stage for the introduction of this notion, it may be helpful to begin with a brief overview of previous approaches to conceptualizing intergroup distrust and suspicion.

Previous Conceptions of Intergroup Distrust and Suspicion

Over the past forty years, a substantial scholarly literature on trust and distrust has accumulated (for representative overviews of the literature, see Barber 1983; Gambetta 1987). Although trust theorists have differed considerably with respect to the emphasis they afford to micro-level versus macro-level determinants of distrust and suspicion, several points of convergence are discernible across these diverse perspectives. First, distrust and suspicion are generally conceptualized as psychological states that are closely linked to individuals' beliefs and expectations about other people. For example, the dispositional inferences individuals make regarding others' intentions and motives are presumed to influence judgments about the trustworthiness of those others. Distrust and suspicion arise when individuals attribute such things as lack of credibility to others' claims or commitments and hostile motives or deceptive intentions to their actions, especially in situations in which uncertainty or ambiguity is present regarding the cause of their behavior (Deutsch 1973; Lindskold 1978). Most conceptions of distrust further assume that psychological states such as fear of exploitation, lack of confidence, and low expectations of reciprocity are significant correlates of distrust (Deutsch 1973; Messick et al. 1983; Tyler 1993).

Suspicion has generally been treated as an important cognitive component of distrust. It has been defined as "a psychological state in which perceivers actively entertain multiple, possibly rival, hypotheses about the motives or genuineness of a person's behavior. Moreover, suspicion involves the belief that the actor's behavior may reflect a motive that the actor wants hidden from the target of his or her behavior" (Fein and Hilton 1994, 168–69). In much of the experimental social psychological literature, especially those studies grounded in game theoretic conceptions of choice behavior, these social inference and attributional processes have been construed as reasonably rational and orderly forms of social inference, consistent with the idea that social perceivers resemble "intuitive scientists" trying to make sense of the social and organizational worlds they inhabit (Kelley 1973).

For example, Julian B. Rotter (1980) and Svenn Lindskold (1978) conceptualize distrust as a generalized expectancy or belief regarding the lack of trustworthiness of other individuals that is predicated upon a specific history of interaction with them. According to this view, when people make judgments about others' trustworthiness (or lack of it), they act much like "intuitive Bayesians" whose inferences are updated on the basis of their prior experience. Research in this tradition has shed considerable light on the conditions under which such "history-based" forms of distrust and suspicion evolve. For example, distrust has been closely linked to patterns of exchange that involve repeated violations of reciprocity (Deutsch 1973; Lindskold 1978; Rotter 1980). Thus when individuals act on faith only to discover that their faith in another has been misplaced, trust declines.

While recognizing the importance of history-based forms of distrust, a number of researchers have noted that other forms of distrust and suspicion appear to be far less rational in their antecedents and origins (Barber 1983; Deutsch 1973; Luhmann 1979). For example, Morton Deutsch (1973, 171) proposes a form of pathological or irrational distrust that he characterizes in terms of an "inflexible, rigid, unaltering tendency to act in a suspicious manner, irrespective of the situation or the consequences of so acting." The pathology of this form of distrust, he notes (Deutsch 1973, 171), is reflected in "the indiscriminateness and incorrigibility of the behavioral tendency." Irrational distrust reflects an exaggerated propensity toward distrust, which can arise even in the absence of specific experiences or interactional histories that justify or warrant it. Irrational distrust represents a form of presumptive distrust that is conferred ex ante on other social actors.

Initial evidence for the existence of this kind of distrust came from ethnographic and field research (Blake and Mouton 1986; Brewer and Campbell 1976; Sherif et al. 1961; Sumner 1906). Subsequent laboratory experiments on in-group bias, using the minimal group paradigm, provide further evidence for it. For example, Marilynn Brewer and her students (Brewer 1979) demonstrate that categorization of individuals into distinct groups can lead individuals to perceive out-group members as less trustworthy, less honest, and less cooperative than other members of their own group, even when those group boundaries are based on arbitrary and transient criteria. According to this perspective, trust often begins and ends at the social category or group boundary.

Although I draw on this previous theory and research in my account of intergroup conflict, I articulate a different theoretical perspective on the determinants of intergroup distrust and suspicion. This conception derives from social information–processing perspectives on social judgment and behavior.

A Social Information–Processing Perspective on Distrust and Suspicion

To understand the dynamics of intergroup distrust and suspicion from a social information–processing perspective, it is useful to start at the level of the individual social perceiver embedded in an intergroup context. I begin by introducing the notion of the intuitive social auditor.

Trust and the Intuitive Social Auditor

As noted earlier, previous models have emphasized that individuals' judgments about others' trustworthiness are anchored, at least in part, on their a priori expectations about others' behavior and on the extent to which subsequent experience supports or discredits those expectations. Robert Boyle and Phillip Bonacich's (1970) analysis of trust development is representative of such arguments. Individuals' expectations about trustworthy behavior, they posit, tend to change "in the direction of experience and to a degree proportional to the difference between this experience and the initial expectations applied to it" (Boyle and Bonacich 1970, 123). The portrait of the social perceiver that emerges from this research is that of an interpersonal bookkeeper, or "social auditor," who attempts to maintain an accurate accounting of past exchanges and transactions.

In their purest form, such models imply a rather straightforward "arithmetic" of trust in which some actions add to the accumulation of trust and others subtract from it. This simple picture is complicated, however, by the fact that systematic biases in social information processing often corrupt the "mental accounting" of the intuitive social auditor. To see where these biases come from, and the effects they exert on social judgment, it is useful to consider how social information processing affects judgments about trust and distrust.

Gerald Salancik and Jeffrey Pfeffer provide a useful perspective on social information–processing theory. They posit that to understand social behavior it is essential to examine the "informational and social environment within which behavior occurs and to which it adapts" (Salancik and Pfeffer 1978, 226). They note that one reason social context is so consequential is that it selectively directs individuals' attention to certain information, making that information more salient and sharpening its impact on individuals' expectations and interpretations of both their own and others' behavior.

Research shows that a variety of goals, not always compatible with one another, affect the way people process social information about other people with whom they are interdependent. In some instances, individuals may be motivated to obtain accurate information about themselves and others on the assumption that such information will be useful in making realistic assessments of how to manage their interdependence with those others more effectively (Ashford 1989; Kelley 1973). In other situations, they may be concerned primarily with obtaining information that will reduce uncertainty regarding their standing in a social relationship (Tyler 1993). In still other contexts, they may want to obtain evidence that will satisfy needs for self-protection (Wood and Taylor 1991), self-enhancement (Brown 1986; Taylor and Brown 1988; Taylor and Brown 1994), reassurance (Kramer 1994), or self-verification (Swann and Read 1981).

In intergroup contexts, any or all of these motives can come into play when individuals from one group interact with members of another. In some situations, for example, it may be most important for individuals to accurately assess the nature of the relationship between their two groups. In the context of an intergroup negotiation, for example, individuals may be most concerned about obtaining accurate information that will help them discern the other group's interests and forge an integrative agreement. In other settings, individuals' paramount concern may be knowing where they stand in the eyes of out-group members, especially if that out-group exercises significant "fate control" over them. For example, assembly-line workers may be highly motivated to know what their managerial counterparts think of their group in general in order to gauge their prospects for promotion. In other contexts, such as those that threaten an individual's sense of self-esteem or self-efficacy vis-à-vis membership in a stigmatized or marginal group, individuals may be motivated to obtain reassuring or self-affirming information.

These divergent goals can affect social information processing by several distinct routes, including their impact on the expectations with which individuals approach their intergroup interactions, the information they find salient during those interactions, and the way they subsequently construe a given interaction and encode it in memory. This portrait of the motivated, vigilant social information processor is useful with respect to understanding what sort of information might affect judgments about trust and distrust. However, it does not help us understand how intergroup cognitions about distrust and suspicion become "decoupled" from actual interactional histories. To see this link, it is useful to introduce the concept of paranoid social cognition.

Paranoid Social Cognition

Early theory and research on paranoid cognition focused almost exclusively on extreme forms of paranoia, such as are typically observed among psychiatric patients in clinical settings (Cameron 1943). On the basis of such observations, Kenneth Colby defined paranoid cognitions as "persecutory delusions and *false beliefs* whose propositional content clusters around ideas of being harassed, threatened, harmed, subjugated, persecuted, accused, mistreated, wronged, tormented, disparaged, vilified, and so on, by malevolent others, either specific individuals or groups" (Colby 1981, 518, emphasis added).

In contrast to clinical theories, recent social psychological research has focused on less extreme forms of paranoid cognition that arise in ordinary social and situational contexts (Fenigstein and Vanable 1992; Kramer 1994; Zimbardo, Andersen, and Kabat 1981). This research proceeds from the intuition that, in milder form, paranoid cognitions appear to be quite prevalent and are often observed even among normal individuals, especially when people find themselves in what they perceive as awkward or threatening social situations. As Alan Fenigstein and Paul Vanable propose, ordinary people "in their everyday behavior often manifest characteristics—such as self-centered thought, suspiciousness, assumptions of ill will or hostility, and even notions of conspiratorial intent—that are reminiscent of paranoia. . . . On various occasions, one may think one is being talked about or feel as if everything is going against one, resulting in suspicion and mistrust of others, as though they were taking advantage of one or were to blame for one's difficulties" (Fenigstein and Vanable 1992, 130–33).

Integrating Colby's definition with this intuition, I define collective paranoia as the response to collectively held beliefs, either false or exaggerated, that cluster around ideas of being harassed, threatened, harmed, subjugated, persecuted, accused, mistreated, wronged, tormented, disparaged, or vilified by a malevolent out-group or out-groups. According to this definition, the perceived source of threat (an out-group or out-groups) and the object of threat (the in-group to which an individual belongs) are both defined at the social group or category level.

It is possible to imagine situations in which a paranoid person maintains pathological suspicion of a personal nature against another person ("him against me") and others involving a group that becomes paranoid about a single individual. There are also situations in which social paranoia is of a personal nature against a group ("them against me"). Finally, there can be paranoia imputed to a group against another group ("them against us"), the case that is at the heart of collective paranoia.

Several psychological phenomena may differentiate these forms of extreme distrust. In particular, the we-them sort that I identify as collective paranoia rests on the bedrock of in-group–out-group differentiation that has been widely studied. When intuitive social auditors do the accounting of transactions that are between-group exchanges, they very likely code them differently from within-group encounters. There is evidence that in-group members are more likely to give other members the benefit of the doubt, manifesting what Brewer (1996, 166) has termed a "leniency bias."

Another factor that tends to maintain and exacerbate distrust and suspicion is what I call the out-group unitization hypothesis, referring to the tendency to treat the out-group as a single unit in the accounting scheme. Out-group unitization reflects the tendency to differentiate less among out-group members than among in-group members when doing the social auditing. As a consequence, a breach of trust from one member of the out-group can be repaid to any other member. If an out-group member insults one, one can retaliate against any other member of the out-group. The target of the retaliation naturally perceives the retaliatory act as gratuitous aggression, further enhancing distrust and suspicion. If an in-group member insults one, one retaliates directly against that person.

Out-group unitization influences the intuitive auditor's accounting with positive exchanges as well as negative ones. If an individual treats an out-group member kindly, the social auditor records the act as a positive contribution not only to their interpersonal relationship but also to the out-group as a whole. One implication is that any member of the out-group should be appropriately grateful, indebted, or appreciative of the act. In contrast, kind acts to in-group members do not create the expectation that other in-group members will be indebted to one's self. The unit for the in-group is the person; for the out-group, it is the group.

Collective Paranoia and Intergroup Relations: Asymmetries in Power and Dependence

Up to this point, I have presented several rather general arguments regarding the impact of social information processing or intergroup distrust and suspicion. Little has been said about the nature of the interdependence or structural relationship between groups. In particular, groups often differ with respect to their power over (or dependence on) other groups. This hierarchic relation, indeed, may be the norm rather than the exception. Hierarchical relationships—those characterized by asymmetries in the power and status of interdependent groups—are among the most important and prevalent forms of social organization. Hierarchy characterizes many forms of intergroup relation, including the relationship between management and labor groups within organizations; between dominant and token social groups; between majority groups in political power and marginal groups seeking power; and between religious and secular sectors in society (see, for example, Fox 1974; Kanter 1977a; Kanter 1977b; Miller 1992). They are also a form of relationship in which the contours and features of collective paranoia are likely to loom particularly large.

The prevalence of hierarchy reflects its many virtues as a form of organizing—virtues that have been long noted by social and organizational theorists. As with many virtues, however, hierarchy enjoys its share of problems, the catalogue of which varies depending upon where in the hierarchical relationship a group happens to be situated. From the perspective of groups that occupy positions of low power or status within a hierarchical social system, the fear of exploitation and chronic suspicion that they are being treated unfairly by those above them are real and recurring concerns. For groups in high-status positions, in contrast, fear that those below them seek to displace them and cannot be trusted unless they are watched closely are common. In conjunction, these divergent concerns about trust are a reminder of the elusive quality of trust in hierarchical relations and the comparative ease with which distrust and suspicion roam over the hierarchical landscape (Barber 1983; Hill 1992; Kanter 1977a; Kanter 1977b; Miller 1992; Tyler and Lind 1992).

Antecedents of Collective Paranoia in Hierarchical Relations

Research on paranoid social cognition identifies several psychological factors that contribute to paranoid cognition. Of particular relevance here is evidence that paranoid social cognition is likely to arise in situations in which individuals feel a heightened sense of self-consciousness, perceive themselves to be under intense evaluative scrutiny, or are uncertain of their status or standing within a social relation (Fenigstein 1979, 1984; Fenigstein and Vanable 1992; Kramer 1994).

Heightened Self-Consciousness

Studies have shown that heightened self-consciousness increases an individual's tendency to make overly personalistic attributions about others' intentions and motives (Buss and Scheier 1976; Fenigstein and Vanable 1992; Kramer 1994). Fenigstein (1984, 861) characterizes this as the "overperception of self-as-target" bias and argues that, because of it, individuals tend to construe even relatively innocuous social encounters in unrealistically self-referential terms. According to this evidence, self-consciousness induces an exaggerated or irrational suspicion that other people are observing and evaluating them. Thus, ironically, an individual's own self-consciousness engenders the perception of being under intense social scrutiny. This tendency, of course, is one of the defining features of a paranoid style of cognition. As Colby (1981, 518) notes, "Around the central core of persecutory delusions [that preoccupy the paranoid person] there exists a number of attendant properties such as suspiciousness, hypersensitivity, hostility, fearfulness, and self-reference that lead such individuals to interpret events that have nothing to do with them as bearing on them personally."

Within the context of intergroup relations, one important factor that can influence self-consciousness is the relational demography (Tsui, Egan, and O'Reilly 1992) that characterizes the broader social context within which the intergroup relation is embedded. All humans possess membership in multiple social categories. As a consequence, they can categorize themselves—and be categorized by others in turn—in a variety of different ways. These include categorizations based upon physical attributes such as age, race, or gender; categorizations based upon socially defined categories such as religion and social class; and organizationally defined attributes, such as institutional affiliation and departmental membership. Recognizing their importance, researchers have afforded a great deal of attention in recent years to exploring how such categorization processes influence social perception within groups and organizations (Ashforth and Mael 1989; Kanter 1977a; Tsui, Egan, and O'Reilly 1992; Wharton 1992).

Several conclusions emerge from research on social categorization. First, social categorization often influences how individuals define themselves in a given social situation. John Turner (1987) uses the term "self-categorization" to refer to these processes and their effects. Self-categorization is affected by the particular social context within which individuals find themselves. In particular, there is evidence that individuals categorize themselves in terms of those attributes that are distinctive or unique in a given setting. For example, if an individual is the only female in a group, her distinctive gender status may be afforded disproportionate emphasis when explaining her behavior, affecting not only how she is seen by others but also how she sees herself. Thus one factor that can enhance self-consciousness is for a person to be unique or distinctive with respect to some obvious characteristic like race or gender (Taylor et al. 1978). Indeed, it is hard to imagine a more potent way to increase the salience of a group boundary or social category than to have "solo status" as a lone woman in an otherwise all-male office. Not only is self-consciousness increased, it is increased about precisely the group characteristics that can lead to group-based attributions for others' behaviors and judgments.

From a cognitive standpoint, the enhanced distinctiveness of the category during social interaction makes gender-based attributions more available during social information processing. Intergroup differences become highly salient explanations for behavior, and the social auditor grows suspicious by crediting pluses and minuses to group rather than individual accounts. As a result, differences tend to become more salient or "loom larger" during subsequent interactions, as well, affecting both social inference processes and the behaviors that flow from them (Cota and Dion 1986; Kanter 1977a, 1977b; Taylor 1981).

The argument that self-categorization on the basis of distinctive or exceptional status produces a heightened form of self-consciousness is consistent with a considerable body of evidence regarding the cognitive and social consequences of "being different" or standing out from other members of a group (Kanter 1977a, 1997b; Tsui, Egan, and O'Reilly 1992; Taylor 1981). In social information–processing terms, one fairly immediate consequence of an individual's awareness of being different from others is that it prompts effortful attributional search for the causes of others' behavior toward him or her while at the same time injecting considerable ambiguity into the social inference process. Such self-consciousness might be expected to be especially pronounced when individuals are uncertain about how much merely "being different" from others influences how they are evaluated and treated.

Perceived Evaluative Scrutiny

A second factor that contributes to paranoid social cognition is the perception that one is under evaluative scrutiny. Research has shown that when individuals feel under moderate or intense evaluative scrutiny, they tend to overattribute others' behavior to personalistic causes (Fenigstein and Vanable 1992; Kramer 1994). For example, to junior faculty members under review for tenure in an academic department, even casual and seemingly benign encounters can take on significant and potentially sinister import because they feel they are under continual evaluative scrutiny by more senior colleagues. Thus the failure of a senior colleague to return a casual hello as they pass one another in the hall may prompt intense rumination on the part of the junior faculty member about the cause or "meaning" of the event ("Did I say something at the last faculty meeting that offended her?" "Does he feel uncomfortable seeing me because he decided to vote against me for tenure?"). The effect of perceiving themselves under evaluative scrutiny thus leads individuals to attribute the behavior of others in overly personalistic and diagnostic terms (that is, as having implications for their standing in the relationship). As a consequence, even when plausible nonpersonalistic accounts are available, individuals who feel under evaluative scrutiny tend to discount the credibility of such accounts in favor of those that are viewed as more self-relevant.

In many respects, token groups exemplify these cognitive dilemmas and difficulties. Token status in a hierarchy is based upon "ascribed characteristics (master statuses such as sex, race, religion, ethnic group, and age) or other characteristics that carry with them a set of assumptions about culture, status, and behavior that are highly salient for majority category members" (Kanter 1977b, 966). In discussing the effects of token status on social perception and interpersonal relations, Rosabeth Kanter (1977a, 1977b) notes that individuals who are members of token categories are likely to attract disproportionate attention from other groups, particularly those who enjoy dominant status in terms of numerical proportions. For example, she observes that females in many American corporations often feel as if they are in the limelight compared with their statistically more numerous male counterparts.

In support of these observations, Shelley Taylor (1981) demonstrates that observers often allocate disproportionate amounts of attention to individuals who have token status in groups, especially when making attributions about group processes and outcomes. Charles Lord and David Saenz provide an important extension of this early work by showing how token status affects the cognitive processes of "token" individuals themselves. Based on their findings, Lord and Saenz conclude that "tokens feel the social pressure of imagined audience scrutiny, and may do so even when the 'audience' of majority group members treat them no differently from nontokens" (Lord and Saenz 1985, 919).

The model of the vigilant social auditor advanced earlier helps explain this pattern. From a social information–processing perspective, individuals in lower-status groups in a social hierarchy are likely to be hypervigilant and ruminative information processors compared with their higher-status counterparts, especially members of those groups on whose judgment they depend. As a consequence of their enhanced vigilance and rumination, they will tend to (over)construe others' behavior as indicative of trust-related concerns.

These arguments imply that individuals in lower-status groups should develop, over time, more elaborate and differentiated mental accounting systems for tracking trust-related transactions. According to this cognitive elaboration hypothesis, we would expect members of social groups who occupy the bottom position in a hierarchical relation to be able to recall more trust-related incidents and behaviors than their superordinate counterparts. Susan Fiske (1993) identifies a number of factors involved in this asymmetry. Her research suggests that people are vigilant and careful information processors when they need to be but often rely on stereotypes and other poorly articulated schemata of others when they can get away with it. She observes that "the power*less* are stereotyped because no one needs to, can, or wants to be detailed and accurate about them. The power*ful* are not so likely to be stereotyped because subordinates need to, can, and want to form detailed impressions of them. The powerless need to try to predict and possibly alter their own fates" (Fiske 1993, 624).

Extrapolating from such evidence and arguments, it might be argued that violations of trust will tend to loom larger than confirmations of trust for those in positions of low power or control in such situations. Several lines of research suggest this hypothesis. First, violations of trust are highly salient to victims, prompting intense ruminative activity and greater attributional search for the causes of the violation (Janoff-Bulman 1992). Second, to the extent that violations of trust are coded as interpersonal losses, they should loom larger than "mere" confirmations of trust of comparable magnitude (for example, failure to keep a promise should have more impact on judgments about trustworthiness than merely keeping it). Finally, cognitive responses to positive and negative events are often highly asymmetrical (Peeters and Czapinski 1990; Taylor 1991). As Taylor (1991, 70) notes, "Negative events produce more causal attribution activity than positive events, controlling for expectedness."

Uncertainty About Social Standing

A third factor that can contribute to the emergence of paranoid social cognition is the level of uncertainty about social standing that social perceivers possess. Recent research on the group value model suggests that people attach great psychological importance to their standing within social systems and social interactions (Lind and Tyler 1988). Standing refers to the "information communicated to a person about his or her status with the group . . . communicated both by interpersonal aspects of treatment—politeness and/or respect—and by the attention paid to a person as a full group member" (Tyler 1993, 148). According to this model, individuals are motivated to determine whether they have been treated fairly and whether they are valued or respected by those on whom they are dependent (Tyler 1993). Consequently, they try to diagnose their standing, using information from exchanges and encounters as clues to whether their standing in the relationship is "good" or "bad."

Because of their ongoing concerns about standing, individuals in lower-status or less powerful groups tend to be proactive information seekers, searching for data that will help them make sense of their place in the social order (Ashford 1989). In doing so, individuals are torn between the desire to obtain accurate information about where they stand in a social system and the desire to obtain reassuring or self-enhancing information (Brown 1991; Brown and Dutton 1995; Sedikides 1993; Strube et al. 1986; Strube and Roemmele 1985; Trope 1983, 1986). As a result, when individuals find themselves in situations in which their self-esteem or positive social identity is threatened, a conflict may arise between the desire to find out where they actually stand in the relationship and the desire to assuage their fears about poor standing or loss of standing.

Cognitive Consequences of Collective Paranoia

One response to a perceived threat about standing is to activate adaptive information search and appraisal. Moderate levels of threat often provoke vigilant information processing about the nature of the threat and the responses that might be taken to reduce it (Janis 1989; Janoff-Bulman 1992; Lazarus and Folkman 1984). When a threat becomes too severe, however, individuals may experience a hypervigilant style of social information processing. This hypervigilant information processing can lead, in turn, to the misconstrual of social information, affecting judgments about another's trustworthiness (Kramer 1995b).

A second response individuals often have to threatening events is dysphoric rumination (Janoff-Bulman 1992). Dysphoric rumination refers to the tendency for individuals to unhappily reimagine, rethink, and relive pleasant or unpleasant events. Research (Lyubomirsky and Nolen-Hoeksema 1993; Kramer 1994; Tesser 1978) indicates a number of reasons why dysphoric rumination might contribute to paranoid social cognition. First, rumination following negative events has been found to increase negative thinking about those events and contribute to a pessimistic tendency in trying to explain them. Dysphoric ruminators appear to engage in worst-case thinking about their troubles and the prospects for resolving them. Second, rumination can increase individuals' confidence in the interpretations and explanations they have generated to explain adverse or threatening events.

This result is ironic and might, at first glance, seem counterintuitive. One might argue that the more individuals ruminate about the causes of their difficulties, the more likely they should be to generate numerous alternative, reasonable hypotheses, leading to decreased confidence in an especially implausible or "paranoid" account of their difficulties. However, as Timothy Wilson and Douglas Kraft (1993, 410) aptly note, "Because it is often difficult to get at the exact roots of [many] feelings, repeated introspections may not result in better access to the actual causes. Instead, people may repeatedly focus on reasons that are plausible and easy to verbalize." Such results suggest the operation of an interesting "cognitive effort" heuristic ("Since I've thought so much about this, it must be true"). Along these lines, Kramer (1994) has demonstrated support for the hypothesis that inducing dysphoric rumination about the motives of others increases distrust and suspicion of them.

Hypervigilance and dysphoric rumination can affect social information processing and threat perception between social groups in at least three ways: through the sinister attribution error, biased punctuation of interactional history, and exaggerated perceptions of conspiracy. The sinister attribution error or bias reflects a tendency to overattribute hostile intentions and malevolent motives to others (Kramer 1994). Individuals should discount the validity of any single causal explanation when multiple, competing explanations for that behavior are available (Kelley 1973; Morris and Larrick 1995). Thus even when they suspect they may be the target or cause of another's behavior, individuals should discount this self-referential or personalistic attribution if other plausible reasons exist.

However, there is substantial evidence that people often make overly personalistic attributions of others' actions even when competing explanations are readily available (Fenigstein 1979; Fenigstein and Vanable 1992; Heider 1958; Hilton, Fein, and Miller 1993; Kramer 1994; Vorauer and Ross 1993). Certain cognitive states, such as self-consciousness, increase this tendency to make overly personalistic and negative attributions (Fenigstein and Vanable 1992; Kramer 1994).

The notion of "biased punctuation" of social interactions refers to a tendency for interdependent decision makers to organize their interpersonal histories in a self-serving fashion (Kahn and Kramer 1990). Thus, in the case of an intergroup conflict, members of group A are likely to construe the history of conflict with another group, B, as a sequence (B,A), (B,A), (B,A), in which the initial hostile or aggressive move was made by B, causing A to engage in defensive and legitimate retaliatory actions. However, actor B punctuates the same history of interaction as (A,B), (A,B), (A,B), reversing the roles of aggressor and defender. The tendency to punctuate a behavioral sequence in a self-serving fashion is a type of social script that has been called the aggressor-defender model (Pruitt and Rubin 1986).

Since defiance is morally acceptable whereas aggression is not, each party to a conflict will frame the interaction so as to make the other party the "first mover," the one who initiated the conflict. Considered in conjunction with the out-group unitization hypothesis mentioned earlier, it is easy to see how an act that is seen as a response by one side can be viewed as an initiation by the other.

Exaggerated perceptions of conspiracy reflect a tendency for individuals to overestimate the extent to which their perceived out-group enemies or adversaries are engaged in coordinated and concerted hostile or malevolent actions against them. Just as biased punctuation of interactional history entails an overperception of episodic or causal linkages between disparate or unconnected events, so the exaggerated perception of conspiracy entails an overperception of *social* linkages among out-group actors. At the core of the exaggerated perception of conspiracy is the tendency to overperceive interdependent connections among the actions of individual out-group members, even when their acts are, in actuality, independent. In the context of intergroup relations, these exaggerated perceptions of conspiracy center around the presumed intentionality of acts of the out-group (that is, actions are construed as *coordinated* attempts aimed at harming one's own group).

Exaggerated perceptions of conspiracy are likely to emerge later in a conflict, after issues have intensified. In these circumstances, group positions are likely to be extreme, including the perception that anyone who is not with our group must be against it. Thus both sides in an intense conflict may perceive objectively moderate positions to be more favorable to the other side (Dawes, Singer, and Lemons 1972; Lord, Lepper, and Ross 1979).

Affective and Behavioral Consequences of Collective Paranoia

There are several affective and behavioral consequences of collective paranoia. First, collective paranoia contributes to a form of affective response that has been called moral aggression. The term has been used to refer to the intense negative reactions individuals sometimes experience when they feel they have been treated in an unfair, unjust, or untrustworthy fashion (see, for example,. Brewer 1981; Campbell 1975; Trivers 1971). The notion of moral aggression reflects a basic intuition about the phenomenology of injustice: people often have a limited tolerance for other people or groups who are perceived to be dishonest or untrustworthy, especially when they believe that they themselves or the groups to which they belong are engaging in more cooperative, trustworthy behavior (Schelling 1958; Wilson 1978). There is evidence that moral aggression is associated with strong anger and a desire for retribution (Bies 1987). Such feelings have been linked to intergroup violence and revenge behaviors (Bies, Tripp, and Kramer 1996).

A second form of behavior driven by collective paranoia is defensive noncooperation. Kramer and Brewer (1986) note that one reason groups "defect" from preserving common resource pools shared with other groups is that they believe others are not doing their fair share. Thus they construe their own noncooperative behavior as defensively motivated—that is, designed to protect their own welfare, even if that means compromising the collective welfare. Such behavior is intended to minimize the risks of exploitation or getting the so-called sucker's payoff. It thus constitutes a form of preemptive defense against the expectation that trust will be violated. Of course, to the extent that each group engages in such acts, the result is a series of reciprocal disappointments and self-justificatory acts that can increase intergroup distrust and suspicion, creating a self-fulfilling prophecy.

Untying the Knot: Reducing Distrust and Suspicion Between Groups

The numerous psychological and social barriers to trust identified in the previous sections, especially when viewed as operating in concert, might seem to mitigate against the prospects of trust ever gaining a toehold, let alone flourishing, in intergroup relations. To be sure, the problem of creating and sustaining trust, especially against the backdrop of a history of mutual enmity or wariness, has proved daunting both in practice and theory. The difficulty was nicely captured in a personal communiqué sent by Soviet premier Nikita Khrushchev to President John F. Kennedy at the height of tensions during the Cuban missile crisis. Khrushchev cautioned Kennedy that the escalating conflict between their countries could be likened to a rope with a knot in its middle; "the harder you and I pull, the tighter this knot [of war] will become," he suggested. "And a time may come when this knot is tied so tight that the person who tied it is no longer capable of untying it" (cited in Kennedy 1969, 81).

There is evidence that the barriers to trust, though formidable, are not insurmountable. A body of literature addresses the question of how trust can be created and the knot of distrust, if not untied completely, can be at least loosened. Among the suggested responses to intergroup conflict of this magnitude are unilateral initiatives that can be undertaken by the negotiating parties themselves, interventions involving third parties, and structural approaches to building trust.

Unilateral Negotiator Initiatives

One way in which interdependent groups can attempt to influence each other is through attempts to change their perceptions and behaviors. This can include efforts to create a climate of mutual trust by attempting both to elicit cooperative behavior from the other group and to communicate one's own group's trustworthiness and willingness to cooperate. Much of the literature on this trust-building process has been motivated by recognition of the circular relation between trust and cooperation (Deutsch 1973): trust tends to beget cooperation, and cooperation breeds further trust. Therefore, if a cycle of mutual cooperation can be initiated and sustained, trust will develop (Lindskold 1978). This trust, in turn, will spur further cooperative acts.

Perhaps the simplest and most direct way to initiate such constructive change in the relationship between two wary groups is for one of the groups to make a gesture that interrupts the status quo. Such an effort is direct in that it immediately alters the pattern of interaction and simple in that it requires no third-party interventions or elaborate structural changes. Early studies pursuing this idea examine the use of unconditional pacifism to elicit cooperative responses. The experimental evidence regarding the efficacy of this strategy, however, is discouraging. At least in the context of laboratory settings, unvarying or unconditional cooperation is puzzling to recipients, and the tendency is to exploit it (Deutsch 1973).

Although strategies of unconditional cooperation yield disappointing results, initiatives that involve contingent cooperation have proved more effective in eliciting and sustaining cooperative behavior. Early studies on this issue involve simple mixed-motives games in which a confederate makes an initial cooperative move, inviting a reciprocal act of cooperation (Deutsch 1973). Subsequent studies in this vein identify specific patterns of reciprocation that are efficacious in such situations. Charles Osgood's (1962) strategy of graduated reciprocation in tension reduction (GRIT) was an early model of such patterns. Osgood's core insight is that a sequence of carefully calibrated and clear signals might initiate a sustainable process of mutual trust and cooperation. One of the appeals of this strategy, and perhaps one reason it attracted so much attention, is that it seemed to offer a mechanism for reducing distrust and suspicion between the nuclear superpowers. Amit Etzioni (1967) uses the GRIT framework to interpret the series of progressively conciliatory exchanges between President Kennedy and Premier Khrushchev in the early 1960s.

Drawing on this theory, Lindskold and others undertook a sustained program of laboratory-based research on the dynamics of trust development (for reviews, see Lindskold 1978, 1986). Several practical recommendations have emerged from this work. First, it is useful for negotiators to announce what they are doing ahead of time and to carry out the initiatives as announced. In addition, it has been suggested that conciliatory initiatives should be irrevocable and noncontingent, so that they will be understood as efforts to resolve the conflict rather than to gain a quid pro quo. They should be costly or risky to oneself, so that they cannot be construed as a cheap trick or a trap. They should be continued for a period of time so as to put pressure on the other party to reciprocate and to give the other party time to rethink its policy. To these recommendations, I would add two others: Unilateral initiatives should be noticeable and unexpected so that they will provoke thought. And their users should try to demonstrate a good and lasting reason for wanting to change the relationship; otherwise such initiatives may be viewed as a flash in the pan.

The GRIT strategy proceeds from a logic of starting small in order to jump-start a trust-building process. An alternative strategy, and one that reverses the logic a bit, involves an attempt by one party to "break the frame" of distrust and suspicion by making a large, dramatic conciliatory gesture. Because it entails such obvious and severe political costs to the negotiator making the initiative, the significance of such a gesture is hard to discount or ignore. An example is Egyptian president Anwar Sadat's trip to Jerusalem in 1978, which paved the way for peace between Egypt and Israel. Sadat stated that the purpose of the trip was to improve Israeli trust in Egypt. Herb Kelman (1985) reports that most Israelis viewed this event as a genuine effort to improve relations. This strategy is not, however, unconditionally effective, and it may produce other than the intended effects. Such initiatives risk alienating important constituents and may undermine a negotiator's credibility and effectiveness with constituents. Moreover, as Sadat's experience demonstrated, this estrangement may sometimes have fatal consequences.

Other studies indicate that cooperation leads to improved interpersonal and intergroup relations. In early studies on this topic, Muzafer Sherif and his colleagues (Sherif et al. 1961) first produced animosity between two groups of boys in a summer camp by having them compete with and exploit one another. They were then able to dispel this animosity in a second phase by having the boys cooperate on "superordinate" goals. Additional research suggests that even the anticipation of cooperation can lead to improved interpersonal and intergroup relations (Deutsch 1973). There are many possible explanations for the positive trust-building effects of cooperation on relationships. Cooperation may lead to reward at the hands of the other party. It may provide favorable information about the other party that would not otherwise be available. It may enhance perceived similarity and break down the conceptual boundary between groups (Brewer and Kramer 1985). Helping the other party may induce positive attitudes, another dissonance-resolving effect.

Such findings suggest that another way groups can build trust through their own actions is to engage in relationship-building activities. Most experienced professional conflict managers recognize that it is often useful to attempt to build a positive personal bond with another party, even if doing so entails some scrutiny by constituents (Deutsch 1973). This approach builds on recognition that trust is a central characteristic of mature and secure relationships in which people are likely to exhibit a combination of problem solving and concession making, which can lead to mutually beneficial, win-win agreements.

Peter Carnevale and Dean Pruitt (2000) have called these sorts of relationships "working relationships." Working relationships are often found between people with emotional ties, such as friends, relatives, or married couples. Working relationships also are common between people with instrumental ties, such as colleagues whose jobs require them to cooperate and negotiators in counterpart relationships. An example of the latter would be a salesperson and a regular client. Working relationships involve three related norms for dealing with mixed-motive settings: a norm of problem solving, which specifies that if both parties feel strongly about an issue, they should try to find a way for both of them to succeed; a norm of mutual responsiveness, which specifies that if only one party feels strongly about an issue or if problem solving fails, the party who feels less strongly should concede to the other's wishes; and a norm of truth in signaling, which specifies that the parties should be honest about the strength of their feelings. Truth in signaling is a necessary adjunct to the norm of mutual responsiveness, preventing people from exaggerating the strength of their needs. In the absence of this norm, neither party will trust the other's statements about issue importance, and the norm of mutual responsiveness will collapse.

Third-Party Interventions and Improvements in Trust Between Groups

It has long been appreciated that third parties can play a significant role in the process of both creating and repairing damaged trust in intergroup relations (Pruitt and Rubin 1986). Mediators inject cooperative norms, routines, and procedures into a negotiation. The effects of such interventions can be direct not only in terms of leading to better exchange of information and consideration of more integrative offers but also in modeling skills that the negotiators may then use themselves. Third parties often take even more active roles in trying to influence the negotiation processes between groups.

Research on the efficacy of different third-party interventions suggests that such interventions can be distinguished by their fundamental assumptions regarding the sources and dynamics of intergroup conflict (Keashly, Fisher, and Grant 1993). Specifically, they argue, third-party interventions involving mediation attempt to resolve conflict by focusing on creatively addressing the substantive issues in a conflict. Third-party consultation, in contrast, focuses on altering the relationship between the parties, including their attitudes and perceptions (or misperceptions). Using an exercise called the Intergroup Conflict Simulation, they demonstrate that both mediation and consultation produced comparable success with respect to resolution of the simulated dispute (a land settlement). However, consultation resulted in groups' expressing more positive attitudes toward one another and perception of the intergroup relationship itself as more collaborative. With respect to trust building, therefore, it may be that consultation can enhance perceptions of the out-group that contribute to higher perceptions of trustworthiness, including credibility, reliability, and benevolence of motives.

Structural Approaches to Creating and Sustaining Trust Between Groups

There is a large body of theory and research, mostly sociological, on institutional approaches to creating and sustaining trust. The Standing Consultative Commission provides one illustration as to how institutional structures can be used to improve and stabilize trust in complex, recurring, high-stakes negotiations, especially when the parties are highly distrustful of each other (for history and overview, see Kahn 1990). The commission was a product of the Strategic Arms Limitation talks begun in 1969 between the United States and the Soviet Union. Thus its creation was a direct result of a specific negotiation (the Anti-Ballistic Missile Treaty of 1972), but its aim was more general: the commission was to contribute to the continued viability and effectiveness of negotiated agreements by resolving questions of interpretation and concerns about compliance if and as they arose. It thus created an institutional mechanism for allowing the parties to reach an initial agreement, even though many details had not been worked out to the parties' respective satisfaction.

In discussing the utility of mechanisms of this sort, Robert Kahn (1990, 161) notes that an important function of such an institution is that it enables the ongoing "interpretation and fleshing out of an agreement that is appropriately general rather than specific in many respects." In a related way, it builds flexibility into the "application of the agreement to new political and technological developments." In this respect, such structures enable the more open-ended, relational agreements exemplified by Japanese negotiations.

Another way of thinking about structural mechanisms for solving dilemmas of trust focuses on the efficacy of incentive systems in inducing trust and cooperation. In these cases, an outside agency (for example, a government) is implemented that either reinforces cooperation (by providing a bonus to those who are most cooperative) or punishes noncooperation (by imposing a penalty on those who are least cooperative). There is evidence that reward systems are more effective in inducing cooperation than penalty systems, though the latter are more effective than no system at all (Carnevale and Pruitt 2000).

Even when the necessary and sufficient conditions for trust do not exist, negotiators may be able to make some progress by simply reducing their dependence on trust. Noting that it is hard for people to cooperate in the absence of trust, Carnevale and Pruitt (2000) argue that, when there is a desire or necessity to engage in negotiation but trust between the parties is low, it may be possible to reduce reliance on trust by making decisions reversible. Hence an escape from any particular commitment is possible should the other party prove untrustworthy.

In support of this logic, Deutsch (1973) has found higher levels of cooperation in a prisoner's dilemma when both parties were free to reverse their decisions again and again until mutually satisfactory outcomes were obtained. In the context of intergroup relationships, such reversibility might be manifested as a rule, either explicitly stated or tacitly assumed, that no agreements are final until all points of contention have been mutually agreed upon by both groups. This rule makes it possible to concede on some issues without full assurance that the adversary will concede on all of the others that await resolution. What is most important, invocation of the rule by one party or the other will not be attributed to bad faith. In other words, backing out of a previous agreement or asking that an issue be revisited will be viewed not as defection but as a legitimate part of the process.

Another strategy for reducing dependence on trust is to fractionate a conflict by decomposing a complex multi-issue negotiation into many small issues, so that the risk associated with reaching agreement on any one issue is relatively low (Carnevale and Pruitt 2000). A negotiator can usually make a tiny cooperative move, even if trust is low, and then wait to see if the other reciprocates before taking the next tiny move. Two negotiators can sometimes move toward settlement using this strategy, each making small concessions that are reciprocated by the other until they arrive at a common position. Much like GRIT, this strategy greatly reduces the perceived risk of misplaced trust. It has the additional benefit, similar to piecemeal reciprocity, that the parties learn that reaching agreement is possible—that it is possible to trust the other along at least some dimensions or with respect to some set of issues. Success on these early and comparatively easy issues may then build momentum and increase confidence on subsequent and more thorny issues, leading over time to greater trust between the negotiators.

Contributions and Implications of the Present Framework

A major aim of this chapter is to suggest a new framework for thinking about the antecedents and consequences of intergroup distrust and suspicion. My arguments regarding the effects of heightened self-consciousness, the perception that one is under evaluative scrutiny, and uncertainty about standing on social information suggest how exaggerated or irrational forms of distrust and suspicion can evolve from social information–processing tendencies that foster the misconstrual of others' actions and motives. The list of factors considered here obviously does not exhaust the possible factors that might contribute to the development of collective paranoia. Rather, it is intended merely to illustrate the kinds of cognitive, structural, and social relational factors that might intensify intergroup distrust and suspicion. However, it draws attention to an important intuition about the psychological dynamics of collective paranoia. In each case, central issues include perceptions of vulnerability and lack of perceived control over important outcomes implied by the presence of powerful evaluative out-groups.

Much of this analysis has proceeded from the presumption that many of the social cognitive correlates of collective paranoia reflect rather ordinary social information–processing goals and motives gone awry. Social and organizational life is an ongoing process of sense making and adaptation: individuals like to know where they fit in a complex social hierarchy. Moreover, when problems arise, they attempt to engage in effective reality testing and problem solving. Group members in social contexts are intendedly rational, vigilant, and discerning social perceivers. They normally engage in constructive attempts to make sense of their environments, and vigilance and rumination are useful strategies for so doing. Thus when occasions arise that threaten a group's security, status, esteem, or perceived control over events, group members engage in an active search for the sources and causes of their difficulties. During such a search, other social groups with whom they are interdependent, especially those that are perceived as powerful or in control of important outcomes, will quite naturally attract attention. Such groups become objects of vigilant scrutiny and rumination.

Of course, all individuals routinely confront sense-making dilemmas. However, for those groups who occupy certain disadvantaged social positions relative to other groups (those who perceive themselves as particularly vulnerable, are uncertain about their standing in the social order, or perceive themselves to be under evaluative scrutiny), these sense-making predicaments are more acute.

It is useful to raise a few caveats about this analysis. First, many of the conceptual labels employed in the model—such as sinister attribution error, paranoid social cognition, and exaggerated perception of conspiracy—may strike some readers as excessively pejorative labels. In effect, they seem to blame the victim by prejudging or assuming an objective reference point against which the cognitions of certain groups fall short. For example, characterizing the cognitive processes of individuals who happen to belong to relatively disadvantaged groups within a social system as paranoid might seem to minimize the legitimacy of their concerns or the validity of their plight.

This is far from the intent of this analysis. Rather, the spirit of the analysis is to suggest some deleterious cognitive and behavioral consequences that are sometimes correlated with certain locations within social hierarchies. To the extent that social locations influence the magnitude and direction of certain social information–processing biases, they may contribute to a potentially debilitating pattern of misperception and misattribution. A better understanding of these irrational bases of distrust and suspicion can be a first step in developing a set of more efficacious behavioral technologies for building and restoring trust between groups.

Relatedly, the label "sinister attribution error" clearly implies a mistaken or flawed process of social inference, again seeming to cast aspersions on the cognitive competence of members of certain social groups. Insofar as research findings reviewed in this chapter do document that psychological processes such as self-consciousness and dysphoric rumination lead to systematic distortions in the attribution and social inference process, the term "error" or "bias" seems quite appropriate. However, it is important that such cognitive errors not be misconstrued as "errors" in a more existential sense. In highly competitive or political social contexts, for example, a propensity toward vigilance with respect to detecting the lack of trustworthiness of a powerful out-group may be quite prudent and adaptive. In such environments, it is often better to be safe than sorry.

Such possibilities prompt consideration of other adaptive functions of collective paranoia. There are several ways in which the psychological processes associated with paranoid cognitions (heightened vigilance, self-consciousness, and rumination) may have adaptive consequences, especially for groups who are relatively disadvantaged with respect to their power or status within a social hierarchy. First, distrust is not always irrational. In the competition for scarce resources and the attempt to gain social power, groups are almost certain to encounter other groups who wish to hold them back, rival groups who seek to displace them, or less powerful but equally ambitious groups seeking to curry favor or mislead them. Although the fears and suspicions of some groups may sometimes seem exaggerated to outsiders, this does not mean that their distrust is necessarily without foundation or foolish. The expression, "Just because you're paranoid doesn't mean they aren't out to get you," often contains more than a kernel of truth.

When viewed from this perspective, psychological processes such as vigilance and rumination may be quite functional. In much the same way that defensive pessimism contributes to a form of adaptive preparedness when individuals anticipate challenging events (Norem and Cantor 1986), so might paranoid cognition help group members maintain their motivation to overcome perceived dangers and obstacles within their social environments (even when those dangers and obstacles seem misplaced or inflated from the perspective of more neutral observers). Moderate levels of social paranoia, including a tendency toward hypervigilance and ruminative information processing, might help them make sense of the social situations they are in and help them determine appropriate forms of adaptive response.

Similarly, in highly competitive social environments, it may prove fatal to underestimate one's competitors. As Andrew Grove (1996, 3), the president and chief executive officer of Intel, once asserted, "Only the paranoid survive." Elaborating on what he meant by this maxim, he added,

> The things I tend to be paranoid about vary. I worry about products getting screwed up, and I worry about products getting introduced prematurely. I worry about factories not performing well, and I worry about having too many factories. I worry about hiring the right people, and I worry about morale slacking off. And, of course, I worry about competitors. I worry about people figuring out how to do what we do better or cheaper, and displacing us with our customers.

In expounding further on the adaptive value of such paranoia, Grove noted, "I believe in the value of paranoia. Business success contains the seeds of its own destruction. The more successful you are, the more people want a chunk of your business and then another chunk and then another until there is nothing left. I believe that the prime responsibility of a manager is to guard against other people's attacks and to inculcate this guardian attitude in the people under his or her management." Both for individuals who are members of groups in power and for those who are members of groups who feel powerless, success and even survival may be contingent on continuous, even if effortful, vigilance regarding emerging threats in the social landscape. A functionalist account of social paranoia emphasizes, therefore, the role such paranoia plays in individuals' attempts at making sense of the potentially perilous environments in which their social actions are embedded. Under the best of circumstances, sense making in social settings is a problematic enterprise, fraught with ambiguity and risk (Weick 1995), but this may be especially true when it comes to deciding whom one can trust, how much, and under what conditions. As the former governor of Texas, John Connolly, once mused, in response to a query regarding President Lyndon Johnson's seeming paranoia as president, "We often hear that someone worries too much. But in some fields, you can't worry too much, especially if worrying means recognizing that things may [go] wrong and planning how to deal with these inevitable setbacks. Those blissful souls who speed so self-confidently along life's straight, smooth highway are often the ones who end up in the ditch when the road suddenly veers" (quoted in Grubin 1991).

By maintaining a heightened, even if (to others) misplaced or exaggerated, sensitivity to the interpersonal dangers that surround them, individuals can maintain their alertness and focus. As J. David Lewis and Andrew Weigert (1985, 969) note in this regard, distrust and suspicion help reduce complexity and uncertainty in social life by "dictating a course of action based on suspicion, monitoring, and activation of institutional safeguards." Along similar lines, the former presidential aide and speechwriter Richard Goodwin (1988, 398) once observed that a predisposition toward paranoia can help individuals remain "on the alert—observing and listening—to discern the hidden intentions of others—their concealed ambitions, weaknesses, greeds, and lusts."

Of course, at the very heart of the sense-making predicament confronting individuals embedded in trust dilemmas of this sort is not simply *whether* to trust or distrust others but also, and especially, *how much* trust and distrust are appropriate in a given situation. In this regard, it is interesting to view the final months in the life of the writer Ernest Hemingway as a cautionary tale. Late in his life, Hemingway began to display many of the classic symptoms of clinical paranoia. He claimed, for example, that the Federal Bureau of Investigation was intercepting his mail and tapping his phone lines. "It's the worst hell. The god damnedest hell," he confided to friend A. E. Hotchner. "They've bugged everything. That's why we're using Duke's car. Mine's bugged. Everything's bugged. Can't use the phone. What put me on to it was that phone call with you. You remember we got disconnected? That tipped their hand.... [Even my] mail [is being] intercepted." Hemingway was also convinced he was under surveillance by the FBI and was being followed by agents. Much to the dismay of his wife and drinking companions, he would sometimes point out various men in dark suits who, he asserted, were FBI agents sent by J. Edgar Hoover to follow his movements and harass him. On one occasion, when friends tried to reassure him that two men sitting across a bar where he was drinking were simply salesmen having a drink, Hemingway angrily retorted, "Of course [they'd say] they're salesmen. The FBI is noted for its clumsy disguises. What do you think they'd pose as—concert violinists?" (Hotchner 1966, 231, 232).

At the time, Hemingway's claims, as well as the vehemence with which they were asserted, were viewed by psychiatrists treating him as compelling evidence of his clinical paranoia. To be sure, Hemingway was suffering from a variety of mental difficulties linked to depression, chronic alcohol abuse, painful physical ailments, and writer's block. However, several decades later, we now know that at least some of Hemingway's perceptions were veridical. Documents released under the Freedom of Information Act have revealed that, in fact, Hemingway was under FBI surveillance and that, at J. Edgar Hoover's instigation, the FBI was engaged in an intense program of surveillance. Moreover, the scope of this surveillance was greater than even Hemingway himself had imagined. Hemingway's FBI file was opened on October 8, 1942 (years before Hemingway even had begun to suspect he was under surveillance) and remained open thirteen years after his death (the last entry was dated January 25, 1974). The file contained 125 pages of single-spaced entries. As it turns out, even his Mayo Clinic phone was bugged (although his physicians viewed Hemingway's "paranoia" about hearing noises on his phone lines as proof of the validity of their diagnosis).

Such ironic realizations bring us full circle, back to what seemed, at the outset of this chapter, to be a fairly sharp distinction between rational and irrational forms of distrust and suspicion. When embedded in sense-making conundrums of the sort Hemingway and those around him struggled with, untangling truth from error with respect to trust is an enterprise often fraught with peril. Although more self-assured organizational perceivers may be bemused—and amused—by the ease with which their paranoid counterparts are lulled into a false sense of insecurity, just as easily they themselves may underestimate the concealed dangers lurking in their organizational environment. They press nonchalantly onward, much like the smug but unknowingly imperiled character in the Brecht play who "laughed because he thought that they could not hit him—he did not imagine they were practicing how to miss him" (cited in Watzlawick, Beavin, and Jackson 1967, 137).

It is this possibility, of course, that draws attention to the other edge of the sword of suspicion. As David Shapiro (1965, 55–58) aptly notes, "Suspicious thinking is unrealistic only in some ways. . . . In others, it may be sharply perceptive. . . . Suspicious people are not simply people who are apprehensive and 'imagine things.' They are, in fact, extremely keen and often penetrating observers. They not only imagine, but also *search*." In his rich and evocative study of the Sicilian Mafia, Diego Gambetta documents how, in such a world, everything must be scrutinized—even luck. For, as Gambetta notes, "there is nothing as suspicious as luck" (Gambetta 1993, 224).

Karl Weick's (1995) thoughtful meditation on the nature of wisdom offers a balanced perspective on how to navigate on the edge of this judgmental razor. In defining wisdom, he quotes John Meacham (1983, 134): "To be wise is not to know particular facts but to know without excessive confidence or excessive cautiousness." Such wisdom, according to Meacham (1983, 134), is best conceptualized as "an attitude taken by persons toward the beliefs, values, knowledge, information, abilities, and skills that are held, a tendency to doubt that these are necessarily true or valid and to doubt that they are an exhaustive set of those things that could be known." As Weick (1995, 134) goes on to elaborate, "Extreme confidence and extreme caution both can destroy. . . . Wisdom . . .

avoids extremes and improves adaptability." In a world of uncertain threats and concealed dangers, a little paranoia can be more than a little prudent, it can even be rational.

A preliminary version of these ideas was presented at the Bellagio Conference on Distrust and Suspicion, Bellagio, Italy, 1997. I am grateful to Marilynn Brewer, Russell Hardin, and David Messick for their contributions to the development of these ideas.

References

Ashford, Susan J. 1989. "Self-assessments in Organizations: A Literature Review and Integrative Model." In *Research in Organizational Behavior*, edited by Larry L. Cummings and Barry M. Staw, vol. 11. Greenwich, Conn.: JAI Press.

Ashforth, Blake E., and Fred Mael. 1989. "Social Identity Theory and the Organization." *Academy of Management Review* 14(1): 20–39.

Barber, Bernard. 1983. *The Logic and Limits of Trust*. New Brunswick, N.J.: Rutgers University Press.

Bies, Robert J. 1987. "The Predicament of Injustice: The Management of Moral Outrage." In *Research in Organizational Behavior*, edited by Larry L. Cummings and Barry M. Staw, vol. 9. Greenwich, Conn.: JAI Press.

Bies, Robert J., Thomas M. Tripp, and Roderick M. Kramer. 1996. "At the Breaking Point: Cognitive and Social Dynamics of Revenge in Organizations." In *Antisocial Behavior in Organizations*, edited by Jerald Greenberg and Robert Giacalone. Thousand Oaks, Calif.: Sage Publications.

Blake, Robert R., and Jane J. Mouton. 1986. "From Theory to Practice in Interface Problem Solving." In *Psychology of Intergroup Relations*, edited by Stephen Worchel and William G. Austin. 2nd ed. Chicago: Nelson-Hall.

Boyle, Richard, and Phillip Bonacich. 1970. "The Development of Trust and Mistrust in Mixed-Motives Games." *Sociometry* 33(2, June): 123–39.

Brewer, Marilynn B. 1979. "Ingroup Bias in the Minimal Intergroup Situation: A Cognitive-Motivational Analysis." *Psychological Bulletin* 86: 307–24.

———. 1981. "Ethnocentrism and Its Role in Interpersonal Trust." In *Scientific Inquiry and the Social Sciences*, edited by Marilynn B. Brewer and Barry E. Collins. New York: Jossey-Bass.

———. 1996. "In-group Favoritism: The Subtle Side of Intergroup Discrimination." In *Codes of Conduct: Behavioral Research into Business Ethics*, edited by David M. Messick and Ann E. Tenbrunsel. New York: Russell Sage Foundation.

Brewer, Marilynn B., and Donald T. Campbell. 1976. *Ethnocentrism and Intergroup Attitudes: East African Evidence*. New York: Halsted.

Brewer, Marilynn B., and Roderick M. Kramer. 1985. "Intergroup Relations." *Annual Review of Psychology* 36: 219–43.

Brown, Jonathan D. 1986. "Evaluation of Self and Others: Self-enhancement Biases in Social Judgment." *Social Cognition* 4: 343–53.

———. 1991. "Accuracy and Bias in Self-knowledge." In *Handbook of Social and Clinical Psychology: The Health Perspective*, edited by C. R. Snyder and Donelson F. Forsyth. New York: Pergamon.

Brown, Jonathan D., and Keith A. Dutton. 1995. "Truth and Consequences: The Costs and Benefits of Accurate Self-knowledge." *Personality and Social Psychology Bulletin* 21(12): 1288–98.

Buss, Daniel M., and Michael F. Scheier. 1976. "Self-consciousness, Self-awareness, and Self-attribution." *Journal of Research in Personality* 10: 463–68.

Cameron, Norman. 1943. "The Development of Paranoiac Thinking." *Psychological Review* 50: 219–33.

Campbell, Donald T. 1975. "On the Conflict Between Biological and Social Evolution and Between Psychology and Moral Tradition." *American Psychologist* 30: 1103–26.

Carnevale, Peter, and Dean G. Pruitt. 2000. *Negotiation in Social Conflict*. 2nd ed. Buckingham, U.K.: Open University Press.

Colby, Kenneth M. 1981. "Modeling a Paranoid Mind." *Behavioral and Brain Sciences* 4(4): 515–60.

Cota, Albert A., and Kenneth L. Dion. 1986. "Salience of Gender and Sex Composition of Ad Hoc Groups: An Experimental Test of Distinctiveness Theory." *Journal of Personality and Social Psychology* 50: 770–76.

Dawes, Robyn M., David Singer, and Frank Lemons. 1972. "An Experimental Analysis of the Contrast Affect and Its Implications for Intergroup Communication and the Indirect Assessment of Attitude." *Journal of Personality and Social Psychology* 21: 281–95.

Deutsch, Morton. 1973. *The Resolution of Conflict*. New Haven, Conn.: Yale University Press.

Etzioni, Amit. 1967. "The Kennedy Experiment." *Western Political Quarterly* 20: 12–23.

Fein, Steven, and James L. Hilton. 1994. "Judging Others in the Shadow of Suspicion." *Motivation and Emotion* 18(2): 167–98.

Fenigstein, Alan. 1979. "Self-consciousness, Self-attention, and Social Interaction." *Journal of Personality and Social Psychology* 37: 75–86.

———. 1984. "Self-consciousness and Self as Target." *Journal of Personality and Social Psychology* 47: 860–70.

Fenigstein, Alan, and Paul A. Vanable. 1992. "Paranoia and Self-consciousness." *Journal of Personality and Social Psychology* 62: 129–38.

Fiske, Susan T. 1993. "Controlling Other People: The Impact of Power on Stereotypes." *American Psychologist* 48: 621–28.

Fox, Alan. 1974. *Beyond Contract: Power and Trust Relations*. London: Faber and Faber.

Gambetta, Diego. 1987. *Trust: Making and Breaking Cooperative Relations*. Cambridge, U.K.: Oxford University Press.

———. 1993. *The Sicilian Mafia: The Business of Private Protection*. Cambridge, Mass.: Harvard University Press.

Goodwin, Richard. 1988. *Remembering America*. New York: Harper & Row.

Grove, Andrew. 1996. *Only the Paranoid Survive: How to Survive the Crisis Points That Challenge Every Career*. New York: Doubleday.

Grubin, David. 1991. *LBJ*. VHS. Written and produced by David Grubin. Alexandria, Va.: PBS Public Broadcasting Service Videos.

Heider, Fritz. 1958. *The Psychology of Interpersonal Relations*. Hillsdale, N.J.: Lawrence Erlbaum.
Hill, Linda A. 1992. *Becoming a Manager*. Cambridge, Mass.: Harvard Business School.
Hilton, James L., Steven Fein, and Dale T. Miller. 1993. "Suspicion and Dispositional Inference." *Personality and Social Psychology Bulletin* 19(5): 501–12.
Hotchner, A. E. 1966. *Papa Hemingway*. New York: Scribners.
Janis, Irving L. 1989. *Crucial Decisions*. New York: Free Press.
Janoff-Bulman, Ronnie. 1992. *Shattered Assumptions: Towards a New Psychology of Trauma*. New York: Free Press.
Kahn, Robert L. 1990. "Organizational Theory and International Relations." In *Organizations and Nation-States: New Perspectives on Conflict and Cooperation*, edited by Robert L. Kahn and Mayer N. Zald. San Francisco: Jossey-Bass.
Kahn, Robert L., and Roderick M. Kramer. 1990. "Untying the Knot: De-escalatory Processes in International Conflict." In *Organizations and Nation-States: New Perspectives on Conflict and Cooperation*, edited by Robert L. Kahn and Mayer N. Zald. San Francisco: Jossey-Bass.
Kanter, Rosabeth. 1977a. *Men and Women of the Corporation*. New York: Basic Books.
———. 1977b. "Some Effects of Proportions on Group Life: Skewed Sex Rations and Responses to Token Women." *American Journal of Sociology* 82(5, March): 965–90.
Keashly, Loraleigh, Roger J. Fisher, and Peter R. Grant. 1993. "The Comparative Utility of Third-Party Consultation and Mediation in a Complex Intergroup Conflict." *Human Relations* 46(3): 371–93.
Kelley, Harold H. 1973. "Causal Schemata and the Attribution Process." *American Psychologist* 28: 107–23.
Kelman, Herb C. 1985. "Overcoming the Barrier." *Negotiation Journal* 1: 213–35.
Kennedy, Robert F. 1969. *Thirteen Days*. New York: Norton.
Kramer, Roderick M. 1994. "The Sinister Attribution Error: Origins and Consequences of Collective Paranoia." *Motivation and Emotion* 18(2): 199–230.
———. 1995a. "Divergent Realities, Convergent Disappointments: Trust and the Intuitive Auditor." In *Trust in Organizations*, edited by Roderick M. Kramer and Tom R. Tyler. Thousand Oaks, Calif.: Sage Publications.
———. 1995b. "In Dubious Battle: Heightened Accountability, Dysphoric Cognition, and Self-defeating Bargaining Behavior." In *Negotiation in Its Social Context*, edited by Roderick M. Kramer and David M. Messick. Thousand Oaks, Calif.: Sage Publications.
Kramer, Roderick M., and Marilynn B. Brewer. 1986. "Social Group Identity and the Emergence of Cooperation in Resource Conservation Dilemmas." In *Experimental Studies of Social Dilemmas*, edited by Henk Wilke, Christal Rutte, and David M. Messick. Frankfurt, Ger.: Lang.
Latane, Bibb, and John M. Darley. 1968. *The Unresponsive Bystander*. New York: Century Crofts.
Lazarus, Richard S., and Susan A. Folkman. 1984. *Stress, Appraisal, and Coping*. New York: Springer.
Lewis, J. David, and Andrew Weigert. 1985. "Trust as a Social Reality." *Social Forces* 63(4, June): 967–85.

Lind, E. Allan, and Tom R. Tyler. 1988. *The Social Psychology of Procedural Justice*. New York: Plenum.

Lindskold, Svenn. 1978. "Trust Development, the GRIT Proposal, and the Effects of Conciliatory Acts on Conflict and Cooperation." *Psychological Bulletin* 85: 772–93.

———. 1986. "GRIT: Reducing Distrust Through Carefully Introduced Conciliation." In *Psychology of Intergroup Relations*, edited by Stephen Worchel and William G. Austin. Chicago: Nelson Hall.

Lord, Charles G., Mark Lepper, and Lee Ross. 1979. "Biased Assimilation and Attitude Polarization: The Effects of Prior Theories on Subsequently Considered Evidence." *Journal of Personality and Social Psychology* 37: 2098–2109.

Lord, Charles G., and David S. Saenz. 1985. "Memory Deficits and Memory Surfeits: Differential Cognitive Consequences of Tokenism for Tokens and Observers." *Journal of Personality and Social Psychology* 49: 918–26.

Luhmann, Niklas. 1979. *Trust and Power*. New York: John Wiley.

Lyubomirsky, Susan, and Susan Nolen-Hoeksema. 1993. "Self-perpetuating Properties of Dysphoric Rumination." *Journal of Personality and Social Psychology* 65: 339–49.

Meacham, John A. 1983. "Wisdom and the Context of Knowledge: Knowing That One Doesn't Know." In *On the Development of Developmental Psychology*, edited by Deanna Kuhn and John A. Meacham. Basel, Switz.: Karger.

Messick, David M., Henk Wilke, Marilynn B. Brewer, Roderick M. Kramer, Patricia Zemke, and Layton Lui. 1983. "Individual Adaptations and Structural Changes as Solutions to Social Dilemmas." *Journal of Personality and Social Psychology* 44: 294–309.

Miller, Gary J. 1992. *Managerial Dilemmas: The Political Economy of Hierarchies*. New York: Cambridge University Press.

Morris, Michael W., and Richard P. Larrick. 1995. "When One Cause Casts Doubt on Another: A Normative Analysis of Discounting in Causal Attribution." *Psychological Review* 102: 331–35.

Norem, Julie K., and Nancy Cantor. 1986. "Defensive Pessimism: Harnessing Anxiety as Motivation." *Journal of Personality and Social Psychology* 51: 1208–17.

Osgood, Charles E. 1962. *An Alternative to War and Surrender*. Champaign, Ill.: University of Illinois Press.

Peeters, Guido, and Janusz Czapinski. 1990. "Positive-Negative Asymmetry in Evaluations: The Distinction Between Affective and Informational Negativity Effects." In W. Stroebe and M. Hewstone, eds., *European Review of Social Psychology* 1: 33–60.

Pruitt, Dean G., and Jeffrey Z. Rubin. 1986. *Social Conflict: Escalation, Stalemate, and Settlement*. New York: Random House.

Rotter, Julian B. 1967. "A New Scale for the Measurement of Interpersonal Trust." *Journal of Personality* 35: 651–55.

———. 1980. "Interpersonal Trust, Trustworthiness, and Gullibility." *American Psychologist* 35: 1–7.

Salancik, Gerald R., and Jeffrey Pfeffer. 1978. "A Social Information Processing Approach to Job Attitudes and Task Design." *Administrative Science Quarterly* 23: 224–53.

Schelling, Thomas C. 1958. "The Strategy of Conflict: Prospectus for a Reorientation of Game Theory." *Journal of Conflict Resolution* 2: 203–64.

Sedikides, Constantine. 1993. "Assessment, Enhancement and Verification Determinants of the Self-evaluation Process." *Journal of Personality and Social Psychology* 65: 317–38.
Shapiro, David. 1965. *Neurotic Styles*. New York: Basic Books.
Sherif, Muzafer, O. J. Harvey, B. Jack White, William R. Hood, and Carolyn W. Sherif. 1961. *Intergroup Cooperation and Competition: The Robbers' Cave Experiment*. Norman, Okla.: University Book Exchange.
Strube, Michael J., Cynthia L. Lott, G. M. Le-Xuan-Hy, Julie Oxenberg, and Ann K. Deichmann. 1986. "Self-evaluation of Abilities: Accurate Self-assessment Versus Biased Self-enhancement." *Journal of Personality and Social Psychology* 51: 16–25.
Strube, Michael J., and Laurie A. Roemmele. 1985. "Self-enhancement, Self-assessment, and Self-evaluative Task Choice." *Journal of Personality and Social Psychology* 49: 981–93.
Sumner, William G. 1906. *Folkways*. Boston: Ginn.
Swann, William, and Stephen Read. 1981. "Self-verification Processes: How We Sustain Our Self-conceptions." *Journal of Experimental Social Psychology* 17: 351–72.
Taylor, Shelley E. 1981. "A Categorization Approach to Stereotyping." In *Cognitive Processes in Stereotyping and Intergroup Behavior*, edited by D. L. Hamilton. Hillsdale, N.J.: Lawrence Erlbaum.
———. 1991. "Asymmetric Effects of Positive and Negative Events: The Mobilization-Minimization Hypothesis." *Psychological Bulletin* 110(1): 67–85.
Taylor, Shelley E., and Jonathan D. Brown. 1988. "Illusion and Well-being: A Social Psychological Perspective on Mental Health." *Psychological Bulletin* 103: 193–210.
———. 1994. "Positive Illusions and Well-being Revisited: Separating Fact from Fiction." *Psychological Bulletin* 116(1): 21–27.
Taylor, Shelley E., Susan T. Fiske, Nancy L. Etcoff, and Audrey Ruderman. 1978. "Categorical Bases of Person Memory and Stereotyping." *Journal of Personality and Social Psychology* 36: 778–93.
Tesser, Abraham. 1978. "Self-generated Attitude Change." In *Advances in Experimental Social Psychology*, edited by L. Berkowitz, vol. 11. San Diego, Calif.: Academic Press.
Trivers, Robert L. 1971. "The Evolution of Reciprocal Altruism." *Quarterly Review of Biology* 46(4): 35–37.
Trope, Yacob. 1983. "Self-assessment in Achievement Behavior." In *Psychological Perspectives on the Self*, edited by Jerry M. Suls and Anthony G. Greenwald, vol. 2. Hillsdale, N.J.: Lawrence Erlbaum.
———. 1986. "Self-enhancement and Self-assessment in Achievement Behavior." In *Handbook of Motivation and Cognition: Foundations of Social Behavior*, edited by Robin M. Sorrentino and E. Tory Higgins, vol. 1. New York: Guilford.
Tsui, Anne S., Terri D. Egan, and Charles O'Reilly. 1992. "Being Different: Relational Demography and Organizational Attachment." *Administrative Science Quarterly* 37: 549–79.
Turner, John. 1987. *Rediscovering the Social Group: A Self-categorization Theory*. Oxford, U.K.: Basil Blackwell.

Tyler, Tom R. 1993. "The Social Psychology of Authority." In *Social Psychology in Organizations: Advances in Theory and Practice*, edited by J. Keith Murnighan. Englewood Cliffs, N.J.: Prentice-Hall.

Tyler, Tom R., and E. Allan Lind. 1992. "A Relational Model of Authority in Groups." In *Advances in Experimental Social Psychology*, edited by Mark Snyder, vol. 25. New York: Academic Press.

Vorauer, John D., and Michael Ross. 1993. "Making Mountains Out of Molehills: An Informational Goals Analysis of Self- and Social Perception." *Personality and Social Psychology Bulletin* 19: 620–32.

Watzlawick, Paul, Janet H. Beavin, and Donald D. Jackson. 1967. *Pragmatics of Human Communication: A Study of Interactional Patterns, Pathologies, and Paradoxes*. New York: W. W. Norton.

Weick, Karl E. 1995. *Sensemaking in Organizations*. Thousand Oaks, Calif.: Sage Publications.

Wharton, Ann S. 1992. "The Social Construction of Gender and Race in Organizations: A Social Identity and Group Mobilization Perspective." In *Research in the Sociology of Organizations*, vol. 1, edited by Samuel Bacharach and Edward J. Lawler. Greenwich, Conn.: JAI Press.

Wilson, Edward O. 1978. *On Human Nature*. New York: Bantam Books.

Wilson, Timothy D., and Dolores Kraft. 1993. "Why Do I Love Thee? Effects of Repeated Introspections About a Dating Relationship on Attitudes Towards the Relationship." *Personality and Social Psychology Bulletin* 19(4): 409–18.

Wood, Joanne V., and Kathryn L. Taylor. 1991. "Serving Self-relevant Goals Through Social Comparison." In *Social Comparison: Contemporary Theory and Research*, edited by Jerry Suls and T. A. Wills. Hillsdale, N.J.: Lawrence Erlbaum.

Worchel, Stephen, and William G. Austin. 1986. *Psychology of Intergroup Relations*. Chicago: Nelson-Hall.

Zimbardo, Philip G., Susan M. Andersen, and Loren Kabat. 1981. "Induced Hearing Deficit Generates Experimental Paranoia." *Science* 212: 1529–31.

Chapter 7

Compensating for Distrust Among Kin

Margaret L. Brown

In a 1973 study of "fictive kinship" among the Merina of Madagascar, Maurice Bloch compares labor exchanges among fictive kin with exchanges among "blood" kin. Contrary to his expectations, the Merina relied on fictive kin more often than on blood kin when seeking agricultural laborers. " 'Real' kinsmen would always come," a villager said, whereas " 'artificial' kinsmen would only come if one kept up the typical kinship behaviour of repeated requests for help. If one did not do so these 'artificial' kinsmen would lapse" (Bloch 1973, 79). "Real" kin were reliable over the long term without needing to be called frequently into action, but fictive kin needed regular, short-term activation lest they forgot the existence and meaning of their exchange relationship.

Real kin in Bloch's study were reliable because of the strength of the moral bond of their relationship. This allowed them to invest time and energy in creating and maintaining relationships beyond the family. In some situations, though, the "moral bond" of kinship cannot be taken for granted and therefore cannot provide the foundation upon which individuals can systematically create relationships of trust with nonkin. Like Bloch, I base my analysis in this chapter on the view that people will expend energy and resources trying to stabilize weak but important ties. In the villages of my study, situated on the Masoala Peninsula on Madagascar's northeast coast, people invest much more heavily in "real" kin relations than in any other type of relationship because the strength of family ties is so uncertain and because family ties provide the central means of access to important types of social, political, and economic resources. For these people, unlike those in Bloch's study, the need to invest in these crucial "real" kin ties so consumes people that they have developed few mechanisms for establishing trust among nonkin.[1] Indeed, the villagers I studied avoid even creating the types of fictive kin relations described by Bloch, claiming they are too costly to establish and of little worth.

In the analysis that follows, trust is understood as the willingness to accept risk based upon stable, positive expectations of a partner's intentions. The problem for social actors is to determine which partners are worthy of trust and in what realms they should be trusted.[2] This is true of kin as well as nonkin, although much writing on trust treats kinship as a special category of relations in which trust is assumed. Many analyses of trust-based relationships suggest that relations among family members are the social relationships most likely to be characterized by trust.[3] To understand why this might be the case, I refer here to two of the more distinct ways of understanding trust in society more generally and apply these approaches to an understanding of family relations. One view is that trust is fundamentally normative, or moral. The other is that trust is fundamentally rational.[4]

Consistent with the normative view of trust is the view that family relations are "moral" relations, in which individuals are expected to share "without reckoning" (Fortes 1969, 1987). In his influential analyses of family relations, the anthropologist Meyer Fortes (1983, 23) considers kinship to be governed by the norm of prescriptive altruism, which he defines as "a rule of conduct that implies recognition of binding mutual interdependence and willingness to forgo what we would regard as selfish gratification for the sake of others." Those analysts who focus on family relations as morally binding emphasize the second part of Fortes's definition—the willingness to forgo self-interest for the sake of another—as the basis of trust within the family. For example, in his book, *Trust: The Social Virtues and the Creation of Prosperity*, Francis Fukuyama frequently invokes the trust that naturally occurs within the family. He writes that family enterprises can thrive in China "because their cohesion is based on the moral and emotional bonds of a pre-existing social group" (Fukuyama 1995, 63). These predetermined moral bonds are supposed to explain why much of social life in many societies is organized around kin-based networks.

Reference to morality implies that the reason kinship coordinates cooperation in these societies is that cooperative endeavors, when supported by morality, require little additional effort; they occur naturally. In Fukuyama's study, in which family bonds are less strong and individuals less bound by a familial "ethos" (such as in Japan, according to his analysis), family members have opportunities and incentives to build trust outside the family. Ultimately, the strength of family ties and the morality (or ethos) of those bonds impede the extension of networks beyond the family. Thus for Fukuyama and others who share his views, familism, or a preoccupation with family ties, is based upon a moral connection (Banfield 1958; Putnam 1993; Yamagishi and Yamagishi 1994).

Some theorists of trust, however, have developed a second line of reasoning that does not rely on ethos or nature and can also be applied to family relations. The arguments put forth by these theorists are more in keeping with the first part of Fortes's definition of prescriptive altruism: "recognition of binding mutual interdependence." Focus on the *recognition* of interdependence moves one from an understanding of trust based in morality to an understanding based in rationality. Russell Hardin's (1993, 1997, 2002) work has most clearly developed this view of trust. In his analysis, if I trust, this means I believe that the trustee's interests encapsulate my own. This could be for any number of reasons. For example, one reason trust might occur more frequently among family members is that they may experience more situations in which their interests coincide simply because of the structural position they share relative to other persons or institutions in their society. It is important to recognize, however, that similar processes must occur in dealing with kin or with nonkin. If I am going to take a risk by cooperating with another person, I must look for indicators of that person's trustworthiness, and that person must find ways to signal to me his or her trustworthiness. Recognition that such processes occur among family members as well as among strangers seems to be missing from much of the literature on trust.[5]

The three cases presented in this chapter show that relying on a moral definition of trust is insufficient even when attempting to understand family relations. Two of the cases focus on processes through which those who wish to be trusted within an environment of widespread distrust attempt to secure the trust of others. In these cases, it is quite clear that the parties involved are aware that they are in mutually dependent positions that nevertheless rest on shaky ground. The third case focuses on the strategies pursued by family members when mutual trust cannot be achieved. All three cases highlight practices that have the effect of setting constraints on realms of interaction, effectively limiting the possibilities for exploitation by untrustworthy family members.

In each of the cases examined here, individuals are engaged in processes of compensating for the distrust that permeates their everyday lives by drawing on available cultural and social resources. They use these resources to construct mechanisms both to facilitate trust in particular types of interactions and to protect themselves from untrustworthy behavior in other interactions. At times, both processes can be seen operating in a single relationship, showing how complex the creation and management of trust can be. One of the points that I hope to make clear through analysis of these cases is the importance of understanding the social and cultural context within which beliefs about risk and trustworthiness are formed. It is in regards to these issues that much of the literature on trust has underanalyzed the relevance of family relations for understanding the development of trust.[6]

It is true that in some contexts, simply knowing that A is a close family member may be enough to encourage me to take risks with her. In those contexts, the relevant signaling mechanisms are simply those that let me know she is family of sufficient closeness to provide me with security in interactions with her. However, what allows me to trust A in this setting is not simply our blood relationship. It is primarily the social norms that I believe guide her behavior in the relationship.[7] Thus besides knowing that A is my kin I will also seek some sort of signals that let me know that she actually subscribes to those norms that I believe would sanction her were she to betray my trust. I believe this is true in all family interactions. The differences lie in the degree to which people initially distrust family, for whatever reasons, and the associated level of risk connected to familial interactions. In all cases, any assessment of the risk involved in a potential interaction must take into account the social and cultural resources all parties have to draw on in signaling and interpreting their intentions toward one another.

The Context of Distrust

In the pages that follow, I present three case studies that show family members attempting to overcome mistrust. These cases all occurred in the villages of Ambatobe and Tanambao, on the northeast coast of Madagascar. One involves a man trying to reestablish trust after betraying his wife. The second is more routine, involving the mechanisms one family has developed to protect property relations among siblings. The third case involves intergenerational conflict between a father and daughter. While no single case study can be entirely representative of all the variation that occurs in everyday social interactions, the combination of the three presented here does provide a view of a range of possible dilemmas and resolutions villagers face. The most unusual case, that of the married couple, exemplifies, through their breach, the informational potential of widely followed social norms, while the most common case, that of the property transactions among siblings, demonstrates the ways that a more widespread trust in an impersonal form of exchange facilitates an otherwise risky transaction among kin.

Three features of life in the villages of Ambatobe and Tanambao make establishing trust among kin a central focus for most villagers. First, kin ties, particularly to elders, provide access to important economic, social, political, and spiritual resources in the local arena. Regarding economic resources, even renting and sharecropping of land most frequently occurs between kin, while inheritance necessarily involves acknowledgment of kinship obligations. Furthermore, elder kin often use gifts and loans of land to mark their commitment to their junior kin and to attempt to extract reciprocal displays of commitment from those kin. In addition to land access, many labor exchanges are also based upon the activation of kinship ties. Perhaps most important, appeals for ancestral intervention always involve elder kin.

The second important feature of village life that makes kinship a focal point for villagers is the weakness or scarcity of other institutions, formal or informal, that might substitute for kin ties should they fail to provide support and security. As mentioned earlier, most labor and land access is provided through kin networks. Although a few villagers rely heavily on wage or salaried work, none is entirely sustained by performing such labor.[8] All households engage in subsistence agriculture for the bulk of their livelihood, cash crops and paid labor providing supplementary income.[9] These villages are relatively remote, with no vehicular access by land and only irregular access by boat. The central town in the region is approximately twenty-five miles north of these villages. No villagers regularly seek work in this town. A few villagers travel daily or weekly to work on a palm plantation about ten miles south of the village. None of those villagers is a head of household, most being dependent children of villagers.

The other wage work performed by villagers is seasonal, involving ebony collecting for an exporter in town. Thus market institutions do not provide a reliable alternative to kin-based access to land and labor. In terms of legal institutions, all forms of dispute resolution in these villages are based upon the belief that kin should provide the primary support for those seeking justice. Before bringing a dispute to village administrative authorities, a villager must first seek assistance from his or her senior kin. Only after satisfying this expectation can villagers take disputes to the local court. Even at this level, however, much of the decision making may rest on arguments made by elders on behalf of their junior kin.

Related to the weakness and scarcity of non-kin-based formal and informal institutions is the general insignificance in these villages of ethnic or other status-based collective identities. This is an important feature of local life because it means that there is no identity beyond kinship that carries social meaning and that might thus provide an alternative or supplementary means of access to local resources. In many other regions of Madagascar, ethnic and class distinctions have become central to social, political, and economic institutions that grant privileges and protection to those members of society who are identified with a particular group while stigmatizing or otherwise discriminating against members of other groups. This phenomenon is not apparent in Ambatobe and Tanambao. This is partially owing to the historical development of the region.

Among the most represented ethnic groups in the region are the Betsimisaraka, who have always been loosely organized with no strong leadership. In addition, the Masoala Peninsula was populated relatively late and by a mixture of people coming from many different regions of Madagascar. Thus no single ethnic group established early control of political and economic resources.

The uncertainty of kin ties is the third feature, besides kin-based access to resources and the absence of other, non-kinship-oriented institutions, that explains why establishing trust among kin is of such great importance to villagers. Relations between children and their parents and other elders are not automatically assured to be mutually supportive. While this is probably true in most societies, uncertainty runs particularly high here for two reasons. First, bilateral reckoning of descent provides children with a number of elders in both the maternal and paternal lines who might provide support.[10] This means that both children and elders have some choices regarding which relationships among their kin they are going to try to strengthen and which they might be willing to let drop. A parent, for example, might show preference for one child over another by granting a gift of land to one while encouraging the other to move elsewhere for their sustenance. A child might indicate his preference for one elder over another by continuing to follow the ancestral food taboos of one while abandoning those of another. In each case, the actions provide information regarding either the assessed or the desired strength of particular kin ties.

A second reason for the uncertainty among kin is the instability of male-female unions and the frequency of what in the United States would be called "blended families." Half of the women in Ambatobe and Tanambao have divorced at least once.[11] Meanwhile, in 67 percent of current marriages, one or both of the partners has a child or children from a previous union. One implication of such household instability is anxiety over property rights. Once a father has acknowledged a child as his own, that child carries throughout his or her lifetime legitimate claims to use or inherit part of any property the father acquired on his own or through inheritance. The child has the same rights to his or her mother's property. Knowledge that potential claimants may return at any time to compete for familial property causes much anxiety between marital partners and among a couple's children. In many cases, this anxiety also prompts children to attempt to strengthen their relationships with their parents or other relevant elders. In doing so, signs of commitment on both sides of the relationship are important.

These three features—the centrality of kin relations, the weakness of other institutions, and the uncertainty of kin ties—shape the world within which villagers interact and attempt to form temporary and long-term alliances. In all instances, villagers are aware that they must establish reliable relationships with some close kin. Their lives depend on it. The problem for them is working out how to determine who is reliable and who is not and how to let their own commitments be known. The cases that follow serve to illuminate the complex ways these problems are worked out.

Conflict Between Husband and Wife

Marital or similar, but nonformalized, relations merit special consideration when discussing kinship. Typically, the literature addressing trust and kinship focuses on presumed "blood" relationships rather than on those based in choice. However, a long tradition in social scientific studies of households has assumed a deep level of integration within households, to the extent that a researcher could talk about a household as a single unit, with no need to specify the reasons behind the members' apparent cooperation on most household issues.[12] This type of study seems to be most congruent with approaches that emphasize the morality of kinship, as a shared pursuit of common interests is taken for granted rather than treated as a question for empirical study. However, recent approaches to household studies have disaggregated households, raising questions regarding how and why consensus is reached in determining the behavior of household members and examining the processes by which individuals pursue their separate interests within marriage.[13] These studies are most in keeping with the view of trust as rationally rather than morally based. For example, the bond that might inspire trust between husband and wife is their mutual recognition that the needs of each are more likely to be met through cooperative interaction with the other.[14] Because approaches to marital relations have so closely resembled approaches to other types of "consanguineal" kinship (kinship based in blood), I include this example as a particular subset of kin relations, based explicitly on choice.

Arnaud came from another village to marry his wife, a native of Tanambao. In the villages of the Masoala Peninsula, it is generally held in low esteem for a man to live off his wife's land; the ideal practice is for a woman to move to her husband's village after marriage. However, for a variety of reasons, Arnaud and his wife decided to live in her village, using land provided by her maternal kin. In order not to be completely dependent on his wife, Arnaud continued working as a salaried laborer in a village ten miles away. Instead of traveling there every day, Arnaud set up house near the work site, in a large village where he had family. He stayed in that village during the week, returning to Tanambao on weekends to be with his wife and children and to help with the farm labor.

Shortly after their marriage, Arnaud began a relationship with a woman in the village where he spent the weeknights. His wife found out and wanted to end their relationship. Although extramarital affairs are common among men in this region, women do not have boundless tolerance for them. Many wives say they are willing to accept such relationships so long as their husbands do not spend a lot of money on their girlfriends. In one discussion with a disgruntled wife, I was informed bluntly that if husbands gave only their bodies to other women, wives would not get upset; it was the clothes and jewelry given to girlfriends that brought them shame and caused jealousy. One way to keep men's extramarital affairs from getting out of control is to prevent husbands from having unfettered access to household money.

Indeed, in all but one of the 150 households in these villages, women control the money. Earnings from cash crops, wage labor, or craft work are placed in a joint pool and kept by the wife. A husband then has to ask his wife for money whenever he wants to buy something. He is expected to explain to her what he wants, and if she agrees to the purchase, she gives him the money. When the wife needs items for cooking or otherwise taking care of the household, she can simply take money from the household fund. Men and women both agree this is the best arrangement for managing their money because men tend to waste money. "If I had the money, I would lose it all on alcohol and women," is a common assertion made by men. Their wives agree. Thus the money-management norm in these villages has helped to decrease the extent to which women have to place trust in their husbands regarding household funds.

Nevertheless, money remains a constant source of tension for many couples, and the increasing availability of salaried labor and other cash-earning opportunities further complicates their relationships. With salaried labor (other than agricultural labor conducted for other villagers), money is often turned over to the worker at a distance from his home village. In some instances, it may require the worker to go to town to pick up a check or to cash a check at the bank. This type of remuneration presents many opportunities for the wage earner to spend the money before returning to the household. The wage earner can go to the bars in town and drink. He can shop at the stores and buy presents to attract women. This is, in fact, what seems to be causing most of the problems in the marriages of those few couples in which the husband works for a salary.[15] It also is a problem for some of the couples in which the husband earns a great deal of money collecting ebony on short-term contracts.

Sales of agricultural produce, such as coffee, cloves, or vanilla, are frequently made in the village to middle merchants who then resell the products in Antalaha. Many times these transactions are conducted in household courtyards. Thus wives are frequently present, if not in charge, when the sale is made. Even if the wife is not present at the time, she knows approximately how much of a crop they have harvested, and she can easily find out the selling price for the crop in the village that day. Therefore, the very process by which most of a household's cash is acquired has built into it the wife's ability to monitor the intake and thereby discourage any significant cheating on the part of the husband.[16] Furthermore, when cash is obtained in the village, there are fewer opportunities and incentives to spend it in ways that would anger wives. This is partly owing to the fact that there are only a few small shops in the villages. However, husbands rarely want to cause their wives to leave them. A man knows that if he were to purchase items for another woman in the village, the gossip would quickly get back to his wife, and he would find little support in the village for causing such public humiliation of his wife. Although men like to have external relationships, they generally try to avoid conducting them in ways that force their wives to acknowledge them.

Arnaud was one of those men who gathered a salary outside the village and had ample opportunity to spend it before returning home. Ultimately, he was trying to maintain two households, giving much of his paycheck to his girlfriend in the distant village while his wife and children worked hard during the week maintaining their rice fields and herding their cattle. His wife could no longer tolerate this imbalance between his household contributions and his household extractions, and she asked for divorce. Despite his wandering ways, Arnaud did not want to lose his wife, and he eventually persuaded her to reconcile. He stopped working in the distant village and began to spend most nights at home with his wife. They started to draw their livelihood primarily from their agricultural produce.

The form of Arnaud's reconciliation with his wife is of particular interest for the subject of this chapter. It is important to remember that in moving to his wife's village and relying on her land for his household's subsistence needs, Arnaud began this relationship in a disadvantageous bargaining position and signaled his inability to support himself comfortably without her. Thus his attempt to reconcile with her occurred within a context of their mutual awareness of the extent of his dependence upon her and a recognition that he had a great deal to lose were he to be caught in a lie.

Arnaud followed a two-part strategy designed to provide further evidence of the credibility of his commitment to his wife. First, he moved back home, thereby changing his access to outside income. This strategy clearly constrained his ability to establish costly relationships with other women. Second, drawing on his knowledge about the implications of widespread practices regarding food taboos, he altered his behavior in a way intended to signal his trustworthiness to his wife.

Food taboos have implications for every villager in Ambatobe and Tanambao. Each child comes into the world with two sets of taboos, one set from the mother and one from the father. These, in turn, can be traced back to preceding generations, so that people speak of carrying the taboos of eight ancestors (the maternal and paternal great-grandparents) as they have been passed down through their children. Having taboos in common is one way individuals recognize common ancestry and thereby a sense of mutual responsibility. The inverse can also be true: dissimilarity in taboo adherence between two individuals can be taken as a sign of their moral distance from one another. By following a particular set of taboos, a person lets it be known who or what is his or her ultimate source of authority.[17] Thus knowing about another's taboo observance helps individuals in a social relationship evaluate the extent to which they might expect their interests to be intertwined.

As mentioned earlier, marriages in these villages are inherently unstable. One practice that contributes to this instability is that married individuals persist in following the taboos of their own ancestors instead of merging their taboos into a common set. Married couples also maintain loyalties to their separate family lines in other ways. For example, each member of the couple keeps separate any property he or she brought into the marriage. They also maintain separate family cemeteries and plan to be buried with their respective fathers—not with one another—when they die. Taboo adherence is thus one among many ways married partners signal to one another where their primary loyalties lie. It is one of the most important ways, however, because of its impact on everyday life.

When a couple marries, they cease to prepare one another's taboo foods in the household kitchen, and they generally avoid eating the taboo foods in one another's presence. However, if either of them happens upon the spouse's taboo food in someone else's home, or at a roadside restaurant, each is free to consume it. When a woman becomes pregnant, she adopts the taboos of her child's father as soon as she is aware of the pregnancy and will continue to follow them until the time she stops breast-feeding. There is no complementary occasion requiring a husband to follow his wife's taboos. It is rare to have anyone suggest that it would be appropriate for a man to follow his wife's taboos beyond respecting them in her presence, in the presence of their children, and in their household. Since the child is never in a position of getting nourishment directly from the man's body, men do not have to be concerned with placing the child in danger.

It could be said that the unequal responsibilities for the child's well-being give men more freedom to be promiscuous. The fact that men never have to adopt the taboos of their wives or of their children's mothers makes it easier for men to have multiple relationships without having to pay a high cost in taboo observance. A woman, on the other hand, is under pressure to acknowledge the father of her child to ensure that she follows the appropriate taboos. Thus a wife who cheats on her husband and becomes pregnant physically bears the signs of that infidelity through her avoidance of particular foods associated with her child's father. It is more difficult for a woman to escape signs of her infidelity.

So what does all of this have to do with Arnaud? Although Arnaud reconciled with his wife and returned to their home to live, the damage had been done, and he knew he had lost some of her trust. Trying to think of ways to convince her that he truly was committed to her, he noted a pattern of behavior in the household of another troubled couple he knew. This couple fought all the time and eventually divorced. The husband, Arnaud said, never showed any respect for the wife, and he often went so far as to prepare her taboo foods in their joint kitchen. Arnaud saw this as part of the problem with that relationship and reflected on his own behavior. He realized that while he never brought his own wife's taboo foods into their household, he did eat them frequently. When he was living in the other village and working at the plantation, he regularly consumed many of her taboo foods.

Arnaud saw this as part of a larger pattern of disrespectful behavior toward his wife. Wanting to convince his wife that he was indeed committed to her, he believed that he would have to alter his behavior in some radical way. As a gesture of his sincerity he decided to adopt her food taboos. He avoided eating her taboo foods all the time, not only in her presence or in their household. This was an intriguing choice, since most men do not follow their wives' food taboos. Local norms certainly do not require it. However, local norms also do not require husbands to be faithful to their wives, and so simply showing himself to be a follower of the standard widespread norms regarding behavior in marriage would not have helped Arnaud in making his case to his wife. He had to convince her that he would be faithful beyond the level expected more broadly by husbands in these villages. Furthermore, owing to his own vulnerability and lack of choices outside of this marriage, his wife could expect him to be willing to make a greater sacrifice for her than would a man who had married in a more traditional way, by bringing his wife to live on his family's land.

Arnaud recognized that the failure to observe common taboos lends instability to a relationship. In seeking to prove to his wife that he would not again disrespect her, as he had in having an affair, he chose taboo observance as the symbol of his respect. That such observance is not expected between a man and wife gave force to his claim of commitment to her and his desire to do everything possible to ensure her well-being. Arnaud was drawing on widely shared cultural and social norms to show how he *differed* from the norm. In most households, it is taken for granted that the couple's commitment to one another goes only so far and that natal family always takes priority. It is also taken for granted that husbands will probably have affairs. This latter fact is often made clear in prenuptial contracts drawn up by marrying couples and their families. Because most spouses follow the norms, displaying their commitment to the dominant belief system, they are not placed in a position of wondering whether a spouse shares these beliefs. Observation of such commitment lends predictability to social interactions.

Between husbands and wives, sharing a value system does not imply the existence of deep trust. In fact, it signals to both parties the limits of their trustworthiness. This is precisely what gives Arnaud's action its meaning: by changing the content of his social behavior, he caused his wife to stop and interpret his actions. "What does this mean, that he is now following my taboos?" She may not have come to the conclusion he desired, but she was pushed, by the sheer anomaly of his behavior, to engage in a conscious process of interpretation. Having once been humiliated and taken advantage of, she would most likely require more convincing to trust a second time. For this reason, Arnaud had to make a move that showed he understood the meaning behind common, everyday practices. He then had to show that he considered his relationship with his wife to differ from the standard village relationships in which those practices were commonplace. His strategies appear to have worked in winning back her trust, as she relented and agreed to give their marriage a second chance.

Distrust Among Siblings

Belalahy is the eldest of his mother and father's children. Each of his parents died in recent years. The common practice in these villages is for children to share land acquired through inheritance. This is especially true of irrigated rice fields, which are economically unsuitable for division and also are imbued with spiritual significance. Sometimes this sharing goes on indefinitely, the number of individuals with nominal rights to the land increasing with each generation. Occasionally, this cycle is curtailed through a land sale, usually between coheirs. This is in keeping with another general trend, which is that most land transfers of any type are conducted between kin.

There are some good reasons why land sale between heirs might be advantageous. For example, because there are few villagewide associations in Ambatobe and Tanambao, villagers have a relatively lower level of systematic interaction with households and families of nonkin than with kin. They therefore have developed fewer mechanisms for establishing trust with nonkin. Sellers of land often continue to maintain some fields near those they are selling and are therefore reluctant to make neighbors of strangers, which might increase the possibility for conflict. Fields and plantations are often contiguous with those of other family members, meaning that a person has already had experience with how those family members behave regarding property issues such as boundaries, water management, and cattle herding in the vicinity. When inherited property is involved, sale always requires the consent of any coheirs to the land, and other family members may not allow sale to someone outside the family. In sum, the preference for selling to family may be rooted in experience with family and lack of experience with nonkin; it does not necessarily rest on any moral attachment to those family members.

In my first interview with Belalahy he mentioned having bought a large parcel of irrigated rice land from his siblings a few years back for 250,000 Malagasy francs.[18] He later explained that he had bought the land from his brothers and sisters because, as the eldest, he was the one among them with the most money. As a family, they were trying to gather the resources for their father's reburial ceremony. Children are expected to host a big feast in honor of their deceased parent four or five years after the death. They must butcher at least one steer to show proper respect for their ancestors. Additionally, they must supply enough alcoholic beverages to appropriately entertain many guests. These ceremonies are costly affairs, but they must be performed to avoid angering the ancestors and inviting ill fortune.

When preparing for such a feast, it is important that the children contribute in roughly equal amounts. This is why Belalahy did not simply spend the money on the ceremony or contribute the steer himself. Instead, his brothers and sisters exchanged part of their share of inherited family land for his money. This is a rather complicated way to reach their desired goal of acquiring a steer. The multistage process this family undertook reveals something about the types of relationships that exist among kin. On the surface, reburial and other such ceremonies have the appearance of representing the unified group interests of the family. However, this case sheds light on the underlying processes that serve to protect individual self-interest in the achievement of the ceremony. There is some sense in which the siblings involved are not so sure their interests converge.

The siblings' desire to have their transactions with one another be explicitly monetized is interesting. Why did they not simply have Belalahy buy the steer, since he had the cash, and then exchange the steer for the land? To answer this question, it helps to note that Belalahy has the upper hand in this relationship because he has the cash. The siblings know they must provide him with something in return for his contribution, and it is normal for that something to be land. However, they would like to control as much as possible the amount he can extract from them. Though no one ever said this to me, they might fear that if they let him buy the steer first, he would buy a more expensive one than the others could afford. They will then still be obliged to compensate him for the purchase. Why might he do this? One reason might be a desire to gain personal control of more of the family rice fields. By conducting the land exchange first, the less powerful brothers and sisters are able to exert greater control over the transaction and prevent Belalahy from using his greater power to extract more land from them than they want to give up.

Belalahy also has reasons to prefer that the exchange take place in cash. Aware of the greater power he holds in his relationship with his brothers and sisters, Belalahy might want to avoid the opportunity for any doubt to be cast on his integrity. Cash exchanges are more transparent than exchanges in kind. Once a price has been agreed on, there is no doubt about the comparable value of the items being exchanged. This is not true of exchanges in kind, which leave more room for doubt about comparative value. Moreover, the exchange of land for cash and then cash for the steer makes the exchanges less open ended: there is no need to rely on a promise of future repayment once a good is acquired. That is one of the advantages of having two stages of cash transactions.

Most villagers believe the type of transaction undertaken by Belalahy and his brothers and sisters is the best way for any type of exchange to occur. They all have more confidence in money than in any other medium of exchange. Of course, this would not seem especially noteworthy if this discussion were not about exchange among family members. When dealing with strangers, money does lessen the cost of exchange. However, in the general understanding, familial ties usually imply more trust. The moral, or normative, view of trust is the most common way of thinking about exchanges within the family. Under this conceptualization of family relations, exchanges are conceived as open ended or, in anthropological terms, characterized by generalized reciprocity (Sahlins 1972). Family members are generally expected to give freely to their kin and trust that they will be treated similarly by the other partner when she or he has the resources. In Tanambao and Ambatobe, the interesting fact is that villagers do not want to leave the exchange relationship unclosed between family members.

In this case, two different processes are at work through the use of cash transactions among kin. First, Belalahy's brothers and sisters use the sale of land to their brother as a means of protecting themselves from potential exploitation by him. By setting constraints on the terms of the exchange, they clarify the extent to which they are willing to accept risk when engaging in property transactions with him. Second, Belalahy uses the medium of cash as a way to reduce his siblings' uncertainty regarding his integrity in the land purchase. By agreeing to this transaction and purchasing the land in advance of the steer purchase, Belalahy sets constraints on his own ability to attempt to renegotiate the terms of the exchange in the future. He thereby makes himself more trustworthy.

Intergenerational Conflict

The next case involves a relationship that crosses generations. This case is somewhat different from the preceding ones in that it does not focus on people trying to establish their trustworthiness where they know it is not taken for granted, as in the cases of Arnaud and Belalahy. However, it is similar in that it involves the attempt to set constraints on possible exploitation or mistreatment by kin. In this case, a father and daughter have given up on trusting each other. Having reached this point, their behavior is now oriented toward protecting themselves and their children from the expected, and perhaps dangerous, untrustworthiness of the other.

Germaine is Claude's only child apart from those he has produced with his current wife. Germaine's mother and father never had a stable relationship together, and as a young child she was sent to be reared by her father's father. Her father took a wife with whom he has several children, some of whom are now adults starting their own households. Germaine married and moved to her husband's village. However, in the early 1990s, she and her husband and children moved back to Tanambao to help her ailing grandfather. She had been her grandfather's primary helper all her life, as his only child, Claude, has been inattentive to his father for much of his life.

Germaine's decision to move her entire family to Tanambao several years after she married is an interesting one. As mentioned earlier, it is highly undesirable for a man to move to his wife's village and live off her family land after marriage. Most women do not desire such a relationship any more than do men, so Germaine's decision to move can be interpreted as a serious sacrifice on her part, signaling her strong commitment to caring for her grandfather. Of course, the move also brought its rewards, and these may have been on her mind as well.

One of the conflicts between Claude and Germaine involves her grandfather's property. Some disputes have involved land, while others involve cattle. The primary point of dispute is that over the years, Claude's father has granted Germaine gifts of land and insisted that she be allowed to use some of the cattle that Claude herds for him. Claude resents this, claiming that she is taking property that rightfully should pass to him. As his father's only child, he feels that he should inherit all of his father's property and then should have the authority to decide how it is divided among his children for use during his lifetime. After his death, they will all inherit equally the land he received from his father.

Now Claude has decided that he will start making gifts of his own property to his other children before he dies. He wants to do this, he says, to avoid arguments among his children after his death. However, this is not entirely convincing. Many people worry that their children will argue over inherited property, yet few challenge local norms of succession by handing out land to their children before they die. In fact, a few elderly people told me they would never dream of giving their land to their future heirs before they died. Otherwise, they asked, how could they be sure their children would continue to help them out and show them respect in their old age? In the particular case of Claude, it is probable that he wants to hand out his land now to reduce the amount of land available to be shared by Germaine, his "zanaka ambelana,"[19] whom he and his wife now view as a competitor for his father's property. Upon his death, Germaine will have rights, along with Claude's other children, to any property he acquired before marriage and any land he inherits from his father.

Germaine clearly thinks that her father is maneuvering to prevent her from sharing in his wealth. When asked what she fears most for the future of her own children, she focuses on the fact that there is no one she trusts to take care of them and to see they get their due. Her grandfather is old, and she and her father have already had many arguments. There are times when she even fears her father, and she therefore worries that he will transfer his animosity toward her to her children.[20] For this reason, along with the problem of her husband's nonnative status, she and her family plan to move their household back to her husband's natal village after her grandfather's death.

As mentioned earlier in this chapter, elder villagers generally avoid making permanent gifts of land to their children. They explained this to me as though it were a kind of safety net, ensuring that their children would be bound to them until their death—and even afterward. On the Masoala Peninsula, when a parent dies, the property does not always pass immediately to the children. Often, inherited land is not divided among the children but is instead used by all of them through some sort of sharing plan. Moreover, whatever land is going to be divided—usually cash-crop plantations or hillside fields—frequently is not divided among the heirs until several years after the parent's death. During these years, the harvests from these fields as well as from the irrigated rice fields are intended to be used to prepare for the parent's reburial ceremony.

The reburial ceremony is perhaps the most important event in a parent-child relationship. In the villages of my research, as in other regions of Madagascar, elders derive their power and authority from the fact that they form a direct link to ancestors. Ancestors can be generous and giving, but they can also be unpredictably violent and vengeful (Cole 1996; Graeber 1995, 1996). Elders provide the mediating link between young kin and this powerful spiritual world. If one of their junior kin falls ill or suffers some other misfortune, an elder may be asked to appeal to their ancestors for help or forgiveness. However, it is also true that elders depend on their children and other close dependents to help them gain honor among the ancestors. The junior kin's role toward this end is to treat their elders with appropriate respect and to faithfully obey all ancestral rules, which reflects well on the training they received from their elders.

The relationship of mutual dependence affects the strategies elders and juniors adopt toward one another. As their children become adults and establish their own households and their own fields, parents recognize that their control over them becomes weaker. However, they can continue to control their children's access to ancestral lands and to already established cash-crop plantations. Thus most parents choose not to give cultivated land to their children. The gifts that parents do make tend to be gifts of fallow land, usually to sons, that the sons themselves plant in cash crops or rice. Such fields have little economic or spiritual significance relative to established plantations and "rizières" (rice fields). For their part, most children are eager to ensure that they in no way are cut out of the family patrimony. Therefore, the promise of property in the future helps to secure relations in the present.

It is in this context that Claude's actions and those of his father are to be understood. His father is going against the local norm by giving property directly to his granddaughter rather than leaving it all to be inherited by his son. This is partially because Claude did not appear to be committed to his father in his early adult years. Claude left home and led a fairly undisciplined life before being brought back to the village by his father. Relations between father and son have been strained for many years. Germaine has been loyal and has cared for her grandfather during various illnesses and now in his old age. Thus Germaine has turned out to be the most reliable junior kin Claude's father has, and he is both rewarding that behavior and also trying to secure her continued loyalty after his death.

From his perspective in the relationship, Claude feels threatened by Germaine. One of the factors affecting his feelings is that his wife does not want his external child, his zanaka ambelana, competing with her children for Claude's property. This is not unusual. In extended interviews with many members of these villages, they frequently remarked upon whether or not their parents had any zanaka ambelana. I found this interesting, since being such a child carries no stigma under most circumstances. Nor is it considered immoral to parent such a child. It became clear through the course of observing and interviewing villagers over several months that the central concern is property. Adult children, interacting with their half siblings, frequently become engaged in disputes about how property should be used and who has rights to decide.

Not every situation involving half siblings results in problems. In cases in which the ambelana children have been well integrated into the family, property is not much in dispute. It is taken for granted that all the children will share the inheritance. However, in cases in which the external children are either unknown to or shunned by the primary family, there is frequently tension concerning who has rights to what, and children and parents alike often discuss ways to protect themselves from the potential future appearance of a zanaka ambelana demanding a share in parental property. Usually, the most concerned party is the spouse who did not parent the child, and such a spouse can influence the decisions a husband or wife makes regarding property.[21]

Claude's history with his father and with his wife have created conditions under which he and his daughter have become incapable of trust, and Claude and his father also do not trust each other. However, each person, Claude, his father, and Germaine, have determined that there are other relationships they can reinforce that can compensate for the weaknesses of their particular parent-child bonds. Germaine fears her father's power to withhold economic and spiritual resources from her and her children, yet she sees no way to reconcile with him. For this reason, she has attached herself more closely to her grandfather. Claude is not fearful of his daughter, but he is jealous of her relationship with his father. He also believes that she is more committed to her grandfather than she is to him. Thus for the dual reason of preventing her from sharing in his wealth and trying to reinforce his relationship with the children of his current wife, he is doling out some of his cultivated land now, before he dies. Claude's father is concerned about his legacy being properly tended and believes he cannot trust his only son to honor him in the necessary ways. He therefore is trying to reaffirm his relationship with Germaine, the family member who has offered him the deepest support in the broadest number of ways over the years.

Conclusion

The three case studies presented here show that securing trust among kin is far from a simple matter, even in a society in which most social, economic, and political relationships are organized around kinship. The tendency in much of the recent social science literature concerning "family-centered" societies has been to assume that what makes those societies family centered is some sort of moral, affective bond, or ethos. These studies do not address the possibility that motivation behind a central focus on family may be quite different, depending upon the context. Some so-called familistic societies may indeed be characterized by strong, altruistic, unconditional attachment to kin. However, the motivation behind other familistic behavior may be the absence of reliable alternatives to kin. From the outside, the societies may look similar, but the underlying processes motivating family-centered behavior are quite distinct from each other. Furthermore, members of the societies would be likely to react differently to similar incentives for economic and political change.

In the standard analysis of the economic and political backwardness of family-centered societies, it is theorized that the strength of family ties prevents family members from seeking political allies or economic partners outside the family (Fukuyama 1995; Granovetter 1973; Putnam 1993). Thus economic or political development programs seeking to encourage individuals to expand their range of trusting social interactions would need to address the fundamental value system that attaches family members to one another. Changing other social, political, or economic institutions without changing the institution of the family would have little impact on development.

These three cases show a society whose family-centeredness rests on weak family ties. This, coupled with the near monopoly on economic and spiritual resources held by family elders, encourages villagers to invest almost exclusively in solidifying and clarifying their family relationships, leaving them little time and few resources to commit to relations with nonkin. One possible implication of these findings is that villagers might be quite happy to break away from their dependence on kin if other reliable institutions were to emerge in the region. One example in support of this hypothesis is the apparent attraction for many young villagers of the teachings of a recently established Lutheran church in the village that teaches them ways to communicate with the spirits without depending upon their elders. Similarly, many young villagers are drawn to working for a salary rather than depending upon family land for their sustenance.

The point I want to make in highlighting the difference between my findings and other studies of family-centered societies is that there are many cases in which family relations require much more work than those other studies would suggest. It may well be the difficulty with which relations among kin are established, rather than the ease, that impedes the development of other types of social relationships. It is impossible to determine which processes and mechanisms are at work simply by observing that a society is family centered. Something must be known about their underlying beliefs and the economic and political context in which those beliefs must be acted upon.

The subject of beliefs and the role that past experience and a socially acquired understanding of social norms play in informing those beliefs has been central to this study. How do people know whom to trust to do a particular thing? Three key ways they make this determination is to rely on past experience with that person or with people like that person, to rely on their beliefs regarding the extent to which their interests and the interests of the other person coincide, and to rely on their understanding of how that person is constrained or not by particular social norms. This latter factor is crucial and needs more attention in future studies of trust. In the analysis presented here, I have tried to show how, within a context of shared social norms, individuals can use their knowledge of the expectations embedded within those norms to predict the commitment of their social partners in particular realms. Similarly, they can use that same knowledge to signal their commitment to others. The cases presented here have all occurred within a context of widespread distrust, but I would argue that people follow similar processes of interpretation and signaling in more trusting contexts. The difference lies in the extent to which the prevailing norms inspire trust.

Finally, these cases, occurring as they do within such a context of distrust, provide the opportunity to see that distrust can indeed be costly. Much has been written about the social costs of mistrust, but little has been done to examine exactly how individuals attempt to compensate for the absence of trust. What is clear from these cases is the costs people bear in setting constraints on others, or even themselves, to establish trust and trustworthiness. The case of Arnaud is particularly enlightening in this regard. The widespread mistrust between husbands and wives prevents most husbands from doing what Arnaud initially did in seeking salaried labor in a distant village. Eventually, his need to show his commitment to his wife caused him to surrender that work. The perceived need for men to be monitored by their wives in monetary matters impedes villagers' abilities to seek economic opportunities beyond the village level, at least insofar as they also desire stable marriages. In the case of Belalahy and his brothers and sisters, it might be suggested that the social conditions that encourage land transfers only between family members set constraints on the ability of sellers to get the best prices for their land, and the knowledge of these constraints may have an impact on the types of investments they make on their land.

These conclusions are not intended to suggest that villagers are irrational or unreasonably conservative. Rather, based on their current access to important economic, political, and spiritual resources and on what is known about the values and commitments of most of the people with whom they interact, their choices make a lot of sense. Those choices, however, do not provide them with a strong foundation for creating lasting relationships with nonkin. That may be the biggest cost of distrust within the family.

Research was conducted in 1995 and 1996. The author acknowledges the generous financial support provided by Institute of International Education-Fulbright, the National Science Foundation (grant SBR 8419644), and the Wenner-Gren Foundation for Anthropological Research (grant 5967).

Notes

1. It is beyond the scope of this chapter to offer an explanation of why the villagers studied by Bloch differ from those in the region of my study. Margaret Brown (1999, esp. chap. 3, and 2004) provides a framework for addressing this question.
2. As Russell Hardin (2002) notes, we rarely simply trust. We trust a person to do a particular thing or set of things. This is frequently overlooked in analyses of trust.
3. One particularly widespread example can be seen in the literature on patron-client ties, in which these ties are understood to inspire trust because they replicate kin relations (for example, Cohen 1969; Eisenstadt and Roniger 1980; Mintz and Wolf 1950).
4. Martin Hollis (1998) offers a third option. He claims that individuals experience different types of trust in different types of relationships. He makes a distinction between normative and predictive trust: the former is based in role-playing, the latter in experience. Thus people trust family because they are in structural positions vis-à-vis one another that would make trust (or trustworthiness) normatively appropriate. When dealing with someone who does not fit into a role that is bound by morality, people must base their trust on experience with that individual, with people like that individual, or with their experience in similar situations. This distinction, however, does not do much to clarify the process by which an individual is judged to be appropriately playing his or her role.
5. Many anthropologists have noted the complexity of kin relations, although they have not done so in the context of analyzing trust. For the reader interested in exploring some of these approaches that challenge the view that kinship naturally leads to moral connectedness, some of the more prominent general examples include works by Fredrik Barth (1959), Edmund R. Leach (1964), and David Schneider (1984). Kinship studies that focus on gender, such as those represented in edited volumes by Jane Collier and Sylvia Yanagisako (1987) and by Mary Jo Maynes et al. (1996), have introduced more systematic analyses of the role power and hierarchy play in kin-based relations. Other anthropologists (Rosen 1984; contributors to Schweitzer 2000). have taken approaches that emphasize the strategic nature of kinship. A third category of study emphasizing the complexity of kin relations is one that focuses on kinship as a relationship that is achieved rather than given at birth (for example, Astuti 2000 and Carsten 1991, 1995). For an interesting overview of the issues of ambiguity and ambivalence in kin relations, see Michael Peletz (2001).
6. Some theorists (for example, Govier 1992, Hardin 1993) have explicitly recognized the problem of trust within families, particularly the potential for abuse by parents or spouses. However, no study has attempted to look to broader social and cultural patterns for an understanding of when and where trust in family might be particularly disadvantageous.

188   Distrust

7. On the importance of the connection between beliefs and social norms, see Jack Knight (2001).

8. Throughout this chapter I discuss the villages in the present tense. The present should be understood to be 1995 to 1996, when I was observing village life and conducting interviews. Many things have surely changed since 1996, and the use of the present tense is not intended to imply otherwise.

9. Note here that in discussing households as part of the kinship domain, I am including kinship through marriage as well as kinship through an assumed genetic relationship. The reasons for making this connection are addressed in more detail in the discussion of the first case study.

10. Bilateral kinship reckoning means that, from the point of view of ego (the person from whom kinship is being traced), kin from both the maternal and paternal sides are given equal weight. In Madagascar, this usually extends three generations, to a person's great-grandparents, commonly referred to as the "eight ancestors." Each person belongs to both maternally and paternally derived lineages and thus holds rights and responsibilities in two groups.

11. I use the terms "husband," "wife," and "divorce" for ease of discussion. In reality, of course, local practices do not exactly match up with these English terms. For example, there are different types of marriages in these villages, but most villagers do not perform any ceremony sanctioned by the state or a Christian church. Instead, they consider a relationship to be characterized by commitment once a couple has moved into a shared house and farmed together. As for divorce, there are structured traditional processes for reconciling a failing marriage or, when that fails, for overseeing the division of property upon the breakup of the marriage.

12. See Jane Guyer (1981) for a review of some of this literature as it relates to African studies.

13. Margaret Brown (2003) provides an extended examination of bargaining within families and households in northeastern Madagascar.

14. A variety of approaches to household studies take this latter point of view. Gary Becker's (1981) work on household economics is an early example. More recent approaches emphasize transaction costs (Pollak 1985), institutional constraints on individual bargaining (Sen 1990), and the importance of social networks (Agarwal 1997) and social norms (Bittman et al. 2003). The common thread tying these studies together is the view that individuals do, to the extent possible, calculate the relative advantages of staying in a marital relationship versus leaving it. Having children in common does not prevent this type of calculation, and children can become the object of the bargaining behavior that goes on between a husband and wife.

15. At the time of my research, a large internationally funded conservation and development project was working with the Malagasy government to create a national park in the region and to develop economic resources in the villages. This project was beginning to employ a few village men on a

salaried basis. The salaries were quite large compared with the average villager's yearly agricultural income.

16. There is much less concern about women cheating or misusing household funds. In general, villagers assume that women will put the concerns of their children over their own personal benefit. Furthermore, if a woman were to use household money to purchase fine clothing or jewelry for herself—and these would be her most likely purchases—she would risk acquiring a reputation that might have negative long-term consequences in dealing with her spouse and with her own family.

17. Michael Lambek (1992) and David Graeber (1995, 1996) have made similar observations about the social implications of taboos in other regions of Madagascar.

18. At the time of the purchase, which was around 1993, one U.S. dollar equaled approximately 1,750 Malagasy francs.

19. "Zanaka ambelana" is the local term for a child who is a product of a relationship outside of the existing or the "primary" marriage The phrase does not imply social stigma, although it can carry information about the legal rights of a child.

20. This fear that hostility will be passed down to future generations is a common concern of villagers regarding all conflicts with other villagers, family or not, and leads most of them to avoid any type of escalation of dispute.

21. In this region of Madagascar, male and female children inherit equally, and they inherit property from both mother and father.

References

Agarwal, Bina. 1997. " 'Bargaining' and Gender Relations: Within and Beyond the Household." *Feminist Economics* 3(1): 1–51.

Astuti, Rita. 2000. "Kindreds and Descent Groups: New Perspectives from Madagascar." In *Cultures of Relatedness: New Approaches to the Study of Kinship*, edited by Janet Carsten. Cambridge, U.K.: Cambridge University Press.

Banfield, Edward C. 1958. *The Moral Basis of a Backward Society*. New York: Free Press.

Barth, Fredrik. 1959. *Political Leadership Among Swat Pathans*. London: Athlone Press.

Becker, Gary. 1981. *A Treatise on the Family*. Cambridge, Mass.: Harvard University Press.

Bittman, Michael, Paula England, Liana Sayer, Nancy Folbre, and George Matheson. 2003. "When Does Gender Trump Money? Bargaining and Time in Household Work." *American Journal of Sociology* 109(1): 186–214.

Bloch, Maurice. 1973. "The Long Term and the Short Term: The Economic and Political Significance of the Morality of Kinship." In *The Character of Kinship*, edited by Jack Goody. London: Cambridge University Press.

Brown, Margaret L. 1999. "Authority Relations and Trust: Social Cohesion on the Eastern Masoala Peninsula, Madagascar." Ph.D. diss., Washington University, St. Louis.

———. 2003. "Relative Commitments: Gender, Kinship, and Power." Unpublished manuscript. Washington University, St. Louis.

———. 2004. "Reclaiming Lost Ancestors and Acknowledging Slave Descent: Insights from Madagascar." *Comparative Studies in Society and History* 46(3): n.p.

Carsten, Janet. 1991. "Children in Between: Fostering and the Process of Kinship on Pulau Langkawi, Malaysia." *Man* 26(3): 425–43.

———. 1995. "The Substance of Kinship and the Heat of the Hearth: Feeding, Personhood, and Relatedness Among Malays in Pulau Langkawi." *American Ethnologist* 22(2): 223–41.

Cohen, Abner. 1969. "Custom and Politics in Urban Africa: A Study of Hausa Migrants in Yoruba Towns." Berkeley: University of California Press.

Cole, Jennifer. 1996. "The Necessity of Forgetting: Ancestral and Colonial Memories in East Madagascar." Ph.D. diss., University of California, Berkeley.

Collier, Jane F., and Sylvia J. Yanagisako, eds. 1987. *Gender and Kinship: Essays Toward a Unified Analysis*. Stanford, Calif.: Stanford University Press.

Eisenstadt, S. N., and Louis Roniger. 1980. "Patron-Client Relations as a Model of Structuring Social Exchange." *Comparative Studies in Society and History* 22(2): 42–77.

Fortes, Meyer. 1969. *Kinship and the Social Order*. Chicago: Aldine.

———. 1983. "Rules and the Emergence of Society." Occasional Paper 39. London: The Royal Anthropological Institute of Great Britain and Ireland.

———. 1987. *Religion, Morality and the Person*. Cambridge: Cambridge University Press.

Fukuyama, Francis. 1995. *Trust: The Social Virtues and the Creation of Prosperity*. London: Hamish Hamilton.

Govier, Trudy. "Trust, Distrust, and Feminist Theory." 1992. *Hypatia* 7: 16–33.

Graeber, David. 1995. "Dancing with Corpses Reconsidered: An Interpretation of *Famadihana* (in Arivonimamao, Madagascar)." *American Ethnologist* 22(2): 258–78.

———. 1996. "The Disastrous Ordeal of 1987: Memory and Violence in a Rural Malagasy Community." Ph.D. diss., University of Chicago.

Granovetter, Mark. 1973. "The Strength of Weak Ties." *American Journal of Sociology* 78(6, May): 1360–80.

Guyer, Jane. 1981. "Household and Community in African Studies." *African Studies Review* 24(2/3, June–September): 87–137.

Hardin, Russell. 1993. "The Street-Level Epistemology of Trust." *Politics and Society* 21(4): 505–29.

———. 1997. "Trustworthiness." *Ethics* 107(1): 26–42.

———. 2002. *Trust and Trustworthiness*. New York: Russell Sage Foundation.

Hollis, Martin. 1998. *Trust Within Reason*. Cambridge: Cambridge University Press.

Knight, Jack C. 2001. "Social Norms and the Rule of Law: Fostering Trust in a Socially-Diverse Society." In *Trust in Society*, edited by Karen Cook. New York: Russell Sage Foundation.

Lambek, Michael. 1992. "Taboo as Cultural Practice among Malagasy Speakers." *Man* 27(2): 245–66.

Leach, Edmund R. 1964. *Political Systems of Highland Burma: A Study of Kachin Social Structure*. London: Athlone Press.

Maynes, Mary Jo, Ann Waltner, Brigitte Soland, and Ulrike Strasser, eds. 1996. *Gender, Kinship, Power: A Comparative and Interdisciplinary History.* New York: Routledge.
Mintz, Sidney W., and Eric R. Wolf. 1950. "An Analysis of Ritual Co-Parenthood (*Compadrazgo*)." *Southwestern Journal of Anthropology* 6(4): 341–68.
Peletz, Michael G. 2001. "Ambivalence in Kinship Since the 1940s." In *Relative Values: Reconfiguring Kinship Studies,* edited by Sarah Franklin and Susan McKinnon. Durham, N.C.: Duke University Press.
Pollak, Robert A. 1985. "A Transaction Cost Approach to Families and Households." *Journal of Economic Literature* 23(2, June): 581–608.
Putnam, Robert D. 1993. *Making Democracy Work.* Princeton, N.J.: Princeton University Press.
Rosen, Lawrence. 1984. *Bargaining for Reality: The Construction of Social Relations in a Muslim Community.* Chicago: University of Chicago Press.
Sahlins, Marshall David. 1972. *Stone Age Economics.* Chicago: Aldine-Atherton.
Schneider, David M. 1984. *A Critique of the Study of Kinship.* Ann Arbor: University of Michigan Press.
Schweitzer, Peter P., ed. 2000. *Dividends of Kinship: Meanings and Uses of Social Relatedness.* London: Routledge.
Sen, Amartya. 1990. "Gender and Cooperative Conflicts." In *Persistent Inequalities: Women and World Development,* edited by Irene Tinker. New York: Oxford University Press.
Yamagishi, Toshio and Midori Yamagishi. 1994. "Trust and Commitment in the United States and Japan." *Motivation and Emotion* 18(2): 129–66.

Chapter 8

Deadly Distrust: Honor Killings and Swedish Multiculturalism

UNNI WIKAN

SWEDEN IS the most liberal of the Scandinavian countries in regard to immigrant groups. It is the only one that defines itself as multicultural in an ideological, not just a descriptive, sense.[1] Sweden pursues a politics of ethnic minority rights that grants some special privileges to immigrant groups so they can practice their own traditions. One example is a law that sets the minimum marital age at fifteen years for girls of non-Western immigrant background. For all others, the legal minimum age is eighteen years. "Immigrant background" may apply even when the girl is Swedish-born and a Swedish citizen. It is her parents' cultural heritage that determines the case. In the other Scandinavian countries, the minimum marital age is eighteen years for all residents, irrespective of background.

One way of characterizing this difference between Sweden, on the one hand, and Norway and Denmark, on the other, is to say that Sweden shows more *trust* in its immigrant population. Sweden apparently has more confidence that families, clans, and communities will act in accordance with the best interests of their members.

This is the only sensible interpretation, in my view, given Sweden's position in the world as an upholder of the best in the liberal tradition. Liberalism seeks to protect individuals from undue harm perpetrated by powerful bodies or agents, be they states, churches, communities, or others. Political liberalism proceeds from the belief that "it is government's performance at the extreme that we have to fear. Hence, we should design government to be safe against extreme performance."

The same might be said for multiculturalism as a political ideology. Risk aversion, not misanthropy, is the issue (Hardin 2002, 74).

Is trust warranted in Sweden's case? Are immigrants in Sweden more liberal minded than in the other Scandinavian countries? A comparative study of forced marriage, commissioned by the Nordic Council of Ministers, might indicate as much: Forced marriage has been a key concern in Norway and Denmark since the early to middle 1990s; in Sweden, it was not an issue at all (Bredal 1999).

Norway's case is interesting in this respect. In 1993 an old law against forced marriage was canceled because deemed superfluous. In January 1995 it was reinstituted. By then, abundant evidence had come to the fore regarding the need for precisely such a law to protect immigrant girls from coerced marriage.[2] How has Sweden escaped the problem? Has it escaped the problem?

Not in the view of Fadime Sahindal, a girl of Kurdish origin who lived in Sweden with her family from when she was nine years old.[3] Fadime was twenty-one years old when she first drew attention to the fate that had been designated for many girls like her: to marry a cousin in Turkey at a young age, about sixteen. In a documentary on her life first shown on Swedish television in May 1998, she expounded on the rationale and prevalence of the practice, and on the suffering inflicted on youngsters who grew up in Sweden and who had to bury their dreams of choosing their own mates. She also pointed to the vested interests that bred new life into a practice of cross-cousin marriage that might otherwise be on the wane: "They will do anything to get a son here!" ("Striptease," reported by Marianne Spanner, *Sämhallsmagasin*, SVT1, May 6, 1998).

In Sweden, as in Norway (and Denmark until 2003),[4] marriage with a resident is like a green card: it provides a visa and all the social benefits of the welfare state.[5] Fadime had gone her own way and paid the price for it. When she became a public figure in Sweden in 1998, it was because she trusted the media to help safeguard her life, after the police, to whom she had appealed, turned her down. They did not believe her story—that male kinsmen were going to kill her simply because she had a Swedish-Iranian boyfriend and that she had been given an ultimatum: never to return to her hometown, Uppsala, or she would not escape alive. Fadime was pained and humiliated by her treatment at the hands of the police. "My story was like a saga to them," she later said, in a speech at a conference in the Swedish Parliament in November 2001. Fearing for her life, she saw media exposure as her last resort. "Perhaps my family will not dare to kill me, when so many people know who I am," she reasoned. Thus it was that in May 1998, the story of Fadime was brought to public attention in a documentary aired on Swedish TV.

To situate Fadime's story in context, some background knowledge on the new multiethnic Scandinavia is in order. Multiculturalism is a concept that can be defined in many ways.[6] Descriptively, it may refer simply to the coexistence of many different ethnic groups within a state or society. The assumption may or may not be that plurality is good and enriching for the society as a whole. Whatever the case, immigrants have come to stay in Scandinavia, where a sizable proportion of residents are now immigrants or of immigrant background. In Sweden, persons of non-Western immigrant background make up about 15 percent of the population. In Denmark and Norway, the percentages are approximately 12 and 9 percent, respectively, Norway now having the fastest relative increase; in Europe, only Austria outstrips Norway in terms of the influx of asylum seekers. Since immigration restrictions were introduced by the western European countries around 1975, most new immigrants enter either as political asylum seekers or on grounds of family reunification (many of them through marriage) (Brochmann 1996). Political asylum is granted only to a few, but many are granted residence (and later citizenship) on humanitarian grounds. Thus in Norway, for example, more than 60 percent of the non-Western immigrants have lived in the country less than ten years. Proportions in Sweden and Denmark are roughly similar (Wikan 2002, 46).

This translates to a steady flow of immigrants hailing from nondemocratic and autocratic regimes entering the liberal welfare states of the Nordic countries. Though some of the countries from which these immigrants come define themselves as democratic (as do most regimes nowadays), *liberal* democracy, grounded in the idea of freedom, liberty, and equality for all citizens and the right to *exit* from illiberal groups, is absent. Most of them—societies in the Middle East and central and southern Asia—abide by hierarchical and strongly patriarchal traditions.

This creates certain dilemmas. In the words of Russell Hardin (2004, 19), "Where should an otherwise liberal state stand on its dealings with illiberal immigrant groups?" On moral and normative grounds, the question may be endlessly debated. In real life, the *consequences* make themselves felt, whether one acts or fails to act. Among those who suffered the consequences was Fadime Sahindal.

On February 4, 2002, Fadime was buried from Uppsala cathedral. Her funeral was attended by the crown princess, the minister of integration, members of Parliament, the archbishop, and other high officials in addition to two hundred members of the Sahindal family and numerous others who had been lucky enough to find seats. Another two thousand watched outside on that cold, rainy day, having come to pay Fadime their last respects. Her funeral was broadcast live on Swedish television.

"Fadime was one of the martyrs of our time," said the bishop in her memorial speech. "Let us thank God for Fadime, that with her courage, strength, and love of life, she has given heart and force to so many" (live documentary of the memorial ceremony for Fadime Sahindal, SVT4,

February 4, 2002). Her words must have sounded like heresy to some of those who were present in the church or watched the ceremony on TV and those who were outraged by the dishonor Fadime had conferred on her family. Fadime was a whore, said her father, when he gave himself up to the police, shortly after the murder.

Fadime was buried in the old graveyard in Uppsala, beside her beloved Patrik Lindesjö. Patrik had died in a car crash in June 1998. It was for him that she paid with her life. With Fadime's death, the disgrace she had caused her family by falling in love with a "Swede," and going public with it, refusing the Kurdish cousin her family had in mind for her, was erased.

"The final solution," her father called it in court. He could not, he claimed, have rid himself of Fadime in any other way: "The problem is over now."[7]

"He must be sick; only a sick man would kill his daughter," said a sister of Fadime to the police. "He had no choice," said some Kurdish men to the media. They would not condemn the murder: bereft of his honor, he had no other option.

Other Kurds took an emphatic stance against the murder, expressing their sincere regrets and distress that once more, a woman of their own heritage had had to pay with her life for her quest for freedom. In the past five years there had been several such honor killings in Sweden, in addition to other such attempts that failed, leaving the victim lame or mutilated (For an account of some of these, see Wikan 2002, 91–100). Most outspoken in their condemnation of the killing of Fadime were Kurdish women's organizations, of which there are several.

The Kurdish minority in Sweden counts about forty thousand people with origins in the Middle East: Turkey, Iran, Iraq, and Syria. The Sahindal family had come from southeastern Turkey in the early 1970s and now has about three hundred members in Sweden. Fadime's father arrived in Sweden in 1981, and his wife and five children followed in 1984. Fadime was then nine years old, she was born on April 4th, 1975, and died on January 21, 2002, barely twenty-six years old.

Fadime's is a classic case of distrust operating at all levels and penetrating everywhere and of the hard work that needs to be done to protect the basic moral values and legal principles that undergird welfare societies. Distrust must be taken in earnest: trust in the goodwill of ethnic minorities and their desire to extend the freedoms of a liberal democracy can in some cases backfire. It can be grossly inappropriate, as it was in Fadime's case.

Refugees who seek political asylum in the West, fleeing from persecution in their homelands, cannot be counted on a priori, to be liberal minded. Oppression nurtures oppression, and the fight for freedom at the national or subnational level does not necessarily translate into a quest for freedom at the personal level or for all categories of person. *My Home, My Prison* is the title of the autobiography of Raymonda Hawa Tawil (1979), an early Palestinian feminist and the mother-in-law of chairman Yasser Arafat. Among Palestinians, as among Kurds, patriarchal traditions and the use of violence in child-rearing practices sometimes combine with bitterness and rage over the group's political fate to breed illiberal, indeed antiliberal, practices.

This does not mean that all Kurds or Palestinians, or only Kurds and Palestinians, display social patterns that undermine liberal welfarism. Violence against women and children is a ubiquitous problem, even in native Scandinavia. It is also prevalent among many ethnic minorities that have found new homes in the West.

Among refugees and immigrants, some people practice customs that undercut freedom and equality for other members of the community. These are customs that are inimical to human rights, including the rights of the child, upon which Scandinavian social welfarism rests. Forced marriage and honor killings are examples of such traditions. In some cases, according to the available evidence, these traditions are being reinforced in the West. It is not just a matter of the export of antihumanitarian, illiberal traditions from some communities in the third world but of the reinforcement or reinvention of practices that are profoundly inimical to human welfare. Fadime suffered the consequences of such practices.

At issue is distrust: of the surrounding society, of one's own children, in one's kin and the power of their revenge for perceived breaches of loyalty, in one's community and its power to shame, and in the polity, the courts, the government, and the media. These responses are not limited to immigrants. Nonimmigrants share many of the same or similar attitudes. Moreover, immigrants are unique individuals with diverse ways of perceiving and relating to the world. Among Kurds in Sweden, as we have seen, reactions to the murder of Fadime ran the gamut from utter condemnation to moderate acceptance and even wholesale embrace. Evidence to be cited later in this chapter underscores this point. Immigrants are unique individuals and must be recognized as such, rather than as products or replicas of "a culture" (Wikan 1999).

Yet Fadime's story carries a message about the future of our multiethnic societies that must be heeded, lest she be truly betrayed. She spent the last four years of her life committed to telling the world that integration of immigrants into Swedish society must be taken in earnest; that looming obstacles to social integration urgently needed attention; that it was, in some cases, a question of countering deadly distrust: unless illiberal minorities were integrated in the polity and civic society, people like her could be made to pay with their lives.

"I know," she said on Swedish TV in 1998, "that I shall face threats to my life until [my accusers'] breath expires. To kill me is the only way my kin can regain their honor and pride." Yet she also hoped that by going public she might gain some security.

It was a forlorn hope. "She underestimated her kinsmen's rage," according to Nalin Pekgul, a member of the Swedish Parliament of Kurdish descent. Pekgul is presently urging the Swedish government to stand up for the liberties and rights of women of immigrant background. She is fierce in her critique of Swedish politicians and intellectuals, as are many other women—and men—of Kurdish descent. In their view, Sweden let immigrant citizens down by failing to combat patriarchy and violence against females.

At least some officials agree. "I have failed," said the Swedish minister of integration, Mona Sahlin, in the aftermath of Fadime's death. "I have failed to take culture in earnest because I was afraid to add fuel to the racist fire" ("Vi har svikitflickorna," interview by Peter Beckman with minister of integration, Mona Sahlin, *Dagens Nyheter* 8, June 2001). She also told how it was her meeting with the sister of another victim of an honor killing, Pela Atrushi, that made her change her view. Pela, a citizen of Sweden, was killed in Kurdish Iraq in June 1999. Her father claimed responsibility for the murder and was sentenced to five months on probation.

Pela's sister, who witnessed the murder, managed to escape to Sweden and told the truth to the police: it was her uncles, Swedish citizens, who had carried out the deed. On their return to Sweden the two men were tried, and in December 2000 they were sentenced to life imprisonment. Were it not for Pela's sister, there would have been no trial in Sweden. She alone stood witness to the atrocity. She now lives in secrecy and has been given a new identity to protect her life.[8]

Again in March 2002, another sister was to brave threats as the sole witness in court against the perpetrator in an honor killing: she was Fadime's sister, Songül, twenty-three years old. She, too, had been urged by her family not to give witness regarding the murder she observed at close hand: Fadime had been killed in her flat.

In the eyes of their kinsmen, Pela and Fadime committed the same crime: they had "become Swedish," an atrocity from the point of view of prominent males of their clan. Both girls wanted to stake out their own paths in life. They wanted to have the freedoms that are considered natural and normal for Swedish girls: the right to self-determination and to choose whom they wanted to marry. To their kin, this bespoke utter disgrace. For girls, such disobedience can be deadly. Fadime's younger brother, Mesut, had a Swedish fiancée with whom he lived part of the week, an arrangement that had persisted for years. In August 1998 he was sentenced to five months in jail for violence against Fadime in public and for threatening her life. Fadime was a whore, he claimed. Clearly, different logics apply for males and females in his community.

Sara, another victim of honor killing in Sweden, was also accused of being "a whore" by her brother and other male kin. Sara was fifteen years old when she was murdered by her brother and a cousin in December 1996. The culprits were sixteen and seventeen years old. Sara's mother tells how her son had threatened to kill Sara a fortnight before the deed: She was a whore, he said, who slept with Swedish boys. "But what about you, don't you sleep with Swedish girls?" the mother wondered. "Yes, but that is different, he is a male; moreover, he would not even think of sleeping with Iraqi girls; it's just with Swedish girls, with whores, that he does it" (cited in Wikan 2002, 91).

In the aftermath of Sara's death, the debate raged in Sweden regarding who and what was to blame for the murder: was it a cultural crime—an honor crime—or an incident of plain violence against women—a universal problem? Now, following Fadime's murder, the debate has been resumed. The Swedish government has taken severe criticism for listening to Swedish liberals (academics and politicians) rather than to those who experience the problems firsthand: immigrants, and immigrant women most of all. Recall the testimony of the minister of integration, Mona Sahlin, in which she stated she had failed to see the problems for what they were until she met Pela's sister.

Sahlin's testimony discloses *her* particular object of distrust: ordinary people, Swedes who might fall prey to racism. She balanced her concerns—concern for immigrant girls and their welfare versus concern with racism and discrimination against non-Western immigrants. The latter had won, until she met Pela's sister.

The stance Sahlin took—to silence critical social issues for fear of nurturing racism—bespeaks distrust in ordinary people's power of reasoning and judgment; it is a mistake she wishes she had not made. Racism is likely to grow when people see their worst fears—and acts exceeding their worst fears—of immigrants actualized. Fadime's case has done untold harm. Facing up to the power of culture to inflict harm on individual lives can reduce racism, I believe, provided measures are taken that foster more benign and liberal attitudes and practices.

The reluctance to embark on such a trail is not unique to Sweden; it resides in other Scandinavian governments as well. But Sweden has been the extreme case, owing to its stated ideology of multiculturalism combined with strict political correctness (see Carlbom 2003; Friedman 1999). Generally, the mistake made by the Scandinavian countries was to assume that a multiethnic and pluralistic society would work itself out to the best of all parties if people were kind and tolerant toward one another. Silencing backfired; problems grew; and all over Scandinavia policies are now being revised.

In Fadime's case, it took four years before the death threats were put into effect. She was killed on January 21, 2002, while visiting her sister,

Songül. Their mother and little sister, Nabile, thirteen years old, also witnessed the crime. The four women had met secretly to pass an evening together before Fadime was to travel to Kenya for half a year to write her master's thesis in social work. Fadime's father (and most probably other male kinsmen) found the women out. He fired three shots at Fadime, at close range. The first hit her in the head and was deadly; he then shot her in the face; the third shot missed.

"My father fired the shots, but I know that the family is behind [it]," Songül said in court. She alone from the family was willing to give evidence. "It was a planned murder, a premeditated act." She had heard her father and other kinsmen (both male and female) saying that Fadime must be killed (testimony given in Uppsala municipal court, March 12, 2002).

The court case took place from March 12 to 15, 2002, in Uppsala. Distrust featured amply in the courtroom and beyond. Besides Songül, three other witnesses from the family were summoned to appear: Fadime's mother, the mother's brother, and a cousin of the father. Testimony of the men was crucial, as it was they whom the father had contacted after the murder and they who then contacted the police; the mother had witnessed the murder of her child.

All three declined to witness in court—the mother on the grounds that she had already told everything she knew to the police; the cousin because he had been a close friend of the defendant for fifty years; the mother's brother on the grounds that he was a close relative (he was also a cousin of Fadime's father and married to his sister).

The cousin was not exempted but claimed complete memory loss, even when the prosecutor asked him to remember how he came to know that Fadime had been killed. After all, it was a special event. "For me, there are no special days," answered the man. He was later convicted of perjury, for which he was sentenced to five months in jail.

On the second day of the trial, the proceedings took a dramatic turn when a kinsman, a nephew of Fadime's father, contacted the police and claimed responsibility for the murder. He said it was he, not the father, who had killed Fadime. The father had wanted to absolve his nephew of responsibility. The nephew gave a vivid account of the disgrace Fadime had caused the whole Sahindal clan by being "a whore." She deserved to be killed, he said; he had no regrets. Songül, he said, is also a whore.

Because of critical faults in the man's testimony, he was dismissed as a liar. On why he tried to take responsibility for the murder, some relatives said that he wanted to be a hero in the family. Truly, murdering for honor's sake, or taking upon oneself responsibility for such a murder, is a heroic act in communities like the one of which the Sahindals were part.

This does not mean there is a consensus to that effect. In each and every honor killing I have researched, some members of the family are beyond themselves with grief and despair at losing a loved one. The murderer himself may be heartbroken, despite believing that he had no choice.

Fadime's father was convicted on the grounds of his own testimony, the testimony of Songül, technical evidence, and what Fadime's mother and sister Nebile had told the police. He was sentenced to life imprisonment and ordered to pay Songül an indemnity of fifty thousand kronor.

"I was sick," said the father in court. "Only a sick man would kill his own daughter." He pleaded with the court to regard him as a sick person and not a criminal. In retrospect, he said, he regretted "that event" (his word for the murder). But he had been tormented by "this Fadime," as he called her, who would not leave him and his family alone. Consider what she had done: gone to the police with accusations that his son and he had mistreated her and threatened her life! His son had been thrown in jail; he himself had been sentenced to fines. She exposed them for all the world to see, using the media to blacken their name.

"What she has done to me, I really don't know how I can explain it to you," he said, exasperated, in court—well aware of the feat of cultural translation needed to get a Swedish audience to sympathize with his plight. "If you had a daughter like this Fadime, you would have wished to shoot her too!" he exclaimed to the prosecutor.

"A man with a primitive and naive mind-set who is cognitively underdeveloped and lacking in empathy" was the judgment of the psychiatric expert. His report, five pages in length, was read in its entirety in court. The words "primitive" and "naive," which under normal circumstances would have provoked antiracists, passed without protest. Rahmi Sahindal is not sick or suffering from depression, concluded the psychiatric report. But he is rigid, inflexible, and obsessed with the disgrace that his daughter had caused him. The verdict characterized Fadime's murder as an execution—a verdict consistent with her father's expressions, the "final solution," and "the problem is over now."

Only one man stood trial, but according to Songül, others were behind the murder. This is also the view of Nalin Pekgul, who warns that Swedish jurisprudence fails to take into account the character of honor killings: that several people stand behind, as it is a question of collective honor, not of the self-regard and social esteem of one man. Honor is joint, and honor killings reflect this fact.

Distrust permeated the Fadime case. It permeated relations within the intimate family, relations between kin, and relations between minority and majority. It pervaded the court proceedings, making even Fadime's mother fear to give evidence in court. Distrust is also epitomized in the failure of the Swedish government to act in time to try to prevent "the final solution." Most important, distrust in government and civic society by immigrants who hail from nations where the state is perceived as the enemy can undercut the values of social liberalism, as we have seen. It takes heart and bravery like Fadime's to look the problems in the face: to recognize that her parents were also victims, not just violators, victims of failed integration policies.

"If Sweden had taken integration [of immigrants into Swedish society] in earnest, this could have been prevented," Fadime told a conference convened in the Swedish Parliament two months before she was killed. In the context, her "this" refers to her having had to choose between liberty and her family; in retrospect, it signals a much graver foreboding.

This was Fadime's legacy: to alert Swedes, and all the world, that people like her parents deserved better than to be alienated from their children and feel at loss in their new society because they feared that for which they had come: to savor liberty and personal well-being. "Poor daddy," she said, three times, on that evening—her final evening—when he came to Songül's door, screaming to be let in. She pitied her mother, too: her mother was given the blame, she said, for Fadime having disgraced the family.

Fadime's mother appears to have betrayed her deceased daughter in court, refusing to bear witness to the murder she had seen with her own eyes. What might have been expected? She had told the police all that she knew. How could she have understood that judges have no access to the police reports but only to what is revealed in court? Even though this was explained to her by way of an interpreter, Fadime's mother had little knowledge of Swedish society, even after twenty years in the country. She lived a segregated life within her own community of kinsfolk, where distrust of the larger society was pervasive. Fadime was dead. Her husband had pleaded guilty. What more was there to say?

But at the appeals stage, there *was* more to say. Once again the trial took an unexpected turn, when the father withdrew his confession. He claimed that his life and that of his family had been threatened unless he took upon himself the responsibility for a murder of which he was fully innocent. An acquaintance, whom he could not identify, he now claimed, was the culprit. Fadime's mother testified in court in support of her husband. It was a heartrending spectacle that I have described and analyzed elsewhere (Wikan 2003). Close friends of Fadime agree with me that Fadime's response would probably have been, "Poor Mama." Distrust is pervasive even within the closest family. The mother had much to fear.

Fadime's story signifies the *risk* of group liberalism. When Sweden, in the spring of 2004, considers a proposal to restrict the minimum age for marriage to eighteen for all citizens, it will be largely in response to Fadime's case. The collective wisdom embodied in the liberal theory of distrust will thus be extended to embrace immigrants in larger measure. The institutions this body of collective wisdom has produced, such as a law making the marriage of minors illegal, are an embodiment of a liberal theory of distrust that will at long last, one hopes, benefit the children of immigrants, too.

Fadime's case has heralded an awakening in Sweden regarding the work that needs to be done to counter the distrust that threatens the well-being of a multicultural society and, with it, the future of social liberalism. In Norway, my own home country, as well, the effect of the Fadime case has been profound, triggering debates and measures—both legal and practical—that have long been needed to protect individual liberty and human welfare.[9]

The legacy of Fadime carries beyond Scandinavia; at stake is a difficult and politically sensitive issue that all liberal democracies must struggle with: how to accommodate "culture" within the polity. What are the limits of cultural tolerance? How can a nation build a plural society that both respects different cultural traditions and requires that citizens abide by a set of common laws and norms?[10]

The great majority of immigrants to western Europe hail from countries where extreme distrust in government prevails—where government is perceived as an enemy to be countervened and resisted through the use of kinship and clan networks and other mechanisms. This fact, though, has received scant attention, considering the implications of such attitudes for the development of political and social trust in liberal democracies. If "general social trust is translated into politically relevant trust" (Almond and Verba 1965, 228), then what of the extreme social distrust that we have seen exemplified in Fadime's case? Where does it lead? "One might well argue that wariness toward government could enhance the development of personal trust relationships," notes Hardin (2002, 85), but such development might also foster autocratic hegemony, as is borne out by Fadime's case. Trust between some members of the community can be nourished concurrently with extreme distrust of others, who are made to bear the brunt of illiberal trust. I have elsewhere (Wikan 2002) made an extensive analysis of such dilemmas and challenges that need to be dealt with, not put aside, in multicultural societies.

The future of social liberalism depends on how these issues are handled—in practice. Honor killings will be condemned by most members of liberal democracies. But the practices and traditions that undergird inhumane acts—whether by immigrants or natives—demand careful attention in the midst of everyday life. This was Fadime's message: it is in the everyday order of events that measures must be taken, and policies instigated, that enable and encourage people like her parents to find their place in a welfare state. Not at the margins, not on the periphery, not in a subgroup that encapsulates itself in distrust of the larger society, but in a vibrant pluralist society that empowers people to discard fear and partake of all the benefits of civic society. Only thus can the common good—freedom, justice, and equality for all—be realized.

Notes

1. On multiculturalism in Sweden, see Carlbom 2003.
2. The story of Norwegian Pakistani Nasim Karim, who was married by force in Pakistan and then managed to escape, was published the following year (see Karim 1996). A brief rendition of her story in English is included in Wikan (2002, 107–16), which presents other case materials and discussion of the problems and policies regarding forced marriage not just in Norway but in other parts of western Europe as well.
3. A full account and analysis of Fadime's case is found in Wikan (2003), which has been translated into Danish and Swedish.
4. In 2003 Denmark passed a new law making twenty-four the minimum age at which a Dane could legally bring in a spouse from abroad. The law applies to all residents, including native Danish citizens, so as not to be discriminatory. It is intended to be a mechanism to counter forced marriage of children and young adults. Evaluations so far suggest that the law has been effective. The Danish government recognizes that, though legal restrictions of this sort may not be the ideal way to address the problem, in the absence of a better alternative the law is the best way available to protect the interests especially of immigrant girls. Boys are also affected, in Denmark as elsewhere in Europe.
5. Family reunification and other issues that are briefly mentioned here are discussed at length in Wikan (2002), which also contains references to other sources.
6. The literature about multiculturalism is vast. I here refer to two key texts, Cohen, Howard, and Nussbaum (1999) and Kymlicka (1995).
7. I attended the court case in its entirety. I have also read the full police report (three hundred pages) of interviews with witnesses, including those who would not give evidence in court. In addition, my data for my presentation and analysis are based on press clippings, talks with some of Fadime's closest kin, and viewing of videos on Fadime. I also watched the funeral on TV.
8. The story of Pela's sister, Breen, has been told with the help of the Swedish journalist and author Lena Katarina Swanberg (2002).
9. For an incisive and pertinent discussion of the undertheorizing of social liberalism within the welfare state, see Hardin (2004). As Hardin (2004, 12) argues, group liberalism, which is advocated by many proponents of multiculturalism, is often profoundly illiberal in that it "liberates one group from the hegemony or control of another group." The Fadime case brings home the point that it is social liberalism, not group liberalism, that is called for (see also Okin 1999).

10. The literature dealing with these issues is vast these days. Permit me to single out a volume to which I contributed: the *Daedalus* (Shweder, Minow, and Markus 2000) issue on "The End of Tolerance: Engaging Cultural Differences", which emanated from an interdisciplinary working group on Ethnic Custom, American Law, and Assimilation under the auspices of the Social Science Research Council, 1997 to 1999. Hardin's (2004, 19–20) gives an answer to the question, "Where should an otherwise liberal state stand on its dealings with illiberal immigrant groups?" that is worth quoting at length: "I do not think that there is a correct answer to such a question if it is essentially normative or moral. But there can be an answer practically, which is that for a universalistic liberal state to support illiberal practices in selected subpopulations is incoherent and likely to be destructive of the survival of the liberal order.... We cannot *in the name of liberalism* protect illiberalism."

References

Almond, Gabriel Abraham, and Sidney Verba. 1965. *The Civic Culture: Political Attitudes and Democracy in Five Nations and Analytic Study*. Boston: Little, Brown.
Bredal, Anja. 1999. *Arrangerte ekteskap og tvangsekteskap i Norden*. TemaNord. Copenhagen: Nordisk Ministerråd.
Brochmann, Grete. 1996. *European Integration and Immigration from Third Countries*. Oslo: Scandinavian University Press.
Carlbom, Aje. 2003. *The Imagined versus the Real Other: Multiculturalism and the Representation of Muslims in Sweden*. Lund: Lund Monographs in Social Anthropology.
Cohen, Joshua, Matthew Howard, and Martha C. Nussbaum, eds. 1999. *Is Multiculturalism Bad for Women?* Princeton, N.J.: Princeton University Press.
Friedman, Jonathan. 1999. "Rhinoceros II." *Current Anthropology* 40(5): 679–94.
Hardin, Russell. 2002. "Liberal Distrust." *European Review* 10(1): 73–89.
———. 2004. "Liberalism and Cultural Diversity." Unpublished paper. New York University.
Karim, Nasim. 1996. *Izzat: For ærens skyld*. Oslo: Cappelen.
Kymlicka, Will. 1995. *Multicultural Citizenship*. Oxford: Oxford University Press.
Okin, Susan Moller. 1999. *Is Multiculturalism Bad for Women?* Princeton, N.J.: Princeton University Press.
Shweder, Richard, Martha Minow, and Hazel Markus, eds. 2000. "The End of Tolerance: Engaging Cultural Differences." *Daedalus, Journal of the American Academy of Arts and Sciences* 129(4, Fall): entire issue.
Swanberg, Lena Katarina. 2002. *Hedersmordet på Pela: Lillasystern berättar*. Stockholm: Bokförlaget Forum AB.
Tawil, Raymonda. 1979. *My Home, My Prison*. Jerusalem: Adam Publishers.
Wikan, Unni. 1999. "Culture: A New Concept of Race." *Social Anthropology* 7(1): 57–64.
———. 2002. *Generous Betrayal: Politics of Culture in the New Europe*. Chicago: University of Chicago Press.
———. 2003. *For ærens skyld: Fadime til ettertanke*. Oslo: Scandinavian University Press.

PART III

THE POLITICS OF DISTRUST

Chapter 9

Distrust and the Development of Urban Regulations

PATRICK TROY

THE HISTORY of regulations relating to urban development in New South Wales, Australia, is largely one of reaction to catastrophe, failure, political contention, and turmoil. The regulatory system presently in place was incrementally and progressively introduced following a sequence of catastrophes and failures to structures and buildings that collapsed or burned down and of epidemics that brought injury, and sickness, and death. Often, regulations were introduced partly as a "moral panic" response to an incident or series of incidents, spurred by public anger and concern at those catastrophes, failures, and epidemics.

The regulations were designed to reduce the distrust or to increase the trust of residents in the strength, integrity, and fire safety of the structures and buildings that make up their cities and the healthfulness of the urban environment. (The discussion here generally uses an everyday, narrow definition of trust and tends to use "trust" and "confidence" interchangeably.) They were also designed to increase residents' trust that government would look after their interests. In some cases the regulations may be described as symbolic acts of government because they had no real content or could have no significant effect in achieving the stated aims of government. They may have been necessary to assuage anxiety or public anger, although later they may have been cited, in the case for deregulation, as evidence of overregulation.

This account of the development of a system in New South Wales to regulate and control the quality of urban space, and even the quantity of it in a given location, applies with appropriate modification and cultural translation elsewhere. This is most obvious in the other Australian cities established as British colonies. Similar concerns in other advanced urban societies, including those with different cultural traditions, would be expected to result in similar regulatory regimes and elicit similar expressions of trust and distrust.

This account focuses on how specific aspects of urban regulation lead to generalized trust and distrust. Many of the regulations employed to control aspects of urban development in New South Wales came in the baggage of those on the First Fleet. They were the regulations in place in England in the late eighteenth century and were imported without modification. The early governors, commencing in 1788 with the first, Arthur Phillip, drew up local regulations broadly covering buildings and city layout. However, in the new settlement those regulations tended to be observed mainly in the breach. Until the Building Act of 1837 (An Act for Regulating Buildings and Party-walls and for Preventing Mischiefs by Fire in the Town of Sydney [8 Will. IV, no. 6]), only spasmodic attempts were made to regulate by local rules the quality of urban development (Troy 1988).

Urban regulations cover all aspects of urban activity and the construction and operation of urban space. For the purpose of this discussion four areas of regulation—structural safety, fire danger, health, and urban planning—have been chosen to illustrate the point, but a similar argument could be made in other areas with equal force.

Each of these areas raises substantive and procedural issues that illuminate considerations of the development of trust and distrust in government and, in some cases, among citizens and corporations. Whether the regulations have substantive effect in achieving the aims for which they are intended may also have an impact on general trust, although this effect may be much harder to establish and would probably take longer to identify. The procedures adopted to determine whether regulations are relevant or how they should be applied and enforced provide obvious opportunities for the development of trust because knowledge of the fairness with which the procedures are applied quickly becomes common knowledge. Any evidence of inconsistency, maladministration, or corruption in the application of regulations quickly becomes corrosive of trust, especially when citizens believe that there has been more than one episode.

Structural safety and fire regulations are examples of areas in which trust can be established ex ante, in that empirical evidence of substantive benefits of regulations can be identified before the regulations are introduced, modernized, or altered. Weaker ex ante evidence can be established for health regulations, though strong ex post evidence has emerged about the impact on health outcomes of strong regulations. Urban planning is an area in which neither ex ante nor ex post evidence can be strongly mounted because of the multiple influences on any outcome. It is an area in which the formulation of regulations relies on negotiation and shared values and is more strongly mediated by general trust in the behavior of other citizens or general belief that the activities of others are mediated by the same set of regulations, administered consistently and fairly.

Trust is strongly evident in the substantive aspects of the first three areas. This trust possibly derives from generally held confidence in the professionalism and seeming scientific basis of regulations in these areas. It ultimately rests on the trustworthiness of the officials, whose qualifications and standing is established by private independent professional institutes. This trust is breaking down, owing partly to the competition between consultants and partly to the trend toward certification of development and to regulations that confine the area of expertise to measurable performance indicators. In the first three areas, individuals can more readily seek legal redress for any damage or injury resulting from failure to comply with regulations because the failures can be more readily connected with observance of the regulations. Procedural trust will also be stronger in areas in which the regulations are more rigid and "scientifically" based.

The weaker causal connection between urban planning regulations and inefficiencies, externalities, and inequalities in development outcomes means it is harder to seek legal redress. That is, it is harder to establish a direct connection between any injury or loss suffered and the action that allegedly produced the effect. This lower certainty of substantive outcomes and greater contestation in arriving at agreed-upon courses of action mean that the benefits to individuals of departure from the agreed-upon norms and conventions increases the probability of procedural distrust. In some circumstances procedural distrust can arise from genuine citizen participation. For example, a neighbor's objection to a proposed development can be properly and legitimately taken into account but rejected in a decision to approve the proposal; the citizen may then feel that the system has failed because his or her view was not adopted. There is not much that can be done about this except to ensure the maximum degree of transparency in the processes.

Structural Safety

The regulations that cover issues of structural safety were first introduced in New South Wales under the Sydney Police Offences Act in 1833 (4 Will. IV, no. 7). The early regulations governing buildings and other structures, especially those relating to their safety, were simply the codification of "best practice" that architects, engineers, and builders had adopted to ensure that their buildings and structures stood up and served the purposes claimed for them. The regulations increased trust in the builders on the part of members of the community. Because the regulations are in place, buyers and occupants can have greater confidence (trust) in the safety of the buildings and structures.

As engineering became more sophisticated and understanding of the behavior of materials improved, the regulatory framework evolved to be based more closely on scientific analysis than on simple empiricism or "practical knowledge." Structures became more complex, and specialized professions developed in relation to materials, components, and different steps in the construction process. Regulations were developed to be applied not only to the completed structures but also, increasingly, to the quality and proper use of the materials and components used in their construction and to the steps in the construction process.

The community implicitly accepts that it cannot allow individuals to build dwellings and other structures that do not comply with the set of regulations relating to structural safety. Even if individuals are themselves prepared to risk their own lives and health or are happy with the amenities of their development, the regulations must be complied with because others will be exposed to those risks without understanding they are so exposed—an example of the problem of imperfect knowledge. Compliance with regulations must be enforced because individual members of the community have less power than the developers and owners taking the risks and are therefore not able to exercise discretion in relation to them. This is obvious in relation to employees of developers and owners.

Imperfect knowledge is especially important because structures typically have long lives and, once built, may be transferred to others who do not know what decisions were made about the set of risks presented by or embodied in them. Moreover, most people cannot, except with extreme difficulty, determine the risk of structural failure. A person could decide to construct a multistory dwelling knowing she was intending to occupy it using light floor loadings. She might be happy with that constraint on the dwelling's use. And of course she might not understand that the dwelling, once constructed—however "solid" it looks—could only be used for light loading activities. When she uses it in a manner other than that for which it was originally intended and thereby produces a collapse, she might realize, all too late, that she did not and possibly could not assess the risks of her original decisions. Imagine, on the other hand, that she dies or vacates the building without leaving careful instructions about the load limits of the floors or that information is withheld from the next occupant. The next occupant might still want to occupy it as a residence but has a large collection of books or a grand piano that, when placed on the second floor, causes it to collapse. The collapse might even be gradual—that is, the safe floor load might only gradually be exceeded, and deflection or deformation leading to collapse might be imperceptibly slow but ultimately catastrophic nonetheless.

Structures are rarely built without a surplus capacity. That is, they have a capacity to bear loads greater than the load for which they are built. The ratio of the potential load the structure is able to bear to the actual load is called the factor of safety (also referred to colloquially as a "factor of ignorance"). That is, in calculating the design load of a structure, the designer makes an estimate of all the factors that might affect the loads the structure will be required to bear and then increases the load-bearing capacity by a set ratio to allow for factors beyond her control. Part of the reason the factor of safety used is seemingly so high in many structures is that the consequence of failure can be so serious. The ratio is increased to take account of the variation in strength of materials used and to unquantifiable variations in the strength of the structure owing to difference between strength "as built" and the theoretical strength of design but also to variations in assessment of load. That is, the actual process of fabrication and construction leads to variation in the built strength of the structure compared with the theoretical calculations. This means that safety factors include an assessment of the probability that the materials will achieve the strength specified and that construction techniques will ensure that the structure will actually develop the design strength or that the structure will be subjected to a particular load configuration that produces the highest stresses.

In the case of materials and structural elements, after years of research, testing, and experience, regulations have been developed that enable designers and engineers to have great confidence that the materials used in the structures they design and build will have the strength specified. There is, as well, a possibility that the materials, structural elements, and so on will not meet the standard required and expected by the designer or builder. In many situations this will be of little or no consequence, but the precise destination of any particular batch of material or structural elements may not or cannot be known, so that it is prudent to adopt a higher factor of safety than might otherwise be necessary. Similarly, the level of supervision of construction affects the "actual" factor of safety the structure develops. Those constructed under tight supervision and care will be closer to the design strength of the structure, and will therefore have a higher actual factor of safety, than those constructed with less care. Some of the loads on a structure are derived from wind pressures, ambient temperature, and dynamic loads (including, for example, earthquakes), which, by their nature, are unpredictable both in level and frequency of occurrence—hence the selection of a large factor of safety. The projected service life is also an influence on the factor adopted.

One problem that emerges with this approach is that it can generate distrust in the regulatory framework. If users find that a structure can actually carry heavier loads than its specified capacity under what they regard as "normal" conditions, they will tend to disregard the regulations. This will be especially so if dynamic forces of unpredictable but low frequency and large magnitude were important factors in the design but their very infrequency or rarity has lulled people into a false sense of security. On the other hand, if the actual strength of the structure is at the low end of the probability estimate (explicit or implicit) of the strength of the structure and it collapses before it reaches its design load, people lose confidence in the regulations.

In practical terms it is virtually impossible to devise regulations that precisely control the strength of structures. There must be some redundancy in the design of structures and overcapacity in their strength to provide for flexibility in their use. Like any system that is overdetermined, structures that are too tightly specified in terms of their strength are in greater danger of obsolescence or failure when subjected to changes in use or load.

The regulations governing structural safety were originally established by the New South Wales government and often by reference to some national standard, but the process of receiving permission to build the structure was usually the responsibility of a local government authority under powers delegated to it by the state government. The local authority frequently had some discretion about the standard employed, especially where some acceptable range in strength was indicated. Adjoining local authorities often adopted different interpretations of the appropriate standards, and this was the source of dissatisfaction among developers and owners when the reasons for higher standards in one compared with another were not clearly explained. The different standards on occasion led to frustration and distrust, especially among those who were operating in the different jurisdictions.

But the greater source of irritation, frustration, loss of trust, and even active distrust lay in the inconsistent, differential application of the regulations in the same jurisdiction. When it became known that some individuals or corporations had been successful in having lower standards applied to their application for permission to build, confidence in the safety of buildings fell, and loss of trust in administration, if not government, followed. On occasion, this success in having lower standards applied was allegedly owing to corruption in the enforcement of regulations. It may also have been owing to the fact that technological advances had made the regulations outdated and that the administration, understanding this, acted to disregard the regulations in advance of their being revised. The New South Wales government has now adopted the Building Code of Australia (Environmental Planning and Assessment Act 1979, Environmental Planning and Assessment [Building Code of Australia] Regulation 1999). This has led to a loss of local flexibility and discretion. The new performance-based regulations are weaker than the earlier regulations and in theory are more expensive to administer because they require continuing monitoring to be effective.

One of the advantages of a regulatory framework developed as a result of the lived experience of communities is that they often result in structures that are robust enough to cope with significant changes in use. They increase trust in the general safety of the urban fabric. But they also increase trust in a totally different way. Because the structures themselves are capable of adaptation for a multiplicity of uses, they provide a sense of familiarity, amenity, continuity, and stability to the community that uses them. They enable the community to develop confidence—trust—in its future because its members acknowledge and know its past. There clearly are limits to this. It would be unfortunate if all old buildings were protected because of a perception that they contributed to a general feeling of trust and confidence. The continued preservation of buildings that are obviously obsolescent and deteriorated may well create a lack of confidence and trust in government. On the other hand, the destruction of heritage items generally creates distrust in government on the part of the community.

Fire

The Building Act of 1837 (8 Will. IV, no. 6) made provision for structural matters but was essentially designed to prevent "mishaps by fire." Under the act, buildings were required to be set back and spaced to prevent the spread of fire from one to another. In one period, when party walls were required to be carried above the roof line of the adjoining buildings, the act led to the creation of the distinctive style of terraced housing in Sydney.

Fire regulations were introduced to reduce the flammability of structures and buildings and to prevent or inhibit the spread of fire between them. The episodic progressive introduction of such regulations usually followed some highly publicized catastrophic event in which lives were lost. Sometimes whole quarters of a city burned down before the situation could be brought under control and the fires extinguished. On other occasions a single building occupied by many people was destroyed, with great injury and loss of life. The resulting public consternation and distress led to demands by civic leaders that "something be done" to ensure that such events "never happen again." Usually these demands were for proscriptive action against the use of certain materials or for rules governing the provision of exits, the width of corridors and stairways, and the maximum number of people who could be accommodated or assembled in buildings of a given size. Highly flammable roofing materials (such as bark) were banned in the infant colony of New South Wales.

Our developer who intended to occupy the building would argue that she should be allowed to use whatever roofing and other materials she might choose and could calculate the risk of fire and behave accordingly in the building. As in the structural safety illustration, some would argue that other users or members of the community could then make their own assessment of the risk of fire from that and every other building and act accordingly. But it is clear that individuals have a limited capacity to assess the fire risks or the way those risks might change with the aging of materials and so on. In any case, developers are usually coy about or even disingenuous in explaining their own interests and how they are affected.

State authorities on which the private fire insurance industry had substantial representation usually established regulations governing fire safety. Local authorities may have responsibility, delegated by the state government, to administer the regulations for smaller structures. Authorities in New South Wales usually were allowed little discretion in the application of fire regulations, and the main source of irritation lay in the rate at which the regulations were revised to take account of new fire-resistant or fire-retardant materials. For larger structures, the Board of Fire Commissioners, until 1989, and then the fire commissioner retained the power to directly approve the design of buildings and the materials used in its construction. Unlike most other areas of urban regulation, authorities retained the power to enter and inspect structures to ensure that equipment or fire doors and so on were maintained in accordance with the conditions set at the time the use of the building or occupation of the structure was permitted, though changes in the use or intensity of use of structures, especially those in public use, those in which the public congregates, or those the public has access to, may be approved.

Fire authorities retained the power to increase the fire standards to be consistent with those in force at the time of the approved change. Developers, owners, and occupants of larger structures occasionally saw this as an unwarranted intervention, but fires occurred with sufficient frequency to ensure that the fire regulations were applied to the highest contemporary standard, and the inspectorate was active enough in pursuing compliance with them that this was an area of urban administration that had the confidence of residents. The private fire insurance industry was involved not only in setting fire safety standards but also in enforcing them. This included refusing to accept liability for damage, injury, or loss of life if, after a fire, it was shown that the structure was not built or operated in accordance with the fire regulations. This ensured a high degree of compliance with the regulations and a high degree of trust that they would be applied consistently. Fire regulations are now covered by the Building Code of Australia and are uniformly applied.

The high level of enforcement of fire regulations may be used to achieve other social objectives. In New South Wales police have used alleged noncompliance with fire regulations to close down activities they believe are closely related to drug dealing. Rigid application of fire regulations have been used to discourage the conversion of large houses to rooming houses, even though they may have fewer occupants in that use than as conventional houses. The alleged failure of buildings to meet fire regulations has been used as a reason to demolish heritage buildings. These uses of fire regulations tend to bring them into disrepute.

Health

Health issues were first covered by provisions in the Sydney Police Offences Act of 1833 (4 Will. IV, no. 7) to prevent "nuisance," but the first major separate initiative covering health regulations came with a Bill for Promoting the Public Health (17 Vict. 1854) introduced into the New South Wales Legislative Council and modeled on the British Public Health Act of 1848. Although the bill never passed, it served to raise the issues for public debate and made the community more aware of health issues. The Sydney Sewerage Act of 1853 (17 Vict., no. 34) provided the city's commissioners with wide powers for all sanitary purposes. The local press had since 1851 campaigned to improve health conditions ("Sanitary Survey of Contemporary Housing," *Sydney Morning Herald*, 1851).[1] However, there was little action until the Municipalities Act of 1867 (31 Vict., no. 12), which "made some provision for common nuisance prosecutions." Before this, the "only redress for the creation of a nuisance was at common law" (Fisher 1982, 73).

In 1875 the Sydney City and Suburban Sewerage and Health Board was established following a dramatic increase in disease and death and numerous representations about the "unclean state of the city" (Fisher 1982, 74). However, no effective measures to improve health conditions followed. Throughout the 1880s public anger at government inaction grew. Finally, in 1896, New South Wales enacted its first Public Health Act (60 Vict., no. 38). Late in the nineteenth century, following disastrous epidemics, the discovery of some of the mechanisms of disease transmission, and the publication of twelve reports in 1875 and 1876 on water, sewerage, and general health by the Sydney City and Suburban Sewerage and Health Board, regulations were introduced to govern the quality of water and the separation of water-borne waste disposal from potable water supplies (Lloyd, Troy, and Schreiner 1992, chap. 3).

Apart from wanting a more secure supply of potable water to meet the demand during unpredictably long dry periods, higher-income groups demanded the imposition of the higher water standards because they could not trust the lower-income residents to voluntarily avail themselves of the higher-quality supplies. They were concerned that the infectious and contagious diseases that followed poor hygiene would not respect administrative boundaries and that their inevitable contact with lower-income people in the normal transactions of urban life would subject them to greater risk of disease. Wealthier citizens determined that, to obtain a healthier environment for themselves, everyone had to have better-quality water. There were, of course, some wealthier citizens who supported the notion of improved public health on purely altruistic grounds. In any case, the only economical way to provide potable water to the city was to provide it for all residents. (The government might also have encountered difficulties had it tried to reserve public waterways and land for water storage to provide a water supply only for the rich.) The introduction of reticulated water supply systems was opposed by lower-income households because of the cost and because of their distrust of the motives of higher-income households in promoting the development of such systems.

The mechanism chosen to finance the development of a reticulated water supply was a property-based tariff system that forced residents to pay for the water supply whether they used it or not (Dingle and Rasmussen 1991; Lloyd, Troy, and Schreiner 1992). The reliance on the tariff was acknowledgment of distrust by higher-income households in the behavior of lower-income households if given an open choice. Reliance on the property-based tariff was also justified by the view that people would have better health and therefore be of lower risk to the health of others if they actually had and were required to pay for better-quality water. The poor felt that they were being conscripted to pay for a water supply system they did not want. While this was undoubtedly true, health standards did in fact rise, and the improvement was shared by those conscripted to pay for the system, confirming the substantive aspects of the health regulations. A similar consideration was involved in the development of a reticulated sewerage system. Disease spread by fecal contamination and poor drainage of dwellings was widespread. Again, health reformers and the richer households sought the development of a reticulated sewerage system to cope with the problem. The decision was made to compulsorily include all dwellings that could be serviced. Poorer households again felt they were being forced to pay for a service they could not afford and benefited mainly the rich. The financing mechanism again was a tariff based on property values, which, in spite of its rationale, was regressive in its impact. Nonetheless, as with the improved water supply, the development of reticulated sewerage systems led to a marked reduction in communicable diseases. The drop in infant mortality experienced in the late nineteenth and early twentieth centuries can be largely attributed to the development of the new reticulated water supply and sewerage systems.

This illustration is cited not to justify the use of an undemocratic method in pursuit of some social "good" but because it draws attention to a paradox frequently observed in many areas of public policy in which the interest of a minority is of value to the community as a whole. The opposition of the lower-income members of the community could be seen, in part, as an information problem, and they may not have been able to recognize the health risks they faced. Had the water supply and sewerage systems been provided on the basis of real capacity to pay, the lower-income members of the community would have had far fewer grounds for distrust of the actions and motives of the rich. As the property-based tariff system varied with property values, higher-income residents tended to pay more, on average, than those with lower incomes. Higher-income households tended to use more water, and in any event the ratio of higher to lower incomes was much greater than the ratio of higher to lower property values, which meant that in relative terms the "capacity to pay" argument used to rationalize the introduction of the tariff system was vitiated. Higher-income households tended to live in the higher areas, which, being on rock, were expensive to excavate; for this reason, the cost of providing sewerage to high-income households was proportionately higher than that for lower-income households. The effect of this for each system was that the poor paid relatively more.

In setting standards, reference may be made to prevailing scientific theories, experience, or prevailing perceptions of what is "a fair thing." The introduction of building ventilation regulations based on miasmatic theories of disease transmission is a good example of regulations that were adopted after disastrous epidemics but were rationalized by reference to scientific "evidence" and argument. (The City of Sydney Improvement Act [42 Vict., no. 25] of 1879 was the first legislation to make provision for all living rooms to be externally ventilated.) That the regulations remained unchanged when the science used to justify them was replaced by a more powerful science indicating that the ventilation requirements under the regulations did not have the desired effect, provides a valuable insight into the process by which regulations are adopted, enforced, and modified. Here was a situation in which the need for regulations to attain a particular health objective was recognized and the technical expertise of doctors and health inspectors was such as to be able to carry the day in setting the regulations.

Subsequently, inertia in a variety of quarters prevented reform of the regulations for an extended period (about ninety years!), even though the scientific basis for the original regulations had been challenged by newer, better science. The regulations were ultimately reformed as they were progressively brought into disrepute and compliance with them fell. Buildings were constructed with the external air vents specified by the regulations, for example, even though all those administering the regulations knew they had no other effect than to make it impossible to heat rooms—although in those regions with high humidity the ventilators helped minimize condensation within them. Health inspectors knew that people illegally blocked the vents and that manufacturers even made special plates to fit over and block them. Builders learned that building inspectors would not hold up their projects simply because external ventilators were left out or improperly installed.

The regulations were ultimately brought into disrepute, making it easier for the "deregulators" to argue that the system should be dismantled. The public wanted healthy buildings, but developers were able to play on the fears of the public, generating distrust in order to have the regulations removed rather than calling for alternative approaches to the same health end. The removal of the requirement to install external ventilators is an illustration of the asymmetrical power of builders and developers compared with residents. Builders and developers actively created the conditions for distrust to be developed and then secured community support for removal of the regulations. Their campaign ultimately led not only to removal of the requirement for external ventilation but also to the reduction in the requirement for habitable rooms in dwellings to be of a specified minimum size.

Urban Planning

Social objectives are enshrined also in regulations designed to mitigate any adverse consequences that might flow from land use decisions of individuals and especially corporations. Unlike urban regulations in other areas, those governing urban planning were not founded in moral panics of the same kind seen in structural safety, fire, and health. They were grounded in the general belief that there was a "better way" of organizing and distributing activities carried out in urban areas, although some advocates of urban planning expressed a concern that without such reforms the market system might generate self-destructive forces.

The first urban planning regulations were introduced by Governor Phillip in 1788. Control over buildings and some land uses was achieved through various clauses in a number of pieces of legislation affecting local administration in the nineteenth century. Significant control over urban land use and planning issues flowed from the passage of the Local Government Act (no. 41) of 1919. The first legislation in New South Wales to establish a strong regulatory framework for urban planning was the Local Government (Town and Country Planning) Amendment Act (no. 21) of 1945.

One of the features of urban planning is that the benefits are couched in terms of "community interest." The regulations used in urban planning are designed to address the externalities arising from individuals' activities. These externalities may be immediate or long term, obvious and quantifiable or indirect and hard to quantify. The benefits from urban planning and the regulatory system employed to pursue its goals, including the reduction of externalities, are often spread over many people, so that the gains to individuals are small. The benefits may also be indirect and take a long time to be revealed, although they may be large and general. Those who can avoid the "discipline" or constraints of planning or have the regulations interpreted in their favor, however, obtain benefits that are large, focused, and immediate, so they have a strong financial incentive to subvert the system to avoid the inhibitions and restrictions that planning regulations might place on their activities.

Although the urban planning system has large ambitions, in many cases the benefits that flow from it are to those who seek to avoid or change regulations in their favor. They are benefits that go to those involved with the flows—the dynamic elements of incremental additions to and changes in the use of urban space. Planning, on the other hand, tends to be focused on the benefits that are attached to the stock—the continued stable equilibrium in the use of urban space. Planning might, of course, be undertaken to accelerate certain kinds of developments in which not everyone gains, although it will invariably be claimed that the community as a whole benefits.

Urban planning in most modern market economies, in which real property may be privately owned, is negative and passive. While the planning system tends to specify what can be done, it does so by a regulatory system that is negative and rarely requires action The regulations supporting the planning system come into play only when some initiative is proposed. Residents frequently become frustrated when they see a site designated for a particular use remain in another use while similar development occurs elsewhere or even nearby. There is a high degree of discretion in the administration of the regulations, which leads to apparent inconsistency in their application. Developments that are unpopular are approved, while desired developments do not occur or do so in less favorable locations. This may be because the market conditions are not propitious. Residents frequently suspect that the owners of the site designated for some desired development are simply waiting to encourage the planners to allow them to undertake some development that is more advantageous than that shown in the plan. They lose faith in the urban planning system and what it promised, and they become distrustful of its administration.

The majority of residents are intent on the quiet use and enjoyment of their small piece of urban space. They tend to have a live-and-let-live approach, preferring to "rub along" with their neighbors. They are often dismayed and spurred to action when they discover that some change in regulations, often quite subtle, that they did not understand at the time or that they felt did not apply to them leads to significant threat to their amenity or the value of their property. The regulatory framework provides a constancy and consistency in their lives, which they take for granted. It gives them confidence. But the changes in regulations, especially those made rapidly, or the actions flowing from them make them feel a sense of impotency that generates a loss of public trust in the system. When their endeavors to recover the situation, to have the regulations restored, meet with failure, their sense of loss turns to distrust; that may be why some people prefer legally binding zoning plans. Their distrust may be heightened by instances of real or imagined corruption as the explanation of failure, when differences in power between residents and developers is sufficient explanation. One illustration of this is the "trial by exhaustion," a situation in which residents battle hard and successfully to defeat a proposal, but the developer persists, objectors fall away for a number of reasons, and approval of the development is ultimately granted, leaving a feeling of distrust among residents.

Planning regulations or land use controls commonly limit the kinds of uses or activities that may be carried out on a particular parcel of land. As a result, they create opportunities for monopoly profits. In situations in which the decision to permit a particular use on a given site is not transparent and/or is not seen to be "fair," the community develops a degree of distrust in or cynicism of the body, usually a local government, that makes the land use decisions.

The confidence that corporations derive from the permission to carry out those uses or activities on a site encourages them to make job-generating investments. The externalities associated with that use or those activities might be understood and acceptable at the time permission to carry them out was granted, but changes in the technologies employed in pursuing those uses or activities might result in different externalities that are not acceptable. Failure by governments to take remedial action leads to loss of confidence in and even development of distrust in the regulatory system.

Urban planning involves substantive and procedural issues that bear on the development of trust. Most publicity is given to failures in procedures, especially those in which discretion is exercised in favor of one individual or corporation over others. This is an obvious source of annoyance, and accusations of impropriety and corruption are made, leading to a loss of confidence and the generation of cynicism and distrust. A more transparent decision process and less-secret negotiations between developers and consent authorities would reduce distrust.

There is, as well, another sense in which procedural issues may lead to distrust. At one level, planning is seen to be an opportunity for citizens to express their views on the kind of city that they would like to have. Accordingly, most planning systems involve a degree of "citizen participation" or consultation at various stages in the drawing up of the plan.

Citizens are invited to make submissions and are encouraged in the belief that their views will be significant in the final plan. The mechanics of the process are such that it is impossible for the planners to reflect the views of all citizens in the plan, and the process of consultation is inevitably long. As a consequence, when the plans are finally drawn up people feel that they have been excluded, that too many "experts" have been involved and their views have not been taken into account. At worst, they feel manipulated and become distrustful of both the process and the planners. Clearly, a better plan-making process would reduce some of this distrust.

Obvious failures in confidence occur when editorialists and critics blame "the planners" for some disaster or dysfunctional outcome when, in fact, the professional town planners actively opposed the development in question but were overruled by their political masters. Here the distortion in the process is not necessarily venality, but it occurs because of a lack of openness in the system, and it leads to loss of trust in the planners. When planning decisions permit development that the public opposes, they may lead to protest.

Protests over freeway developments, public housing projects, and the siting of hazardous chemical plants are a good example. The politicians at the center of such decisions invariably seek to blame "the planners," and the public tends to focus on them because it is the planners who usually have the task of "explaining" the decision. In administrative cultures like that operating in New South Wales, where public servants cannot participate in public debates without the express permission of ministers at the risk of losing their positions, it is easy for the public to remain uninformed or ill informed. This increases the probability that the public will not have all the relevant information needed to make an accurate assessment of issues. It increases the speculation that impropriety or corruption are factors in play, thus increasing distrust in the process of administration and government. The planners are more likely to be around long after the politicians responsible for the decisions have departed the scene, so they may be able to "set the record straight" after the event, but this is usually too late. In this situation, a short communal or collective memory aids those who seek to incorrectly allocate blame or responsibility. In many situations, "the planners" are in a no-win situation with a consequential loss of trust in the system. In other situations "the planners" may have helped create the distrust because they have tailored their advice to what they believe or are told the politician wants.

Many planning systems, including that in New South Wales, allow appeals against planning decisions, although not usually against rezoning. These appeals create opportunities for the development of both trust and distrust. Frequent successful appeals by developers to the courts tend to lead to loss of trust in the planning system on the part of residents.

Similarly, frequent failed appeals to the courts by residents against planning decisions also tend to lead to distrust in the system. These results are often associated with the different abilities of those appearing before the appeals courts to hire legal representation. Developers typically have more resources than individual residents or residents' groups and often more than the local authorities against whose decisions they enter appeals.

But failures of a substantive kind can also lead to loss of confidence. The loss of confidence may flow from an apparent failure of urban planning to deliver the benefits claimed for it. The counterfactual of what would have happened without the existence of planning regulations is usually impossible to establish, but the expectations developed because of the claims made for urban planning can never be reached in any dynamic system. A large part of the postmodernist explanation for the failure of postwar urban planning lies in its failure to meet the expectations created by the promise of the plan. The process of developing the plan and seeking its public acceptance is necessarily slow, whereas changes in economic and political processes and in social mores and behavior have proved to be astonishingly fast. The conflict implicit in these two temporal dimensions will often be submerged, or not well understood, but frequently find expression as a lack of confidence or trust in urban planning.

Another aspect of urban regulation was the way owners were constrained to build within the curtilage and air space of their own land. Early in the life of the colony the governor introduced regulations to ensure that individual landowners and entrepreneurs did not build where it would obstruct the space designated as a future roadway.

Regulations were also introduced under the Sydney Police Act of 1833 (4 Will. IV, no. 7) to prevent people from erecting buildings or structures that infringed on the space of public thoroughfares or adjoining private land by obstructing or overhanging public thoroughfares. However, individuals who constructed buildings in locations that, while not obstructing the movement or access of others, were extralegal or impermissible, and may well have been illegal, were then able to enlist the necessary political power to provide post hoc approval for the construction.

Similar action is taken in relation to people who carry out an activity that is extralegal or even illegal but who establish a habitual use. Then, if no objections have been raised, they are able to establish a prescriptive right to continue that use. This legitimation of activity or development after the event is a method that has evolved in both advanced and less developed countries. It was used by early settlers in Australia, who "squatted" on land and were then able to have their use of it legitimated. More recently it has been employed by leaseholders in Canberra who carry out activities that are beyond those set in their lease purpose clauses but are legitimated by poor administration of the leasehold system. It is perhaps more understandable in less developed countries, where communities of squatters from rural regions develop on the outskirts of major cities and are subsequently regularized to give the squatters legal rights to the land. In both more and less developed countries, however, the practice tends to lead to cynicism about governance and to distrust in regulations.

This is different from the continuation of existing uses that were begun lawfully—for example, a quarry or factory commenced before the existence of any planning laws saying a quarry or factory was not permitted. In advanced urban economies authorities cannot just say, "We have now changed the rules, so close down." Either the owners or operators of the quarry or factory can be compensated to cease activities or the authorities can ensure there is no expansion or intensification. If the activities are abandoned, the authorities may then ensure they are not resumed.

Regulatory System

The regulatory system is designed to meet three objectives:

1. To ensure that products and processes meet some settled quality standard;
2. To minimize or eliminate externalities from the manufacture or use of products or processes;
3. To ensure that the community's objective of ensuring equity, including equitable access to services, is met, whether the equity is in outcomes, opportunity, or process.

The first objective seeks to minimize the problems of information flows in imperfect markets because individuals cannot know all they need to know about products and processes they use. Pursuit of this objective is designed to simultaneously guarantee that products and processes meet some specified performance standard and, in constructing a set of penalties for noncompliance, to eliminate free-rider problems with the manufacture and sale of such products or processes. The second objective is to ensure that the impact on others or on the environment of the use of products or processes is minimized. Regulations are needed because individuals may not know, or even care, what the negative externalities of such products or processes are, but others need to be protected. The third objective is to ensure reasonable fairness in the treatment each citizen receives at the hand of government—that everyone has the same degree of safety in the buildings they use, the same protection from fire, the same confidence in the water they drink, and so on.

All three objectives may be pursued for a variety of economic and noneconomic or social reasons (Jessop 1990; Colebatch 1991; Boyer 1990). All three are pursued in the belief that, initially at least, they should create or increase trust in the system of governance. However, unless they are pursued consistently, they create distrust among affected individuals, leading to a climate or communal attitude of distrust. To ensure that trust in the system of governance is developed, residents need to know that the regulations are being applied and that the objectives they were designed for are being achieved. This implies that there is a need to keep regulations under review and to maintain an open system to guard against their abuse.

The Development of Trust and the Case for Regulations

Distrust in the regulatory system and even the system of governance will be even greater when the externalities associated with the activities to be regulated are not understood at the time regulations are introduced but are subsequently found to be unacceptable. Community members will complain that governments should act to protect them and that, in situations in which the consequences of the externalities associated with an activity or land use are unknown, they should act with caution. Citizens feel that governments are in a position to know or have the resources to assemble the intelligence, which they cannot, and that it should use this intelligence to protect their interests.

The regulations used to specify the acceptable uses or activities to be carried out at specific locations are simultaneously seen by some to be too general while by others to be too specific, to be too flexible or excessively rigid and so unable to accommodate the dynamic nature of commercial and industrial activities. Some argue that performance-based regulations would be able to provide adequate controls in that situation. The problem with all regulations based on land use controls, whether performance based or not, is that it is not possible to predict the ways in which the externalities will change or whether there will be a change in attitude about what is acceptable.

Residents might, for example, decide that a particular level of discharge of liquids, gases, or particulates is acceptable, but subsequent research shows the substance to have serious health consequences. The corporation responsible for discharge of the substance might still be within the terms of the original performance agreement and can therefore be forced to change only with extreme difficulty. Residents might accept a particular level of traffic generation at one time, only to find that growth of other related activities or changes in traffic generation has produced unacceptable levels of congestion. Those administering regulations can become frustrated because they have done their best in one situation at a particular time only to find that the rate of change of information and community expectations and perceptions have been more rapid than could have been foretold. They feel "damned if they do and damned if they don't." Those critical of them frequently do not care to try to understand the historical context in which the regulations were developed, or they may cynically use the general lack of understanding in pursuit of their own political ambitions.

Distrust and the Development and Administration of Regulations

Some might say that in choosing to construct her multistory building to be able to carry only low loads or with more flammable materials, our developer was exercising her right of choice and that the community ought not attempt to protect people from themselves. They would argue that on grounds of consumer sovereignty she should be allowed to "buy" whatever level of safety she desires and, if she so chooses, to advise people what that was. They might also argue on the same grounds of primitive or vulgar notions of consumer sovereignty that other members of the community ought to make their own decisions about whether to use such building. Elements of this argument can be seen in property transactions: when she comes to sell her building, the rule of caveat emptor applies. It is the responsibility of the potential buyer to discover the limitations or condition of the building. In most cases, however, it is extremely difficult for individuals, including experts, to discover the strength of a structure and the care taken in its construction after it has been built.

Those who use the consumer sovereignty argument hold that an individual who is adversely affected by the failure of buildings to have the appropriate strength, be resistant to fire, or be healthful can always seek remedy in common lawsuits. They can seek redress under common law for any wrong experienced at the hands of others by, for example, suing for damages. This is theoretically true. The practical effect of this approach, however, is that the contest is often between parties of unequal strength, and the courts become jammed with such cases. The resulting frustration and lack of certainty breeds distrust in the institutions of the community. It has been argued that the predominance of the notion of consumer sovereignty in the nineteenth century led to chaos and a flow of cases in the courts that threatened to undermine the basis of the common law system, which, in turn led to the introduction of urban regulations (Sedley 1996). The introduction of regulations not only secured the stability of the common law system, it also led to a fairer treatment of individuals who were, or were at risk of, being adversely affected by structures that were safety, fire, or health hazards.

Proponents of deregulation tend to take a simplistic position in arguing that consumer sovereignty should prevail and the market should, in effect, set the standards under which society operates. They argue that this is more democratic and reflective of social values and attitudes than standards set by "bureaucrats." The consumer sovereignty argument is usually made on the basis of perceived short-term individual benefit. The benefit is usually economic and to the exclusion of other considerations. It denies long-term effects and assumes that the individual not only can but does know all that needs to be known to make a decision. It denies any sense of community engagement or individual or collective responsibility, especially for the externalities that might arise from the decision.

It might be possible for individuals, or hired experts, to make some assessment of the safety of a small number of structures—their dwellings, the bridges they cross on their way to work, the buildings in which they work. But the notion that such assessments can be made by all individuals for all the structures they use or enter during the course of their normal urban life is risible in the extreme. It is more efficient for regulations to ensure safety than for all individuals to hire their own consultants. The argument that standards are set by "bureaucrats" is instructive. It implies that only individuals can make good decisions and all decisions should therefore be left to them; that "there is no such thing as society" (for a strong statement of this view, see Cobin 1997). It also implies that the bureaucrats' political masters do not have control over the design or regulations or of their administration. The ultimate development of the consumer sovereignty argument is that there would be no regulations but there would be a high level of distrust between citizens. The fact that individual members of a community cannot be relied upon to "do the right thing" is amply demonstrated by the introduction of sanctions and the employment of inspectors to identify transgressions and to enforce compliance. That is, the development of the regulatory framework was based on the notion that people could not be trusted to act in the interests of others or, indeed, their own longer-term interests.

An interesting feature of the deregulatory argument is that as soon as the developer seeks to insure a building against structural collapse or fire or the risk of people suing for damages arising from injuries sustained in using the building, insurance companies begin to establish a regulatory framework covering structural safety, fire, and other risks. They develop a form of privatization of regulations. Clients and firms then insist on government regulation or backing for those regulations because they cannot trust other companies to compete with them on even terms. Thus the level of distrust in self-regulation or in the operation of the market leads to pressures by the private sector for the introduction of regulations to ensure that their interests are protected. The market itself seeks regulations as a way of minimizing the free-rider problem and increasing the level of ontological security in the system. Dominant players in the market will establish an informal set of regulations designed to maximize their profits and to protect their corporate interests, which might not coincide with those of the community.

The realities of market imperfections or inefficiencies, including imperfect knowledge and the inability of most people to obtain or assess the knowledge that is available, leads to a demand for regulations to protect individuals and to minimize externalities arising from the construction and operation of buildings. Regulations may be seen as the efficient way of providing the information essential for the safe conduct of the rich variety of activities carried out in urban areas. If the private certification of procedures are extended to planning decisions, the enforcement of regulations becomes even harder.

The paradox that people nonetheless might distrust the regulations or their implementation simply introduces a tension that can be seen as a productive, healthy, necessary condition to keep the regulations continuously under review. The distrust or skepticism in the system thus acts to ensure that the regulations are dynamic. So long as the regulations are reviewed and are more or less in line with new knowledge and or community expectations (which tend to demand higher standards), the level of distrust will not become corrosive of confidence. Distrust is a matter of degree: low-level distrust or skepticism is a necessary condition for the introduction and review of regulations, but when some higher level of distrust (usually unpredictable but dependent on the political situation) is reached it becomes corrosive to the system of governance, and the regulatory system breaks down, leading to chaos and inequality.

Governments can be gulled by well-organized, focused lobbying into changing regulations, especially when they are faced with acute problems of economic management. Politicians anxious to retain power can be convinced (especially if their reelection is funded in whole or in part by those promoting change) that removing or modifying the regulations will "solve" their problems. The climate for such changes can be created by skillful use of the media. The absence of research to back the claims of those seeking deregulation is no barrier to action by the government, especially when those who appear to know or have some special authority vested in them give the advice. The sectional source and nature of the advice is ignored, but as the changes in regulations work their way through the system without producing the claimed benefits, observers take a cynical view of the government and develop a deep distrust of it, its processes, and its policies.

Sectional interests almost invariably oppose the introduction of regulations designed to shape or control their activities. In New South Wales, developers and builders vociferously opposed every attempt to introduce building safety, fire, health, and urban planning regulations, arguing that they would increase the cost of building. The regulations probably did that, but the community nonetheless saw a wider benefit. On occasion, vested interests were able to use delaying tactics in the democratic process to ensure that the regulations were not promulgated. In some cases, it took years to devise and introduce regulations. Often, there were repeated similar disasters before regulations could be introduced to remedy particular problems. Popular sentiment was often overturned or ignored by the legislature because of the power of vested interests. This led to cynicism and distrust in regulations as a means of achieving social objectives. Vested interests have often been strong enough to ensure that regulations have not been enforced, thus creating distrust in the system of enforcement.

Ian Ayres and John Braithwaite (1992) might claim that this was to be expected. Whatever the case for a particular set of regulations, whether they are effective in their design or in their administration depends on the political situation at the time. That is, the effectiveness of a particular set of regulations is a function of the continuous interplay of forces in favor of regulation and those adversely affected by them in the short run. Those affected in the long run, such as homeowners, should have the same interests in high standards of housing safety, fire, and health and in their enforcement as those in favor of regulations.

Lower attention to enforcement in one period might be followed in the next by strong administrative backlash if some failure has occurred resulting in death or injury and the government feels that to regain authority it has to take exemplary action. In other words, the political compact that results in tacit agreement to ignore regulations is inherently unstable if the grounds of the compact are not transparent and publicly accepted. It should be noted, however, that the regulatory backlash often seems to fall away quickly. This is a situation that breeds distrust both on the part of people who are regulated and those who demand regulation.

Discussion

Distrust in government resulting from its activities in regulating urban development arises

1. when regulations get out of date because of changed understanding, behavior, or expectations;
2. when developers and others are able to evade the regulations and residents feel they have not been consulted, when they see the regulations as being capriciously or inconsistently applied, or when they feel the system is being abused;
3. when individuals feel frustrated in their work or general activities and they find the regulations invasive.

It would be misleading to conclude from this that dissatisfaction with urban regulations or their administration is central to the degree of confidence people have in their governments. The daily reminder residents have as they confront points of congestion, experience inefficiency in the urban system, see housing developments that offend their sense of amenity, or observe flagrant displays of decision making that has regressive effects may serve to turn their fatalistic acceptance into hardened cynicism or active distrust. It would be hard to deny, however, that the general level of trust or distrust must affect the level of trust in urban regulations. The level of distrust in the community, however, is now such that the level of distrust in urban regulations probably equals that in other areas.

The first source of distrust is bound to occur, given the episodic nature of the introduction and review of regulations, but it need not lead to disabling levels of distrust in government, although it could lead to anguish and despair before the regulations are amended or modernized. The second source of distrust might, for example, simply be a function of the planning system that favors individual rights in real property—that is, the distrust is a symptom of the system of private ownership of land, in which case it is bound to occur and need not produce a major level of distrust in the system of governance as a whole, although it might produce a general feeling of disillusionment. The third source is important because it represents the continuing tension between social protection and the notion of community, on the one hand, and individual self-interested desires, on the other.

While these sources of distrust might have some local salience and even be generally prominent on occasion, it seems improbable that they are the main or critical sources. These are likely to be secondary causes, the primary causes being those discussed elsewhere in this volume (see, especially, chapter 1), although it should be remembered that community contact with urban regulations is increasing as people become more aware of and concerned for their local amenity and environment. Certainly people are becoming more concerned with unequal or inconsistent application of rules, and this leads to distrust of the system and the rules. Administrative culture and performance have been more important in generating trust or distrust if only because the community's contacts with urban regulations are infrequent and their awareness of them is low, whereas in areas like taxation, welfare, health, education, and the conduct of business, the level of contact is more frequent and citizens' awareness higher. That is, distrust is more likely to be related to the general experience of members of the community with their government in those areas in which they have frequent contact or exposure. Those societies or administrations in which bureaucrats have a good reputation and are seen to act fairly encourage trust. It could be argued from this that those societies in which the bureaucratic systems are being weakened will experience an increase in distrust and that this may well be reflected early in the distrust associated with urban regulation.

Conclusion

The mechanics of the way the community's desire for protection is translated and given administrative form may itself be a source of skepticism and, ultimately, distrust. In most cases, the instruments that aim to meet the community's concern over safety, fire, and health, for example, are not acts of Parliament but regulations that may be made under an act and attached to it as a schedule. The argument in favor of this process is that it makes the establishment and updating of regulations easier because, although they must be tabled in the Parliament for a short time and are liable to be disallowed by a vote in one or another of the houses of the Parliament, the process of change is less cumbersome and less fraught with danger of being ignored than if the same objective were expressed in an act of Parliament. But this same ease of introducing regulations can be used to quickly remove them with little public debate.

The regulations governing the production of urban space have one feature that is unlike most other regulatory systems in that the devising and enforcement of the regulations have very long-term effects. The individuals who are regulated are usually those engaged in the production of urban space, in the case of structural safety, fire, and health regulations, and those who carry out various activities, in the case of urban planning regulations. Those who demand regulations want protection from the builders of structures or those engaged in a variety of urban activities and whom they believe are not much exercised by considerations of the externalities of their actions. Although regulations are seen by some as cumbersome and may be subject to change by the Parliament, in the development of urban space they are preferable to statutory rules and state policies and plans that may be merely made by a minister or official and published. There is no scrutiny by Parliament and often no opportunity for input by the community. Increasingly this has been the course adopted by governments. Its main attribute is speed, but its cost is lack of scrutiny and debate by both Parliament and the community, leading to profound distrust, especially when the promised benefits of development are not realized.

Distrust develops when the scientific basis of building standards is superseded but the regulations are not updated. Distrust might also emerge because the buildings and structures built under the regulations are not maintained. That is, while the regulations covering buildings and structures may well have been properly applied at the time of construction, as a result of aging and deterioration they no longer meet the accepted standards of safety. The building owners and managers have failed in their duty of care if, by economizing on maintenance, the buildings and structure no longer provide safe conditions. This is a common problem where building and structure owners are forced to choose between the construction of new buildings and structures or maintaining those existing. Deterioration and decay leads to loss of confidence in the enforcement of regulations. Distrust may also appear when there is capricious or inconsistent application or enforcement of regulations, such as those covering control of urban development. In situations in which the actions of government appear to favor one developer or group of developers over residents, distrust is generated.

It may be that individuals desire a degree of certainty and reliability that the political and economic system does not or cannot deliver. They seek stability, security, and predictability in their personal lives and in their community. They are social beings who have an obvious self-interest but who have and want to have a sense of engagement with and obligation and commitment to others, though they may seem incapable of fully accepting that the society in which they live is inherently dynamic and focused on the individual. When economic and social processes produce outcomes, such as the breakdown in the regulatory system, that undermine their own stability, threaten their security, and make the situation uncertain for their community, they tend to lose trust in the system. When they are particularly grievously affected, this loss of trust can rapidly turn to active distrust and cynicism.

This raises the question of whose distrust matters in urban regulation. Whose distrust gets listened to? The existence and operation of professional bodies served initially to increase trust in urban regulations, but as their authority has weakened distrust with the development and application of urban regulations has increased. Distrust on the part of developers and entrepreneurs has been given additional weight as the role of government has been challenged and reduced. This, in turn, has meant that the relative power of residents has been reduced and accompanied by an increase in distrust. The cultivation of distrust or, at the least, of an articulated skepticism by citizens in governments and their close and comfortable relationships with corporations might be necessary in the reconstruction of competent and trustworthy governments. Such skepticism might serve to force governments into devising ways of informing citizens of issues and proposed responses in a transparent manner.

What can be observed in examining urban regulations in a situation in which real property is privately owned is that they are founded on distrust—distrust by the community that individuals and corporations will not voluntarily act in the interest of others, distrust by the community that regulators may act in an inconsistent or improper manner, and distrust by the citizens that governments may act on the encouragement of powerful interests to citizens' own disadvantage.

Notes

1. This was a series of reports over an extended period in 1851.

References

Ayres, Ian, and John Braithwaite. 1992. *Responsive Regulation: Transcending the Deregulation Debate.* New York: Oxford University Press.

Boyer, Robert. 1990. *The Regulation School: A Critical Introduction.* Translated by Craig Charney. New York: Columbia University Press.

Cobin, John M. 1997. *Building Regulation, Market Alternatives and Alloidal Policy.* Aldershot, U.K.: Avebury.

Colebatch, Hal. 1991. "Getting Our Act Together: A Case Study in Regulation and Explanation." Paper presented at the Fifteenth World Congress of the International Political Science Association, Buenos Aires (July 21–25).

Dingle, Tony, and Carolyn Rasmussen. 1991. *Vital Connections: Melbourne and Its Board of Works, 1891–1991.* Melbourne: McPhee Gribble.

Fisher, Shirley. 1982. "The Pastoral Interest and Sydney's Public Health." *Historical Studies* 20(78): 73–89.

Jessop, Bob. 1990. "Regulation Theories in Retrospect and Prospect." *Economy and Society* 19(2): 153–215.

Lloyd, Clem J., Patrick N. Troy, and Shelley Schreiner. 1992. *For the Public Health: The Hunter District Water Board, 1892–1992.* Melbourne: Longman Cheshire.

Sedley, Sir Stephen. 1996. "The Common Law and the Constitution." Radcliffe Lectures, University of Warwick, England.

Troy, Patrick N. 1988. "Government Housing Policy in New South Wales, 1788–1900." *Housing Studies* 3(1): 20–30.

Chapter 10

Coping with Distrust in Emerging Russian Markets

VADIM RADAEV

THE MARKET is not confined to a set of transactions among anonymous actors, according to the new institutionalist theory and economic sociology. It is constituted by complex institutional arrangements that help market actors cope with uncertainty and opportunism. The market formation also includes elements of interpersonal trust and trust in institutions, which are necessary for stabilization of the market relationships.

How do market actors decide to act if the level of trust is low? In what ways does distrust in business relations influence entrepreneurial strategies? What kinds of arrangements are created to enforce business contracts and develop trust among business partners?

Issues of trust and distrust in business relationships are explored in this chapter from the standpoint of the new institutionalist theory (Fligstein 1996; North 1992; Williamson 1985), marrying this approach with the literature on trust (Gambetta 1988; Hardin 2001; Rose-Ackerman 2001a; Stompka 1999). Trust is defined here as the belief that other agents will act in a predictable way without special sanctions.

On the empirical side, I use survey data to demonstrate how frequent infringement of business contracts produces interpersonal distrust among business partners in Russia. Given the inability of public institutions to enforce business contracts, Russian entrepreneurs have had to introduce a variety of methods for contract enforcement. Entrepreneurs try to protect themselves from opportunism by taking precautionary measures, checking up on their future business partners, and building closed business networks. Trust formation in a low-trust society starts

234 Distrust

at the interpersonal level in different market segments and develops further at the institutional level.

Data Sources

The analysis presented in this chapter is based primarily on two data sources: a standardized survey of nonstate enterprise managers and entrepreneurs and a set of in-depth interviews. In the survey, conducted from November 1997 to January 1998, 227 completed questionnaires were collected from the heads of nonstate enterprises in twenty-one regions (mainly in the central European parts of Russia). All main areas of economic activity were represented. Selected basic parameters of the surveyed enterprises and entrepreneurs are presented in the appendix to this chapter (for a detailed description of research outcomes, see Radaev 1998a, 2001a). In-depth interviews, conducted from May 1997 to April 1998, focused on the emerging areas of nonstate businesses. A total of ninety-six interviews were recorded, including repeated interviews with twenty-seven respondents of an earlier survey, conducted in 1993 by the Center for Political Technologies.

I also refer to the outcomes of two previous surveys: a survey of 277 Moscow entrepreneurs conducted, in 1993, with the help of the research team of the Institute of Economics at the Russian Academy of Sciences (Radaev 1997) and a 1996 survey of the heads of 887 small enterprises and 210 medium and large enterprises, conducted at the First Russian Congress of Small and Medium Enterprise representatives (Radaev 1996).

Honesty and Tensions in Business Relations

What are the personal features that are most highly valued in business partners today? This open-ended question was put to the Russian entrepreneurs. Almost forty characteristics were noted. An overwhelming majority—79 percent—ranked honesty and trustworthiness as the most important quality in a business partner (see table 10.1). This is in contrast with the qualities normally cited in describing "the real entrepreneur"—intuition, intellect, creativity, and motivation (Radaev 1997, chap. 6).

In addition to concerns with honesty, entrepreneurs also care about practical rules of business conduct, like timely payments and reliability in general. All in all, this concern reflects serious tensions that exist in relationships among business partners.

We asked entrepreneurs whether in the past year they had had any disputes in their relations with other firms and clients that could not

Table 10.1 Most Important Personal Features of Business Partners

Feature	Percentage
Honesty, trustworthiness	79
Responsibility, reliability	29
Professional skills, competence	19
Accuracy, precision	12
Initiative	8
Financial sustainability	4
Gender, ethnicity	1
Work experience, other	2

Source: Author's compilation.
Note: N = 227

be easily resolved. Forty-three percent of our respondents gave a positive answer. More tensions were observed in medium and large companies than in small companies (table 10.2). Heads of privatized firms and firms having state-owned assets complained of disputes more often than heads of newly established private firms. As for sector divisions, the firms in the areas of finance, market services, and industrial production more frequently reported problems with their business partners.

These data point to a high level of opportunism in business relationships. The main source of this problem comes from the frequent infringement of business contracts, which leaves Russian businesses vulnerable to risk and uncertainty. We analyzed the spread of opportunistic behavior by the market segment and entrepreneurial group. To measure the

Table 10.2 Tensions with Partners and Clients, by Type of the Firm Characteristics

Characteristic	Percentage Reporting Tensions in the Last Year
Size of firm	
Large and medium	54
Small	40
Type of firm	
Privatized	54
Newly established private	40
State-owned assets	
Yes	56
No	40

Source: Author's compilation.
Note: N = 227

236   Distrust

Table 10.3   Rate of Contract Infringement in Russian Business (Percentage)

	Frequency of Infringement		
	Often	From Time to Time	Rarely
In Russian business in general	49	43	8
In one's personal experience	32	50	18

Source: Author's compilation.
Note: N = 227

level of opportunism in relationships among business partners we presented our respondents with two questions:

1. How often are business contracts violated in Russian business today?
2. How often do you face contract infringement in your own business activity?

Our data confirm a high level of opportunism. Nearly everyone (92 percent) responded that infringements of the business contracts did happen in Russian business generally (table 10.3). Forty-nine percent of the entrepreneurs responded that contract infringement occurs frequently, and only a negligible portion (8 percent) saw no infringement problem at all. These results are supported by our previous research findings (reported in Radaev 1996, 74–76). The personal experience of our entrepreneurs strongly correlated with their general attitudes on this measure of opportunistic behavior. A vast majority of entrepreneurs (82 percent) reported that they had faced contract infringement in their own day-to-day business activity. One third (32 percent) said they had that experience frequently (table 10.3).

Our data indicate that contract infringements are largely responsible for tensions among business partners. The more often entrepreneurs report having confronted opportunism in contract relations, the more they complain of tensions in their market relationships (table 10.4). Data of the in-depth interviews we conducted also confirm that contract infringement presents a serious problem for Russian entrepreneurs.

It would be reasonable to assume that the level of opportunism differs across market sectors and firm characteristics. Table 10.5 gives the percentage of entrepreneurs reporting frequent contract infringement by characteristics of their firms. Again, larger companies appear to confront opportunism more frequently than small firms. Fifty-seven percent of heads of large and medium enterprises reported that contract violations occur often in Russian business dealings, and 40 percent

Table 10.4 Tensions with Partners and Clients Within the Past Year, by Frequency of Contract Infringement (Percentage)

	Frequency of Contract Infringement		
	Often	From Time to Time	Rarely
	In Russian business generally		
Have tensions	53	37	16
Do not have tensions	47	63	84
	In personal experience		
Have tensions	59	39	23
Do not have tensions	41	61	77

Source: Author's compilation.
Note: N = 227

Table 10.5 Rate of Contract Infringement, by Enterprise Characteristic (Percentage)

	Frequency of Infringement	
Characteristic	Often in Russian Business	Often in Personal Experience
Size of enterprise		
Large and medium	57	40
Small	47	30
State-owned assets		
Yes	58	36
No	47	31
Age of enterprise		
Established (privatized) before 1996	52	35
Established (privatized) in 1996 or 1997	41	25
Sector		
Industrial production	56	38
Construction, transportation	47	47
Wholesale trade	62	43
Retailing, catering, consumer services	47	30
Finance, market services	61	44
Science, health care, culture	44	20
Other	42	26

Source: Author's compilation.
Note: N = 227

reported frequent occurrence in their personal experience. The situation appears to be slightly easier for the managers of small firms: 47 percent reported frequent contract violations in Russian business in general, and 30 percent reported frequent occurrence in their personal experience. The incidence of difficulties with partners and transactions is certainly higher for larger establishments, which makes the probability of market failures higher as well.

Comparing firms by sector division, the most pessimistic views are expressed by managers of firms in the area of finance (44 percent of respondents point to the frequency of the contract infringement problem), construction and transportation (47 percent), and wholesale trade (43 percent). The problem seems to be less acute in the areas of retailing, catering, and consumer services (30 percent) and science, health care, and culture (20 percent). This may be because an entrepreneur whose clients pay in cash, as they do in retailing and other consumer services, is able to impose immediate control over transactions, given that consumer credit in Russia is underdeveloped. Entrepreneurs who are paid through bank transfers, on the other hand, are more vulnerable to payment delays and various tricks. It is noteworthy that across sectors, with the exception of construction and transportation, the two measures of the contract infringement reflecting general estimations and personal experience differ by 15 to 20 percent across sectors. General estimations may be more negative because of interventions of the mass media and common-sense discourse describing Russian business dealers as unreliable. Estimations made from personal experience are less negative.

There are also variations by entrepreneurial group. Owners of businesses are more sensitive toward unreliability in their business partners. A more critical attitude is also reflected by entrepreneurs with higher education and higher "human capital" (measured as a combination of different professional skills). As for gender divisions, male entrepreneurs seem to experience contract violations more often than female entrepreneurs (87 and 70 percent, respectively) (table 10.6). This could simply reflect the fact that men normally occupy higher risk segments of the markets in Russia than women.

Distrust in Persons and Institutions

The cause of the chronic payment arrears between enterprises is a subject of continuous debate among Russian experts. Some say they result from the macroeconomic instability and rigid monetarist policies of the Russian government. Others argue that they are largely an outcome of conscious opportunistic strategies of enterprise managers "seeking their self-interest with guile," in the terms of Oliver E. Williamson

Table 10.6 Rate of Contract Infringement, by Entrepreneur Characteristics (Percentage)

Characteristic	Frequency of Infringement	
	Often in Russian Business	Often in Personal Experience
Owner of the firm	51	34
Manager of the firm	42	27
Males	52	35
Females	41	25
University degree	46	16
No university degree	50	35
Low- and medium-level human capital	45	25
High-level human capital	55	43

Source: Author's compilation.
Note: N = 227

(1985). Both factors might contribute to distortions in the payment systems. In any case, the situation produces serious institutional effects, creating distrust among business partners.

In a business environment in which opportunism is widespread, as it is in Russia, reciprocal trust is difficult to establish. Distrust is displayed in the attitude toward newcomers and market invaders; regular partners are considered to be more or less reliable. However, even in long-term partnerships distrust is a serious problem. The head of a real estate firm expressed the dominant feeling: "I do not trust entirely . . . anyone in business."

This statement can be seen to reflect not only rule-based trust but also affect-based trust—trust founded on personal ties with family and friends (Rose-Ackerman 2001a). These strong ties are obviously preferred to relations with strangers, and many entrepreneurs start their businesses relying on relatives and friends. However, in the experience of the entrepreneurs we interviewed, over the course of years even affect-based trust was largely undermined. "It does not matter," said one manager of a firm selling medical equipment, "if you have very confidential relations with somebody and that somebody loves you tenderly. Payment arrears . . . happen easily." The head of an advertising agency noted, "In those few special cases when I stepped back from the principle of prepayment I was punished severely. . . . And it was my personal acquaintances who did that to me."

These entrepreneurs seem to have had similar experience with foreign companies. Western companies have a reputation in Russia for being more open and more reliable (which is partially true), and for many years it was a matter of high prestige for Russians to have business partners from the West. Nevertheless, after dealing with foreign companies, some of the Russian entrepreneurs we spoke with found the experience frustrating, especially given their initial high expectations. In the end, our entrepreneurs expressed no fundamental difference in attitude toward domestic and foreign business partners. "We do not trust Western partners," the head of a tourist business said, "because they do not always follow their obligations." The head of a group of companies noted that "we used to check up [on] our Western partner more thoroughly than the Russian one."

The main reason for Russian distrust of Western companies came to light during our interviews. When perestroika commenced, a great many Western business people were attracted to the emerging Russian markets as a land of opportunity. At the beginning, it was difficult to distinguish between swindlers and reputable business people simply by checking their credit histories and reputations because information channels were not well developed in Russia. Many Russian entrepreneurs fell victim to their initial one-sided trust in Western business. It was not until Russian entrepreneurs had some experience with Western firms that they became more cautious and selective in their dealings with them.

Interpersonal distrust can be managed with the help of trust in institutions. Third parties are sometimes able to resolve disputed issues. If they are reliable, institutions can encourage reciprocal trust among business partners, as well.

Traditional economic theory is largely based on the assumption of "legal centralism," which posits the existence of effective legislation and relatively costless state and arbitration control that enforces rules (Williamson 1985, chap. 1, sec. 2). The weakness of this assumption is evident, especially in case of Russia, in which public institutions are not effective in imposing sanctions against opportunism and malfeasance. Opinion polls demonstrate relatively low trust in institutions in Russia compared with other countries (Rose-Ackerman 2001b).

When confronting a case of malfeasance on the part of their business partners, only 24 percent of Russian entrepreneurs said they would bring the issue before the arbitration court. Most businessmen (55 percent) would instead try to negotiate and persuade their partners by informal means. Eleven percent of the entrepreneurs we interviewed would use force to compensate their losses.

Our findings partially coincide with those of another 1997 study of 328 Russian enterprises (Hendley, Murrel, and Ryterman 1999). According to this study, 56 percent of the enterprise leaders preferred to hold meetings with their business partners to prevent or resolve problems, compared with the 25 percent who would appeal to the arbitration court. This closely correlates with our findings, though, contrary to our conclusion, the researchers conclude that legal methods of enforcement are preferred to private methods. To some extent this difference could be explained by the prevalence of privatized enterprises (77 percent) in their sample. The managers of the privatized establishments in our survey did say that they appealed to the arbitration courts more frequently.

The number of formal appeals of Russian entrepreneurs to the arbitration court started to increase in the mid-1990s (Sapsai 1997), a trend that has continued in recent years. Still, a large number of entrepreneurs prefer informal ways of dispute settlement. There are several reasons for this. First, the court has proved to be one of the most corrupt institutions in Russia, widely used for asset stripping and aggressive mergers. Second, the Russian courts are not independent from the government officials and are frequently used as a political instrument. For these reasons, distrust of the courts among business leaders in Russia runs deep at present. Third, arbitration procedures are time consuming and costly. Fees may amount to 1.5 to 5 percent of the disputed sum, making arbitration especially costly for small firms. Fourth, owing to many gaps in existing legislation, there is no guarantee that justice will be established. Fifth, even in the event of success in the court, losses are not necessarily covered. Court executives are few, and as a rule they are not very efficient. They often fail to reach a defector. According to the opinion of the head of a trading firm, "It is worth [it] to appeal to the arbitration court only if you deal with the reputable business organization."

The head of a production and trading firm gave us one more remarkable argument for avoiding court procedures: "By appealing to the court you can ruin your relationships. . . . It is not a usual way of doing things. There are two categories—'us' and 'them.' All state authorities involving tax inspections and arbitration court are viewed as 'them.' It is a bad policy to address them." Thus in addition to the inefficiency of arbitration procedures and high transaction costs there are informal boundaries of "customary law" that persuade entrepreneurs to resolve delicate issues among themselves. This logic of negative solidarity—pitting "us" (businessmen) against "them" (authorities) is still influential. And formal appeals to the state are frequently judged on moral grounds as attempts to break somebody down. This example illustrates how trust in public institutions can undermine, rather than strengthen, interpersonal trust.

These attitudes of Russian businessmen are not unique. For instance, an older study of business relations in the United States finds that entrepreneurs tended to settle disputes without appealing to court. The lawsuits for breach of contract are rare, because suing a partner is considered a poor strategy (Macaulay 1992, 273–74, 279) Still, the Russian case is substantially different. In the developed Western countries, negotiations are based on subtle references to existing legal codes. Even if actual sanctions are not imposed, these references provide fertile ground for effective informal agreements. In the case of Russian business, references to means of force are more effective than the latent threat of legal sanction (Radaev 2001b).

Coping with Distrust in Business Relations

The main question this chapter addresses is this: How do entrepreneurs decide to act if their business partners are not entirely reliable and the third parties responsible for dispute settlement are not trusted? According to our interview data, malfeasance in business relations has been on the decline in the past decade. One of our respondents, the head of an investment firm, observed that "the problem of reliability of partners . . . always exists in business. However, it [is] less demanding now."

Does this mean that honesty is starting to pay off? I would argue that this is not the case—or at least not the main reason. Confronting opportunism and malfeasance, Russian entrepreneurs have had to take precautionary measures to secure their business contracts. These include imposing methods of private ordering, checking up on their potential business partners, and building closed business networks. According to the head of a trading firm, "The number of violations has decreased, for the number of business ties has diminished. Before, [an entrepreneur] gave money to somebody and it was not paid back. He was running all around saying that he was cheated. Now he does not give money, and nobody lets him down. So there is nothing to complain [about]. The situation is different." Notes the head of a construction firm, "Everyone is now more cautious than before." Experience does not make people more trustful. Rather, it makes them more cautious.

Russian entrepreneurs maintained control over transactions in a number of ways. They started by signing discriminatory formal contracts—requiring prepayments, for example. In the case of transactions with the new partners, prepayments were considered a compulsory instrument. "Partial prepayment is the only real guarantee," remarked the head of a trading and production firm.

They also initiated deals with some minor probing contracts or divided the transfers into several stages to ensure successful outcomes. If the probing contracts proved to work successfully, business partners increased the volume of the delivered goods and services step by step.

In spite of these efforts, no formal contract provides perfect protection from the opportunism of market agents. First, the culture of formal business contracting is not highly developed in Russia so far. Second, formal contracts are not able to cover all necessary issues and anticipate all possible intervening factors. Third, having signed a contract the entrepreneur still is by no means secured from violations. The firm could simply disappear after getting its payment—take the money and run. "No doubt it is necessary to sign contracts in any case," noted the head of a real estate firm. "But all the same, implementation of this contract depends on the person." "Informal word weighs much more than any signed contract in our market," remarked the head of an investment company. The use of informal practices of contract enforcement are obviously not limited to Russia. The following is a quotation from the older study mentioned earlier: "Businessmen often prefer to rely on 'a man's word' in a brief letter, a handshake, or 'common honesty and decency'—even when the transaction involves exposure to serious risks" (Macaulay 1992, 269). Clearly, the status of the firm and the personality of the entrepreneurs play an important role here. If formal contracting is not able to secure positive outcomes, the entrepreneurs in our study checked up on their potential partners thoroughly before getting involved into business transactions. Various replies from respondents addressed this practice. "We used to check up [on] every new partner thoroughly and for the long time. And if we start working with him or her we ensure the conditions, which provide sufficient guarantees for us" (head of the group of companies). "We do not sign serious contracts before checkups and do not deal with the new partners [until the background checks have been completed]" (head of a holding company). "It is possible to have a business without checkups. But in this case one has to be alert and expect failures. It is necessary to calculate risks and be ready for something. It takes more energy to make a transaction. One is supposed to ensure each step from a variety of failures" (head of a retail-shop network). At the beginning of the 1990s, in the absence of reliable and systematic sources of business information, entrepreneurs took the full risk of malfeasance on the part of their partners. Today, opportunities for getting data on financial sustainability and business reputation of the economic agents are much more extensive. The data on potential business partners is collected from official and commercial registers and databases. Foreign partners are checked up on through the embassies and trading offices of the large firms in the other countries. "It was impossible before," said the head of an industrial production firm. "Now we are dealing with the Ministry of Home Affairs and banks. They can make inquiries about any client for us." The head of an investment firm noted, "We have got opportunities for checking up [on] firms and their founders. There are long 'black lists' already. Besides, the system of 'hoarding and running away' is now not so widespread in the territory of Russia." Economic agents in the markets do not meet one another as perfect strangers, and their contract relationships are not confined to formal economic exchange. "Faceless contracting is thereby supplanted by contracting in which the identity of the parties matters" (Williamson 1986, 185).

It is important to underline that background checks on potential partners are not confined to mere technical and impersonal acts of data collection. Many important decisions are based on face-to-face meetings, during which subjective evaluations of the partner's reliability are made. Thus the Russian entrepreneur learns to be a good psychologist. Personal characteristics of business partners matter when an entrepreneur runs the risk of opportunistic actions on an everyday basis. "It is necessary to have a great life experience to work without checkups," observed the head of a network of retail shops. "If such an experience is lacking, it is better to make inquiries, though business information is objective only . . . 50 percent [of the time]. There is no other way of making inquiries but via people, who are often very subjective."

All in all, big transactions are safeguarded by prior checkups. But even after getting positive information, entrepreneurs are still cautious. Noted the head of an investment company, "A sufficient number of partners has been already checked up. It is not a problem to find out anything you like. You are not able to come to the business from nowhere anymore. Nobody would give you anything like it was before." "There are small contracts on thirty thousand and big contracts on three hundred thousand [dollars]," remarked another. "No one would make a deal on three hundred thousand with a newcomer right away."

Data collection costs both time and money. But even a detailed inspection cannot guarantee positive outcomes. Contracts are largely enforced through personal business networks, through which social capital is accumulated (Coleman 1988). A "business network" can be defined as a stable and relatively closed set of interpersonal links among regular business partners. It is based on a combination of formal control and informal exchange of services. These networks play an increasing part in Russian business. Three of the entrepreneurs we interviewed noted the importance of their business networks. "We are giving goods in credit only to permanent clients. We would never give it to any others. . . . If you make purchases you should deal through your own acquaintances. Otherwise, you have no guarantees. They will sell distorted goods to you" (head of a wholesale firm). "It is vitally important to have permanent partners now. They are valuable not because they pay back on time but because they pay back in principle" (head of a firm selling fuel). "One-day firms disappeared among suppliers. . . . We have also changed. We did not make alliances before. Now we are very active in making alliances with our Russian partners. And we have our joint projects. We would never do it before because they would cheat you and never get the work done" (head of a computer firm).

Over the past few years, Russian entrepreneurs have become more selective in dealing with newcomers and outsiders. They reasonably prefer to stay within their own business networks, excluding "invaders." One of our respondents, who heads up several firms, noted the narrowing range of his business contacts: "We are dealing with [a] smaller and smaller number of people. Some time ago one could disseminate a hundred personal cards just to somebody. Now we do not use cards because we do not meet new people. And even if you are introduced to somebody new it is done via those with the high reputation. The circle has not closed down completely but it is extending very slowly."

Business networks are often not institutionalized in any formal way. The existing business associations and unions, though numerous, are not influential, and membership in them does not dramatically alter the firm's prospects. At least in our data, membership in these entrepreneurial associations does not correlate with the main variables describing contract relationships (Radaev 1996, 1998a).

Business networks no doubt are established to overcome distrust among business partners. What sort of trust is built through these networks? As mentioned earlier in this chapter, the new Russian entrepreneurs initially tended to start up their businesses with friends and personal contacts. Of the 277 Moscow entrepreneurs we surveyed in 1993, 42 percent started up with personal acquaintances, 23 percent with friends and relatives, 17 percent with relatives, and 11 percent with new or "nearly new" agents (Radaev 1993, 7–8). Given the uncertainty of formal and informal rules, business startups were largely built upon affect-based trust. A serious shift has occurred over the past decade, when many initial business teams were dismantled and former partners started up their own firms. Friendships in this new environment became an obstacle to efficient leadership. According to our interviewees, both business relationships and friendships began to fall apart. The head of a law firm said that "good acquaintances, as a rule, [will] let you down in [most] cases," and the head of a trading firm noted "a fundamental truth in business: those will survive who will understand that [they] must end with friendships [at] the right moment."

Thus affect-based trust has largely been replaced with reputation-based trust. Strategic alliances are increasingly built not on personal and kin relationships but more on recognition of the professional and managerial skills and business reputations. Firms and their leaders are divided into those that are "respectable" (and will not let one down) and unknowns (with whom one should be cautious). Thus business networks are used to disseminate information on unreliable business agents and to build up reputations. The head of a marketing department told us that "nobody would deal with a man who has cheated once. . . . If the sum [lost] is not significant, he will be just blacklisted as an unreliable partner." "Information is transferred instantly," said the head of a commercial bank. "And in case of contract infringement you run a risk of losing all your partners. . . . As soon as you fail to fulfill serious obligations, you find [that your] resources [are cut off] and your bank is closing down." Honesty may not pay in every case, but by and large it begins to pay off within closed business networks. The networks lower risks, help to overcome interpersonal distrust, and produce a sort of segmented business ethics.

General logic begins with informal private ordering, through which, over time, closed business networks are established. These, in turn, help create elements of interpersonal trust. Market actors start with affect-based trust and move, over time, toward reputation-based trust. As trust based on reputation is strengthened, trust in public institutions develops.

Conclusions

Most Russian entrepreneurs require honesty and trustworthiness from their business partners. This requirement reflects tensions existing in the market relationships. These tensions originate from the widespread infringement of business contracts owing to opportunism and malfeasance. Frequent infringement of business contracts creates interpersonal distrust among business partners, backed by the low trust in public institutions in response to their ineffectiveness and dependence on certain political and business interests.

Given the inability of the public institutions to enforce business contracts effectively, Russian entrepreneurs have had to take measures to secure their contracts. These include private ordering and thoroughly checking up on their potential business partners. Entrepreneurs also try to protect themselves from opportunism by building up relatively closed business networks. Reciprocal trust within business networks moves gradually from affect-based trust to trust based on reputation. In general, trust formation starts at the interpersonal level and is maintained by means of the informal private ordering and closed business networks. This interpersonal trust, which originated in different market segments, increasingly contributes to the development of trust in public institutions.

The author and research team of the Center for Political Technologies, Moscow, conducted the surveys. The U.S. Centre for International Private Enterprise (CIPE) funded the research. I would like to thank Igor Bunin, Rostislav Kapelyushnikov, Alexey Zudin, and Natalia Nazarova, of the Center for Political Technologies, and Vladimiz Gubernatorov, of the Russian Federation Chamber of Commerce and Industry, for valuable support in the implementation of the project.

Appendix: Basic Parameters of the Sample

	Percentage
Firm Type	
Privatized state firms	18
Newly established private firms	82
Firm Size	
Small	79
Medium and large	21
Sex of Entrepreneur	
Male	75
Female	25
Education of Entrepreneur	
University degree	83
No university degree	17
Ownership Status of Entrepreneur	
Owner of enterprise	79
Manager of enterprise	21
Business Associations	
Member	28
Nonmember	72
Location of Enterprise	
Moscow	19
Other	81

References

Coleman, James. 1988. "Social Capital in the Creation of Human Capital." *American Journal of Sociology* Suppl. 94: 95–120.

Fligstein, Neil. 1996. "Markets as Politics: A Political-Cultural Approach to Market Institutions." *American Sociological Review* 61(4, August): 656–73.

Gambetta, Diego, ed. 1988. *Trust: Making and Breaking Cooperative Relations*. Oxford, U.K.: Basil Blackwell.

Hardin, Russell. 2001. "Conceptions and Explanations of Trust." In *Trust and Society*, edited by Karen Cook. New York: Russell Sage Foundation.

Hendley, Katherine, Peter Murrel, and Randy Ryterman. 1999. "Law Works in Russia: The Role of Legal Institutions in the Transactions of Russian Enterprises." Unpublished manuscript.

Macaulay, Steve. 1992. "Non-Contractual Relations in Business: A Preliminary Study." In *The Sociology of Economic Life*, edited by Mark Granovetter and Richard Swedberg. Boulder, Colo.: Westview Press.

North, Douglass C. 1992. *Institutions, Institutional Change and Economic Performance*. Cambridge: Cambridge University Press.

Radaev, Vadim. 1993. "Rossiiskie predprinimateli—Kto oni (Na primere Moskvy)" (Russian entrepreneurs—Who are they [The example of Moscow]). *Vestnik statistiki* (9, September): 3–13.

———. 1996. "Maly Biznes i Problemy Delovoy Etiki: Nadezhdy i Realnost" (Small business and business ethics: Hopes and reality). *Voprosy Ekonomiki* (7, July): 72–82.

———. 1997. *Ekonomicheskaya sotsiologiya: Kurs lektsii* (Economic sociology: A lecture course). Moscow: Aspect Press.

———. 1998a. *Formirovaniye novykh rossiiskikh rynkov: Transaktsionnye izderzhki, formy kontrolya i delovaya etika* (Formation of new Russian markets: Transaction costs, forms of control and business ethics). Moscow: Center for Political Technologies.

———. 1998b. "Regional Entrepreneurship: The State of Small Business." In *A Regional Approach to Industrial Restructuring in the Tomsk Region, Russian Federation*. Paris: Organization for Economic Cooperation and Development.

———. 2001a. "Entrepreneurial Strategies and the Structure of Transaction Costs in Russian Business." In *The New Entrepreneurs of Europe and Asia: Patterns of Business Development in Russia, Eastern Europe and China*, edited by Victoria Bonnell and Thomas Gold. Armonk, N.Y.: M. E. Sharpe.

———. 2001b. "Entreprise, protection et violence en Russie à la fin des annees 1990." In "Le crime organise en Russie: Nouvelles approches," edited by Gilles Favarel-Garrigues. *Cultures et Conflits* (42, Summer): 47–68.

Rose-Ackerman, Susan. 2001a. "Trust, Honesty and Corruption: Reflection on the State-Building Process." *Archives of European Sociology* (3): 526–70.

———. 2001b. "Trust and Honesty in Post-Socialist Societies." *Kyklos* 54(2–3): 415–44.

Sapsai, Boris. 1997. "Systema i mekhanizmy razresheniya khoziaistvennykh sporov" (System and mechanisms for settling economic disputes). *Predprinimatelstvo v Rossii* (3): 5–14.

Stompka, Peter. 1999. *Trust: A Sociological Theory*. Cambridge: Cambridge University Press.

Williamson, Oliver E. 1985. *The Economic Institutions of Capitalism: Firms, Markets, Relational Contracting*. New York: Free Press.

———. 1986. "The Economics of Governance: Framework and Implications." In *Economics as a Process: Essays in the New Institutional Economics*, edited by Richard N. Langlois. Cambridge: Cambridge University Press.

Chapter 11

Distrust as a Trade Impediment: European Trade Policy Toward Nonmarket Economies

CYNTHIA M. HORNE

DISTRUST BETWEEN potential trading partners can prevent the establishment of trading relations or decrease the flow of trade between existing trading partners. Distrust can impede the broadening and deepening of trade relations, even if institutional structures are in place to foster credible trade commitments.

In its effects on trading relations, distrust is quite different from lack of trust. In trade, no partner is completely trustworthy. A belief that the other side has one's best interests at heart is not necessary for the establishment of trading relations. Each party assumes that the other is acting in his or her own self-interest and is involved in the trading relationship because of the reward, material or otherwise, to be derived. Since all countries assume the other is out to enhance its self-interest, there is a certain lack of trust even between the closest trading partners. Few would argue that countries enter into trading relations out of pure altruism. However, the fact that self-interest motivates countries to engage in trade does not prevent the establishment and continuation of trading relationships.

The effect on trade relations of distrust of the incentives, interests, and capabilities of trading partners is much different from that of simple lack of trust. To be consistent with the ideas developed by Edna Ullmann-Margalit (chapter 3) in this volume, I am proposing an understanding of distrust somewhere along her continuum between lack of trust and distrust. With this in mind, I draw a distinction between lack of trust and distrust. It is possible for one country not to trust another because of lack of complete information, insufficient institutional constraints, or knowledge that trade is generally motivated by self-interest. This lack of trust may or may not prevent the establishment of a trading relationship. However, distrust involves an active lack of trust, a belief that the other has antagonistic interests and will act to harm one. This is consistent with the intentionality component of Ullmann-Margalit's understanding of distrust. In this case, an active lack of trust prevents countries from engaging fully, if at all, in trade relations for fear of the adverse effects of such relations.

In this chapter I define distrust as a belief about the interests, incentives, and capabilities of some agent on which one relies for something (Gambetta 1988b; Ullmann-Margalit, chapter 3 in this volume).[1] As Russell Hardin (chapter 1 in this volume) outlines, there are three parts to distrust, just as there are three parts to trust relations: agent A trusts (or distrusts) agent B to do X (Hardin 1998; Levi 1998). In determining whether one will trust another to do something, one considers the intentions, incentives, interests, and competence of the other as well as the institutions constraining certain behaviors (Levi 2000). In the end, however, no amount of coercion, institutional constraint, or monitoring can guarantee that an individual will behave as one desires. Hence one makes a probabilistic assessment about the actions of the other and decides whether to make oneself vulnerable to the other—that is, whether to trust or not (Coleman 1990; Gambetta 1988a).

I apply this cognitive understanding of trust to the European Union's trade relations, examining how the European Union (agent A) distrusts formerly communist countries (agent B) to trade fairly (issue X). I approach questions of distrust on a state-to-state level. While most of the other chapters in this volume take a micro-level approach to distrust, given the nature of the puzzle, I analyze *trust* at an aggregated level. States can distrust other states. Trade officials who make policies for states can develop and harbor distrust based on social and institutional constraints and render policies "as if" they held such national- or state-level beliefs. Therefore, I am making an assumption that personalized interactions are not required to create distrust.

The extraordinary methods used by the EU to apply antidumping laws to formerly communist countries, or so-called nonmarket economies, illustrates the difference between distrust and lack of trust.[2] The EU singles out formerly communist countries as different from other developing countries and treats them differently under its antidumping trade rules. It would be erroneous to claim that the EU "trusts" other developing countries to trade fairly or not to dump their goods. It would also be a stretch to argue that the EU trusts that other developing countries

Figure 11.1 Annual European Union Antidumping Cases Initiated Against Nonmarket Economies, 1980 to 2000

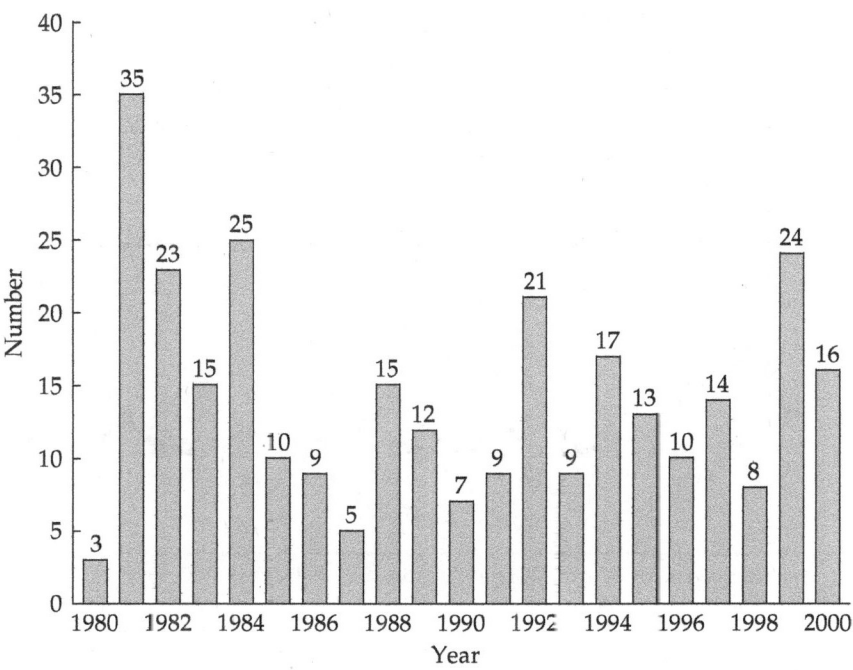

Source: European Commission (1983, 1984, 1986, 1987, 1989, 1990, 1995, 1996, 1997b, 1998, 1999, 2001).

have the EU's best interests at heart with regard to trade relations. However, since the EU does not actively distrust other similarly situated developing countries, such as Indonesia or India, these countries are subject to a host of different trade rules than nonmarket economies who are distrusted.[3] In this case, lack of trust and distrust result in two different policy paths, one leading to unusually high levels of trade discrimination. The differential manner in which the EU applies its antidumping laws to nonmarket economies illustrates the causal role of distrust in hobbling trade relations.

This differential treatment of nonmarket economies (NMEs) results in discriminatory trade protection. Levels of trade protection are high in both relative and absolute terms. From 1980 to 2000, almost three hundred antidumping cases were initiated against imports from NMEs or former NMEs (see figure 11.1), although imports from NMEs represent only a fraction of all trade.[4] Moreover, relative to other country groupings,

Figure 11.2 Cross-Group Comparison of European Union Antidumping Cases, 1980 to 2000

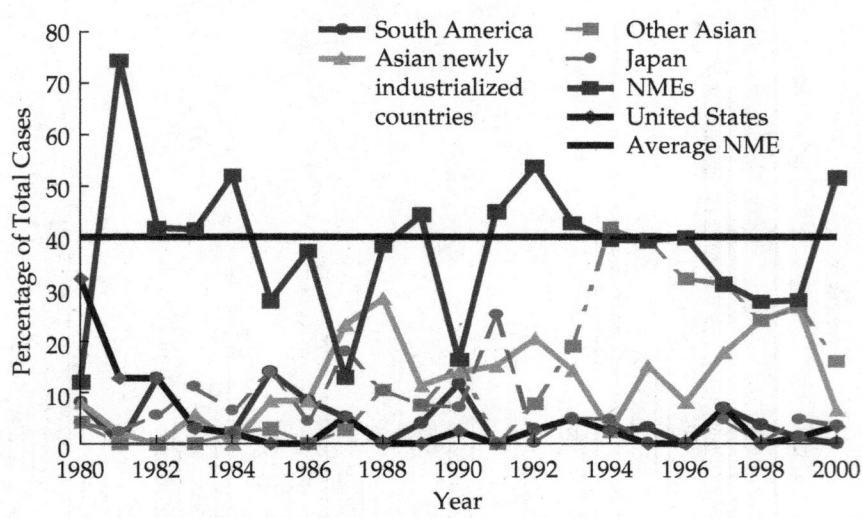

Source: European Commission (1983, 1984, 1986, 1987, 1989, 1990, 1995, 1996, 1997b, 1998, 1999, 2001).

NMEs account for an unusually high percentage of antidumping cases (see figure 11.2; for country groupings, see the appendix to this chapter). What explains the EU's unusual patterns and high levels of trade protection against NMEs?

Antidumping laws are designed to protect domestic firms from unfairly priced competing imports. Low pricing can drive other fairly competing firms out of business and allow competitors to gain monopoly control of a market. Antidumping laws, rather than other forms of trade protection, were selected as the topic of this chapter because they are highly formalized, highly legalized trade rules. Because of the extensive bureaucratic oversight over the administration of the laws and the extensive formal codification of the implementation of the laws, they are some of the least likely trade laws to be politically manipulated.

In this chapter I examine trade cases since 1991, after the fall of the Soviet Union and since the start of widespread economic and political reforms throughout the region. Despite EU contentions that antidumping laws are above political manipulation and do not target certain countries or country groups, nonmarket economies have experienced unusual patterns of trade protection. These trade cases are used here to advance the argument that distrust of nonmarket economies causes the

EU to interpret the application of trade laws in a consistently discriminatory manner.

History of Distrust of Trade with Nonmarket Economies

During the cold war, nonmarket economies were assumed to pose an extraordinary trade threat owing to the structure of their domestic economic and political institutions and their hostile interests toward the West. The EU distrusted the incentives, intentions, and capabilities of NMEs and therefore believed that special extraordinary rules had to be established to safeguard European industries from the potential effects of unfair trade with NMEs. The special NME designation allowed the United States and EU to apply trade rules to Poland, Russia, and China that were different from those to which developing countries like Bangladesh, Hong Kong, and Brazil were subject. These different antidumping laws resulted in more restrictive treatment of NME exports than those from other countries.

There are three broad reasons why the EU developed an active distrust of nonmarket economies during the cold war: strategic, institutional, and ideological (Gaddis 1972; Paterson 1973; Rees 1967; Schlesinger 1967). First, the West looked upon communist expansion as a direct threat to capitalism. Therefore, on a strategic basis, it was rational for the West to develop a belief about antagonistic communist interests. Second, the communist bloc had domestic economic and political institutions that might appear to threaten the West. It was assumed that the domestic structure of centrally planned economies not only gave NMEs a purported unfair trade advantage but also gave them an incentive to dump goods and disrupt Western markets (Holzman 1987; Marer 1984, 129).[5]

Third, the cold war was an ideological confrontation as much as, if not more than, a security confrontation. An ideology premised on the demise of capitalism was understandably distrusted by the liberal, democratic West (Lenin 1932; Marx and Engels 1848/1978, 19–20). The cold war was fought not only with nuclear weapons but also with trade weapons and beliefs about the other side (Larson 1985, ix). Trade was yet another venue for the ideological struggle between communism and capitalism. The West developed a belief that nonmarket economies had an interest in dumping their goods to hurt Western industries. "In the West, dumping by Socialist countries [was] often viewed as a deliberate conspiracy to disrupt Capitalist markets and discredit free enterprise" (Wilczynski 1969, 138). Therefore, the practice of dumping was an important element in the ideological and trade warfare between the East and the West.

Ideological differences, institutional differences, and strategic differences all combined to create in the West an active distrust of trade with NMEs. To be consistent with the terms used in this volume, the EU distrusted nonmarket economies in the issue area of trade as a result of these ideological, institutional, and strategic differences. This distrustful relationship spawned special rules, laws, and regulations to monitor trade.

Antidumping policy was one of the trade policies specifically targeted against imports from communist countries. Beliefs about the other side factored significantly into the creation of antidumping laws for these countries and in their actual application. In fact, both the United States and the EU considered "communist" to be synonymous with "nonmarket economy." Hence Yugoslavia was considered a market economy because it was not part of the communist bloc. As such, the labels "nonmarket" and "market" did not necessarily reflect the actual structure of the economic system. Nonmarket was a label used by the West to separate friend from foe. It was strongly affected by beliefs the West had regarding the capabilities, intentions, and incentives of the communist bloc.

Antidumping Trade Laws

Dumping, as defined by European Community regulations, is the "selling of a product in the Community at a price below its 'normal value' " (European Commission 1998, 3). This means that if the "export price [of a product] to the Community is less than a comparable price for the like product, in the ordinary course of trade, as established for the exporting country," then the product is being dumped (COM Doc. [EC] 384/96, OJL 03/06/96, art. 1 [2]).[6] As previously mentioned, antidumping laws are designed to redress dumping as an unfair trading practice. The underlying belief is that dumped goods can put suppliers selling at normal value out of business, thereby hurting domestic industries, precipitating unemployment, and promoting the development of monopolies.[7]

The European Union has specified that antidumping laws should not be used for political purposes. To remain legitimate, these laws must be trade policy tools, not purveyors of industrial policy or beholden to interest group politics. In a speech by the European Commission's vice president, the EU outlined the objective nature of antidumping legislation. "EU legislation on antidumping is a strict legal system which does not give very much room for discretion by the Commission when judging the various aspects of the cases" (quoted in Laurent 1996). Antidumping laws and practices constitute a form of "secondary legislation" confirmed by European Court of Justice decisions, stressed Sir Leon Brittan, vice president of the European Commission (Laurent

1996). This, combined with the strict standards imposed by the joint agreement on antidumping between the General Agreement on Tariffs and Trade (GATT) and the World Trade Organization (WTO), removes room for political considerations in antidumping determinations.

The EU contends that antidumping laws are politically neutral, meaning they should not penalize or target certain countries or groups of countries. Sir Leon Brittan, as vice president of the European Commission, has stressed that "there is absolutely no question of conducting some sort of industrial policy" nor of targeting countries or groups of countries with antidumping laws (Agence Europe 1997). Therefore, by choosing to analyze trade relations between the EU and formerly communist countries through the lens of antidumping trade regulation, I am analyzing the *least likely* trade case for overt political manipulation.

Determining Fair Trade: The Analogue Country Method

The European Commission is the agency in the European Union charged with administering antidumping laws for all the countries. The commission conducts investigations of products that are alleged to have been dumped in the EU and makes determinations regarding what a fair or "normal value" for an imported product should be. This is of particular importance because it is on this crucial value that the presence or absence of dumping is determined.

Determination of normal value is particularly tricky involving trade cases with nonmarket economies. Normal value is typically based on the prices paid in the "ordinary course of trade." For example, if the exporter in a country produces tables, the price of similar tables sold domestically constitutes the normal value for that product. The normal value of the product is then compared with the export price of the product to determine whether dumping has occurred. There are various procedures and rules designed to determine normal value if the exporting country does not produce tables for internal consumption or if there are problems associated with using the domestic prices of an exporting country. This is the situation faced by nonmarket economies. For this reason, special rules and procedures have been developed to determine what constitutes the "normal value" of products from nonmarket economies.

An analogue method was developed by the United States and later codified and adopted by all GATT signatories as a way to determine normal value in NME antidumping cases (European Commission 1997a, 3).[8] The analogue country method adjusts for the problem that prices in nonmarket economies do not reflect the forces of supply and demand. Instead of using the domestic prices of production in the nonmarket economy, the prices of production are valued in an analogue country, in other words, a country price proxy. This means that all the costs of production—factor inputs such as land, labor, and capital—are valued by looking at the prices in a third-country "market" surrogate (COM Doc. [EC] 384/96, art. 2[7]).

In practice, this means that the EU solicits domestic price information, factors of production information, and general microeconomic data from similar types of companies in "market economies." The costs of production of the analogue are substituted for the costs of production in the nonmarket economy to arrive at dumping amounts. For example, in a case involving ice skates from Hungary, Czechoslovakia, and Romania, the prices incurred by Yugoslav producers of ice skates were used as analogues to calculate dumping margins against Hungarian, Czech, and Romanian imports (COM Doc. [EEC] 85/143, OJL 52, 22/02/85).[9]

Common analogues for nonmarket economies include Korea, Thailand, Brazil, India, Malaysia, and Indonesia (see table 11.1, final column). These countries tend to be the most appropriate proxies in terms of wage levels, sophistication of industry development, size of export and import markets, and technological development. They are also subject to antidumping investigations themselves, which means that often the EU is able to force the industries in those countries to provide information that can then be used in similar cases against nonmarket economies.

European antidumping regulations require only that the analogue be selected "not in an unreasonable manner," de facto leaving much discretion in analogue selection to the trade agency (COM [97] 677 final-97/0368 [ACC], OJC 70/98). The choice of analogues has been the subject of much debate, both within the European Commission and in the academic community, because the selection of an analogue has profound implications on the prices that are used in determining the existence of dumping (Fine 1988; Tharakan and Waelbroeck 1994).

Many factors are often cited in the selection of an analogue, including wage comparability, level of modernization, similarity of product, similarity of production method, similarity of access to raw materials or factors of production, and volume of domestic sales. However, in practice the most important factor is the ability to obtain information.[10] There are many problems associated with obtaining confidential firm-level information from analogues to be used in other antidumping cases. Analogues rarely comply voluntarily with the EU's requests for information. This often means that an analogue involved in a concurrent or recent antidumping investigation will be used to price the costs of production in a nonmarket economy. However, since the analogue is already guilty of dumping, using its costs of production necessarily guar-

Table 11.1 Sample of Affirmative Antidumping Cases Against Nonmarket Economies Using Developing Countries as Analogues, 1990 to 1999

Case	Nonmarket Economies	Product	Analogue
EC No. 2093/91, OJL 18/07/91	China	Small-screen TVs	Hong Kong
91/522/EEC, OJL 02/10/91	Soviet Union	Artificial corundum	Yugoslavia
91/522/EEC, OJL 02/10/91	Hungary	Artificial corundum	Yugoslavia
91/522/EEC, OJL 02/10/91	Czechoslovakia	Artificial corundum	Yugoslavia
EC No. 3433/91, OJL 28/11/91	China	Pocket lighters	Thailand
EC No. 1189/93, OJL 15/05/93	Hungary	Seamless iron pipe	Croatia
EC No. 1189/93, OJL 15/05/93	Poland	Seamless iron pipe	Croatia
EC No. 710/95, OJL 01/04/95	China	Color TVs	Singapore
EC No. 2022/95, OJL 23/08/95	Russia	Ammonium nitrate	Poland
EC No. 2022/95, OJL 23/08/95	Lithuania	Ammonium nitrate	Poland
EC No. 5/96, OJL 04/01/96	China	Microwave ovens	Korea
EC No. 584/96, OJL 03/04/96	China	Iron or steel pipe fittings	Thailand
EC No. 2208/96, OJL 18/11/96	China	Unbleached cotton	India
EC No. 1490/96, OJL 30/07/96	Belarus	Polyester fiber	Taiwan
EC No. 119/97, OJL 24/01/97	China	Ring binders	Malaysia
EC No. 165/97, OJL 01/31/97	China	Footwear	Indonesia
EC No. 981/97, OJL 31/05/97	Russia	Seamless iron pipe	Czech Republic
EC No. 1786/97, OJL 17/09/97	Ukraine	Silicon carbide	Brazil
EC No. 1931/97, OJL 04/10/97	Russia	Unalloyed zinc	Poland
EC No. 1931/97, OJL 04/10/97	Kazakhstan	Unalloyed zinc	Poland

(Table continues on p. 258.)

Table 11.1 *Continued*

Case	Nonmarket Economies	Product	Analogue
EC No. 1931/97, OJL 04/10/97	Ukraine	Unalloyed zinc	Poland
EC No. 1931/97, OJL 04/10/97	Uzbekistan	Unalloyed zinc	Poland
EC No. 2380/98, OJL 23/01/98	China	Leather handbags	Indonesia
EC No. 393/98, OJL 20/02/98	China	Metal fasteners	Taiwan
EC No. 904/98, OJL 30/04/98	China	Fax machines	Korea

Source: Data from European Commission and European Council (1980–2001).

antees that the nonmarket economy will be found guilty of dumping as well. Thus information problems affect the fairness of the antidumping determinations against NMEs.

The EU sometimes chooses dubiously relevant information from analogues over information provided by industries in nonmarket economies based on the *presumption* that information supplied by NME firms is not accurate. The EU has a policy of rejecting information from nonmarket economies unless that information can be verified by multiple sources. Since this is rarely possible with any developing country, given limitations in accounting practices, technology, and the presence of informal exchange mechanisms, this policy is particularly onerous on NMEs. Such a presumption about the inherent inadequacy of information does not exist with other developing countries. This presumption about the inadequacy of even verifiable information is rooted in the EU's distrust of nonmarket economies. In practice, information supplied by Polish firms in 1993 or Czech industries in 1994 is presumed to be incomplete or misleading, and information from analogue Thai or Indonesian or Indian firms is substituted. In the absence of "perfect information" from the nonmarket economies, the presumption of distrust holds, according to the findings of Ullmann-Margalit (chapter 3 in this volume). This is consistent with Roderick Kramer's concept of individuals as "hypervigilant . . . social information processors" (chapter 6 in this volume). In cases involving NMEs, trade officials are especially vigilant in scrutinizing and double-verifying information. They do not follow such procedures in cases involving other types of developing countries. As a result, they find more problems with NME information than with similar types of information from other developing countries. Not surprisingly, the information problems become yet one more validation of the need to continue to distrust NMEs. Presumptions that the information supplied will not be adequate result in the disregard of viable information and the acceptance of questionable information from third-country price proxies.[11]

The analogue method was originally used because the capabilities and interests of nonmarket economies appeared threatening to the West. Today, trade officials continue to use the analogue-country method, despite its anachronistic application, relying on presumptions to direct the manner in which the laws are interpreted and implemented.

Alternative Explanations of Trade Protection

"Trust is a peculiar belief predicated not on evidence but on the lack of contrary evidence," notes Diego Gambetta (1988a, 234). His observation can well be applied to the EU's attitude toward nonmarket economies. The manner in which the EU applies antidumping laws to nonmarket economies is a function of the EU's opportunity, interests, and distrust of the motives and incentives of nonmarket economies. If the EU lacked either opportunity or interest to manipulate trade laws, then there might be no problem. Given the loose wording of article VI of the GATT regarding trade with NMEs, there is certainly opportunity for some political manipulation. Given the power of certain domestic interest groups in the EU that support trade protection, there is also some interest in generalized trade protection. However, while opportunity and interest are necessary conditions to explain EU antidumping policy, they are not sufficient. To understand the EU's behavior, one also needs to discuss distrust. This ideologically driven distrust continues to permeate trade relations between the EU and nonmarket economies.

International political economy, public policy, and comparative politics provide myriad possible alternative hypotheses to a distrust hypothesis. Testing all possible alternatives is beyond the scope of this chapter. I address three of the most robust alternative explanations of trade protection: import penetration and economic interest arguments, institutionalist arguments, and bureaucratic inertia arguments.

Import penetration arguments would contend that the EU imposes high antidumping duties on NMEs because nonmarket economies pose a particular threat to the EU market as a function of the latter's high import volumes. Perhaps relative to other countries, NMEs export more to the EU or flood the EU market with low-cost goods, thereby necessitating higher levels of trade protection. For example, if the EU

Figure 11.3 European Union Imports from Nonmarket Economies Compared with Antidumping Cases Against Nonmarket Economies, 1980 to 2000

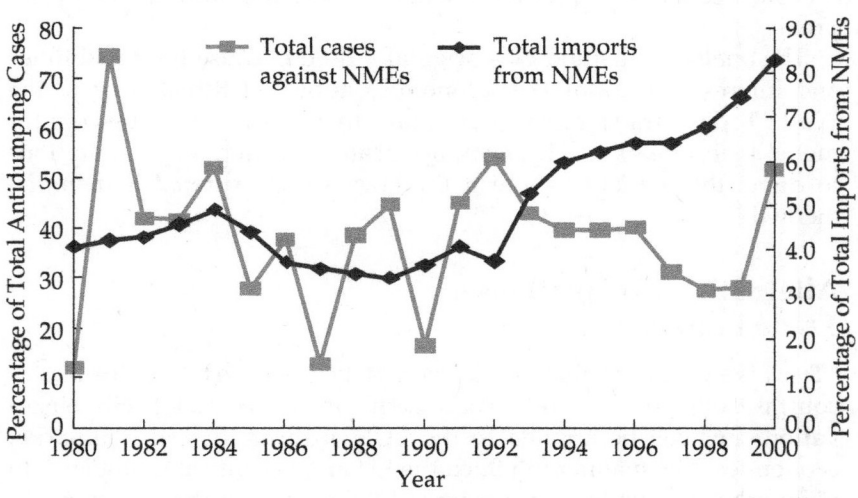

Source: International Monetary Fund (1997); European Commission (1983, 1984, 1986, 1987, 1989, 1990, 1995, 1996, 1997b, 1998, 1999, 2001).

uses antidumping laws to counter unfair trade, there should be a direct relationship between the volume of trade and the number of antidumping cases. This means that as nonmarket economies increase their exports to the EU, one might expect to see an increase in the number of cases launched against them. Import penetration argument yields the first alternative hypothesis: *The greater the import penetration, the greater the number of antidumping cases.* Trade data do not validate this expected economic relationship, however. Nonmarket economies account for only a small percentage of trade, a share disproportionate to the percentage of antidumping cases launched against them. In the post–cold war period alone, NMEs comprised 40 percent of EU antidumping trade cases but only 5 percent of imports (figure 11.3). There is no positive relationship between the percentage of total antidumping cases and the percentage of total imports into the EU accounted for by nonmarket economies, as the import penetration hypothesis would predict. The scatter plot in figure 11.4 tracks the percentage of total imports and the percentage of total antidumping cases by country group (see the appendix to this chapter for country groupings). For all country groupings other than NMEs there is a direct, positive relationship. As predicted, increased import penetration is correlated with increased use of trade

Figure 11.4 Ratio of Imports to Antidumping Cases, by Country Grouping, 1980 to 1999

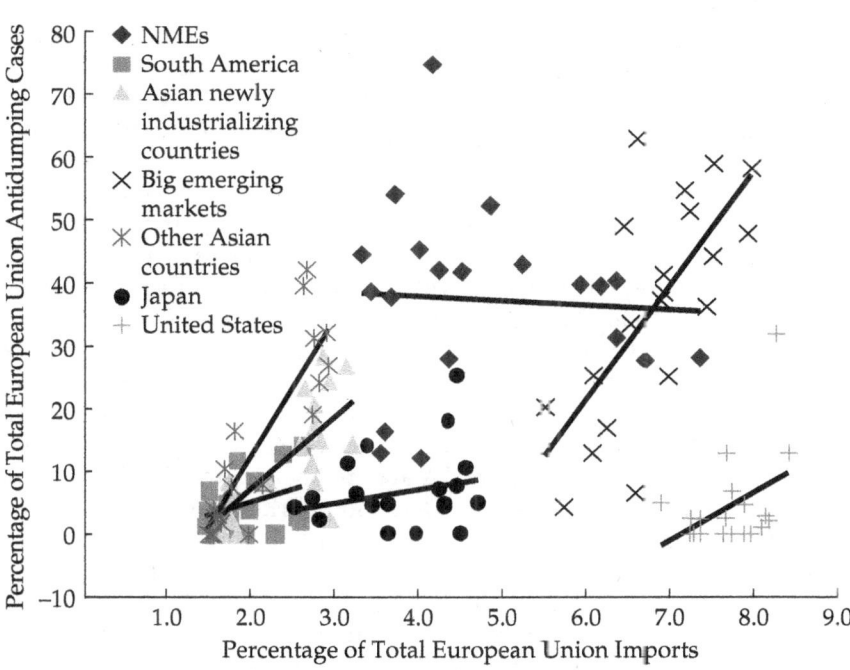

Source: International Monetary Fund (1997); European Commission (1983, 1984, 1986, 1987, 1989, 1990, 1995, 1996, 1997b, 1998, 1999, 2001).

protection. However, this does not hold true for NMEs. They are the only grouping with a negative regression line, demonstrating a highly unusual trade pattern. The EU's use of antidumping regulations against NMEs is not consistent with its use of this form of trade protection against other country groups, irrespective of commodity or time.

Even on the same antidumping cases, with the international economic environment, the product, the domestic interests groups, and the political climate held constant, when developing countries like Malaysia and India are analyzed side by side with nonmarket economies, nonmarket economies have substantially higher antidumping margins and are almost always found guilty of dumping.[12] A top trade official at the European Commission confirmed (in our interview) that it was no accident that in almost every antidumping case the nonmarket economy is found guilty of dumping. In fact, he contended that positive affirmations of dumping were assured in cases against nonmarket economies, owing to the method used by the European Union to determine dumping. This is strong evidence that nonmarket economies are actively discriminated against.

Moreover, nonmarket economies do not pose an extraordinary threat to European trade that would necessitate applying extraordinary antidumping laws to them or finding ways to manipulate the laws to negate an NME comparative advantage. Nonmarket economies do not have unlimited export capacity capable of flooding European markets even in "sensitive sectors" (Brenton and Di Mauro 1998) and have not increased their exports to Europe, which might have triggered trade protectionism (Eichengreen and Kohl 1998). In sum, none of the simple economic criteria can predict or explain the manner in which nonmarket economies are treated under antidumping laws.

Institutionalist arguments might suggest that the EU maximizes its possibilities for trade protection within the institutional constraints set by the WTO. That is, perhaps nonmarket economies are subjected to higher levels of trade protection than are other developing countries because most developing countries are members of the WTO and most nonmarket economies are not. Once nonmarket economies become members of the WTO, they are considered "market oriented" and as such should and will be treated differently. This argument would be consistent with the suggestions of both Kramer and Deborah Larson (chapters 6 and 2 in this volume, respectively), who argue that institutions or other constraints on parties in distrustful exchange relations might help to overcome distrust. The institutionalist argument yields the second alternative hypothesis: *Once nonmarket economies become members of the WTO, there should be a decrease in trade protectionism against them.* There are two problems with this hypothesis. First, WTO membership for nonmarket economies does not necessarily decrease the incidence of dumping or decrease antidumping margins against formerly communist countries. Cases against Poland, the Czech Republic, and Hungary have increased since they have been reclassified as market economies and inducted into the WTO. Second, WTO membership and "market orientation" are not synonymous, as this theory suggests. For example, the Kyrgyz Republic is a member of the WTO but is still labeled a nonmarket economy by the United States and the EU, and it continues to be treated differently from other types of developing countries in antidumping cases. Membership in the WTO has done nothing to protect the Kyrgyz Republic from this discriminatory treatment. Conversely, Lithuania was considered a "market-oriented economy" by the EU in 1998, and yet it did not receive WTO membership until 2001 (WTO 2002). In sum, membership of nonmarket economies in the WTO does not present an institutional constraint on the EU's actual application of antidumping laws.

Finally, it might seem plausible that bureaucratic inertia can explain why the EU continues to treat nonmarket economies differently from other types of developing countries. During the cold war, nonmarket economies were substantially different and posed a security and possibly economic threat to the West. Perhaps the laws and regulations have simply failed to keep up with the pace of transitions in these countries. The bureaucratic inertia argument yields the third alternative hypothesis: *Nonmarket economies continue to be discriminated against because the formal institutions and rules governing the adjudication of antidumping laws have not yet been changed.*

However, the problem with the administration of antidumping laws is not that trade-related bureaucracies have been unable to change to reflect the market reforms in transitional economies. On the contrary, the EU has continued to adjust the application of its antidumping laws to nonmarket economies since the beginning of reforms in the region. New regulations have developed to improve the transparency and fairness of the laws.[13] The laws are being changed to allow nonmarket economies to realize a comparative advantage in trade. Neither the laws nor the procedures for administering antidumping cases have remained the same. The real puzzle is why, in spite of the changes in transitional economies, the EU maintains and perpetuates through *continued innovation* inefficient methods of administering antidumping laws on imports from nonmarket economies.

The evidence presented against the three alternative hypotheses, loosely derived from rationalist assumptions, does not suggest that the European Union fails to behave rationally by seizing opportunities to discriminate against trade with nonmarket economies. In fact, if there were no opportunities to discriminate against nonmarket economies, then discrimination would not exist. So opportunity and interest are two necessary but not sufficient conditions for explaining EU behavior. However, the findings suggest that the European Union does not appear to be a simple rational opportunist. Traditional theories of international political economy fall short in explaining the pattern of trade protectionism.

Nonmarket Economy Antidumping Cases in Practice

> I too often have the impression that there are some states, China for instance, which are unpopular here, so that things are applied to them that are not applied to others.
> —EU official, in oral comments before the European Parliament ("Questions Nos H-0379/97 ... and H-0380/97" 1997)

So what, then, explains the EU's pattern of anti-dumping use against non-market economies? Empirical evidence supports the theory that distrust impedes the establishment of mutually advantageous trade relations between the European Union and nonmarket economies. In spite of EU policy affirmations that antidumping laws are apolitical trade laws, an analysis of cases against nonmarket economies provides evidence to the contrary. In selecting an "appropriate" analogue, the EU is supposed to focus on factors such as wage comparability, level of technological development of the industry, similarity of production profile, comparability of access to raw materials, and total imports and exports to ensure comparability between the nonmarket economy and the analogue. By focusing on these types of factors, the EU should be able to arrive at an analogue country that is a reasonable proxy for the nonmarket economy. In practice, this should mean that the EU uses developing-country analogues that are producers of similar goods, such as India, Pakistan, Malaysia, Taiwan, and Indonesia (table 11.1). In theory, this would allow the possibility of finding comparable wage levels and levels of economic development between the analogue and the nonmarket economy for the purposes of the antidumping case.

As discussed earlier in this chapter, there are many problems associated with the use of the analogue-country method, even when reasonably comparable developing countries are selected as surrogates for nonmarket economies. However, in a variety of cases the EU has not chosen developing countries as surrogates. In fact, highly advanced market economies, including member nations of the Organization for Economic Cooperation and Development (OECD), are often used as surrogates for cases against nonmarket economies, in spite of EU official policy that acknowledges that such advanced economies are ill suited to serve as cost proxies (see the final column in table 11.2).

For example, Canada, the United States, Norway, and even the entire European Union have been used as third-country analogues in cases against NME exports. This is a particularly egregious deviation from the intent of the antidumping laws. Since nonmarket economies necessarily compete on price to break into new markets, and since the types of goods they tend to export are labor or energy intensive, the use of advanced industrialized democracies as market analogues guarantees positive antidumping determinations. In essence, the use of these types of surrogates negates the possibility of finding that a nonmarket economy has a natural comparative advantage in the production of any good. A review of a few cases will elucidate this problem.

In the case of *Unwrought Magnesium from Russia and Ukraine* (EC 1347/96, OJL 12/07/96), the pricing of labor became a central point of disagreement. The United States, Japan, and Norway were initially considered as analogues for the pricing of Russian and Ukrainian inputs,

Table 11.2 Sample of Affirmative Antidumping Cases Against Nonmarket Economies Using OECD Member Countries as Analogues, 1990 to 1999

Case Number	Country	Product	OECD Analogue
EC No. 1937/90, OJL 07/07/90	China	Typewriter ribbon	EU
EC No. 3642/92, OJL 14/12/92	Poland	Ferrosilicon	Norway
EC No. 3068/92, OJL 24/10/92	Ukraine	Potash	Canada
EC No. 3068/92, OJL 24/10/92	Russia	Potash	Canada
EC No. 3068/92, OJL 24/10/92	Belarus	Potash	Canada
EC No. 821/94, OJL 13/04/94	China	Silicon carbide	United States
EC No. 821/94, OJL 13/04/94	Poland	Silicon carbide	United States
EC No. 821/94, OJL 13/04/94	Russia	Silicon carbide	United States
EC No. 821/94, OJL 13/04/94	Ukraine	Silicon carbide	United States
EC No. 821/94, OJL 13/04/94	Norway	Silicon carbide	United States
EC No. 137/96, OJL 27/01/96	China	Chamottes	United States
EC No. 600/96, OJL 04/04/96	China	Coumarin	United States
EC No. 1006/96, OJL 05/06/96	China	Powdered carbon	United States
EC No. 1347/96, OJL 12/07/96	Russia	Unwrought magnesium	Norway
EC No. 1347/96, OJL 12/07/96	Ukraine	Unwrought magnesium	Norway
EC No. 1347/96, OJL 12/07/96	Kazakhstan	Unwrought magnesium	Norway
EC No. 2496/97, OJL 16/12/97	China	Silicon metal	Norway
EC No. 449/98, OJL 27/02/98	Belarus	Potassium chloride	Canada
EC No. 449/98, OJL 27/02/98	Russia	Potassium chloride	Canada
EC No. 449/98, OJL 27/02/98	Ukraine	Potassium chloride	Canada

(*Table continues on p. 266.*)

Table 11.2 *Continued*

Case Number	Country	Product	OECD Analogue
EC No. 771/98, OJL 09/04/98	China	Tungsten carbide	United States
EC No. 2402/98, OJL 07/11/98	China	Unwrought magnesium	Norway
EC No. 603/99, OJL 20/03/99	Czech Republic[a]	Polypropylene binder	United States
EC No. 603/99, OJL 20/03/99	Hungary[a]	Polypropylene binder	United States

Source: Data from European Commission and European Council (1980–2001).
[a] In these cases the countries had been reclassified as market economies, but surrogates were still used in determining normal value.

and Norway was finally selected. The European Commission argued that because Norway was a significant producer of this product, had an efficient production process, enjoyed low-cost electric energy, and was similarly situated to Russia and Ukraine with respect to access to raw materials (sea water and dolomite), Norway would be an adequate analogue (COM Doc [EC] 2997/95, OJL 23/12/95, art. 20). Differences in the quality and purity of Norwegian output and Russian and Ukrainian output were ignored, even though the lower purity of Russian and Ukrainian output would certainly have lowered its market price. Moreover, Russian producers argued, Norwegian labor costs were not comparable to labor costs in Russia, and use of Norway as an analogue would result in unfair dumping determinations (COM Doc. [EC] 1347/96, OJL 12/07/96, art. 16).

In response to criticism regarding the inappropriate labor pricing, the European Commission argued, "It is clear that such natural comparative advantages cannot include advantages either in costs or prices by the nonmarket economy country companies" (COM Doc. [EC] 2997/95, OJL 23/12/95, art. 35). The commission then specifically named such costs that do not constitute a comparative advantage: "A number of claims put forward by the exporters concerned cannot be accepted, as such claims related to certain cost advantages, in particular with respect—to production labor costs;—depreciation costs;—environmental costs;—selling expenses;—and raw material costs" (COM Doc. [EC] 2997/95, art. 36). Therefore, the Russian and Ukrainian producers' claims that they enjoyed a comparative advantage in access to raw materials, energy efficiency of production process, and staff levels in the companies were rejected. In effect, the commission summarily rejected the proposition that low labor costs could constitute a comparative advantage in the production of a commodity from nonmarket economies.

The commission then went even further in interpreting what constitutes a comparative advantage. It subsequently imposed its interpretation of correct energy and environmental policies on the constructed cost of production for Russia and Ukraine. The commission explained that not only would it use Norwegian labor costs but it would also make adjustments to the Russian and Ukrainian costs to take into consideration energy and environmental policies that they *should have* followed (COM Doc. [EC] 1347/96, OJL 12/07/96, art. 27).

In sum, the European Commission ruled that not only were Russia and Ukraine not allowed to treat cheap labor as a comparative advantage they also were not permitted to waste energy or pollute in the production of products for export. After imposing antidumping duties on Russian and Ukrainian magnesium imports, the volume of imports fell by 49 percent and the value of imports fell 55 percent (COM Doc. [EC] 1002/98, OJL 14/05/98, art. 47). This is not surprising, given the high antidumping duties arrived at after pricing energy, environmental protection, and labor costs using Norwegian domestic costs of production as the analogue.

In a similar case, *Unwrought Magnesium from China*, the commission ruled that the large and conveniently located reserves of raw materials, low investment, low labor costs, and low costs of production that characterized the Chinese industry either could not be quantified or were not considered "relevant" to determining the export value of Chinese goods (COM Doc. [EC] 2402/98, OJL 07/11/98, art. 9). Norway was again used as an analogue country to calculate labor and other costs, and dumping duties were consequently imposed on Chinese exports.

In the case *Powdered Carbon from China*, the costs of environmental protection became an antidumping issue (COM Doc. [EC] 1984/95, OJL 15/08/95). In this case, the United States was used as a price surrogate. In determining what would constitute a fair value of powdered carbon imports from China and what price of imports from China would not injure European producers, the costs of environment-friendly production methods were included. European producers had updated their production methods to decrease environmental pollution, and this was considered the standard to which Chinese exporters should comply. Because they did not, estimates of Chinese production costs were revalued appropriately. In this case, U.S. domestic prices for labor and access to raw materials were used to price Chinese exports to the EU, and costs of environmental protection as well as raw materials usage were added on top. The resulting antidumping margin of more than 70 percent caused the expected drop in Chinese exports (COM Doc. [EC] 1984/95,

OJL 15/08/95, art. 57). This case sets an interesting precedent, by which European policies about the environment are imposed on exports from nonmarket developing countries.

In the case of *Potassium Chloride from Russia, Belarus, and Ukraine*, Canada was chosen as the analogue country. "The Russian and Belarussian mines [claimed they] enjoyed natural comparative advantages in terms of access to raw materials, production process, proximity of production to customers and special characteristics of the product, i.e. the size of the reserves, the general characteristics of the mines, and their geographical location, and finally the characteristics of the ore" (COM Doc. [EC] 449/98, OJL 27/02/98, art. 32). The EU rejected these claims of a natural comparative advantage and argued that none of these claims could be "clearly demonstrated and evaluated in terms of cost" (COM Doc. [EC] 449/98, OJL 27/02/98, art. 34). The largest cost in the production of potassium chloride is transportation—namely, getting the ore from the mines to market (art. 29). In spite of the differences in transportation costs between Russia and Canada, the prices of Canadian rail and road transport were applied to Russian, Ukrainian, and Belarussian calculations of normal value, and, not surprisingly, a positive duty was assessed.

Even the European Parliament questioned the fairness of using Canada as an analogue in this case, citing the incomparable production costs between Canadian firms and Belarussian, Russian, or Ukrainian firms (European Parliament 1996). The parliament also highlighted how this method inflated the duties levied on nonmarket economy exporters. In this case, dumping margins of almost 60 percent were levied on Russian, Ukrainian, and Belarussian exports (COM Doc. [EC] 449/98, OJL 27/02/98).

There are many cases in which advanced industrialized countries are used as market surrogates for nonmarket economies (see table 11.2). This is done in spite of European Union policies that the United States and other OECD countries should not be used as analogue countries to determine surrogate prices for nonmarket economies. Using advanced OECD countries as analogues necessarily negates any comparative advantage nonmarket economies might have in labor costs (Laurent 1996). The European Foreign Trade Association has lobbied against commission antidumping determinations, arguing that antidumping laws are being manipulated "to abusively counteract the lawful comparative cost advantages enjoyed by developing countries" (Agence Europe 1996). In this incident the European Foreign Trade Association was referring to a case against China, in which China was unable to demonstrate a comparative advantage in the production of handbags because of the use of the analogue-country methodology (Council Regulation [EC] No. 1567/97, OJL 02/08/97).

In 1998 a series of changes were made to antidumping laws as applied to China and Russia. These changes were designed to increase the fairness and transparency with which antidumping laws were applied to these countries by taking into consideration their extensive market reforms (COM Doc. [EC] 905/98, OJL 30/04/98, art. 1).[14] China and Russia were removed from the list of "state-trading countries." This does not mean that they are now considered market economies for the purposes of antidumping laws (a fact repeatedly emphasized in various interviews with trade officials at the European Commission, Directorate General I [DGI], Fall 1999). The removal of Russia and China from the list of nonmarket economies simply means they are now considered "hybrid regimes" (European Commission 1998, 7). As such, the EU pledges to consider in future antidumping cases whether the firms involved are market oriented.

With these changes, the commission promised to "take a more *systematic approach to issues of individual treatment and natural comparative advantage*" of Russian and Chinese enterprises (italics added for emphasis; European Commission 1998, 7). Nonmarket economies should see in this legal change a ray of hope that they might be able to assume their place in the international division of labor by contributing labor- or energy-intensive goods. However, given that the aforementioned cases *Unwrought Magnesium from China* and *Potassium Chloride from Russia, Belarus, and Ukraine* took place during or after the ratification of this legal change to take comparative advantage into account, it does not appear that the change will preclude the use of OECD-analogue prices for energy, labor, and environmental costs in antidumping cases against nonmarket economies.

Interviews with top-ranking trade officials and officials in charge of external relations at the European Commission revealed a widespread distrust of the information supplied by nonmarket economies and the extent of their reforms.[15] Trade officials vehemently denied that labor supply, energy resources, or the use of the environment could constitute a comparative advantage for nonmarket economies, although they could in cases involving developing countries. The EU official charged with overseeing external relations with China could come up with no comparative advantage that China might enjoy. Officials charged with administering antidumping duties could find no potential comparative advantage of nonmarket economies. In effect, the trade officials were committing what Kramer (chapter 6 of this volume) describes as "sinister attribution error," ascribing hostile intentions and malevolent motives to NMEs despite a lack of supporting evidence.

Because there is sufficient latitude built into the trade laws to allow officials to adjudicate antidumping cases in accordance with their interpretations of comparative advantage, trade officials can render their decisions based on presumptions about NMEs (European Court of Justice 1996, II-875). In these cases, presumptions and distrust of NMEs dominate decision making. As Ullmann-Margalit explains (chapter 3 in this volume), in the absence of adequate reasons for dealing with NMEs with trust, a presumption of distrust is the "default rule." Presumptions about the NMEs' lack of reform, presumptions about the different and possibly threatening organization of their economies, and presumptions about the intrinsic problems of free trade with these countries supersede actual information about the scope and extent of reform in these transitional economies.

It must be remembered that other developing countries are not treated like nonmarket economies. The same labor, environmental, or energy standards are not applied to India, Pakistan, Egypt, Indonesia, Thailand, and other developing countries. The EU does not use its antidumping laws to thwart the practices of many developing countries that have low labor rates or subsidized, state-owned, and inefficient energy production or those that pollute or abuse the environment as a result of their production for export. The EU accepts that these types of "comparative advantages" are low-value-added, short-term practices to help developing countries earn capital in the international division of labor. Nonmarket economies are held to a different standard of development than other types of developing countries.

Conclusion

A distrust hypothesis helps explain the discriminatory nature of trade relations between the European Union and nonmarket economies. The EU does not simply lack trust toward nonmarket economies but is actively engaged in distrusting these countries. The EU fails to apply the same onerous trade procedures to other types of developing countries, not because the countries are necessarily adhering to certain environmental, labor, and energy use standards nor because developing countries are necessarily more market oriented than so-called nonmarket economies. The EU may not "trust" India, Bangladesh, and Indonesia's trade incentives, but it does not actively distrust them. It is distrust that prompts the EU to apply different rules and procedures to nonmarket economies than to other types of developing countries. These extraordinary rules and procedures are deemed necessary because of uncertainty about the interests, incentives, and capabilities of nonmarket economies. Similar uncertainty surrounds the interests, incentives, and capabilities of developing-country trading partners, but they are not subjected to the same onerous institutional arrangements. This points to the different implications of a lack of trust versus active distrust on trade relations.

The EU's distrust of nonmarket economies is evident not only in the actual trade case law discussed in the previous section but in the interviews as well. Trade officials harbor a generalized dislike for nonmarket economy countries, which were described as "unpleasant to visit," "backward," "different from the West and certainly not European," "not trustworthy," and subject to possibly deceptive motives and economic arrangements.[16] These unfounded yet powerful beliefs fuel the lingering perception that NMEs are threatening and that trade officials must therefore be "hypervigilant" in the administration of those trade cases (Kramer, chapter 6 in this volume).[17]

Distrusting nonmarket economies changes the manner in which the EU investigates their cases. The burden of proof is higher for nonmarket economies than for other developing countries because the presumption of distrust dominates decision making. This is consistent with the predictions of Ullmann-Margalit (chapter 3, this volume). Because it distrusts the capacity, intentions, and interests of nonmarket economies, the EU presumes that their domestic economies must be noncompetitive and not market oriented. This presumption of nonmarket activity has proved to be an impossible hurdle for nonmarket economies in transition to cross.

For example, in the case of trade with developing countries like Taiwan and South Korea, EU trade officials acknowledged a certain "darkness about their economic practices," but this "darkness" remains unexplored because there is an overarching presumption that market forces are at work.[18] There is no such presumption with nonmarket economies. In fact, an opposite presumption dominates decision making: the presumption that nonmarket forces permeate economic relations.

To use Ullmann-Margalit's terminology, in this case the "default rule" is a presumption of distrust. The presumption of nonmarket activity causes the EU to adjudicate NME antidumping cases differently from other similar cases involving developing countries. The presumption of distrust causes EU trade officials to review each piece of information supplied by NMEs with a fine-tooth comb and therefore to find the problems or inconsistencies in information for which they are searching. As Kramer (chapter 6 in this volume) notes, distrust of NMEs causes trade officials to be "hypervigilant . . . social information processors." In the end, this results in more onerous treatment of nonmarket economy imports than imports from other developing countries, because trade with those countries and information from those countries is not similarly scrutinized or questioned.

The broader policy implication is that the presumption of distrust directed toward nonmarket economies undermines the ability of the EU to establish mutually beneficial trade relations with these countries and further its foreign policy objectives vis-à-vis these transitional countries. In this case, distrust results in an outcome neither party wants: nonmarket economies are prevented from fully integrating into the international political economy, and the EU is prevented from realizing its foreign policy objectives to foster peace and trade with these countries.

Changing the EU's beliefs about the perceived threat posed by nonmarket economies may prove a challenging hurdle, but it is one with many mutual rewards. In this volume, both Kramer (chapter 6) and Larson (chapter 2) discuss various devices to decrease distrust. Kramer highlights the utility of relationship-building activities, unilateral initiatives, and third-party intervention. Margaret Levi, Matthew Moe, and Theresa Buckley (chapter 5 in this volume) and Larson stress the capacity of third-party institutions to build trust or overcome distrust. In the case of trade with NMEs, there has been some movement along all of these lines. The EU's association agreements with NMEs are clear attempts to build closer relationships. The WTO is an example of third-party intervention in trade relations between the countries. Internally motivated changes within the EU designed to make the trade laws "fairer" to NMEs are unilateral initiatives to improve trade relations. However, thus far these have been insufficient to overcome the presumption of distrust. The EU's differential treatment of nonmarket economies in relation to antidumping cases is a reminder about the temerity of distrust, once in place, and the difficulty in predicting change or moving from the suboptimal distrust equilibrium to a potentially more advantageous one.

Appendix: Country Groupings, U.S.- and EU-Constructed Aggregates

Asian Newly Industrialized Countries (Four Countries)

Hong Kong, Singapore, South Korea, Taiwan

Big Emerging Markets (Fifteen Countries)

Argentina, Brazil, Brunei, Hong Kong, India, Indonesia, Malaysia, Mexico, Philippines, Singapore, South Korea, South Africa, Taiwan, Thailand, Turkey

Europe (Fifteen Countries)

Austria, Belgium, Denmark, Finland, France, Germany, Ireland, Italy, Netherlands, Norway, Portugal, Spain, Sweden, Switzerland, the United Kingdom

Nonmarket Economies (Twenty-five Countries)

Albania, Armenia, Azerbaijan, Belarus, Bulgaria, China, the Czech Republic, Estonia, Georgia, the German Democratic Republic, Hungary, Kazakhstan, the Kyrgyz Republic, Latvia, Lithuania, Moldova, Poland, Romania, Russia, the Slovak Republic, Tajikistan, Turkmenistan, Ukraine, Uzbekistan, Vietnam[19]

Other Asian Countries (Twenty Countries)

Afghanistan, Bangladesh, Bhutan, Brunei, Burma, Cambodia, India, Indonesia, North Korea, Laos, Macao, Malaysia, Maldive Islands, Mongolia, Nepal, Pakistan, Philippines, Sri Lanka, Thailand, Vietnam

South America (Ten Countries)

Argentina, Bolivia, Brazil, Chile, Colombia, Ecuador, Paraguay, Peru, Uruguay, Venezuela

Notes

1. This is consistent with Ullmann-Margalit's understanding of distrust as a function of three conditions: intention, right reason, and competence.
2. The term nonmarket economy is both a political and an economic designation. It only refers to countries that were or are communist. While in some circles the term is being replaced by "transitional economies," "nonmarket economies" remains the official term still used by both U.S. and EU trade agencies.
3. By similarly situated I mean developing countries at similar levels of economic development, with comparable wage and income levels and similar production profiles. Countries considered by the European Union to be similarly situated include Malaysia, Indonesia, Egypt, Brazil, Argentina, South Korea, and India.
4. In keeping with the procedures followed by the European Commission, before the dissolution of the USSR in 1991, each antidumping case was counted as one case (not fifteen cases or one for each republic). Since 1991, antidumping cases are counted against each country involved in a case.
5. For discussions of the alleged unfair trade advantages enjoyed by centrally planned economies, see Gregory and Stuart (1990), 163–250; Kornai (1992), 262–92, 333–51; and Murrell (1990), 25–42.
6. For source of all EC case numbers, see European Commission and European Council (1980–2001).
7. There is a substantial body of literature critiquing the economic basis for antidumping laws, as embodied by Jacob Viner and the Chicago school (see Anderson 1993; Miranda 1996; Tharakan 1999; and Wares 1977).

8. While EU antidumping laws are specific to the EU, they are not arbitrary, and they largely conform to the international standards specified in article VI of the GATT. However, the rules and procedures do leave considerable room for discretion on the part of GATT signatories.
9. Note this interesting political example: Yugoslavia is classified as a market economy and is used as analogue for the parallel cases against nonmarket economies.
10. Various interviews with senior trade officials at the European Commission, Directorate General I (DGI), Brussels, Fall 1999. I assured my interviewees anonymity; therefore no full names and no full titles are cited.
11. Various interviews with trade officials in the department of Antidumping Investigations, European Commission, DGI, Brussels, Fall 1999.
12. Interviews with trade officials in antidumping investigations, European Commission, DGI, Brussels, Fall 1999. For examples of recent cases, see *Steel Wire Ropes and Cables* (EC 1796/99, OJL 17/08/99); *Color Televisions* (EC 2584/98, OJL 02/12/98); and *Potassium Permanganate* (EC 1507/98, OJL 16/07/98).
13. Examples include the market-oriented industry test, changes in the status of China and Russia, new rules for individual treatment of firms, and special association agreements with Eastern Europe.
14. If a firm in China or Russia can prove with documented evidence that all of its inputs are market determined, then its domestic prices will be used in antidumping investigations. It is believed that this would allow Chinese and Russian firms to demonstrate a comparative advantage and would result in substantially lower antidumping margins if dumping were to be found. Given that the criteria are onerous, trade officials do not think that Russia or China will be able to demonstrate the existence of a market-oriented industry in a transitional economy. In fact, many U.S. and EU "market" trading partners would not be able to pass the formal and informal criteria of the tests (discussion with trade analyst at European Commission, DGI, Brussels, Fall 1999).
15. Interviews with various heads of unit and directors in the European Commission, DGI, Brussels, Fall 1999.
16. Compilation from various interviews with trade officials and heads of units in European Commission, DGI, Brussels, Fall 1999.
17. It would be interesting (though outside the scope of this study) to discern the mechanisms by which individuals in the trade agencies are socialized and instructed to adopt the generalized distrust beliefs. Understanding the mechanisms of transmission would point to ways to ameliorate the problem.
18. Interview with trade official in Antidumping Investigations, European Commission, DGI. Brussels, Fall 1999.
19. The Czech Republic, Hungary, Poland, and the Slovak Republic were removed from classification as nonmarket economies in 1992, Bulgaria and Romania in 1994, and Estonia, Latvia, and Lithuania in 1998.

References

Agence Europe. 1996. "FTA Criticizes Anti-dumping Proceedings on Handbags and Satchels Originating in China." *Europe Daily Bulletins*, no. 6748 (June 14, 1996).

———. 1997. "At Anti-dumping Seminar, Sir Leon Brittan Announces a New, More Flexible System for Price Undertakings." *Europe Daily Bulletins*, no. 6902 (January 29, 1997).

Anderson, James. 1993. "Domino Dumping II: Anti-dumping." *Journal of International Economics* 35: 133–50.

Brenton, Paul, and Francesca Di Mauro. 1998. "Sensitive Industrial Products Between the CEECs and the EU." *World Economy* 21: 285–304.

Coleman, James. 1990. *Foundations of Social Theory*. Cambridge, Mass.: Belknap Press of Harvard University Press.

Eichengreen, Barry, and Richard Kohl. 1998. "The External Sector, the State, and Development in Eastern Europe." In *Enlarging Europe: The Industrial Foundations of a New Political Reality*, edited by John Zysman and Andrew Schwartz. Berkeley: University of California Press.

European Commission. 1983. *First Annual Report of the Commission to the European Communities on the Community's Anti-dumping and Anti-subsidy Activities (Submitted to the Council and the European Parliament by the Commission)*. COM(83) 519 final. Brussels: Commission of the European Communities.

———. 1984. *Second Annual Report of the Commission of the European Communities to the European Parliament on the Community's Anti-dumping and Anti-subsidy Activities*. COM(84) 721 final. Brussels: Commission of the European Communities.

———. 1986. *Third Annual Report of the Commission to the European Parliament on the Community's Anti-dumping and Anti-subsidy Activities*. COM(86) 308 final. Brussels: Commission of the European Communities.

———. 1987. *Fourth Annual Report of the Commission to the European Parliament on the Community's Anti-dumping and Anti-subsidy Activities*. COM(87) 178 final. Brussels: Commission of the European Communities.

———. 1989. *Sixth Annual Report of the Commission on the Community's Anti-dumping and Anti-subsidy Activities*. COM(89) 106 final. Brussels: Commission of the European Communities.

———. 1990. *Seventh Annual Report of the Commission on the Community's Anti-dumping and Anti-subsidy Activities*. COM(90) 229 final. Brussels: Commission of the European Communities.

———. 1995. *Twelfth Annual Report from the Commission to the European Parliament on the Community's Anti-dumping and Anti-subsidy Activities (1993)*. COM(95) 16 final. Brussels: Commission of the European Communities.

———. 1996. *Fifteenth Annual Report of the Commission of the European Communities to the European Parliament on the Community's Anti-dumping and Anti-subsidy Activities*. Brussels: European Commission.

———. 1997a. *Communication from the Commission to the Council and the European Parliament on the Treatment of Former Non-market Economies in Anti-dumping*

Proceedings and a Proposal for a Council Regulation (EC) No. 384/96. Brussels: European Commission.

———. 1997b. *Sixteenth Annual Report from the Commission to the European Parliament on the Community's Anti-dumping and Anti-subsidy Activities.* Brussels: European Commission.

———. 1998. *Seventeenth Annual Report from the Commission to the European Parliament on The Community's Anti-dumping and Anti-subsidy Activities.* Brussels: European Commission.

———. 1999. *Eighteenth Annual Report from the Commission to the European Parliament on the Community's Anti-dumping and Anti-subsidy Activities.* Brussels: European Commission.

———. 2001. *Anti-dumping and Anti-subsidy Statistics Covering the Year 2000.* Brussels: European Commission.

European Commission and European Council. 1980–2001. "Case Rulings." *Official Journal L and C.* Available at: http://europa.eu.int. Accessed on January 29, 2004.

European Court of Justice. 1996. "Climax Paper Converters Ltd. v Council of the European Union." Case T-155/94, September 18, 1996, II-873-919.

European Parliament. 1996. "Written Question P-2790/96 by Pierluigi Castagnetti (PPE) to the Commission; Subject: Anti-dumping duties on imports under Council Regulation." EEC 3068/92. Brussels: European Commission.

Fine, Frank. 1988. "EEC Antidumping: The Problem of Imports from State-Trading Countries." *Law and Policy in International Business* 20: 91–107.

Gaddis, John Lewis. 1972. *The United States and the Origins of the Cold War, 1941–1947.* New York: Columbia University Press.

Gambetta, Diego. 1988a. "Can We Trust Trust?" In *Trust: Making and Breaking Cooperative Relations,* edited by Diego Gambetta. New York: Basil Blackwell.

———, ed. 1988b. *Trust: Making and Breaking Cooperative Relations.* New York: Basil Blackwell.

Gregory, Paul, and Robert Stuart. 1990. *Soviet Economic Structure and Performance.* New York: Harper Collins.

Hardin, Russell. 1998. "Trust in Government." In *Trust in Governance,* edited by Valerie Braithwaite and Margaret Levi. New York: Russell Sage Foundation.

Holzman, Franklyn. 1987. "A Comparative View of Foreign Trade Behavior: Market Versus Centrally Planned Economies." In *The Economics of Soviet Bloc Trade and Finance,* edited by Franklyn Holzman. Boulder, Colo.: Westview Press.

International Monetary Fund. 1997. *Direction of Trade Statistics Yearbook.* Washington, D.C.: International Monetary Fund.

Kornai, Janos. 1992. *The Socialist System: The Political Economy of Communism.* Princeton, N.J.: Princeton University Press.

Larson, Deborah Welch. 1985. *Origins of Containment: A Psychological Explanation.* Princeton, N.J.: Princeton University Press.

Laurent, Patrick. 1996. *Anti-dumping Policies in a Globalizing World.* Speech presented to the Swedish Minister for Foreign Trade (November 5, 1996). Stockholm: European Commission, Directorate General for Trade.

Lenin, Vladimir I. 1932. *State and Revolution.* New York: International Publishers.

Levi, Margaret. 1998. "A State of Trust." In *Trust and Governance,* edited by Valerie Braithwaite and Margaret Levi. New York: Russell Sage Foundation.

———. 2000. "When Good Defenses Make Good Neighbors." In *Institutions, Contracts, and Organizations: Perspectives from New Institutional Economics*, edited by Claude Menard. Colchester, Eng.: Edward Elgar.

Marer, Paul. 1984. "United States Market Disruption Procedures Involving Romanian and Other CPE Products, With Policy Recommendations." In *New Horizons in East-West Economic and Business Relations*, edited by Marvin Jackson and James Woodson. New York: Columbia University Press.

Marx, Karl, and Friedrich Engels. 1848/1978. "The Manifesto of the Communist Party." In *The Marx-Engels Reader*, edited by Robert Tucker. New York: W. W. Norton.

Miranda, Jorge. 1996. "Should Antidumping Laws Be Dumped?" *Law & Policy in International Business* 28(1): 255–88.

Murrell, Peter. 1990. *The Nature of Socialist Economies: Lessons from Eastern European Foreign Trade*. Princeton, N.J.: Princeton University Press.

Paterson, Thomas. 1973. *Soviet-American Confrontation: Postwar Reconstruction and the Origins of the Cold War*. Baltimore, Md.: Johns Hopkins University Press.

"Questions Nos H-0379/97 by Mr. Bertens and H-0380/97 by Mr. Gahrton on EU policy toward China." 1997. *European Foreign Policy Bulletin* (97/317, June). Available at http://www.arc1.ive/efpball. Accessed June 1999.

Rees, David. 1967. *The Age of Containment: The Cold War, 1945–1968*. London: St. Martin's Press.

Schlesinger, Arthur. 1967. "Origins of the Cold War." *Foreign Affairs* 46: 22–52.

Tharakan, P. K. Mathew. 1999. "Is Anti-Dumping Here to Stay?" *World Economy* 22: 179–206.

Tharakan, P. K. Mathew, and Jean Waelbroeck. 1994. "Antidumping and Countervailing Duty Decisions in the EC and in the US: An Experiment in Comparative Political Economy." *European Economic Review* 38(1): 171–93.

Wares, William. 1977. *The Theory of Dumping and American Commercial Policy*. Lexington, Mass.: D.C. Heath.

Wilczynski, Jozef. 1969. *The Economics and Politics of East-West Trade*. New York: Frederick Praeger.

World Trade Organization. 2002. "About the WTO: The Organization's Members." Available at: http://www.wto.org/english/thewto_e/whatis_e/tif_e/org6_e.htm. Accessed on January 29, 2004.

Chapter 12

Terrorism and Group-Generalized Distrust

RUSSELL HARDIN

TERRORISM RAISES two important issues in trust. First, obviously, is the problem of how terrorists can cooperate in extraordinary actions that put themselves at great risk. Second is the problem of how a society—even one with standard liberal protections of civil liberties—can avoid becoming the object of the pervasive distrust of those subcommunities, domestic and foreign, from which terrorists might come. The two problems interact in that the devices for securing cooperative commitments among potential terrorists run counter to the plausible visions of society that include strong protections of civil liberties. In these visions, civil liberties are needed to protect individuals from abuse by the state at various levels of government. It is through its justice system, not through protections of civil liberties, that the state must protect individuals from one another.

In the United States, the second of these problems is especially acute because of the long history of slavery based on race and the resultant racism that has pervaded both laws and mores. Just because there is a severe problem of racism in the United States, protections of civil liberties must be universalized to cover everyone, and the actual language of civil liberties is universalistic. To put African Americans under surveillance or to arrest and search them far more often, proportionately, than whites, especially in cities in which police forces are dominated by whites, is bound to exacerbate racism. Indeed, discrimination by officials and by ordinary citizens may exacerbate the problem of subcommunal organization that enables intracommunal cooperation in hostility toward the dominant social group.

Now we face the possibility of a new version of discriminatory stereotyping that might be at least statistically justified. That is, the odds are that the most grievous terrorist attacks that Americans face in the present era will come from Arab and Islamist fanatics, although, as we know all too well, right-wing Caucasian Americans such as Timothy McVeigh and right-wing militias are the next most likely source (see Stern 1996). (In England, Spain, and some other democratic nations, the greatest threats may be domestic minority groups, not foreigners who import their terrorism.) Part of the source of popular fear of Islamist fanatics is that they isolate themselves in exclusionary communities where we cannot know them and, perhaps more important, they cannot know us. They can sustain beliefs in such communities that would seem lunatic for anyone in the larger society (Hardin 2001). Their isolation, coupled with suspicions about their actual beliefs and motivations, may provoke a form of generalized distrust of everyone from their general background, the vast majority of whom are unlikely to become terrorists. We may call this group-generalized distrust.

Efforts to prevent terrorist attacks, however, are not like efforts to control ordinary crime, and they may undercut the regime of civil liberties that depends on the assumption that miscreants actually have interests—largely material—that are shared by the larger society. Much of social order is built on relationships of trust that cannot hold between a self-isolated terrorist group and ordinary citizens. Pervasive distrust of a potentially terrorist group may seemingly give the state license to take extraordinary, illiberal actions that might be well received by the majority of citizens, who do not think their own liberties are at risk from actions against members of identifiable groups from which terrorists are most likely to come. Against this relatively smug stance, however, one might note that the extremist militia groups in the United States claim to be defending their own civil liberties. Given the government's disastrously violent attack on the radical Branch Davidian community in Waco, Texas, on April 19, 1993, we cannot easily say they are wrong (see Boyer 1995).

In this discussion, I assume the encapsulated-interest model of trust, as discussed in chapter 1. The focus is on groups as well as individuals, with groups and their members commonly the objects of trust or distrust and with individuals in the large society trusting or distrusting them. If one were to do survey research on the distribution of distrust of groups, one would wish to have responses to questions about members of identifiable groups as well as responses to questions about various groups as groups. For example, a woman might generally react differently toward women and toward men on many ordinary issues having nothing to do with gender per se (Cook, Hardin, and Levi 2004, chap. 2). If she is an American citizen and she meets two anonymous strangers, one of whom has certain identifying characteristics of an American and the other of whom has foreign characteristics, she might deal with them very differently. In particular, she might more readily take the risk of relying on the first and be somewhat more wary of relying on the second for some minor matter.

If the other person has a heavy accent and Middle Eastern facial features, she might be only slightly more wary of that person than of the first person in dealing with some minor matter of the moment. But she might be extremely wary of the *group* from which the second person comes. She might therefore even want quite different policies for dealing with the different groups from which these two "anonymous" strangers come. We know from varied contexts that people can have a more positive view of individuals from a group than they have of the group. Many Americans, for example, nearly revile government bureaucrats as a class, even though they often think well of all the bureaucrats with whom they have had any dealings (Klein 1994). There must be many Americans who have trusted Arab American associates but who generally distrust Arabs as a group.

The Epistemology of Close Communities

How do terrorists who are embedded in a foreign society cooperate? Cooperative communal ties are organized in two substantially different ways (Cook and Hardin 2001; Fischer 1982). First, small, close communities tend to be governed by general norms of cooperativeness, norms whose requirements can be vague and ill defined and can be subjectively asserted by members of the community. The norms can require different things of different people, depending on their likely capacities. For example, if your family suffers some hardship, your neighbors might do distinctively different things to help you get through the hard time. Some of us might cook for you, others might take care of your children when needed, and so forth. Second, in more complex settings, such as urban areas, many relationships are organized through networks that are relatively specifically concerned with particular kinds of cooperation or cooperation on particular kinds of issues.[1]

Norms of communal cooperation are effective only to the extent that members of a group or community want to continue as members. In this respect, such norms, although vague in their range, are similar to trust as encapsulated interest. Such trust generally depends on the trustworthiness induced by the desire to maintain the relationship. Network organization of cooperation can be governed by overlapping dyadic encapsulated-interest trust relationships and by reputational effects that are a proxy for such trust relationships. Hence such trust relations are a substitute for traditional communal norms for contexts in which the norms would no longer work because the web of dense interactions that both defines and enforces the norms is absent. When cooperation is organized by communal norms, it can become highly exclusionary, so that only members of the community can have cooperative relations with those in the community. In such a case, the norms of cooperativeness are norms of exclusion (Hardin 1995, chap. 4).

For many fundamentalist groups, continued loyalty to the group and its beliefs is secured by isolating the group and its members from many other influences, so that relations within the community are governed by extensive norms of exclusion. When this happens, it is not only trust relations but also basic beliefs that are constrained. If I encounter no one with contrary beliefs, my own beliefs will tend to prevail by inertia and lack of questioning. There are many strong, extreme beliefs about religious issues as well as about lots of other things. Many of these views have to be wrong for the simple reasons that they differ from one another and that each denies the truth of the others. The two matters for which such staunch loyalty to unquestioned beliefs are politically most important are probably religious and nationalist commitments (see Hardin 1997, 2001). Such beliefs are often maintained by blocking alternative views and by sanctioning those within the group who stray.

Consider a very peaceful group, the devoutly religious Amish, who live mostly in the Midwest of the United States and into Canada. The Amish are not hostile to others but merely want to continue in their own ways (this is evidently true at least for older adults), and they are very nearly apolitical. The old-order Amish of Wisconsin have long striven to protect their children against corruption of their beliefs by taking them out of school at the age of fourteen. Wisconsin law requires education through the age of sixteen, and Wisconsin officials attempted to force Amish children to continue in school by fining parents who took their children out of school early. (The fines were not large.) In a famous Supreme Court case (*Wisconsin v. Yoder et al.*, 406 U.S. 205–49), Amish leaders won the right to stop public education of their children at the age of fourteen. The Amish and the Supreme Court opinion both argued that further education was likely to corrupt Amish children's beliefs. They therefore concluded that the constitutional separation of church and state meant that Amish children could not be forced to expose their beliefs to such severe tests (also see Hardin 1995, 201–3).

It is widely supposed that such narrow views cannot readily be sustained by many people if they are constantly exposed to different views. Often, the reason people alter their views about ordinary matters is that they experience things that run counter to their beliefs or they deal with people who question their beliefs. Indeed, this was the forcefully articulated view of Amish leaders in Wisconsin. They well understood that keeping their children away from the broader American culture was virtually essential to keeping them in the faith.

Even more forcefully, the English philosopher G. E. M. Anscombe (1981) says that unless children are taught some of the more incredible articles of Catholic faith at a very early age, they will have a hard time ever coming to believe them. Only someone gifted with a child's magical thinking can accept, for example, the story of transubstantiation, by which an ordinary wafer becomes the flesh of Christ and a sip of ordinary wine becomes the blood of Christ (Anscombe's own example). Tell this to an adult who has not previously heard of it, and you are likely to be met with astonished incredulity that anyone could possibly hold such a belief. Once taught at an early enough age, however, a person might survive adult reasoning without loss of the seemingly implausible belief. Someone intimidated by the invocation of the cross throughout childhood might still be motivated by its image in later life, even after giving up many of the beliefs associated with the meaning of that cross. The mere symbol of the cross can seemingly chastise and energize people.

Extremist and fundamentalist groups are often able to block such corrective devices as come from interactions in the larger society. Some of the terrorism on the ground in the Middle East seems to fit easily with the usual view that isolation is important in strengthening and sustaining extremist beliefs. Terrorist training commonly takes place in isolated camps, such as those of al Qaida, in which there is no contrary view and every individual is constantly reinforced in the group's belief system. There might be few broader social influences that are discussed or that can survive in the face of constant hortatory indoctrination as well as fairly substantial deprivation of kinds of social interaction that most people enjoy (see, for example, Barbara Crossette, "Living in a World without Women," *New York Times,* November 4, 2001, sec. 4, p. 1).

All of this works because most of what anyone knows comes from hearsay, from such "experts" as a neighborhood gossip, a newspaper, or, in exceptional cases, an encyclopedia or other authoritative source. What isolation from other influences does is give us a crippled epistemology. We are unable to come to know many things, and we have no reason to reconsider the things we think we know.

On this account, maintenance of extremist beliefs depends on embedding the believers in a closed community. It need not be entirely closed, just mostly. For example, an Amish farmer might know several non-Amish with whom he deals commercially. But he does not immerse himself in their communal life, and he knows little of it. Members of the extremist militias of Idaho, Michigan, Montana, and Wyoming are very isolated from other influences. Their friends are other militia members. The Unabomber led the life of a nearly complete loner; he evidently had no further influences on his beliefs beyond the things he chose to read. But he was a loner in the further sense that he was not part of a larger, more threatening movement of terrorists who might wreak far greater harm than any ordinarily equipped loner.

Our embeddedness in an exclusive community can both enable and constrain us. It enables us to rely on fellow group members in ways and to a degree that would be implausible in the larger society outside our community. There is a bit of truth in the chief normative claim of communitarianism, which is that community can be very supportive of us and make daily life more congenial and comfortable and is therefore in some sense good for us. It offers us the epistemological comforts of home (Hardin 1995, 54, 77, 89–90). Another bit of truth in communitarianism, which, however, has negative implications, is that community can suppress us and keep us in line in ways that make little sense except that they are the ways of the community. Communities can destroy individuals and their lives. Communitarian philosophers in our time see the good side of community as overwhelmingly, even definitively, good, and they are virtually blind to the potentially harmful side of it (Hardin 1995, chap. 7). There is a brutal and unavoidable conflict inherent in the idea of exclusionary communities in which adults secure their own values by constraining their children's future values.

Narrowing one's associations to others in an isolated extremist group cripples one's epistemology by blocking out general questioning of the group's beliefs (Hardin 2001). To an outsider, those beliefs might be utterly crazy, as Anscombe (1981) grants for her own Catholic beliefs. Indeed, virtually all strong religious beliefs sound crazy or silly to those who do not share them. Committed believers in each of the three major monotheistic religions spawned in the Middle East hold views that exclude the possibility that the other two sets of religious beliefs could be true. Christianity and Islam are proselytizing religions, and they have come into mortal conflict therefore. Stringent versions of Islam and Judaism require religious control over civic life and, because they both hold the land that is now Israel as holy, they come into mortal conflict. Indeed, insofar as Western ideas influence secular politics in Islamic societies, stringent versions of Islam are in conflict with purveyors of such secular politics, including the West—especially the Anglo-Saxon West, which has not merely purveyed ideas but has even installed and supported secular regimes in the Middle East.

Social scientists and historians might explain the prevalence of certain religious beliefs, but their explanations are likely to render the content of the beliefs contingent on historical accidents rather than on theological truths. Although the truth of their beliefs surely matters to those who are deeply religious, they do not seem to think that their beliefs need to be shown to be true; they simply know them to be true.

True believers are not typically scientifically interested in how they got their beliefs.

Generalized Trust, Generalized Distrust

There is a fairly extensive literature on so-called generalized trust, that is, trust in the anonymous or general other person, including strangers, whom we might encounter, perhaps with some restrictions on what issues would come under that trust. (This discussion draws on Hardin 2002.) Evidence for such generalized trust comes primarily from three standard survey questions in the General Social Survey. One of these is, "Generally speaking, would you say that most people can be trusted, or that you can't be too careful dealing with people?" People commonly answer that most people can be trusted; or, on a multilevel scale, they choose a relatively high level of confidence in others' trustworthiness. It is all too easy to read such responses very loosely. If I say I can trust most people most of the time, I may merely be saying I trust most of *those I do actually deal with* most of the time. Of course, that is partly why I deal with them and not lots of other people whom I would not trust most of the time (I might actively distrust some of them and be agnostic about others).

In principle, however, the idea of generalized trust has two odd features. First, it sounds more nearly like an account of simple *expectations* than an account of trust. In this account, I supposedly think everyone is reliable to some degree, independently of who they are or what relationship I have with them. I think this of them the way I might think the typical person would behave in certain ways in various contexts. This sounds more like optimism about the cooperativeness of my fellows than trust in them. Moreover, at best, such optimism is likely to be about specific kinds of people, so that it depends on stereotyping. I therefore call it group-generalized trust.

Second, when survey respondents say they trust most people most of the time, this is almost surely an elliptical claim. They do not mean that, if a random stranger on the street were to ask for a loan of, say, a hundred dollars, they would trust that person to repay and would therefore make the loan. Hence even this open-ended answer to a badly framed, vague question is almost certainly just a loose way of saying they would trust most people within somewhat narrow limits. Moreover, it is also elliptical in its reference to "most people." Few of the respondents would genuinely trust just anyone much at all. Even if I trust most of those I deal with most of the time, that is because most of the time there is little at stake in my dealings with them—I would not trust many of them for very high stakes. My trust is of you to do X, and making X a large matter can drastically affect whether I would trust you.

The survey results cannot be read to show that there is genuinely generalized trust. The respondents are forced by the vagueness of the questions to give vague answers, and it is a misdescription to label their responses as generalized trust. In Julian Rotter's (1967) interpersonal trust scale, discussed in chapter 1 of this volume, there is no room for a category of generalized trust, even in his psychological view that some people are inherently more trusting than others. That his scale divides into three independent factors suggests, indeed, that trust must vary according to the stereotypical character of the potential objects of trust, whether they are, for example, parents, professionals, politicians, or strangers (Wright and Tedeschi 1975). It would not be hard to frame survey questions that would allow us to multiply these categories.

At best, in any case, generalized trust must be a matter of relatively positive expectations of the trustworthiness, cooperativeness, or helpfulness of others. It is the stance of, for example, the child who has grown up in a benign environment in which virtually everyone has always been trustworthy. That former child now faces others with relatively positive expectations by inductive generalization (see Hardin 2002, chap. 5). The value of quasi-generalized trust is the value of such an upbringing: It gives us the sense of running little risk in cooperating with others, so that we may more readily enter into relationships with them. Of course, such generalized optimism is a value only if others are relatively trustworthy.

Why speak of generalized trust? In any real-world context, I trust some more than others, and I trust any given person more about some things than about others and more in some contexts than in others. I may be more optimistic in my expectations of others' trustworthiness on first encounters than you are, but apart from such a general fact I do not have generalized trust. I might also typecast many people and suppose some of the types are likely to be trustworthy enough to justify the risk of cooperating with them, other types less so, and still others not at all. However, this is far short of generalized trust. It is merely optimism about certain others. Such optimism from typecasting makes rational sense, just as typecasting of those whom one might employ makes rational sense as a first, crude indicator of competence or commitment. This is the rationale in Gary Becker's (1971) analysis of discrimination in hiring.

Many, maybe even most, claims for generalized trust can readily be restated as claims that, in contexts in which trust generally pays off, it makes sense to risk entering into exchanges even with those whom one cannot claim to trust in the encapsulated-interest sense—because one does not yet have ongoing relationships with them nor does one have reasons of reputation to trust them. This is not a claim that one trusts those others but only that one has relatively optimistic expectations of being able to build successful relationships with certain, perhaps numerous, others (although surely not with just anyone). Hence generalized trust seems likely to be nothing more than an optimistic assessment of trustworthiness and a willingness therefore to take small risks on dealing with others whom one does not yet know. That assessment would be corrected if the optimism proved to be unwarranted because people and agencies in the relevant context proved not to be generally trustworthy.

Whereas generalized trust or group-generalized trust makes little or no sense (other than as a claim of optimism), group-generalized distrust in many contexts makes very good sense. If I am Jewish, Gypsy, or gay, I have good reason to distrust all officers of the Nazi state and probably most citizens in Nazi Germany as well. American Indians of the western plains had very good reason to distrust whites. During Slobodan Milosevic's wars and pogroms, Serbs, Croatians, and Muslims in what was then Yugoslavia had increasingly good reasons to distrust most members of the other groups, especially while the latter were acting as groups. Blacks in the United States have long had good reason to distrust white police officers, not only in the South but in many northern cities as well. In all of these cases, distrust is defined by the belief that members of the other groups and their representatives are hostile to one's interests. Trust relationships between members of these various groups are the unusual cases that require explanation; the relatively group-generalized distrust is easy to understand and justify. In all of these particular cases, the proportion of those from another group who were not to be trusted was generally quite large—or, in the Yugoslav case, it became quite large very quickly after various atrocities and brutalities.

Consider just one of these archetypal cases. In the American South during the days of Jim Crow segregation laws and practices, white police forces and courts intimidated and harassed blacks. Ordinary white citizens often were also abusive and scornful toward blacks. But frequent lynchings must have had an especially detrimental effect on race relations and on the prospects for interracial trust. From 1883 to 1960, the awful era of lynching in the United States, an estimated 4,742 blacks died at the hands of lynch mobs. That is far more than the number of people killed and even seriously injured in all the terrorist attacks on Israel or in the attacks of 11 September in the United States. A recent book displays photographs of uncounted whites—numbering into the thousands at single events—celebrating or merely spectating at these lynchings (Allen et al. 2000; see also McMurtry 2000). Some of the photographs derive from postcards that were made and sold at the events and then mailed to others. One of these postcards, plate 26, pictures a crowd around the charred remains of Jesse Washington, who was lynched in Waco, Texas, in 1916. The postcard is inscribed, "This is the barbecue we had last night my picture is to the left with a cross over it your son Joe." In the face of such events, generalized distrust of whites by blacks must have been pervasive—and perhaps still is.

In the current circumstances of mostly Arab and Islamic terrorism against Israel and the West, it is surely a tiny fraction of all Arabs and Islamists who are genuinely a threat, but the scale of their threat may make many Israelis and Westerners wary of virtually all Arabs and Islamists, because what bothers them is roughly the product of the likelihood of doing harm and the scale of the harm that is likely. Moreover, many who are not prospects for taking terrorist action evidently sympathize with and even support those actions (see, for example, Lynsey Addario, "Jihad's Women," *New York Times Magazine*, October 21, 2001, pp. 38–41). In current conditions, Arabs are more likely than, say, Africans or Chinese to be terrorists against Westerners.

On the encapsulated-interest theory of trust, I cannot trust the members of a circumscribed community and they cannot trust me, because we are not involved in ongoing relationships that we could sustain to our benefit. We might distrust each other, but we could not trust each other. Mere statistical doubt in the likely trustworthiness of the members of some identifiable group can be sufficient to induce distrust of all members of the group with whom one has no personal relationship on which to have established trust. Such distrust would be group-generalized distrust. This statistical doubt can trump relational considerations and can block the initial risk taking that might allow for a test of another individual's trustworthiness by stereotyping that individual as primarily a member of some group. If there are many people with whom one can have a particular beneficial interaction, narrowing the set by excluding certain stereotypes is efficient, and we commonly do such things in many contexts.

Unfortunately, however, systematically excluding on the basis of ethnicity or race becomes pervasively destructive of community relations. If my group has statistical grounds for doubting the motivations of many members of your group and hence for generally distrusting your group, my group's behavior is apt to give your group grounds for distrusting us. Distrust feeds distrust. Perhaps, in a cruel reverse, distrust begets untrustworthiness that ex post might be seen to justify the distrust, whereas trustworthiness begets trust that is justified by the trustworthiness (Hardin 2002, chap. 2).

Moreover, trust and distrust are likely to be asymmetric. A single betrayal may typically be enough to establish distrust, whereas a string of successful instances of cooperation may be required to develop trust. Moreover, once distrust is established it may take overwhelming counterevidence to induce trust again, whereas it may take no more than a single betrayal to wreck an ongoing trust relationship. This asymmetry is familiar from our experience with reputations. A good reputation can be wrecked easily, but a bad one is very hard to overcome (Good 1988, 43; Hardin 2002, chap. 4). Responses to terrorist actions that generally attack a minority group, such as Arab Americans, may therefore set relations back substantially and encourage the establishment of group-generalized distrust.

Terrorist Communities

Terrorist communities seem likely to be merely special cases of exclusionary groups more generally. They are, of course, special in their purposes, but they may also be special in the small size of their face-to-face communities. Terrorism that is well organized, as opposed to the anarchically, individually motivated terrorism of the Unabomber, poses a potentially grievous problem. Terrorists, almost by definition, seem to identify strongly with a particular community and see some other community as hostile to their own community's prospects. For that reason, they are likely to find it natural to live in exclusionary groups. Therefore, there is likely to be little evidence of their role in the society they wish to attack.

An astonishing fact about the Unabomber is that he was evidently able to sustain his views and his energies while living as a loner. Already, that suggests problematic sanity. The terrorists who attacked the World Trade Center and the Pentagon seemingly lived in very small communities of sometimes only two people. In some ways, the Internet allows individuals and small groups to be quite isolated while nevertheless maintaining substantial contact with others of like mind. Islamic terrorists in the West can be almost completely isolated individually while maintaining nearly instant, frequent contact with one another and with groups in the Middle East, Pakistan, or, formerly, Afghanistan.

Immigrants who join an extant subcommunity of fellow nationals are likely to be integrated into a stable set of values and commitments and are likely to find that their interests depend in large part on building and maintaining good relations within that community. They are likely to experience an analogue of what sociologists in the Marxist tradition call embourgeoisement. When workers begin to partake of the pleasures of the bourgeoisie—owning houses and cars and having their children educated—they tend to adopt bourgeois values and become conservatively concerned with maintaining and maybe advancing their status within the system (Goldthorpe et al. 1969). Then they cease to be revolutionary, and, indeed, they may even cease to vote for workers' parties in democratic elections. Part of the life of the "sleepers"—dedicated terrorists living in the country they plan eventually to attack in some way—is to avoid any analogue of embourgeoisement by avoiding the development of rich ties to others in the society in which they await their day of violence. Rich relationships in the larger society might block the prospect of ever adopting terrorist commitments for those not already part of a terrorist group.

Civil Liberties

In the historical development of liberal theory from Thomas Hobbes to our time, order is prior to all else. This was true for Hobbes (1651/1968) because he thought that the choice citizens faced was one between anarchic chaos and rigidly controlled order. It is implausible that Western democracies risk falling into radical internal disorder of the kind that disrupted Hobbes's world in seventeenth-century England. The behavior of ordinary citizens and politicians in highly developed democracies suggests that they have little or no fear that they are threatened with the chaotic disorder that Hobbes thought justified an all-powerful state. Indeed, we are the inheritors of a tradition of opposing state power insofar as it is directed against citizens. Because we have mastered the problem of internal order that worried Hobbes, we can give our attention to other issues, including, dramatically, civil liberties that protect us not from one another (the job of the state) but from the state itself, to keep it from overstepping its bounds while protecting us from one another. There might be some risk of Hobbesian disorder from external terrorism, although even this seems unlikely in any developed democracy other than, perhaps, Israel. Israel might face such a risk because the proportionate scale of terrorism that it faces is far greater than that faced by any other democratic nation.

In the face of contemporary terror on a dramatic scale, it would be a mistake to assert the priority of civil liberties over every other concern in principle. Clearly, Hobbes's concern with survival comes first. Without basic survival, civil liberties have no meaning. The basic achievement of social order is essentially a coordination problem, not a problem of deep conflict or of shared values, as various theorists have surmised. Once we are coordinated on a system of order, few citizens would put that order at risk as the price of achieving any particular policy. Only a deeply conflictual issue, such as slavery in the United States before the Civil War or divisive class conflict, is likely to justify, for many people, putting order at grave risk (Hardin 1999, 9–12).

In the face of threats from hostile exclusionary groups that solidify their beliefs through isolation and thereby engender potentially deep distrust, it is not psychologically reasonable to expect people actually to believe that the full program of civil liberties that protect citizens should be invoked on behalf of members of a potentially terrorist group. Because the language of such protections is overwhelmingly universalistic, many citizens quoted in the recent American press and many of those with whom I speak, especially students in my classes on law and morality, democracy, and nationalism, find themselves being inconsistent in arguing both for the maintenance of civil liberties and for the strong surveillance of Arabs in the United States and restrictions on their travel or immigration to the United States. If the vocabulary of civil liberties distinguished between citizens and noncitizens, who might be seen as in limbo while establishing the credentials for deserving citizenship, it might be easy for these same people to defend civil liberties for citizens without wavering while demanding different treatment of noncitizens. The painfully tainted history of race relations in the United States makes it difficult to treat groups differently in the law. The law must be universal. This history therefore probably makes it difficult even to treat noncitizens differently from citizens in many respects.

Indeed, for most of a century, civil liberties law in the United States has largely been defined by the group-level conflict of racism, especially in the criminal law, laws regulating state provisions of various benefits such as education, and in some categories of regulatory law governing travel, real estate, and other housing. There have also been issues of political liberties in the heyday of anticommunism and in the era of anarchism in the early twentieth century and with respect to ethnic groups during the two world wars, when Americans of German and later of Japanese and Italian descent were subjected to abusive surveillance and even internment. But year to year for many decades, much of civil liberties law has been about protection of blacks accused of or under trial for crimes of various kinds and blacks abused by various government officials. Many of the resultant civil liberties doctrines might never have arisen except for the abuses of racism on the part of officials of various governments, local, state, and federal.

The original Bill of Rights addresses abuses—especially those perpetrated by the English crown against its own citizens at home and in the colonies—in the period before the enumeration of rights of citizenship under the U.S. Constitution. Nations that adopt new constitutions today typically put rights protections first, rather than appending them at the end as an afterthought. But they would not include some of the protections dear to the generation of James Madison because they have no recent history of relevant abuses, such as the stationing of government troops in private homes.

One way to avoid group discrimination is through surveillance that discovers and then monitors particular individuals because of their suspect activities. It is frequently remarked that the United States suffered a major failure of intelligence gathering before September 11,

2001. The implication is usually that the Central Intelligence Agency failed to monitor plans abroad. But there was also arguably a failure of domestic intelligence. That massive failure raises a hard question: Do Americans want the kind of surveillance that we once had under J. Edgar Hoover's Federal Bureau of Investigation? Hoover used the power of the FBI to go after groups that he thought were anti-American, including civil rights activists, civil libertarians, and anti–Vietnam War activists. In his time, everyone who participated in even the most peaceful civil rights or antiwar activities was photographed repeatedly; the photos were shown to informants to identify the people; and files were amassed on all so-called activists. The files on the terrorists who bombed southern black churches were reputedly far less extensive.

Hoover was a thoroughly indecent man with gross power who blackmailed public officials to keep himself in power far beyond retirement age. One can imagine a version of the FBI that could do surveillance but would focus only on genuinely hostile groups and individuals. But we cannot easily guarantee that such an FBI would not also abuse its powers while maybe failing to find and watch terrorists. Democratic control of government works through openness and oversight. A surveillance organization cannot be open or openly overseen, and there is no way to guarantee that it will act only on its mandate. It is difficult to square civil liberties with pervasive secrecy in governmental proceedings.

Depending on what kind of people the terrorists are, there are several distinct problems in controlling terrorism: the production of terrorists in Libya, Afghanistan, Pakistan, Montana, and other places (many of whom were trained in their necessary skills, although not likely their beliefs, by the American Central Intelligence Agency, in Pakistan, and the American military, in Vietnam); their entry into the United States; and their communal maintenance in the United States. The first of these is largely a matter of foreign policy and is not particularly germane to the problem of civil liberties in a nation that the terrorists might target. (Part of U.S. foreign policy is to encourage and even demand that other nations protect civil liberties—or human rights. One might expect the current administration to relax such demands in favor of strenuous action against presumed terrorists.) The second is a problem of differentiating between those who come into the society either as ordinary visitors or potential immigrants and those who come for hostile purposes. The third is probably the one that most requires something like FBI surveillance and that therefore implicates civil liberties.

Again, the main purpose of protecting civil liberties is to block state action against individuals. The problem we face with terrorists is more nearly the problem that Hobbes supposed is fundamental for social order: protecting each of us against the others. Until we have social order and such protections of our safety, we are not likely to be concerned with civil liberties because such liberties could not even be defined absent a state as their target. Hobbes could be considered foundational for modern liberal theory, which developed further through the writings of John Locke, David Hume, and Adam Smith and which, in a sense, culminated in the work of James Madison in creating the U.S. Constitution. Although Madison saw that constitution as an embodiment of liberal protections of individuals, many of his contemporaries wanted such protections to be made explicit in amendments that make up the Bill of Rights. These amendments were added to the Constitution a few years after its ratification. Already at the time of that constitution, Americans had achieved such a successful level of social order that civil liberties had become a greater concern. A distressing fact of our time is that international terrorism has undercut the nearly universal support of strong protections of civil liberties.

A Hobbesian state uses simple sanctions to deter individuals from de facto cheating their fellow citizens, for example, through theft. Relatively limited state power is evidently adequate to enforce a high level of social order when the chief violations of that order come from simple self-interest. When the state must deter fanatical actions, such simple, low-grade sanctions may be inadequate. Hobbes saw aristocratic glory seekers in his era as people who enjoyed the exploits of fighting and who therefore were not fit citizens for a world of social order (Hardin 1991).[2] His response to them was to anathematize them, to declare them enemies and therefore make it acceptable for citizens to kill them with impunity if they would not leave. He had a similar view of how to deal with religious fanatics who insisted that everyone be subjected to their own views. His society succeeded in living past the massive, violent disruptions of his century. The aristocrats of future generations mellowed and gave up glory seeking. Religious fanatics sometimes left England for Holland or the Americas and sometimes simply withdrew from the political fray. Had both groups persisted in the behaviors that wrecked life for vast numbers during the seventeenth century, the later concern with civil liberties could not have arisen.

Legal action against ordinary miscreants has two aspects: backward looking and forward looking. It is backward looking when it punishes a particular action; it is forward looking when it deters action from even happening. Backward-looking punishment of ordinary crimes acts simultaneously to help deter future crimes. Punishment of acts of fanatical terrorism is likely to have little or no deterrent effect. The retributivist school of thought holds that criminal law should be backward looking, not forward looking. Such law should be not about deterrence but about punishment of wrongdoing. This view is often associated with the view that what counts as a crime is not merely conventionally determined by what the law says but is a moral wrong per se and thereby deserves punishment. This general view does not easily fit such problems as terrorism, especially suicidal terrorism. Punishment after the fact is often irrelevant (not always—those who planned and carried out the 1993 bombing of the World Trade Center were tried and sentenced to long jail terms). Even when it is not irrelevant, our overwhelming concern is to deter terrorism. The only effective deterrence is de facto total deterrence. For example, the only ways to deter suicide bombers are to stop them in their tracks and jail them or to block their entry in advance.

The liberal state is not well designed for the latter form of deterrence. Indeed, the liberal state is not well designed for the kinds of surveillance needed for either form of deterrence. The liberal state was designed to achieve a high level of social order without massively infringing the liberties of ordinary citizens. The Nazi state, the states of many military juntas, and the state of many fundamentalist regimes, such as that in Saudi Arabia, can adopt the draconian devices that suppress such fanatical actions. They presumably make many errors of commitment—killing or otherwise suppressing the innocent—while killing and suppressing those who might have been destructive if allowed to run free. As its central purpose, a regime of civil liberties is designed to protect against such errors of commitment, which wreck the lives of the innocent. Even for the prosecution of ordinary crimes, errors of commitment are seemingly common, as is suggested by recent uses of DNA evidence to exonerate many men on death row in various states of the United States.

The idea of protecting civil liberties was to protect those for whom the social order is beneficial. People who benefit from the social order will generally not attempt to wreck it. Citizens who build their lives on the extant social order are likely to acquiesce in government actions to maintain that order. They will be supportive of well-directed policy action and of a criminal justice system that seems to work properly. Most citizens will also acquiesce in government secrecy in certain matters, such as strategic planning during wartime and weapons designs, and in some degree of police surveillance through checking identity cards such as driver's licenses or passports.

Most citizens might even acquiesce in such activities as those of J. Edgar Hoover's relatively abusive FBI. But opposition to such activities is apt to be substantial, so substantial as to disrupt loyalties in the society. In the United States, moreover, Congress is likely to be perturbed by such secrecy and the actions it cloaks. A police force that is abusive in such ways cannot get fully voluntary compliance from citizens, many of whom will not give it information or other assistance it needs to function successfully. Furthermore, opposition to such a police force can transmute into more general opposition to the regime.

Concluding Remarks

Who were the men and perhaps women who organized and carried out the attacks on the World Trade Center and the Pentagon in September 2001? If their narrowly focused, extreme beliefs required sustenance from the community in which they lived and with whom they shared their beliefs, then there must be a significant number of others living in Florida, New Jersey, and maybe other places such as Minnesota, because some of these people had evidently been in the United States for many years. In the news coverage so far, people are reported to say some of them were friendly and polite. But no one says any of them was a friend. They seem to have managed to keep themselves apart.

Were they like the Unabomber—individuals living in our society but almost totally isolated, holding strong beliefs and dealing with almost no one? Or were they more nearly like the Amish—a community with close relationships, one that provided constant affirmation of and support for their beliefs? If they and others who might follow them are like the Unabomber, they will be hard to find and track. Indeed, it will be extremely difficult even to identify any of them before they act. If they are like the Amish, their communities in the United States might be located, and we might come to understand their goals.

We might suppose that they are more like the communal Amish than the isolated Unabomber. Some of them needed to use the American world of flight training to become competent to do what they did, so they had to move in and out of the larger American society, and they had to be here for a moderately long time. Hence they were involved in some limited networks in the larger society as necessary to sustain themselves, to learn to fly, and to use other resources to help them in their planning and execution of their horrendous actions. But they were evidently otherwise isolated from that society. Their isolation made them less known and even knowable. Had they had richer relationships in the larger society, they might have been identifiable, but then their motivations might also have been or become different, so that there would have been nothing of special public interest to know them for.

We evidently face Hobbes's problem of groups that are misfit for society because they wish to destroy it rather than to benefit from it. But we face that problem in the era of strong protections of civil liberties, and we would be aghast at Hobbes's own solution to his problem, which would be to kill or drive out committed terrorists (if we could identify them). Western liberal societies cannot adopt such a Hobbesian domestic policy without harming and maybe even wrecking themselves (although in Afghanistan we have adopted the equivalent of a Hobbesian foreign policy). We have our commitment to civil liberties because we long ago overcame our problems of grievous social disorder and were therefore able to focus our efforts on less destructive issues than those of religious fanatics and aristocratic glory seekers. The religious fanatics among current terrorists seem fanatical at levels that the various Protestant sects of Hobbes's time could not have rivaled. Some of the current terrorists might be more nearly romantic glory seekers than religious fanatics. Indeed, Osama bin Laden has seemed in his videotapes to be playing rather than to be deeply religiously motivated, although that appearance may be little more than a trick of his personality.

Western liberal democracies overcame their own problems of disorder primarily through economic advances that led to the quasi embourgeoisement of the large majority of all citizens. In part, it is that economic success that is now the target of terrorist actions. Because terrorists' goal is destruction rather than something more nearly like theft, liberals have no incentive system that can overcome their urges. Treating them as criminals if they are caught in planning or carrying out attacks makes sense ex post, but the threat of such sanctions will play little or no role in motivating them ex ante. Our issue is almost entirely that ex ante problem. It is not an entirely novel problem, but it is entirely novel to face it in an advanced liberal democracy that has no theory or institutional devices for dealing with it.

It is disheartening that the contemporary problem of Islamic terrorism provokes, in a new form, the old problem of pervasive group-generalized distrust of a particular ethnically defined group within the society. More generally, the ongoing threat of massive terrorism is likely to be highly corrosive to a liberal society. The example of Israel suggests grim possibilities. Israeli politics has drifted toward support of those who favor draconian policies and very nearly a police state that cannot be sustainable but that may block other possibilities. At the very least, civil liberties in the face of substantial terrorist threats will be more constrained than in the past. Although some proponents of civil liberties seem to frame them in absolutist terms, they are only of value once we have secured survival. If survival is at stake, the niceties of civil liberties are of less urgent concern. When a tiny fraction of an identifiable group is likely to wreak horrendous harms, the product of the small probability and the scale of the harm seems to lead to group-generalized distrust that is statistically justified and that may lead to strong support for antilibertarian policies that work against all the members of the group.

Notes

1. On the change from small community to urban life, see Watters (2003).
2. See Hobbes (1651/1968, chap. 15, 209); and Hardin (1991). Don Herzog (1989, chap. 3) supposes that the nobility were the target of this worry because, contrary to Hobbes's ground principle for his laws of nature, they were not interested in seeking or enjoying peace but actually preferred strife, in which they could achieve glory and honor.

References

Allen, James, Hilton Als, John Lewis, and Leon F. Litwack. 2000. *Without Sanctuary: Lynching Photography in America*. Santa Fe, N.M.: Twin Palms.

Anscombe, G. E. M. 1981. "On Transubstantiation." In *Ethics, Religion and Politics*. Minneapolis: University of Minnesota Press.

Becker, Gary S. 1971. *The Economics of Discrimination*. 2d ed. Chicago: University of Chicago Press.

Boyer, Peter J. 1995. "Children of Waco." *New Yorker*, April 15, pp. 38–45.

Cook, Karen S., and Russell Hardin. 2001. "Norms of Cooperativeness and Networks of Trust." In *Social Norms*, edited by Michael Hechter and Karl-Dieter Opp. New York: Russell Sage Foundation.

Cook, Karen S., Russell Hardin, and Margaret Levi. 2004. *Cooperation Without Trust?* Unpublished manuscript.

Fischer, Claude S. 1982. *To Dwell among Friends: Personal Networks in Town and City*. Chicago: University of Chicago Press.

Goldthorpe, John H., David Lockwood, Frank Bechhofer, and Jennifer Platt. 1969. *The Affluent Worker in the Class Structure*. Cambridge: Cambridge University Press.

Good, David. 1988. "Individuals, Interpersonal Relations, and Trust." In *Trust: Making and Breaking Cooperative Relations*, edited by Diego Gambetta. Oxford, U.K.: Basil Blackwell.

Hardin, Russell. 1991. "Hobbesian Political Order." *Political Theory* 19(2, May): 156–80.

———. 1995. *One for All: The Logic of Group Conflict*. Princeton, N.J.: Princeton University Press.

———. 1997. "The Economics of Religious Belief." *Journal of Institutional and Theoretical Economics* 153(1): 259–78.

———. 1999. *Liberalism, Constitutionalism, and Democracy*. Oxford, U.K.: Oxford University Press.

———. 2001. "The Crippled Epistemology of Extremism." In *Political Extremism and Rationality*, edited by Albert Breton, Gianluigi Galeotti, Pierre Salmon, and Ronald Wintrobe. Cambridge: Cambridge University Press.

———. 2002. *Trust and Trustworthiness*. New York: Russell Sage Foundation.

Herzog, Don. 1989. *Happy Slaves*. Chicago: University of Chicago Press.

Hobbes, Thomas. 1651/1968. *Leviathan*, edited by C. B. Macpherson. London: Penguin.

Klein, Daniel B. 1994. "If Government Is So Villainous, How Come Government Officials Don't Seem Like Villains?" *Economics and Philosophy* 10(1): 91–106.

McMurtry, Larry. 2000. "Hometown America's Black Book." *New York Review of Books*, December 21, 28–30.

Rotter, Julian B. 1967. "A New Scale for the Measurement of Interpersonal Trust." *Journal of Personality* 35(4): 1–7.

Stern, Kenneth S. 1996. *A Force upon the Plain: The American Militia Movement and the Politics of Hate*. New York: Simon & Schuster.

Watters, Ethan. 2003. *Urban Tribes: A Generation Redefines Friendship, Family, and Commitment*. New York: Bloomsbury.

Wright, Thomas L., and Richard G. Tedeschi. 1975. "Factor Analysis of the Interpersonal Trust Scale." *Journal of Consulting and Clinical Psychology* 43: 470–77.

Chapter 13

Corruption, Distrust, and the Deterioration of the Rule of Law

GABRIELLA R. MONTINOLA

WHEN THE U.S. Supreme Court ruled against a recount of the Florida ballots in the November 2000 presidential race, Albert Gore, the candidate who would have to concede defeat, and his close supporters accepted the decision calmly. Although there were street demonstrations for both candidates, they remained nonviolent. Nor were there serious attempts to destabilize the new administration.[1] When the Philippine Supreme Court issued a resolution effectively legitimating the impeachment of incumbent president Joseph Estrada in January 2001, the ousted president left the presidential palace only after military officers made clear their intention to support the new regime. A few months later, thousands of Estrada supporters stormed the palace, protesting his treatment by the new president and demanding that he be reinstalled. The ensuing battle between police and protesters lasted for more than twelve hours and resulted in at least a hundred casualties and five deaths (Sindayen 2001).

What accounts for the different reactions in the two countries? One possibility is that most Americans, including supporters of the losing candidate Gore, have confidence in the overall impartiality of the U.S. justice system, if not the impartiality of this one particular decision. In a survey performed in 1999, 77 percent of respondents expressed confidence in the U.S. Supreme Court (National Center for State Courts 1999). Most Filipinos, in contrast, do not have confidence in their system of justice. Another possibility is that the stakes of losing an election in the United States, while significant in terms of power and prestige, are not so threatening to one's well-being that the losing candidate would expect serious retribution.² This is not the case in the Philippines. Despite his relatively lenient treatment to this point, Estrada, who is currently under indictment for corruption, has reason to distrust the politicians who decided to impeach him and the Supreme Court justices who legitimated that impeachment.

In this chapter, I provide a general argument for the emergence of distrust in government institutions and between fellow citizens that provides an explanation for events, such as those just described. I argue that the structure of incentives and opportunities faced by public officials determines in large part whether they will uphold the rule of law or engage in corrupt activity, and that the level of corruption in a system influences individuals' trust assessments of both government officials and fellow citizens. The argument is then illustrated by focusing on a specific institution—the Philippine Supreme Court, whose rules were redesigned with the adoption of a new constitution in 1987, whose members' behavior has been perceived as substantially more corrupt than that of justices in the decades shortly after Philippine independence in 1946, and whose members have lost the confidence of a majority of Filipinos.

Incentives, Opportunities, and Corruption in Government

Interest in the causes and consequences of government corruption has surged in the past decade, in large part for pragmatic reasons. The simultaneous democratization and economic liberalization of several developing and formerly communist countries in the 1990s did not generate the salutary effects initially expected by advocates of democracy and free markets (Dethier, Ghanem, and Zoli 1999; Sachs and Pistor 1997). A closer look at the ailing countries suggests that it was not political or economic liberalization per se that led to instability and economic stagnation but rather the corruption in government that accompanied the opening.

The merits of different theories of corruption have been reviewed elsewhere (Bardhan 1997; Azfar, Lee, and Swamy 2001), as have the different definitions of corruption (Lancaster and Montinola 1997). Suffice it to say the current conventional wisdom attributes corruption—here defined as the misuse of public office for private-regarding concerns[3]—to the structure of incentives, opportunities, and costs faced by individuals. This institutional approach suggests that individuals are motivated in large part by self-interest (which may include the well-being of family and close associates) and that their behavior depends on the costs and benefits they expect to incur by their actions within particular contexts.[4]

Corrupt behavior is clearly not restricted to transactions involving government. It occurs within numerous settings, including private corporations and nonprofit organizations. But government is particularly susceptible to corruption because it has the power to allocate scarce, often singular, benefits (Rose-Ackerman 1999), and when a single entity controls the supply of a product, that entity will have incentive to reduce output and raise prices to increase profits. A government official with sole control over the distribution of a specific type of license has a similar incentive: to demand an additional "fee" over the government's stated price for each license. Given the opportunity, the official is likely to act upon that incentive unless the potential costs of demanding such a fee outweigh the benefits he or she expects to accrue.

Often, there is more than one official whose function is to distribute a particular government benefit. For example, if one is applying for a business license and is confronted with a demand for a bribe, one can withdraw and reapply in hopes of dealing with an official who does not demand a bribe. But a significant number of benefits—indeed, the most lucrative ones—tend to be unique items, such as government contracts and corporations being privatized. The power to allocate these items provides strong incentives to engage in corrupt behavior. Moreover, the potential profits from these government benefits are sufficiently high to provide the individuals competing for them an incentive to pay bribes.

A government could altogether forgo the distribution of particular benefits and allow the private sector to supply the specific commodity, but this is not always feasible. The provision of many public goods is insufficiently profitable to induce the private sector into the market. As a result, there is an incentive in every government for public officials to engage in corrupt behavior.

Since all incentives for corruption cannot be eliminated, one remedy implied by the institutional approach is to counter them with mechanisms that limit opportunities for corrupt transactions. Such opportunities can be minimized by increasing transparency. The media, if not cowed or completely controlled by government, plays an important role in this regard (Peters and Welch 1980). Corruption in Italy, for example, drew sufficient outrage to spur reform after the media made it big news (Rose-Ackerman 1999; Giglioli 1996). In a cross-country empirical study, Daniel Lederman, Norman Loayza, and Rodrigo Reis Soares (2001) find that high levels of corruption are associated with low levels of press freedom. Similarly, Josephine Andrews and Gabriella Montinola (2004) show that countries with strong civil liberties have higher levels of the rule of law. Publication of clear standards and procedures for government contracts and the sale of government corporations is a second means of increasing transparency. If government clients are well informed about requirements for successful applications, and bids are made public, then any impropriety by officials is more likely to be exposed, and officials have less opportunity to take advantage of clients (Manion 1996).

Aside from limiting opportunities, institutional theory suggests that increasing costs to both parties in the corrupt transaction is also necessary to control corruption. Increasing costs requires more than simply increasing the severity of penalties. It requires mechanisms enforcing accountability—mechanisms that provide key actors with the capacity and "political will" (incentive) to ensure punishment of offenders.

In the case of politicians, elections serve as the primary mechanism of accountability. If constituents can replace politicians who engage in corruption, politicians are more likely to refrain from corrupt behavior, assuming they are interested in reelection (Rose-Ackerman 1978).[5] If officials are clearly voted out of office for corrupt behavior, those voted into office will have obvious incentives to ensure punishment of outgoing corrupt officials. They will also have incentives to dismiss corrupt bureaucrats. Indeed, Barbara Geddes (1994) argues that a high probability of losing power, which occurs when opposing parties or coalitions of parties in the legislature have nearly equal proportions of seats, is sufficient to induce politicians to create independent bureaucratic agencies that are less susceptible to corruption.

Within the structure of government, most relationships are hierarchically structured, with agents accountable to principals. But the ultimate principals within government tend to be politicians, who are accountable to the electorate.[6] For example, lower-level bureaucrats are accountable to managers, who have the incentive and capacity to punish those who engage in corrupt behavior. These managers, higher-level bureaucrats, are ultimately accountable to the executive, an elected official. Bureaucrats are also subject to oversight by legislators, who may not have the capacity to dismiss corrupt officials but who do have the incentive to expose bureaucratic corruption if officials act against the interests of legislators' constituents (Calvert, McCubbins, and Weingast 1989). Thus the power of the bureaucracy is ultimately constrained by the line of accountability between voters and politicians.

What constrains members of the judiciary, who are rarely, if ever, elected officials? In the lower courts, judges have monopoly control over the outcome of the cases they hear; thus they have incentives to engage in corrupt behavior. But two mechanisms hold judges in the lower courts accountable. First, individual judges at this level can be prosecuted for corruption by the executive branch. Second, the decisions of lower-court judges are subject to review by courts at higher levels, at which time any impropriety may come to light, and the possibility that a judgment will be overturned reduces the amount that litigants are willing to pay to win their cases.[7] Hence at the lower levels of the judicial branch, if corruption occurs, its incidence may be high (there are likely to be numerous lower courts hearing a substantial amount of cases each year), but the amount of each bribe is likely to be minimal.

Decisions of the highest court in the land are typically concerted; they require the concurrence of more than a single judge. In such a system, no judge has monopoly power over the outcome of a case, and thus incentives for corruption are lower. But judges of the highest courts are generally not subject to prosecution by the executive branch. They tend to be subject to impeachment by the legislature, a relatively difficult measure to impose. Furthermore, the decisions of the Supreme Court are final, and cases that reach this highest court are likely to be highly consequential for the litigants. Thus the incentives for litigants to bribe judges should be pronounced. What other mechanisms might constrain these judges from corrupt activity?

I suggest that probity in the high courts is a function of two mechanisms. First, the need to bribe more than one justice makes it more costly for litigants. As Susan Rose-Ackerman (1999, 145) suggests with respect to the legislative process, having to purchase more than one decision point is "both expensive and risky because just one honest official can undermine the entire effort."[8] The second, and arguably stronger, mechanism preventing corruption is the incentive structure of judges, given that the source of the judicial branch's power primarily derives from its reputation and status within society (Caldeira 1986; Gibson, Caldeira, and Baird 1998). In any given case, it will be in the interest of individual justices to accept bribes in exchange for decisions, but all justices would be better off if the Court's reputation for fairness and integrity is maintained. If justices expect to work together on the Court for many years, as work by Robert Axelrod (1984) implies, they will be more likely to cooperate with one another in maintaining the authority and prestige of the Court. Thus an important mechanism for enforcing accountability among justices of the highest court is a self-enforcing one, their interest in the reputation of the Court.

In sum, institutional theory suggests that corruption in government will be high when the following three conditions hold:

1. Public officials have power to allocate scarce benefits, creating incentives for both officials and the individuals seeking such benefits to engage in corrupt behavior;
2. Opportunities for corrupt behavior are substantial, owing to lack of transparency in government procedures;
3. The costs of corrupt behavior are minimal because of the absence of mechanisms enforcing accountability and disproportionately lenient penalties.

Effects of Corruption on Trust Assessments

Work on the issue of trust—and, in particular, trust in government—has paralleled the growth in the literature on corruption. However, there does not appear to be a consensus on conceptualization of "trust" and "distrust." Following Russell Hardin (1998, 2001) and Edna Ullmann-Margalit (chapter 3 in this volume), in this chapter I view trust and distrust as cognitive assessments of encapsulated interest and ill-being, respectively, involving three elements: a truster, a trustee, and a specific issue or range of issues on which the former trusts or distrusts the latter. This conceptualization implies that an individual cannot "trust" an institution in the strict sense of the word because this would involve attributing to an institution the intention of specifically promoting one's interest. As Ullmann-Margalit notes, "a necessary condition for institutional trust worthy of its name is confidence in the fairness and impartiality of the institution." However, this definition allows for "distrust" in an institution, in that it is possible to believe that an institution is intentionally designed to promote one's ill-being. Moreover, the conceptualization allows for trust or distrust in particular role holders within an institution and generalized distrust in members of identifiable groups.

To my knowledge, few systematic studies have examined the relationship of corruption and trust assessments.[9] But the implication of recent work on trust suggests that governments permeated with corrupt officials will generate distrust in government, lack of trust between officials within government, and lack of interpersonal trust between fellow citizens.

Corruption and Distrust of Government

To understand how corruption leads to generalized distrust of government, consider the simple scenario of a government official demanding a bribe before he processes an application for a business license. He is clearly engaging in corruption—deviating from his normal duty for personal pecuniary gain. He is also suggesting that if the applicant does not pay the bribe, he intends to act against her interests—for example, by delaying the processing of the application. Faced with a government official demanding a bribe, the applicant therefore has grounds to distrust that particular official in the matter of her application.

Will distrust in this particular official generalize to distrust of government? The answer hinges on whether the behavior of the official is considered aberrant or the norm. If it is considered aberrant behavior, and the official is punished, then the applicant has evidence that the government as an institution is acting according to its stated rules, and this will give her grounds for confidence in her government as a whole. But if the applicant has reason to believe that such an official will not be punished even if the unlawful behavior is reported, she will have little confidence in government. Moreover, if the information she gleans from direct interaction with government officials, as well as other sources, such as personal contacts and the media, suggests that corrupt behavior is widespread among government officials, then the applicant will have grounds for inferring that officeholders at higher levels of the hierarchy of government are inclined to act against her interests also, unless they too are bribed. Thus the applicant would have grounds to distrust all government officials—effectively, government in general. This dynamic of distrust is similar to that discussed by Patrick Troy (chapter 9 in this volume) in his work on the implementation of urban regulations.

Let us return to the original scenario between the government official and the woman applying for a license. If the applicant decides to pay the bribe, knowing that she may be applying for other licenses in the future (that is, in hopes of establishing an ongoing relationship that will be beneficial to her), then the initial interaction, assuming it is beneficial to both parties, forms the basis for trust between the actors. It would not be in the interest of either party to report the other. The information each party holds about the other's corrupt behavior is a mechanism encapsulating the interest of each party in the other's interest.[10] Does this trust generalize to trust in other government officials?

The answer is no. Trust in specific government actors engendered by complicity in a corrupt transaction does not generalize to trust in other officeholders. Trust requires knowledge that the trustee intends to act on the truster's behalf. In the case of corrupt behavior, the interest of an applicant is encapsulated in the interest of a government official only after they engage in their first corrupt transaction. Since bribery is clearly an illegal act, there is always the probability of exposure and punishment. Thus an individual who has engaged in corrupt transactions with a specific official attempts to bribe other officials only if the odds of interacting with an official favorably disposed to accepting bribes is high enough to offset the potential costs of being exposed and punished for attempting to bribe a public official. Indeed, an individual who engages in corrupt transactions with specific officials is likely to distrust other officials if he or she has grounds to believe that the latter already has trusting relationships with others whose interests might conflict with his or her own.

So far, the discussion has focused on the effect of corruption on trust assessments of government when the official initiates the corrupt transaction. Are the implications different if the initiator is the citizen? If the applicant initiates the corrupt transaction by offering a bribe, and the official denounces it, in a system with low levels of corruption the official has no grounds to distrust the individual. The applicant cannot harm the official by reporting the incident because it was she who initiated the transaction. But in a system of widespread corruption, the official has grounds to believe that the applicant will try to find a way to bypass the need for the official's approval and, in the process, induce the official's superiors to disfavor him. The official therefore has grounds to distrust the rejected applicant, and this distrust will generalize to all applicants who, the official has grounds to believe, have the ability to bypass his authority.

Thus corrupt transactions that benefit specific citizens and officials may lead to trusting relationships between parties to corrupt transactions, but these relationships do not generalize to other government officials. On the other hand, corrupt behavior, whether initiated by government officials or by citizens, if exposed but left unpunished, is likely to cause distrust in government officials and in government in general.

Corruption and Lack of Trust Within Government and Among Citizens

Does corruption affect trust between officials within government and trust between citizens? Consider first the effect of corruption on trust assessments of officials within government. Governments are hierarchical organizations of principal-agent relationships. As Gary Miller (2001) notes, were it possible to structure principal-agent relationships such that there is no incentive to shirk, trust would not be an issue at all. But perfectly efficient incentive schemes are impossible to design, and it is reasonable to expect that at times, members of an organization will act according to their individual interests in ways that conflict with those of the organization. If superiors consistently punish even the slightest infraction, then government officials have clear signals about acceptable behavior, and in time, mutual trust regarding responsibilities to one another and to the organization may emerge. But if superiors tolerate low-level corrupt activity, such as bribes that bureaucrats might demand to process an application, that tolerance signals lack of incentive or capacity to punish corrupt behavior and is likely to lead to corruption directly harmful to the organization, such as the practice of accepting bribes in exchange for lowering customs tax rates.[11] Supervisors in a system once permeated by corruption find it difficult in the future to "trust" bureaucrats to refrain from corrupt behavior, even if, through draconian sanctions, they can deter most bureaucrats from actually engaging in corrupt behavior.

Finally, in addition to lack of trust between government officials, corruption engenders lack of trust between citizens. As Margaret Levi (1998) notes, a government that can credibly commit to implementing policies in a nonarbitrary fashion facilitates interpersonal trust by solving information, monitoring, and enforcement problems, thereby lowering the costs of making oneself vulnerable to strangers and increasing the probability that strangers will engage in transactions that, if beneficial to both parties, will then be a basis for trust. A government whose officials expect bribes will almost always be perceived as acting arbitrarily. Even if there appear to be certain regularities in corrupt regimes, such as an implicit understanding regarding the size of bribes, the illegal and clandestine nature of corrupt transactions inhibits the emergence of trust. In any given instance, for example, a government contractor might lose a bid without ever understanding why. He will never be certain whether his bribe was not high enough or whether other "arbitrary" factors were considered. Moreover, the arbitrary way in which laws will be upheld because undisclosed factors may affect judicial decisions deters transactions that might lead to beneficial outcomes and consequently minimizes the probability of trusting relationships between citizens. This is clearly demonstrated in Russia, as discussed by Vadim Radaev (chapter 10 in this volume).

There have been apparently predictable yet corrupt regimes, such as the Suharto regime in Indonesia or perhaps the political machines in American cities. But I suggest that in these regimes, predictability is perceived by only a small group of individuals who have personal relations with the ruler, not unlike clients of the Mafia as described by Diego Gambetta (1993).[12] Just as criminal action provides a basis for trust between the Mafia and their clients, it is certainly feasible for corrupt transactions to be the basis for trust. But just as the existence of a Mafia creates distrust between those within and outside the organization, those who are not part of the ruler's network of relations are likely to distrust those who are. Furthermore, while the conditions that allow for stable relationships based on corrupt transactions have not yet been fully specified, I submit that they are highly restrictive. Assuming that investors value predictability, the empirical evidence on corruption and investment suggests that corruption and predictability are not correlated.[13]

In sum, I argue that widespread government corruption is likely to lead to distrust of government, lack of trust between officials within government, and lack of interpersonal trust, even distrust, between fellow citizens. In the following section, I illustrate the argument linking structures of incentives and opportunities, levels of corruption, and trust assessments in the context of a specific government institution—the Philippine Supreme Court.

A Case of Institutional Distrust: The Philippine Supreme Court

Although the argument linking incentives, opportunities, corruption, and distrust should apply to all branches of government, the judicial branch presents the most intriguing contradictions. While it is expected to check both the executive branch and the legislature, the judiciary has no direct control over the means of force to ensure implementation of its decisions.[14] Furthermore, the public has no direct control over the judiciary; judgeships are generally not elected positions. Yet it is the institution on which the public must rely when conflict arises between citizens or between citizens and other branches of government. Thus, whether or not a decline in trust in "government" is a grave problem for democracy (and much of the literature on trust has focused on this issue), popular assessments of the judicial system are critical to establishing the rule of law and stable democracy. Understanding the conditions that affect those assessments is of great import.

The judicial system of the Philippines, and in particular its Supreme Court, is interesting for three reasons. First, the Philippine system was patterned after the American system, which has been in place for more than two hundred years, but the Philippine Supreme Court is clearly not functioning in the same way as its model. This presents a challenge for institutional theory. Second, perceptions of the Philippine judicial system—and, most likely, its actual behavior—have changed over time. During the first twenty-five years of Philippine independence, the Supreme Court appeared to be a highly respected institution; its members were lauded in the press as judges of integrity (Teodoro Locsin, "Men of the Year: The Rule of Law," *Philippines Free Press*, January 4, 1964, pp. 1 and 8). Today, a majority of Filipinos view their Supreme Court as yet another government institution permeated with corruption and their judges, in general, as unworthy of trust. Given the importance of judicial systems for the functioning of democracy, this change in performance is a puzzle worthy of investigation. Finally, given its recent transition from authoritarian to democratic rule, the experience of the Philippines could provide valuable lessons for other fledgling postcommunist and developing-country democracies.

Assessments of the Philippine Judicial System

The judicial system of the Philippines at independence in 1946 grew out of the system established by Americans when they took control of the Philippines in 1898. The Judiciary Act of 1948 adopted by the first Philippine Congress stipulated no essential changes to the structure and powers of the judiciary set up by the colonial government (Narvasa 1998). The Philippine Supreme Court comprised one chief justice and ten associate justices, who as a group had final appellate review over all cases and original jurisdiction in a few specific situations. The justices were nominated by the Philippine president and confirmed by a Commission of Appointments consisting of twelve senators and twelve members of the House of Representatives, elected by each house, respectively, on the basis of proportional representation of the political parties therein.[15]

Until 1972, the Philippine Supreme Court appeared to be a highly respected government institution. While there are no surveys of the general population, it was lauded by numerous contemporary American and Filipino observers. Neal Tate (1992) cites the following observers and their praises. The former Philippine Supreme Court justice George Malcolm observed, in 1957, "Since the inauguration of the Republic of the Philippines in 1946, the [Supreme] Court has retained the confidence of the people" (107). In 1964 the American scholar of Philippine politics Jean Grossholtz called the Supreme Court "the most important legitimizing institution in the Philippines" (107). According to the Jesuit sociologists Francisco Araneta and John J. Carroll (in 1968), "[The Supreme Court] is a special repository of the Filipino's faith in legitimacy and legality" (108). Finally, the Filipino journalist Yan Makabenta (in 1968) observed, "We are a nation that has ... grown skeptical of anyone who occupies a public office, but there remains somehow that curious faith in the high Court" (107). The Supreme Court apparently elicited this praise for its decisions upholding the rule of law even "against the 'pleasure' of the President" (Teodoro Locsin, "Men of the Year: The Rule of Law," *Philippines Free Press*, January 4, 1964, p. 1).

In 1972 President Ferdinand Marcos declared martial law in the Philippines, ostensibly to restore order to a nation he claimed was on the brink of anarchy.[16] By then, a majority of the Court justices had been appointed by Marcos and concurred in a judicial opinion that effectively justified Marcos's dictatorship. Although Marcos did not abolish the courts, as he did the Congress, as Tate (1992, 117) notes, "the [Supreme] Court ... openly defaulted on its ability to consider allegations of human rights failures ... or to challenge the president in any other significant way."

Marcos was deposed in 1986 when various opposition groups and military rebels joined forces against him in what came to be known as the "People Power" or "EDSA" revolution.[17] Corazon Aquino, who had run against Marcos in an election that he called suddenly, was declared president. The vast majority of Filipinos were elated with the ouster of Marcos. They expected the new regime to resolve the injustices that Marcos had inflicted on them and to solve the country's economic problems.

Once firmly in power, Aquino quickly assembled a convention to draft a new constitution that would, among other issues, significantly strengthen the powers of the judicial branch and increase the number of Supreme Court justices, in hopes of preventing any future chief executive from manipulating the Court, as Marcos had, and overthrowing democracy. She also called for the "courtesy resignations" of all members of the Supreme Court, whom she believed supported the Marcos regime. Ultimately, she reappointed five members of the Court who had served under Marcos, judging their sentiments to have been sufficiently far from those of the former dictator. Aquino then filled the remaining Supreme Court positions with her close supporters, anti-Marcos human rights activists, and career judges (Tate 1992, 118).

Did the renewed Supreme Court evoke the same sentiments as its pre–martial law counterpart? A series of surveys performed by the private, nonprofit research institution Social Weather Stations (SWS) from

1989 to 2000 suggests not.[18] While only a few questions in the surveys focused specifically on the Supreme Court, the Court has full supervisory power over the lower courts, and therefore perceptions of courts at all levels ultimately reflect on the performance of the highest court in the land.

In a 1993 survey of a randomly selected national sample of twelve hundred adults, the SWS found that while only 14 percent of respondents expressed personally knowing of a judge who had received a bribe, 49 percent believed that "many" or "most" judges could be "bought or bribed." Furthermore, when asked whether they considered corruption in the "Court of Justice" to be "big, small or none [nonexistent]," 46 percent of respondents chose "big." It is unclear whether respondents were referring to the incidence of corruption or the size of bribes, but the survey responses indicate that a plurality of the population viewed the judicial system as corrupt.

A large majority of respondents in this nationwide survey were of the lower classes. The SWS categorizes socioeconomic status in terms of three groups, ABC, D, and E, which correspond approximately to the upper and middle classes, the poor, and the destitute, respectively.[19] Approximately 9 percent of respondents to the survey were from the upper and middle classes, 62 percent were poor, and 29 percent were destitute. But the sentiments expressed in the nationwide survey were not limited to the lower classes.

A similar survey, carried out in 2000, targeted a random sample of top-level managers, 204 from "top-fifteen-hundred" firms (the largest in the country) and 400 from medium-sized and small enterprises. In this survey, when asked to name a government agency perceived to be corrupt, only 2 percent of respondents identified the Supreme Court, but when asked to name a government agency perceived to be without corruption, only 4 percent of respondents identified the Supreme Court. These responses were not simply owing to the open-ended nature of the questions. The Bureaus of Customs and Internal Revenue were clearly prominent in the minds of enterprise managers as corrupt agencies. The two bureaus were identified as corrupt by 74 percent and 72 percent of respondents, respectively. The Department of Social Works and Development topped the list of agencies without corruption, named by 12 percent of respondents; 41 percent of respondents, when asked for agencies without corruption, replied "none."

Perhaps most telling on the performance of the judicial system are the SWS surveys of six hundred lawyers and one thousand judges carried out from 1994 to 1996 (Mangahas et al. 1996). Lawyers surveyed were from firms in the region around Manila (National Capital Region) and one province from each of the three main regions of the Philippines: Luzon, Visayas, and Mindanao. Judges surveyed were from trial courts at all levels of the judicial branch. In these surveys, the SWS found that when respondents were asked what they thought of judges, 31 percent of lawyers agreed that "very many" or "many" judges were corrupt. Judges, however, disagreed; only 6 and 7 percent of regional and municipal trial court judges, respectively, responded that "very many" or "many" judges were corrupt. When the tables were turned and respondents were asked what they thought of lawyers, 40 percent of lawyers agreed that "very many" or "many" lawyers were corrupt, while only 19 percent of judges rated lawyers in the same way.

When given the names of courts at various levels and asked "at what level do you find corruption among judges," the Supreme Court was specified by 17 percent of lawyers from the National Capital Region, 13 percent of lawyers from the three provinces, 26 percent of regional trial court judges, and 11 percent of municipal trial court judges. Apparently, those closer to the Supreme Court in location or within the judicial hierarchy are more likely to be critical of the high court. Finally, when asked if they were aware of a case in their area in which a judge had taken a bribe, 48 percent of lawyers responded in the affirmative. Although not all lawyers' and judges' responses matched those of the general population, they were disconcerting, considering that they were the responses of individuals likely to have firsthand knowledge of corruption in the courts.

Does this picture change dramatically when survey questions focus on trust assessments? In these same surveys, the SWS also posed questions regarding trust. While not all questions were phrased to capture all three elements of trust used in this chapter, the responses provide insight into assessments of the different groups in society.

In the 1993 national survey, the SWS found that only 45 percent of respondents found "many" or "most" judges "trustworthy," and when asked if they expected "the eventual court decision to be just," fewer than 50 percent of respondents answered in the affirmative. When given an additional stimulus focusing on socioeconomic status and asked whether they agreed that "rich or poor, people ... receive equal treatment in court," fewer than 43 percent agreed. These responses suggest not only that a substantial number of individuals lacks confidence in the judicial system but also that a large plurality expects the courts to discriminate according to litigants' socioeconomic status.

Somewhat surprisingly, and not particularly reassuring for democratic rule, perceptions regarding equal treatment in 1993 differed from those in 1985, the year before democratization, and the changes vary according to socioeconomic status. In general, the number of upper-class and middle-class respondents who perceived the courts to be dispensing equal treatment increased from 40 percent in 1985 to 48 percent in 1993, while the number of lower-class respondents who thought that socioeconomic status was not a factor dropped by 8 percent. Apparently, democratization has not led to the perception of more equal treatment in courts. If the perception that judges are dispensing just rulings and treating people in court equally regardless of income is necessary for people to have confidence in the judicial system, then these surveys do not present optimistic pictures.

Nor does the survey of top-level enterprise managers provide a rosier picture. When asked to rate the Supreme Court in terms of its sincerity in fighting corruption in the public sector, only 11 percent of respondents rated the Supreme Court as "very sincere." Forty-seven percent of respondents rated the Court as "somewhat sincere," but 22 percent were "undecided." Four organizations received higher net sincerity ratings than the Supreme Court: the Asian Development Bank, the World Bank, big foreign businesses, and the Department of Social Welfare and Development.[20] Top-level managers appear to have more confidence in foreign actors than in the Supreme Court.

Interestingly, when asked how much their corporations would be willing to spend to fund a program to reduce public sector corruption, the median amount specified by enterprise managers was 1 percent of their corporation's net income. But when asked to name any individual, agency, or organization that could be "trusted to manage [this] anticorruption program fund," there was no clear consensus on who could be trusted. The top two candidates named in this open-ended question received support from only 8 percent of respondents, but the Supreme Court was identified by only 1 percent of respondents. Twenty-two individuals and entities received more support than the Supreme Court, suggesting that the latter did not inspire much confidence. Moreover, 27 percent of respondents either provided no answer or answered that there were no individuals or groups that could be trusted to manage an anticorruption program fund, suggesting that many enterprise managers trusted neither government officials nor fellow citizens. Since respondents to this particular survey are top-level managers, they are most likely highly educated and of the upper and middle classes. Lack of consensus on any single entity in this open-ended question is unlikely to derive from ignorance of the possibilities.

Finally, the Supreme Court does not fare as badly in the SWS surveys of lawyers and judges, but the judicial system as a whole does not exhibit characteristics of "trustworthiness." Around 80 percent of lawyers and judges expressed positive opinions of the Supreme Court, saying that they were "very satisfied" or "somewhat satisfied" with its performance. Moreover, only 21 percent of judges agreed that "the Supreme Court tends to side with the Executive Branch," suggesting that the Court is perceived as being independent from the branch of government over which the framers of the 1987 constitution were most concerned.

But lawyers are not so sanguine about the judicial system. Sixty-five percent of them described court decisions as "unpredictable," although it is unclear which particular courts they had in mind. Lawyers also appeared to concur with the lower classes: only 48 percent agreed that "poor people can get justice." Moreover, from 62 to 74 percent of lawyers perceived that each of the following factors influences a judge's decision: "a judge's fraternity and sorority connections," "pressure from politicians," "public attention," "the professional reputation of lawyers," and "ties with relatives and friends." Whether or not judges' decisions are truly influenced by these factors, the perception that they are suggests that a large number of lawyers do not expect the judges they encounter in courts to decide cases mainly, if not solely, on the basis of the facts of the cases and the law. These perceptions have led not only to a loss of confidence in the judicial system but also to distrust between citizens whose interests are on the line. As an aide to one litigant before the Supreme Court stated, "When [the governor] thought the other side was maneuvering, he wanted to move also. . . . If we [hadn't] maneuver[ed], we would have lost. . . . [The opposing litigant] was outbidded [sic]" (cited in Coronel 2000, 222).

Sources of Corruption and Trust Assessments

Filipinos' confidence in their current judicial system has declined since the pre–martial law period. While it is impossible to provide comparative evidence on the actual incidence of and amounts exchanged in corrupt transactions, it is difficult to dismiss the stark differences in perception between the pre–and post–martial law courts as completely unfounded.[21] The press during both periods can be characterized as free— indeed, often irresponsibly critical.[22] The pre–martial law press exposed countless corruption scandals involving politicians, including incumbent presidents, but as has been noted, journalists lauded justices of the Supreme Court.[23] One might argue that perceptions of corruption have changed because the lower classes are better informed today about their rights and more active in politics owing to the mobilizational efforts of the many nongovernmental organizations in the country.[24]

But as demonstrated earlier in this chapter, while the lower classes perceive discrimination in courts based on socioeconomic status, perceptions of high levels of corruption are not limited to any one class. Top-level management, lawyers, and judges are all likely to be of the upper and middle classes, and most are likely to have personal connections with some judges, if not the wherewithal to pay bribes. Yet a majority of them are clearly dissatisfied with the arbitrary nature of the corrupt court system. As a senior partner in the country's largest law firm stated in a letter to the chief justice in 1997, "In my 37 years of practice I have never seen the image of the Supreme Court and the court system sink to such levels in the eyes of the business community" (cited in Coronel 2000, 229). Those thirty-seven years encompassed the period before, during, and after authoritarian rule.

Why has the Court's behavior changed? An institutional theory of corruption centers on changes in structures of incentives, opportunities, and costs, and this is, in fact, what has changed in the Philippines. The 1987 constitution adopted after the Marcos regime was deposed stipulates new rules for the judicial system, which have led to an increase in corruption or, at best, perceptions of corruption and arbitrariness of the system.[25] Four changes, in particular, have increased judges' incentives and opportunities for corruption.

First, the 1987 constitution expands the scope of jurisdiction of the Supreme Court. It gives the Supreme Court the "*duty* . . . to settle actual controversies involving rights which are legally demandable and enforceable, and to determine whether or not there has been *grave abuse of discretion . . . on the part of any branch or instrumentality of the Government*" (art. VIII, sec. 1, emphasis added). This provision was intended to prevent the Court from refusing to hear politically controversial cases, as it often had during the Marcos regime.[26] But as Haynie (1998, 464) suggests, it has made the Court's approval "a necessary hoop through which all congressional and executive actions must pass." Given the significance of these cases, the provision increases incentives for corruption.

Second, the Philippine Constitution (art. VIII, sec. 4) allows the Supreme Court to sit en banc, in two divisions of seven justices, three divisions of five, or five divisions of three. The Supreme Court currently sits in three divisions. This provision was adopted to ensure timely decisions, given the Court's substantial docket, but it also increases incentives to engage in corruption. As mentioned earlier, having fewer decision points lowers the costs of corruption. Indeed, if as Sheila Coronel (2000) reports, only those assigned to write the majority opinion ("ponentes") actually study cases while the rest decide to concur or dissent based on the presentation of the ponente, then there is only one decision point to be bought. Given the substantial sums involved in most cases that reach the Supreme Court, that single justice's control over the outcome provides him or her with substantial incentives to accept bribes in exchange for a favorable decision.[27]

Third, the 1987 constitution (art. VIII, secs. 2, 3, 6, 10) provides the judiciary with much greater autonomy from the executive and legislative branches. Appropriations for the judiciary may not be reduced from that of the previous year and must be automatically and regularly released. The new constitution also prohibits the Congress from reorganizing the judiciary in a way that would undermine judges' tenure. Nor can judges be transferred without the approval of the Supreme Court. These provisions are crucial because they prevent both the executive and the legislature from pressuring judges. Philippine presidents have often used control over the release of funds appropriated by the legislature to create support for their agendas (Cariño n.d.; Montinola 1999b). But one provision affording the courts more autonomy has weakened a mechanism holding judges accountable. The Supreme Court now has the power to appoint and supervise all officials and employees of the judiciary and to discipline the Integrated Bar of the Philippines, a power that was previously under the purview of the Justice Department of the executive branch.[28] The chief justice's supervisory power includes control over resources to all judges, including the special prosecutor, the ombudsman, who is empowered by the Constitution (art. XI, sec. 9[1]) to "investigate on its own, or on complaint by any person, any act or omission of any public official, employee, office or agency, when such act or omission appears to be illegal, unjust, improper, or inefficient." Not surprisingly, as Haynie (1998, 463) argues, since administration of the courts switched from the executive to the judicial branch, the Court has been perceived as "protecting its own when . . . [it determines] that there is insufficient evidence of malfeasance" in the judiciary.

Finally, and most important, the procedure for appointment to the Supreme Court has been changed under the 1987 constitution. In the previous system, Supreme Court justices were nominated by the president and required confirmation by a Commission on Appointments. Under the current system, the president appoints one of at least three individuals nominated by a Judicial and Bar Council (JBC); confirmation by the Commission on Appointments is no longer required. The JBC is composed of four ex officio members—the chief justice, the secretary of justice, a senator, and a member of the House—and four regular members—a representative of the Integrated Bar, a professor of law, a retired member of the Supreme Court, and a representative of the private sector. The four regular members of the JBC are appointed by the president for four-year terms with the approval of the Commission on Appointments. The terms of the first set of regular members were staggered so that every year there is a new member on the JBC (Philippine Constitution, art. VIII, secs. 8, 9).

The change in appointment procedure was intended to reduce politicization of the judiciary and increase the role of merit in the selection process (Haynie 1998, 468). Instead, it has made the appointment process less transparent and placed a great deal of power in the hands of two individuals, the president and the chief justice. The president dominates the selection process through his authority to appoint five of the eight members of the council. The chief justice influences the selection of justices through his participation on the JBC and his discretion over the compensation of its regular members. The current appointment system has thus concentrated power in the president and the chief justice, both of whom, once in office, are relatively unconstrained. Philippine presidents are limited to a single term; therefore, like chief justices, once they are in office, impeachment is the only mechanism holding them accountable.[29] As mentioned earlier, concentration of power and lack of transparency increases incentives and opportunities for corruption.

The new appointment process has also affected the most important mechanism of accountability, the interest of Supreme Court justices in maintaining the reputation of the Court. Both the pre– and post–martial law constitutions stipulate a mandatory retirement age of seventy years for all judges. Unless countered by other mechanisms, this provision creates incentives to take advantage of one's public office as one approaches retirement age. This provision did not appear to present a serious problem in the pre–martial law period. Membership in the pre–martial law Supreme Court was relatively stable, inducing justices to consider their longer-term interest in maintaining the integrity and effective power of the Supreme Court. The average tenure of justices during the 1960s was twelve years; most justices appointed to the Supreme Court at independence in 1946 had served during the colonial period. The average tenure of justices on the Supreme Court since 1986 is seven years.[30]

More important, chief justices of the Supreme Court during the period preceding the imposition of martial law tended to spend several years as associate justices before being promoted.[31] The chief justices of the 1950s and 1960s had held positions on the Court for at least ten years before promotion. Only the first post–martial law chief justice, who held office from 1986 to 1988, had similarly lengthy experience on the high court. Notably, his stewardship of the Court is highly praised (Tate 1992, 120–21; Haynie 1998, 462). Since 1988, the Supreme Court has had four chief justices. Of the chief justice in office from 1991 to 1998, a period during which the Supreme Court's reputation was at its lowest, a lawyer from a major firm noted, "He has no moral authority because his colleagues suspect him of doing all sorts of things. And . . . he suspects his colleagues of all sorts of things" (cited in Coronel 2000, 229).

The short tenure of recent justices is, of course, a result of the transition from authoritarian rule to democratic government. The Supreme Court had to be built effectively from scratch. This makes the appointment process all the more important. If the Supreme Court is to regain the confidence of the population, the selection process must be transparent enough to allow public scrutiny, even though justices are not elected, and mechanisms of accountability between the public and those appointing justices must be in place. This is not to say that the previous appointment process was without problems. Indeed, the very fact that Marcos, who was legally elected president twice (1965 and 1969), was able to stack the Court during his two terms suggests problems existed. These problems lay in the organization of the Congress rather than in the appointment procedures per se.

A third problem related to the appointment process and short tenure of recent justices is the limitation of retirement benefits. Justices often expect and do return to private practice when they reach the mandatory retirement age of seventy. This expectation presents justices on the court with incentives to collude with future law partners and affords retired justices with opportunities to influence sitting justices' decisions. As Haynie (1998, 469) notes, retired justices "roam freely in and out of sitting justices' offices, even those assigned to cases for which the former justice is counsel." The revolving door generated by the appointment procedure, together with the mandatory retirement age, impedes the emergence of a self-enforcing equilibrium of cooperation among justices to maintain the reputation of the Court.[32]

In sum, many institutional rule changes embodied in the 1987 constitution were adopted to counter what appeared at that time to be the greatest threat to the country's newly restored democracy—an all-powerful executive. But, as often happens, the changes led to unintended consequences—an increase in incentives and opportunities for corruption throughout the judicial system and, ultimately, Filipinos' loss of confidence or, more seriously, their distrust in the Supreme Court and the judicial system more generally. To be sure, not all Philippine Supreme Court justices and lower-court judges engage in corrupt activity. There continue to be justices in the Philippines with reputations for integrity, and it is possible that after a sufficient number of years under the able stewardship of a chief justice perceived to be incorruptible, the Supreme Court could regain the confidence of the Filipino public. But systemic corruption—or, in the language of game theory, a corrupt equilibrium—is difficult to perturb (Bicchieri and Rovelli 1995). The perception of widespread corruption, whether based on personal experience or on media reports, is sufficient to provide grounds to distrust government, to distrust fellow citizens, and to continue to depend on corrupt means to ensure one's well-being.

Implications for Emerging Democracies

The rule of law requires a state strong enough to implement laws that protect citizens from one another and external forces but not so strong as to be able to violate the rights of citizens. States that violate the rights of identifiable groups of citizens are likely to engender the distrust of those groups but might still provide the rule of law for those not discriminated against. White citizens in South Africa under apartheid, for example, probably had confidence that the state would uphold the rule of law in cases of conflict between white citizens and would not violate white citizens' rights. But a state permeated with government officials engaged in corrupt activities will appear arbitrary to all citizens, if not always, at least most of the time. It will be incapable of upholding the rule of law. Consequently, it will be distrusted by citizens, unable to induce citizen compliance in the provision of public goods, and unlikely to facilitate transactions between strangers, limiting the possibilities for trusting relationships to emerge.

In this chapter I argue that the Supreme Court of the Philippines became susceptible to corruption because of changes to the structure of incentives, opportunities, and costs faced by justices embodied in the 1987 constitution. Given the Supreme Court's role as the ultimate arbiter of conflicts between citizens and between citizens and the state, the public's loss of confidence in the Court owing to the increase in actual (or perceived) corruption is a serious blow to the establishment of, and adherence to, the rule of law. Studies on U.S. courts (Tyler 2001; Tyler et al. 1997) show that individuals are more likely to accept court decisions when they believe procedures have been fair, a condition that corruption undermines. Compliance with other demands of government, such as military service, has been shown to depend on the degree to which citizens perceive the government to be trustworthy (Levi 1997). As Gambetta (1993) and Federico Varese (2001) show, lack of confidence in the legal system promotes the emergence of organizations that work outside the law, such as the Mafia. Furthermore, corruption has been shown to have undermined regime legitimacy in Latin American countries (Seligson 2002). While there are no empirical studies that explicitly link levels of corruption, regime legitimacy, and the breakdown of democracy and the rule of law, corruption is almost always one of the rationales provided by coup makers upon their assumption of power.

Ironically, the 1987 Philippine constitution was designed to strengthen the judicial branch in hopes that the courts would strengthen the rule of law. Instead, it created a Supreme Court whose members are selected in a nontransparent manner and are held accountable only by the mechanism of impeachment and conviction by the legislature. The dearth of mechanisms holding Supreme Court justices accountable might not present a problem where legislatures are effective veto players. But the Philippine legislature is extremely weak; it has been the weakest branch of government since independence because neither the pre- nor post–martial law constitutions has fostered the development of cohesive, clearly differentiated political parties (Montinola 1999a, 1999b). Until political parties with differentiated ideologies provide voters with clearer choices, the Philippine Congress will be a poor check on other branches of government,[33] and the state will remain susceptible to corruption and incapable of upholding the rule of law.

The lesson for emerging democracies from the Philippine experience is the need to create state institutions—executive, legislative, and judicial branches of government—with both the incentive and the genuine capacity to hold one another accountable. Sufficient care should be given to incentives generated by the selection process for each of the three branches. Only then will the state implement laws nonarbitrarily and ultimately elicit the confidence of citizens. The difficulty is that the executive and judicial branches may be easily strengthened by fiat, but the legislature is not. Strengthening legislatures involves creating conditions for the emergence of ideologically differentiated parties. What those conditions are remains an open issue.

The author gratefully acknowledges the helpful comments of Stacia Haynie and Robert Jackman and the research assistance of Ryan Dudley, Alan Alegre, and Joan Mosatalla, of SALIGAN, and Mia Mangalindan, of the Social Weather Stations.

Notes

1. However, there have been numerous debates on the validity and implications of the U.S. Supreme Court's action by legal scholars in law review journals.
2. See Marc Plattner (2001) for a more nuanced discussion of the public reaction to the 2000 presidential election outcome.
3. This definition is from Joseph Nye (1970).
4. The first scholars to develop the institutional approach, also referred to as the economic theory of corruption, were Robert Klitgaard (1988) and Susan Rose-Ackerman (1978). See Rose-Ackerman (1999) for a more recent, comprehensive discussion of the approach.
5. Gabriella Montinola and Robert Jackman (2002) show that while political competition affects a country's level of corruption, the effect is nonlinear. Corruption is typically lower in dictatorships than in countries that have partially democratized. But once a threshold has been passed, democratic practices inhibit corruption.
6. There is a growing literature on corruption that uses the principal-agent framework first applied to governments by Klitgaard (1988) and Rose-Ackerman (1978).
7. A similar argument is made by Fred McChesney (1997) with respect to rent seekers and legislators.
8. See also Andrews and Montinola (2004), which argues that systems with more veto players are less likely to pass corrupt legislation.
9. Recent exceptions are work by Rose-Ackerman (2001), Mitchell Seligson (2002), Donatella Della Porta (2000) and Susan Pharr (2000).
10. Diego Gambetta (1993) discusses the effectiveness of this mechanism for creating trust between mafiosi and their clients, who are expected to perform some criminal activity to show that in the future they can be trusted. See also Varese (2001).

11. Andrei Shleifer and Robert Vishny (1993) refer to the former as corruption without theft and the latter as corruption with theft.
12. See also World Bank (2002), which shows that corruption is mainly a problem for medium-sized firms rather than large firms because the latter have connections to top political leaders.
13. For empirical evidence of corruption and investment, see, for example, Mauro (1995).
14. See Alexander Hamilton's (1788/1992) "Federalist 78."
15. The 1935 constitution (art. VIII, sec. 5) does not specify what proportion of votes in the commission was required for confirmation.
16. Events leading up to and shortly following Marcos's declaration of martial law are described in numerous sources. See, for example, accounts by Amando Doronila (1992) and David Wurfel (1988).
17. Events leading up to the "People Power" revolution are well documented. See, for example, Mercado (1986) and Javate-de Dios, Daroy, and Kalaw-Tirol (1988).
18. The SWS performs periodic surveys on the issue of corruption. As expected, responses change from survey to survey, but they tend to paint the same picture. For more details on the results of these surveys, see the institution's website (www.sws.org.ph; accessed on January 29, 2004).
19. This classification is based on indicators such as the quality of one's home and appliances (Arroyo 1990).
20. The net sincerity rating equals the sum of the ratings for very sincere and somewhat sincere minus the sum of the ratings for somewhat sincere and very insincere.
21. Stacia Haynie (1998) and Sheila Coronel (2000) provide specific examples of Supreme Court decisions that have led to allegations of corruption.
22. See Wurfel (1988) on the pre–martial law period and Haynie (1998) on the post–martial law period.
23. For a few examples of critical articles, see Montinola 1999b.
24. It should be noted that the SWS surveys show some misinformation among the general population regarding legal principles (Mangahas et al. 1996, 26). On the recent, vigorous growth of civil society groups, see Alegre (1996), Coronel Ferrer (1997) and Wui and Lopez (1997).
25. Many of the institutional changes discussed here are also discussed in Haynie (1998) as leading to "politicization" of the Court.
26. Neal Tate (1992) suggests that strengthening the Supreme Court was a surprising move on the part of the Aquino government, given that the institution had let the country down by legitimating the dictatorship, but it is reasonable to believe that a stronger Court may not have been so intimidated.
27. This problem of case assignment to divisions and the possibility of influencing particular ponentes was highlighted in two high-profile cases. In

1992 counsel for the leading supplier of domestic and international telecommunications services in the Philippines, a party to a case before the Supreme Court, was alleged to have penned the opinion of the ponente for the case. Although no hard evidence was ever unearthed, the ponente's early retirement soon thereafter fueled the belief that he was guilty of wrongdoing. In 1994 a decision over control of a jai alai franchise rendered by one division of the Supreme Court was reversed one year later by another division reviewing the same case (see Haynie [1998, 466–67] for a more detailed description of both cases).

28. Membership in the Integrated Bar of the Philippines is required in order to practice law.
29. The difficulty of imposing this mechanism was illustrated in the recent impeachment of Estrada. It was the fact that he was almost surely going to be acquitted by a slim majority in the Senate that led to the military stepping in and effectively settling the issue.
30. Tenure of justices was calculated from data collected and provided to me by Joan Mosatalla of Sentro ng Alternatibong Lingap Panligal (SALIGAN) in the Philippines.
31. Ricardo Paras was promoted to chief justice after ten years on the Court and served for ten more years. Cesar Bengzon was promoted after fifteen years and served as chief justice for five years. Roberto Concepcion, appointed as chief justice in 1966 during Marcos's first term as president, was the exception. Notably, he resigned in 1973, not long after Marcos declared martial law.
32. This problem is similar to that of political parties, although a different set of institutional rules impedes political parties from developing clearly differentiated reputations (Montinola 1999a).
33. One might argue that the impeachment of Estrada is a sign of the legislature's strength, but this would be ignoring the fact that Estrada was ousted by extraconstitutional means (Bernas 2001).

References

Alegre, Alan G. 1996. *Trends and Traditions, Challenges and Choices.* Quezon City, Phil.: Ateneo University Press.

Andrews, Josephine T., and Gabriella R. Montinola. 2004. "Veto Players and the Rule of Law in Emerging Democracies." *Comparative Political Studies* 37(1, February): 55–87.

Arroyo, Dennis M. 1990. "The Usefulness of The ABCDE Market Research System: A Means to Check Social Welfare and Class Attributes." *Social Weather Bulletin* 90(11–12, June): 1–16.

Axelrod, Robert M. 1984. *The Evolution of Cooperation.* New York: Basic Books.

Azfar, Omar, Young Lee, and Anand Swamy. 2001. "The Causes and Consequences of Corruption." *Annals of the American Academy of Political and Social Science* 573(1, January): 42–56.

Bardhan, Pranab. 1997. "Corruption and Development: A Review of Issues." *Journal of Economic Literature* 35(3, September): 1320–46.

Bernas, Joaquin G. 2001. "From One-Man Rule to 'People Power.' " *Ateneo Law Journal* 46(1, June): 44–65.

Bicchieri, Cristina, and Carlo Rovelli. 1995. "Evolution and Revolution: The Dynamics of Corruption." *Rationality and Society* 7(2): 201–24.

Caldeira, Gregory. 1986. "Neither the Purse nor the Sword: Dynamics of Public Confidence in the Supreme Court." *American Political Science Review* 80(4, December): 1209–26.

Calvert, Randall L., Mathew D. McCubbins, and Barry R. Weingast. 1989. "A Theory of Political Control and Agency Discretion." *American Journal of Political Science* 33(3, August): 588–611.

Cariño, Ledevina. n.d. "Pork Barrel in Review: Strategic Position and the Pork Barrel." Unpublished manuscript.

Coronel, Sheila S. 2000. "Justice to the Highest Bidder." *Betrayals of the Public Trust: Investigative Reports on Corruption*, edited by Sheila S. Coronel. Quezon City, Phil.: Philippine Center for Investigative Journalism.

Coronel Ferrer, Miriam, ed. 1997. *Civil Society: Making Civil Society*. Quezon City, Phil.: Third World Studies Center.

Della Porta, Donatella. 2000. "Social Capital, Beliefs in Government, and Political Corruption." In *Disaffected Democracies: What's Troubling the Trilateral Countries?*, edited by Susan J. Pharr and Robert D. Putnam. Princeton, N.J.: Princeton University Press.

Dethier, Jean-Jacques, Hafez Ghanem, and Edda Zoli. 1999. "Does Democracy Facilitate the Economic Transition?" Working paper 2194. Washington, D.C.: World Bank Policy Research.

Doronila, Amando. 1992. *The State, Economic Transformation, and Political Change in the Philippines, 1946–1972*. New York: Oxford University Press.

Gambetta, Diego. 1993. *The Sicilian Mafia: The Business of Private Protection* Cambridge, Mass.: Harvard University Press.

Geddes, Barbara. 1994. *Politician's Dilemma: Building State Capacity in Latin America*. Berkeley: University of California Press.

Gibson, James, Gregory Caldeira, and Vanessa Baird. 1998. "On the Legitimacy of National High Courts." *American Political Science Review* 92(2, June): 343–58.

Giglioli, Pier Paolo. 1996. "Political Corruption and the Media: The Tangentopoli Affair." *International Social Science Journal* 48(3, September): 381–94.

Hamilton, Alexander. 1788/1992. "Federalist 78." *The Federalist Papers*. Washington: The Library of Congress. Available at: http://memory.loc.gov/const/fed/fedpapers.html. Accessed on January 30, 2004.

Hardin, Russell. 1998. "Trust in Government." In *Trust and Governance*, edited by Valerie Braithwaite and Margaret Levi. New York: Russell Sage Foundation.

———. 2001. "Conceptions and Explanations of Trust." In *Trust in Society*, edited by Karen Cook. New York: Russell Sage Foundation.

Haynie, Stacia. 1998. "Paradise Lost: Politicization of the Philippine Supreme Court in the Post-Marcos Era." *Asian Studies Review* 22(4, December): 459–73.

Javate-de Dios, Aurora, Petronilo Bn. Daroy and Lorna Kalaw-Tirol, eds. 1988. *Dictatorship and Revolution: Roots of People's Power*. Metro Manila, Phil.: Conspectus.

Klitgaard, Robert E. 1988. *Controlling Corruption*. Berkeley: University of California Press.

Lancaster, Thomas D., and Gabriella R. Montinola. 1997. "Toward a Methodology for the Comparative Study of Political Corruption." *Crime, Law and Social Change* 27(3/4): 185–206.

Lederman, Daniel, Norman Loayza, and Rodrigo Reis Soares. 2001. "Accountability and Corruption: Political Institutions Matter." Unpublished manuscript.

Levi, Margaret. 1997. *Consent, Dissent and Patriotism*. New York: Cambridge University Press.

———. 1998. "A State of Trust." In *Trust and Governance*, edited by Valerie Braithwaite and Margaret Levi. New York: Russell Sage Foundation.

Mangahas, Mahar, Antonio G. M. La Viña, Steven Rood, Athena L. Casambre, and Dennis M. Arroyo. 1996. *Monitoring the State of the Judiciary and the Legal Profession*. Quezon City, Phil.: Social Weather Stations.

Manion, Melanie. 1996. "Corruption by Design." *Journal of Law, Economics, and Organization* 12(1, April): 167–95.

Mauro, Paolo. 1995. "Corruption and Growth." *Quarterly Journal of Economics* 110(3): 681–712.

McChesney, Fred S. 1997. *Money for Nothing: Politicians, Rent Extraction, and Political Extortion*. Cambridge, Mass.: Harvard University Press.

Mercado, Monina Allarey, ed. 1986. *People Power: The Philippine Revolution of 1986: An Eyewitness History*. Manila, Phil.: James B. Reuter, S.J., Foundation.

Miller, Gary. 2001. "Why is Trust Necessary in Organizations? The Moral Hazard of Profit Maximization." In *Trust in Society*, edited by Karen Cook. New York: Russell Sage Foundation.

Montinola, Gabriella R. 1999a. "Parties and Accountability in the Philippines." *Journal of Democracy* 10(1, January): 126–40.

———. 1999b. "Politicians, Parties, and the Persistence of Weak States: Lessons from the Philippines." *Development and Change* 30(4, October): 739–74.

Montinola, Gabriella R., and Robert W. Jackman. 2002. "Sources of Corruption: A Cross-Country Study." *British Journal of Political Science* 32(1, January): 147–70.

Narvasa, Andres R. 1998. "Judicial Power in the Philippines: Its Governance, Structure, and Independence." *Ateneo Law Journal* 42(2): 213–41.

National Center for State Courts. 1999. *How the Public Views the State Courts: A 1999 National Survey*. Williamsburg, Va.: National Center for State Courts.

Nye, Joseph. 1970. "Corruption and Political Development: A Cost Benefit Analysis." In *Political Corruption: Readings in Comparative Analysis*, edited by Arnold J. Heidenheimer. New York: Holt, Rinehart and Winston.

Peters, John, and Susan Welch. 1980. "The Effect of Charges of Corruption on Voting Behavior in Congressional Elections." *American Political Science Review* 4(3, September): 697–708.

Pharr, Susan J. 2000. "Officials' Misconduct and Public Distrust: Japan and the Trilateral Democracies." In *Disaffected Democracies: What's Troubling the Trilateral Countries?*, edited by Susan J. Pharr and Robert D. Putnam. Princeton, N.J.: Princeton University Press.

Plattner, Marc. 2001. "The Trouble with Parties." *Public Interest* (143, Spring): 27–44.

Rose-Ackerman, Susan. 1978. *Corruption: A Study in Political Economy*. New York: Academic Press.

———. 1999. *Corruption and Government: Causes, Consequences, and Reform.* New York: Cambridge University Press.

———. 2001. "Trust, Honesty and Corruption: Reflection on the State-Building Process." *Archives of European Sociology* 42(3): 27–71.

Sachs, Jeffrey D., and Katharina Pistor. 1997. *The Rule of Law and Economic Reform in Russia.* Boulder, Colo.: Westview Press.

Seligson, Mitchell A. 2002. "The Impact of Corruption on Regime Legitimacy: A Comparative Study of Four Latin American Countries." *Journal of Politics* 64(2, May): 408–33.

Shleifer, Andrei, and Robert W. Vishny. 1993. "Corruption." *Quarterly Journal of Economics* 108(3, August): 599–617.

Sindayen, Nelly. 2001. "Back to the Streets: When Mobs Besieged Her Residence and a Coup Was Attempted, President Arroyo Showed Her Steel. Can She Make Peace with the Masses?" *Time International* 157(19, May): 18.

Tate, C. Neal. 1992. "Temerity and Timidity in the Exercise of Judicial Review in the Philippine Supreme Court." In *Comparative Judicial Review and Public Policy*, edited by Donald W. Jackson and C. Neal Tate. Westport, Conn.: Greenwood Press.

Tyler, Tom R. 2001. "Public Trust and Confidence in Legal Authorities: What Do Majority and Minority Group Members Want from the Law and Legal Institutions?" *Behavioral Science and the Law* 19: 213–35.

Tyler, Tom R., Robert J. Boeckmann, Heather J. Smith, and Yuen J. Huo. 1997. *Social Justice in a Diverse Society.* Boulder, Colo.: Westview Press.

Varese, Federico. 2001. *The Russian Mafia: Private Protection in a New Market Economy.* New York: Oxford University Press.

World Bank. 2002. *Anti-Corruption in Transition: A Contribution to the Policy Debate.* Washington, D.C.: World Bank.

Wui, Marlon A., and Ma. Glenda S. Lopez, eds. 1997. *State/Civil Society Relations in Policy-Making.* Quezon City, Phil.: Third World Studies Center.

Wurfel, David. 1988. *Filipino Politics: Development and Decay.* Ithaca, N.Y.: Cornell University Press.

Index

Boldface numbers refer to figures and tables.

absolute rulers, 89–90
accountability, of government institutions, 317–18
action, default rule for, 70
affect-based trust, Russian markets analysis, 239, 245
African Americans, 278, 286–87
al Qaida, 282
alternatives, control over and power, 87
Amish, 281, 294
analogue method, of fair trade determination, 255–59, 264, 267–68
Andrews, J., 300
Annual Report of the National Labor Relations Board (NLRB), 122
Anscombe, G., 282
antidumping laws and cases, of European Union, 25–26, 250–52, 254–55, **257–58,** 260–70
Aquino, C., 308
Araneta, F., 308
arms control agreements, 44, 52
Armstrong, J., 68
Arrow, K., 131–32
Assad, B., 36–37
asymmetries, 39, 64–65, 87–94, 287–88
Atrushi, P., 197
Australia, urban development analysis. *See* urban development, regulation of in Australia
Axelrod, R., 302
Ayres, I., 228

Bahr, E., 53
Barth, F., 187n5
Bayesian information processors, 46, 50, 137
Becker, G., 188n14, 285
Becker, L., 85, 102
Belarus, EU antidumping cases against, **257, 265,** 268
beliefs: changeability of, 46, 50–51; conditions for trust, 62, 66; of exclusionary groups, 281; formation of, 40–41; Hebrew word for, 62; paranoia defined as, 140; and social norms, 185–86
benevolence, 103n13
Bengzon, C., 320n31
Beria, L., 49
betrayal, 38
bias: of groups, 43–44, 138, 141; of NLRB, 113, 122, 132
biased punctuation, 148
Bill for Promoting the Public Health (1854) (Australia), 215
Bill of Rights, U.S., 292
Bloch, M., 167–68
Bonacich, P., 138
Boyle, R., 138
Braithwaite, J., 228
Branch Davidian incident, 279
Bretton Woods agreements, 53–54
Brewer, M., 138, 141, 150
Brittan, L., 255
Brown, M., 187n1, 188n13
Building Act (1837) (Australia), 213

Index

Building Code of Australia, 212–13, 214
building regulations, in Australia, 208, 209–13, 216–18
Bulgaria, EU trade classification, 274n19
bureaucratic corruption, 301
Bush (George H. W.) administration, 46, 50
Bush (George W.) administration, 52, 55
business relationships, 91, 94–101. *See also* Russian markets

Canada, as EU trade analogue, 268
capitalism, 253
Carnevale, P., 153, 155
Carroll, J., 308
The Cassini Division (MacLeod), 103n6
Catholicism, 282
Chamberlain, N., 114
cheating, 46, 52
child-parent distrust, 181–84
China, 51, 168, **257–58,** 265–69
Christianity, 283
Churchill, W., 36, 46
civil liberties: and control of terrorism, 27, 278–79, 289–94, 295; and corruption, 300
class distrust, 79
cognitive assessment, trust as, 3, 8
cognitive consequences, of collective paranoia, 147–49
Colby, K., 140, 143
Cold War, 41, 50, 253, 263. *See also* Soviet Union-U.S. relations
Coleman, J., 131–32
collective paranoia: adaptive functions of, 157–60; affective and behavioral consequences of, 149–50; cognitive consequences of, 147–49; definition of, 141; psychological factors, 142–47; summary of analysis, 17–18
Collier, J., 187n5
communism, 41, 253–54
communitarianism, 283
community interests, 218–19
comparative advantage, 266–67, 268, 269

competence, 8, 63, 67
complete distrust, 81n4
Concepcion, R., 320n31
confidence, 66, 77
conflict, as justification for distrust, 41–42
Connolly, J., 158
conspiracy, exaggerated perceptions of, 149
Constitution, Philippines (1987), 313–14, 317
Constitution, U.S., 290, 292
consumer sovereignty, 225
continuum, of trust and distrust, 37, 60–62
contracts: enforcement of, 10; moral contracts, 97; in Russia, 53, 235–39, 242–46
Cooke, W., 112–13, 114, 130
cooperation: among groups, 151, 152; and asymmetries of power, 88, 92, 93; of close communities, 280–81; incentives for, 52; model for institutions, 109
Coronel, S., 313, 319n21
corruption: definition of, 299; of governments, 11, 29–30, 299–306; and institutional distrust, 79; of Philippine Supreme Court, 309–16; of Russian courts, 241
court systems: corruption constraints, 301–2; in Israel, 78; in the Philippines, 309–16; in Russia, 53, 240–42
credible commitments, 86, 89–94, 108–9, 131
criminal law, 292–93
Croatia, 42, 44
Cuban Missile Crisis, 39, 150
cultural tolerance, 202
culture, 93, 101
Czechoslovakia, EU antidumping cases against, **257**
Czech Republic, 262, **266,** 274n19

Dasgupta, P., 131–32
data sources: generalized trust, 284–85; NLRB study, 122; Philippine Supreme Court, 308–12; Russian markets, 234

default rule, 70
defensiveness, 47
defensive noncooperation, 150
democracy, 75–76, 318n5
Denmark, 193, 194, 203n4
deregulation, arguments for, 225–28
DeSoto, H., 111
deterrence: with nuclear arms, 37, 46, 48; of terrorism, 292–93
Deutsch, M., 137–38, 155
developing countries, EU's policies toward, 250–51, 253, 261, 262, 270
discrimination, 78, 251, 270, 278–79, 290–91
distrust: as complement of trust, 3–4; complete distrust, 81n4; continuum, 37, 60–62; definition of, 35, 250; errors of, 37–38, 42–49; vs. fear, 36; full distrust, 67–68; generalized distrust, 286–88; good vs. bad distinction, 54; and inability to trust, 35–36; of institutions, 75–76, 78–79; justification for, 40–42; methods for overcoming, 49–54; presumption of, 69–75; prudence of, 38–42, 157; rational vs. irrational forms, 137–38, 160; soft vs. hard distrust, 72–73; theories of, 9–12; three-part relationship with trust, 36–37. *See also specific entries*
Dobrynin, A., 39
Dore, R., 95–96
Dulles, J., 36, 37–38
dumping, definition of, 254
Dunn, J., 38
Durbin Watson test, NLRB analysis, 133n5
dysphoric rumination, 147–48

East and West, 21
East Germany, 49
economic conditions, and NLRB filings, 121
economic models, 94, 131
economic transactions, 74
Egypt, relationship with Israel, 152
Eisenhower administration, 34, 37, 49
elections, 301
embourgeoisement, 288–89, 295
emerging democracies, law requirements, 316–17
emotions, 36, 66
employment, 45–46, 106–10. *See also* unions and unionization
encapsulated-interest account: description of, 6–7, 39; government corruption analysis, 303; and power, 85–89, 102; vs. "right reason" component, 80n2; terrorism study, 279, 285, 287
Enron scandal, 38, 81n7
equilibrium, and credible commitments, 95
errors, type I or type II, 9, 37
Estonia, 274n19
Estrada, J., 298, 320n29, 33
Etzioni, A., 151
European Commission, 255, 261, 264, 266, 267. *See also* European Union, trade policies toward nonmarket economies
European Foreign Trade Association, 268
European Union, trade policies toward nonmarket economies: antidumping laws and cases, 250–52, 254–55, **257–58**, 260–70; fair trade determination, 255–59; historical background, 253–54; research considerations, 249–52; summary of analysis, 25–27; trade protection arguments, 259–63
evaluative scrutiny, 144–46
exclusion, norms of, 281
exclusionary groups, 280–84. *See also* terrorist groups
expectation, vs. trust, 35, 284
experience, 40, 50
extremist groups, 280–84. *See also* terrorist groups

fair trade determination, European Union, 255–59
familiarity, 65–66

families: binding mutual interdependence within, 169; complexity of relationships, 187*n*7; loyalty within, 65; as moral relationship, 168–69; presumption of trust in, 74; Russian markets analysis, 239; as working relationship, 153. *See also* Madagascar study, of distrust among kin; marriage
FBI (Federal Bureau of Investigation), 159, 291
fear, 36
Federal Bureau of Investigation (FBI), 159, 291
Fenigstein, A., 140, 143
feudalism, 90
Fielding, H., 68
fire insurance industry, in Australia, 214
fire regulations, in Australia, 208, 213–15
firms, power asymmetries within, 91, 94–101. *See also* Russian markets
Fiske, S., 146
Flanagan, R., 113, 114, 120, 126–27
forced marriage, 193, 203*n*2
Fortes, M., 168
free-rider problem, 226–27
French machine production, 14, 97–98
friendship, 45, 239, 245
Fukuyama, F., 168–69
full distrust, 67–68
full trust, 62–64

Gambetta, D., 160, 259, 306, 317, 318*n*10
game theory, NLRB analysis, 116–20
Geddes, B., 301
General Agreement on Tariffs and Trade (GATT), 255, 259, 274*n*8
generalized trust and distrust, 28, 284–88
General Social Survey (GSS), 284–85
Germany, 42, 48, 49, 52–53
Gibbon, E., 89
Giuliani, R., 28
Glorious Revolution, 90

goals, 51, 139–40
Golden, M., 116
goodwill, 95, 96
Goodwin, R., 159
Gorbachev, M., 10, 50, 51
Gore, A., 298
Gould, W., 112
government corruption, 11, 29–30, 299–306
government institutions, accountability, of, 317–18
government power, 89–90
government regulation, 4–5, 22–23, 111. *See also* National Labor Relations Board (NLRB); urban development, regulation of in Australia
government trust and distrust, 4, 31–32
Graeber, D., 189*n*17
Great Britain, 36, 86, 90
GRIT (graduated reciprocation in tension reduction), 50, 151–52
Grossholtz, J., 308
group distrust: dangers of, 43–44; hierarchical relationships, 142; and individuals' reasoning, 17, 280; of institutions, 79; leniency bias, 141; out-group unitization, 141; reduction methods, 150–54; research considerations, 136–38; social information-processing perspective, 138–41. *See also* collective paranoia
group liberalism, risk of, 201
groups: bias of, 43–44, 138, 141; categorization process, 143–44; cooperation among, 151, 152; relationships between, 142; token status within, 145. *See also* terrorist groups
group trust, facilitation of, 154–55
Grove, A., 158
GSS (General Social Survey), 284–85

hard distrust, 72
Hardin, R., 36, 39, 80*n*2, 85, 87, 169, 187*n*2, 194, 203*n*9
Hart, K., 25

Haynie, S., 319n21
health regulations, in Australia, 208, 215–18
Hebrew, words for trust, belief, and faith, 62
Helper, S., 103n16
Hemingway, E., 159–60
Herzog, D., 295n2
Hobbesian theory, 73, 289, 292, 294–95
Hollis, M., 187n4
honesty, 45–46, 50–51, 234
honor killings, in Sweden, 192–202
Hoover, J., 291
Hugo, V., 74
Hume, D., 79
Hungary, **257**, 262, **266**, 274n19
hypervigilance, 147–48

identification with others, 40
immigrants, 192–202, 288–89
impersonality, 77
import penetration argument, for trade protection, 259–62
incentives, 52
information, and belief formation, 40
information processing: Bayesian criteria, 46, 50, 137; and group distrust, 138–41, 145–46, 147, 258
institutional theory, of government corruption, 299–302
institutions: and intention, 12, 64, 76–77, 78, 79, 80; Philippine Supreme Court, 306–16; post-World War II agreements, 53–54; research considerations, 75–76; for trust facilitation, 154. *See also* corruption; National Labor Relations Board (NLRB)
Intel, 158
intentions: and full distrust, 67; and full trust, 10–11, 63, 64; of institutions, 76–77, 78, 79, 80; of more powerful actors, 92
interests, 38, 67–68
intergenerational conflict, 181–84
Intergroup Conflict Simulation, 153–54
intergroup distrust. *See* group distrust
Internal Revenue Service (IRS), 24, 28–29
international relations: security dilemma model, 47–48; shared interests, 51–52
interpersonal relationships, 5
intuitive social auditor, 138–40, 145
IRS (Internal Revenue Service), 24, 28–29
Islam, 51, 279, 283, 287
Israel: Oslo agreement, 51; peace talks with Egypt, 152; and Syria, 36–37; terrorism in, 289, 295; ultra-orthodox's view of Supreme Court, 78
Italy, 14, 98–101, 300

Jackman, R., 318n5
Japanese weavers, 14, 95–97
Johnson administration, 158
Judiciary Act (1948) (Philippines), 307

Kahn, R., 154
Kanter, R., 145
Karim, N., 203
Kazakhstan, EU antidumping cases against, **257**, **265**
Kelman, H., 152
Kennan, G., 41
Kennedy, R., 39
Kennedy administration, 39, 50, 150
Khrushchev, N., 39, 49, 150
kin. *See* families
Kipling, R., 68
Kissinger, H., 49
Klitgaard, R., 318n4
Knight, J., 87
knowledge, requirement for, 35
Kraft, D., 148
Kramer, R., 44, 76, 148, 150, 258
Kurdish immigrants, in Sweden, 192–202
Kyrgyz Republic, 262

Labored Relations (Gould), 112
labor issues, 45–46, 106–10. *See also* unions and unionization

labor pricing, EU antidumping cases, 266–67
Lambek, M., 189*n*17
Landrum-Griffin Act (1959), 111, 122
Latvia, 274*n*19
law: criminal law, 292–93; EU antidumping laws and cases, 250–52, 254–55, **257–58,** 260–70; in the Philippines, 306–16; requirements for, 316–17; in U.S. vs. Philippines, 298–99. *See also* court systems
Leach, E., 187*n*5
Lederman, D., 300
leniency bias, 141
Les Miserables (Hugo), 74
Levi, M., 90, 305
Lewis, J., 159
liberalism, 4, 192, 202, 203*n*9–10
Lindskold, S., 137, 151
Lithuania, **257,** 262, 274*n*19
Loayza, N., 300
Local Government Act (1919) (Australia), 218
Local Government Amendment Act (1945) (Australia), 218
Lord, C., 145
Lorenz, E., 97
loyalty, 65
lynching, 286

machinery producers, in France, 97–98
MacLeod, K., 103*n*6
Madagascar study, of distrust among kin: background information, 169–73; conclusions, 184–86; intergenerational conflict, 181–84; marital conflict, 173–78; research considerations, 167–68; siblings, 178–80; summary of analysis, 18–20
Mafia, 42, 160, 306
Makabenta, Y., 308
Malcolm, G., 307
Malenkov, G., 49
manufacturing, subcontracting relationships in France and Italy, 97–101

Marcos, F., 308, 320*n*31
markets, 233. *See also* Russian markets
marriage: in Denmark, 203*n*4; forced marriage, 193, 203*n*2; loyalty in, 65; Madagascar study, 172, 173–78, 188*n*11; in Sweden, 192, 193, 201; as working relationship, 153
Maynes, M., 187*n*5
Meacham, J., 160
media, 300
mediators, 42, 51, 153–54
Merina people, of Madagascar, 167
Merton, R., 9, 47
military, 10, 36
Miller, G., 90–91, 92, 93, 133*n*3, 305
Milosevic, S., 42, 286
minority groups, 65
misplaced trust: cost of, 34–35; protective measures for, 37, 49–54; as self-disconfirming prophecy, 47
Moe, T., 113, 114, 120, 126–27
monarchies, 89–90
monitoring, 45–46, 290–91
Montinola, G., 300, 318*n*5
moral aggression, 149
moral contracts, 97
morality, 5, 168–69
Morgan, E., 4
Morgenbesser, S., 80*n*1
Mosatalla, J., 320*n*30
motivation, 8
multiculturalism, 193–94, 198
mutuality, 65
My Home, My Prison (Tawil), 196

National Labor Relations Act (NLRA) (1935), 108
National Labor Relations Board (NLRB): board members, 113; data sources, 122; disposition of cases, 128–31; drawbacks of, 110–11; and economic conditions, 121; establishment of, 108; model for filing activity, 114–21; research considerations, 111, 112–15; role of, 111; summary of analysis, 14–17; transaction costs, 126–27; trends, 123–26, **128**; and union density, 121–22

NATO (North Atlantic Treaty Organization), 39, 53–54
negative thinking, 147
networks, Russian markets, 244–45
9/11/01. *See* September 11, 2001
Nixon administration, 49
NLRB (National Labor Relations Board). *See* National Labor Relations Board (NLRB)
nonmarket economies (NMEs): countries included in, 273; definition of, 273n2. *See also* European Union, trade policies toward nonmarket economies
normative trust, 187n4
North, D., 86, 90, 92, 131–32
North Atlantic Treaty Organization (NATO), 39, 53–54
Norway: as EU trade analogue, 264, 266; forced marriage, 193, 203n2; immigrant population, 194; as intermediary for negotiations between rival states, 51; social liberalism debates, 202
nuclear arms, 37, 44, 46, 48, 52
nuclear test bans, 49, 50

Office of Management and Budget, 122
Organization for Economic Cooperation and Development (OECD) countries, as EU trade analogues, 264, **265**, 268, 269
Osgood, C., 50, 151
Oslo agreement (1993), 51
Ostpolitik, 52–53
out-group unitization hypothesis, 141

packaging machinery production, in Italy, 98–101
Palestine Liberation Organization (PLO), 51
Palestinians, illiberal practices of, 195–96
paranoia, 36, 140, 142–47, 157–60. *See also* collective paranoia
Paras, R., 320n31
parent-child distrust, 181–84

Park, B., 46
patron-client ties, 187n3
Pekgul, N., 197, 200
Pfeffer, J., 139
Philippine Supreme Court, 29, 30, 298–99, 306–16, 317
Phillip, A., 208, 218
Poland, **257**, 262, **265**, 274n19
police power, 27
political bias, of NLRB, 113, 122, 132
politicians, corruption of, 301
power: asymmetries of, 13, 87–94; definition of, 87; and encapsulated-interest model, 85–89; and stereotypes, 146; in subcontracting relationships, 94–101; and trust violations, 146
predictive trust, 187n4
press, freedom of, 300
presumption, of trust or distrust, 69–75, 270, 271
prisoner's dilemma (PD), 72, 73, 155
problem solving, 153
proof, of trustworthiness, 50
property rights, in Madagascar, 172
Pruitt, D., 153, 155
psychological theories, of trust, 7, 8, 136–37
punishment, of terrorists, 292–93
Putin, V., 52

racial profiling, 27–28
racism, 198, 278
Reagan administration, 51, 52, 126
reciprocal relationships, 47, 102n1, 239, 240
reciprocity, violations of, 137
regulation, government, 4–5, 22–23, 111. *See also* National Labor Relations Board (NLRB); urban development, regulation of in Australia
relational concept, trust as, 87
relationship-building exercises, 152–53
relationships, interpersonal, 5
relationships, value and power of, 87–89
reliance, 66

religious beliefs, 282, 283
Republican presidential leadership, and NLRB filing activity, 124, 125–26
reputation: and credible commitments, 93; as inhibition for lying and cheating, 39; of Japanese weavers, 96, 97; in labor-management relationships, 110; Russian markets analysis, 245–46; in subcontracting relationships, 101
reward systems, 154
"right reason" component, 63–64, 67
Romania, 274n19
Roosevelt (FDR) administration, 36, 46
Rose-Ackerman, S., 302, 318n4
Rothbart, M., 46
Rotter, J., 8, 137, 285
Russia: court system, 53; EU antidumping cases against, **257**, 264, 265–67, 268, 269; nuclear arms reduction treaties, 52; relations with U.S. after 9/11/01, 51. *See also* Soviet Union-U.S. relations
Russian markets: contract enforcement measures, 242–46; contract infringement problem, 235–39; data sources, 234; relationships with western companies, 239–40; summary of analysis, 24–25; survey of personal features valued in business partners, 234–38; survey sample, 247; use of courts to resolve issues, 240–42

Sadat, A., 152
Saenz, D., 145
Sahindal, Fadime, 193, 194–202
Sahlin, M., 197, 198
Sako, M., 96
Salancik, G., 139
Samson and Delilah, 68–69, 74
Scharpf, F., 38
Schelling, T., 13
Schneider, D., 187n5
scrutiny, evaluative, 144–46

security dilemma model, 47–48
self-binding agreements, 53–54
self-categorization, 143–44
self-consciousness, 45, 143–44, 148
self-distrust, 68
self-fulfilling prophecy, 47
self-interest, 168, 249
self-trust, 68
Semlinger, K., 101
September 11, 2001: Bush (George W.) on, 55; Giuliani on, 28; relations with China and Russia following, 51; terrorists involved in, 294; U.S. government's handling of intelligence prior to, 32, 290–91
Serbs, 42, 44
Shapiro, D., 160
shared interests, 51
Sherif, M., 152
Shevardnadze, E., 41
Shleifer, A., 319n11
shock, use of as tool for overcoming distrust, 49–50
siblings, Madagascar study, 178–80
signaling, 153
Slovak Republic, 274n19
"small steps" approach, 52–53, 155
Soares, R., 300
social auditors, 138–40, 145
social capital, 81n8, 244
social categorization, 41, 143–44
social class distrust, 79
social information-processing perspective, 138–41, 145–46, 147, 258
social norms, 97, 185–86
social order, 289, 292
social standing, 146–47
Social Weather Stations (SWS), 308–12, 319n18, 24
soft distrust, 72
Soviet Union-U.S. relations: arms control agreements, 52; belief systems behind, 41; Cuban Missile Crisis, 39, 150; Dulles on, 34, 37–38; Eisenhower on, 34; end of Cold War, 50; nuclear arms, 37, 44, 46, 48, 52; nuclear test bans, 49; post-

World War II Germany, 48; as self-disconfirming prophecy, 9–10; Standing Consultative Commission, 154; Thatcher's influence, 51; trade legacy of Cold War, 253, 263; Truman on, 41; U-2 surveillance plane incident, 49. *See also* Russia
Spielmans, J., 112
Stalin, J., 41, 43, 46, 48
Standing Consultative Commission, 154
state, power of, 89–90
status quo, interruption in, 151
stereotypes and stereotyping, 27–28, 43, 146, 279
Strategic Arms Limitation talks, 154
structural safety regulations, in Australia, 208, 209–13
subcontracting relationships, power asymmetries within, 94–101
substitutability, principle of, 77
Supreme Court, U.S., 298
surveillance, 45–46, 290–91
survey data: generalized trust, 284–85; Philippine Supreme Court, 308–12; Russian entrepreneurs, 234–38, 247
suspicion, 137, 160
Sweden, honor killings in, 20–21, 192–202
Sydney City and Suburban Sewerage and Health Board, 215
Sydney Police Offences Act (1833), 209, 215, 222
Sydney Sewerage Act (1853), 215
Syria, 36–37

Taft-Hartley Act (1947), 111, 112, 122
Tate, N., 307, 308, 319*n*26
Tawil, R., 196
Taylor, S., 145, 146
Tedeschi, R., 8
terrorism, control of and civil liberties, 27, 278–79, 289–94, 295
terrorist groups: characteristics and tactics of, 280–84, 288–89, 294; generalized distrust of, 287–88; isolation of members, 281, 282

Thatcher, M., 51
theories, of trust and distrust, 6–12
third parties, 42, 51, 153–54, 272
thresholds, 51
time horizons, and credible commitments, 92
token status, 145
trade protection, arguments for, 259–63
trade relationships, 249. *See also* European Union, trade policies toward nonmarket economies
traits, 10, 46
transaction costs, of NLRB, 126–27
Truman administration, 41, 48
trust: asymmetrical nature of, 64–65; belief conditions, 66; continuum, 37, 60–62; definition of, 35, 168, 233; encapsulated-interest account of, 6–7, 39, 80*n*2, 85–89, 102, 279, 285, 287, 303; errors of, 37–38; vs. expectation, 35; and familiarity, 65–66; fragility of, 74; full trust, 62–64; generalized trust, 284–86; inability to, 35; in institutions, 75–78; mutuality, 65; negation of, 11, 66–69; and personal interests, 38; presumption of, 69–71; risks of, 38; theories of, 6–9; three-part relationship with distrust, 36–37. *See also specific entries*
Trust: The Social Virtues and the Creation of Prosperity (Fukuyama), 168–69
trust scale, 8
trustworthiness, value to Russian entrepreneurs, 234

Ukraine, EU antidumping cases against, 257–58, 264, 265, 266–67, 268
Ullmann-Margalit, E., 303
Unabomber, 288, 294
unfair labor practices, 113, **123, 124**
unfairness, 78
unilateral negotiator initiatives, 150–53

unions and unionization: NLRB complaints, 121–22, 124; NLRB's popularity with, 132; and power, 107, 110; and productivity, 131. *See also* National Labor Relations Board (NLRB)
United Nations, 53
United States: and China, 51–52; civil liberties and control of terrorism, 278–79, 289–94; as EU trade analogue, 267; institutional trust in, 75; justice system, 298; and NATO, 39; nuclear arms reduction treaties, 52; and Russia, 51. *See also* Soviet Union-U.S. relations
urban development, regulation of in Australia: arguments for and against, 225–28; background, 207–9; fire, 213–15; frustrations of, 224–25; health, 215–18; objectives of, 223–24; sources of distrust, 228–31; structural safety, 209–13; summary of analysis, 22–23; urban planning, 218–23
urban planning, in Australia, 208–9, 218–23
U-2 surveillance plane incident, 49
Uzbekistan, EU antidumping cases against, **258**

Vanable, P., 140
Varese, F., 317
Vishny, R., 319n11
vulnerability, 47

Wagner Act (1935), 108
water supply standards, in Australia, 215–17
weavers, Japanese, 95–97
Weber, M., 90
Weick, K., 160–61
Weigert, A., 159
Weingast, B., 86, 90, 92
West Germany, 52–53
Wikan, U., 203n2–3, 5
Williamson, O., 94, 131, 238–39
Wilmar 8, 112
Wilson, T., 148
wisdom, 160–61
women, honor killings of by immigrants in Sweden, 192–202. *See also* Madagascar study, of distrust among kin
working relationships, 153
work stoppages, NLRB data, 130–31
World Trade Organization (WTO), 255, 262, 272
Wright, T., 8

xenophobia, 43

Yanagisako, S., 187n5
Yugoslavia, 42, 254, 274n9, 286